READING AND NOT READING
THE FAERIE QUEENE

Reading and Not Reading
The Faerie Queene

SPENSER AND THE MAKING OF
LITERARY CRITICISM

CATHERINE NICHOLSON

PRINCETON UNIVERSITY PRESS
PRINCETON & OXFORD

Copyright © 2020 by Princeton University Press

Requests for permission to reproduce material from this work should be sent to permissions@press.princeton.edu

Published by Princeton University Press
41 William Street, Princeton, New Jersey 08540
6 Oxford Street, Woodstock, Oxfordshire OX20 1TR

press.princeton.edu

All Rights Reserved
ISBN: 978-0-691-17678-9
ISBN (pbk.): 978-0-691-19898-9
ISBN (e-book): 978-0-691-20159-7

British Library Cataloging-in-Publication Data is available

Editorial: Anne Savarese and Jenny Tan
Production Editorial: Ellen Foos
Jacket/Cover Design: Chris Ferrante
Production: Brigid Ackerman
Publicity: Alyssa Sanford and Katie Lewis
Copyeditor: Cathryn Slovensky

Jacket image: Sir Guyon reading, from *The Faerie Queene*, book II, canto X. Ed. Thomas J. Wise (1859–1937), illustrated by Walter Crane (1845–1915), London: George Allen, 1895–1897 / Courtesy of the University of Toronto, Robarts Library

This book has been composed in Arno

Printed on acid-free paper. ∞

Printed in the United States of America

10 9 8 7 6 5 4 3 2 1

CONTENTS

List of Illustrations vii

	Introduction: General Ends and First Essentials	1
1	"The Falsest Twoo": Forging the Scholarly Reader	26
2	Una's Line: Child Readers and the Afterlife of Fiction	50
3	Mining the Text: Avid Readers in the Legend of Temperance	108
4	Half-Envying: The Interested Reader and the Partial Marriage Plot	145
5	Reading against Time: Crisis in *The Faerie Queene*	176
6	Blatant Beasts: Encounters with Other Readers	216
	Coda: Reading to the End	241

Acknowledgments 261
Notes 263
Index 299

LIST OF ILLUSTRATIONS

1. "View of Mr. Alcott and the children conversing," Bronson Alcott, *Conversations with Children on the Gospels*, 1836.   60
2. Benjamin West, *Una and the Lion (Mary Hall in the Character of Una)*, 1771. Oil on canvas, 66¼ × 86⅛ in.   84
3. Thomas Watson, print, 1897, after Joshua Reynolds, *Una and the Lion (Portrait of Elizabeth Beauclerc)*, 1782.   85
4. George Stubbs, *Una and the Lion (Portrait of Isabella Saltonstall)*, 1782.   86
5. Etching after William Hilton II, *Una Entering the Cottage*, 1832.   86
6. Lithograph after William Edward Frost, *Una Alarmed*, 1843.   87
7. William Edward Frost, *Una among the Fauns*, 1848.   87
8. Gold coin, "Una and the Lion," 1839.   88
9. Joseph Pitts, *The Vision of the Red Cross Knight*, statuary porcelain, produced by John Rose, ca. 1850.   89
10. Frontispiece, M. H. Towry, *Spenser for Children*, illustrations by Walter Jenks Morgan, 1885.   94
11. Cover image, *Spenser's "Faerie Queene,"* illustrated by Walter Crane, 1897.   95
12. Frontispiece, N. G. Royde-Smith, *Una and the Red Cross Knight*, illustrated by T. H. Robinson, 1905.   96
13. Title page, N. G. Royde-Smith, *Una and the Red Cross Knight*, illustrated by T. H. Robinson, 1905.   97
14. "Una and the Lion," in Andrew Lang, *Red Romance Book*, 1905.   98
15. Cover image, Jeanie Lang, *Stories from "The Faerie Queen" Told to the Children*, illustrated by Rose Le Quesne, 1906.   99

READING AND NOT READING
THE FAERIE QUEENE

INTRODUCTION

General Ends and First Essentials

The generall end . . . of all the booke is to fashion a gentleman or noble person in vertuous and gentle discipline.
—EDMUND SPENSER, *THE FAERIE QUEENE*, 1590

The first essential is, of course, not to read *The Faery Queen*.
—VIRGINIA WOOLF, "THE FAERY QUEEN," 1947

NEAR THE end of book 2 of *The Faerie Queene*, Edmund Spenser's Knight of Temperance, Sir Guyon, enters the library of a virtuous maid named Alma, spies a book titled the *Antiquitee of Faery Lond*, and settles down to read. Seventy stanzas later, he is still at it: "Guyon all this while his booke did read, / Ne yet has ended, for it was a great / And ample volume" (2.10.70.1–3).[1] His sojourn in Alma's library marks a rare interval of calm in the knight's otherwise tempest-tossed career, but the quiet of the scene is misleading: in a poem that persistently identifies hermeneutic skill with heroic action, the meaning of reading itself proves unsettlingly hard to parse. For the *Antiquitee* is no page-turner; on the contrary, it consists of a comically monotonous litany of the descendants of one Elfe, progenitor of faerie kind: Elfin, Elfinan, Elfinell, Elfant, Elfar, Elfinor, Elficleos, Elferon, and so on. Guyon's absorption in it is thus rather baffling: Is he truly fascinated by the faerie genealogy, or have its repetitious rhythms lulled him into a stupor? Is he engaged, enthralled—or merely bored stiff? And what do the fixity and intensity of his gaze portend for his allegorical function in the poem: Is reading without end an exemplary feat of temperate self-mastery or an uncharacteristic lapse into self-indulgent excess? What, finally, are the implications for us: Is Guyon a cautionary figure for the reader of Spenser's poem, our parodic double, or an aspirational ideal? The uncertainties of the episode can't be resolved or evaded, pressed home by an odd, interlinear shift in tense—"Ne yet *has* ended"—that fleetingly conjoins Guyon's experience to our own. However we interpret it, the conjunction is a timely one: two books, twenty-two cantos, more than a thousand stanzas, and some ten thousand lines into *The Faerie Queene*—which is to say, not quite a third of the way through—we might well pause to wonder about the motives and merits of readerly persistence. What is this great and ample volume, and why are *we* still reading it?

It is the peculiar and discomfiting genius of *The Faerie Queene* to call reading into question. Few works have a greater capacity to inspire pleasure, few do more to tax readers' patience, and none, perhaps, has a stronger propensity to fill them with self-doubt. Written at a moment when right reading was at once a stringently regulated ideal and, in Anthony Grafton's words, a "complex and protean enterprise," *The Faerie Queene* invests the work of interpretation with extraordinary, even existential, power: in the densely coded, relentlessly violent world of Spenser's poem, learning to read in the precise fashion that a particular text or occasion requires is the means to narrative survival.[2] As a consequence— and as those of us who study and teach the poem are fond of pointing out— *The Faerie Queene* is filled with testimonies to the necessity of readerly judgment, intuition, and tact. In addition to books like the *Antiquitee*, the inhabitants of Spenser's fictive universe scrutinize prophecies, spells, letters, inscriptions on walls, tapestries, armorial sigils, the workings of divine providence, the features of the faerie landscape, and each other's faces; they live, move, and have their being in a realm of infinite signifying potential—and limitless opportunities for distraction and confusion. Readers of *The Faerie Queene* thus continually read alongside and over the shoulders of readers in *The Faerie Queene*, sharing in their perplexity, profiting from their insights, and learning from their mistakes. As Judith Anderson writes, "the poem itself . . . teaches us at once how to read and how vital this process is."[3] That doubling of interpretive effort imbues the experience of the poem with a rare sense of dynamism and depth: like some vast and versified hall of mirrors, the poem repeatedly confronts us with the image of our engagement with it, and summons us to do better. But it can be unnerving, too. For all its faith in the transformative power of reading well, *The Faerie Queene* is a showcase of hermeneutic excess and incompetence, its pages littered with botched encounters between readers and texts. And as Guyon's ceaseless and possibly pointless contemplation of *The Antiquitee of Faerie Lond* suggests, the poem subjects reading to a deeply skeptical accounting, weighing its costs and benefits with an exacting eye; as often as not, reading comes up short.

The vertiginous, self-deprecating wit of the figure of the still, still-reading Knight of Temperance is an index of the lengths to which Spenser's poem will go in order to anticipate and share in the imagined scene of its reception: even our boredom and exhaustion have a place in its pageant of readerly dispositions. To put it another way, it can be extraordinarily hard to come up with a response of *The Faerie Queene* that doesn't in some way seem to have been scripted—and often also challenged, rebuked, amended, revised, or discarded—in advance. And yet the poem retains a fundamentally welcoming stance toward the contributions of readers. Its intricacy and immensity may be overwhelming, but they yield a fractal-like distribution of interest: famously difficult to comprehend, *The Faerie Queene* is nonetheless susceptible of interpretation at every scale. As Isabel MacCaffrey observes, "open-endedness is built into [*The Faerie Queene*] both formally and thematically because, by calling attention to the process whereby we understand the fiction itself, it sheds light upon the process whereby all understanding takes place."[4]

Spenser's name for this iterative, looping, dialectical process of understanding—the reading of reading, as we might call it—is "discipline." In the "Letter of the Authors expounding his whole intention in the course of this worke," addressed to Sir Walter Raleigh and appended to the 1590 first edition, the poet famously declares that the "generall end" of his poem "is to fashion a gentleman or noble person in vertuous and gentle discipline." The vagueness of the indefinite article—is the object of the poem's fashioning imaginary or real, a singular abstraction or anyone who happens to pick it up?—is the point: *The Faerie Queene* works by concentrating abstract qualities in particular fictive beings and inviting individual readers to identify themselves with broadly universal types. The result is a deliberate blurring of instruction and entertainment, purpose and whim. Rather than delivering his moral precepts straight, Spenser explains, "I conceived [they] should be most plausible and pleasing, being coloured with an historicall fiction, the which the most part of men delight to read, rather for variety of matter, than for profite of the ensample."[5] In an elaboration of the age-old alchemy of profit and pleasure ascribed to poetry by Horace and others, *The Faerie Queene* works to transform instincts of enjoyment common to any literate person—an appetite for narrative, a sympathetic interest in the experiences of fictional characters—into mechanisms of moral, spiritual, and intellectual refinement, aiming at a perfect synthesis of desire and skill. The allegorical champions of each book are the exemplary results of this fashioning, but so, too, at least in theory, are the readers who accompany them on their adventures: their discipline begets our own.

That, in a rather different sense than Spenser intended, is one of the central claims of this book. As scholars have long recognized, when it appeared in print in the 1590s, the epic grandeur, formal intricacy, and moral seriousness of *The Faerie Queene* played a crucial role in transforming the writing of English from a merely useful or amusing pursuit to a legitimate vehicle of eloquence, ambition, and national identity—though the poem was also maligned for its allegorical obscurity and stylistic oddity.[6] But in the decades and centuries that followed, that same obscurity and oddity helped to make the reading of English into a discipline in the modern sense of the word: a specialized body of knowledge with its own proprietary techniques of research, analysis, interpretation, and commentary. Indeed, the very features that curbed the poem's influence as a model of literary practice made it an ideal object of literary analysis. Conspicuously eccentric and yet inarguably important, *The Faerie Queene* proved a reliably generative source of critical judgment and scholarly inquiry. Moreover, the stresses it placed—or was perceived to place—on readers' abilities and expectations yielded a crucial sense of distinction among them, between amateurs and experts, mere literacy and literary criticism, reading as pastime and reading as profession.

When we say that *The Faerie Queene* teaches us how to read, then, what we really mean is that it teaches us—and helps us teach others—how to read in specific and rarified ways. When students begin her course on Spenser, Judith Anderson explains,

> while they are natively bright enough, they have not learned (or been taught) to pay attention to the words, sentences, or logical sequences of writing. Perhaps more significantly, they are not aware in a conceptual sense that such features of their reading might be useful, interesting, even enlightening. . . . [They] desire to read only realistically—characterologically, so to speak—and not simply to ignore, but to want to ignore, alternative and especially complicating dimensions of significance in the hope that these unfamiliar, puzzling things would go away.[7]

The Faerie Queene, however, refuses to submit to such pedestrian longings: "Ill-informed efforts to read . . . autonomously, psychologically, or novelistically" fall flat, while failures to attend to the dense verbal circuitry result in embarrassing mistakes. "There is," Anderson concludes, "nowhere successfully to hide in it": "we either engage . . . the reading process it models" or "get lost in ways of which we cannot avoid becoming aware."[8] Other contributors to the 2003 special issue of *Pedagogy* in which Anderson's essay appears make similar claims for its capacity to turn ordinary students into English majors, or to show them why they might prefer art history or engineering instead.[9] This function as a divining rod of readerly promise and commitment is one that *The Faerie Queene* has long assumed in the study of English—for as long, indeed, as that study can be said to have existed at all. Beginning in the decades just after the poet's death and thanks in part to the influence of his own former schoolmaster, Richard Mulcaster, an early advocate for classroom instruction in English language and literature, the exemplary role once exclusively played by classical authors like Virgil and Cicero was increasingly open to vernacular poets.[10] As Richard Frushell writes in his study of eighteenth-century grammar schools, "the English major was born and the course set for curricular and canonical change in the schools largely because of the growing popularity, ubiquity, and importance of such native models for imitation as Spenser."[11] There is another side to this story, however: the progressive isolation of *The Faerie Queene* from the broadly, if aspirationally, accessible realm of what Gerald Graff calls "general culture" to the proprietary domain of literary scholarship.[12] Indeed, one of the primary aims of this book is to elucidate the process by which Spenser's conception of readerly discipline informed and eventually gave way to our own, such that the moral and intellectual challenges of interpreting *The Faerie Queene* became almost exclusively identified with the attainments of a professional class, and the poem itself all but illegible without them. The result is an unusually complex, almost parasitic interdependence of reader and text, the identity and integrity of each reliant on the exceptionality of the other.

The application of my argument in this book is thus wider than it might seem—as capacious, in fact, as the oppositional poles of my title suggest. To the extent that we identify literature as our disciplinary home and criticism as its constitutive act, I argue, we bear the imprint of Spenser's fashioning, whether we read *The Faerie Queene* or not. But that claim is not meant to reify the poet's own account of how his poem works, for the mechanisms by which *The Faerie Queene* has wrought its influence on readers are by no means as smooth or well regulated as the 1590 "Letter of the Authors" suggests. On the contrary: those who have sought in *The Faerie Queene* the gentle and virtuous fashioning promised by the poet have frequently found themselves struggling in the grip of less benign reactions, from boredom and bafflement to irritation, outrage, obsession, intoxication, and sheer exhaustion. Indeed, for many—perhaps most—of Spenser's readers, the experience of his poem has been the opposite of disciplined: not a steady progress toward understanding but a wild careening from one error or embarrassment to another.

That pattern of reaction and overreaction is both *The Faerie Queene*'s signature effect on readers and its distinctive contribution to the history of literary criticism. For as Anderson testifies, it is precisely the errors and embarrassments to which its readers are prone that make the poem such an effective disciplinary tool. Striving to moderate the excesses and correct the defects of other readers, a long line of critical custodians and scholarly guides have developed ever more elaborate protocols for understanding and enjoying it, and ever more stringent guidelines for how it can't or shouldn't be read. In the process, they have stumbled into errors and embarrassments of their own, providing fodder for future corrections, admonitions, and prohibitions. Along the way, the ability to read *The Faerie Queene* properly has become identified with a growing and contradictory list of readerly endowments: intellectual sophistication and childlike innocence; historical expertise and a taste for anachronism; the willingness to proceed slowly and carefully, with an eye for verbal nuance, and a capacity to digest vast quantities of verse at one go; a blithe disregard for critical fashion and an ease with the lexicon and etiquette of a scholarly elite. But the values attached to such attainments are not inherent or immutable, and their association with Spenser's poem is anything but stable. In the course of its reception history, *The Faerie Queene* has also been identified with such dubious readerly tendencies as laziness, immaturity, bad taste, amoral aestheticism, rank partisanship, special pleading, and the sophomoric pleasures of calling other readers out—in short, with what one might call the *indiscipline* of literary criticism. Even as it plumbs the origins of some of our most cherished disciplinary norms, from editorial objectivity to the care and handling of old books, the history of Spenser's readers also offers the discipline's current denizens a more expansive, less idealized perspective on its defining act: a vantage point from which it is possible to conceive of reading as neither a heroic achievement nor a solipsistic indulgence, but a practice open to improvisation, prone to unintended consequences, and subject to unforeseen detours and reversals.

Spenser's immersion in the pedagogical, intellectual, and hermeneutic ferment of humanism and the Reformation no doubt made him sensitive to such reversals. Certainly it made him doubtful of the ease with which readerly values could, or should, be transmitted: as Jeff Dolven has shown, *The Faerie Queene* is studded with confrontations between would-be teachers and their obstinate or wayward pupils.[13] What is more, the poem itself perpetually models or solicits interpretive strategies it then dismisses as false, inadequate, or unnecessary; reading perpetually begets not reading. Disabling though it may seem, this self-contradictory impulse serves as both a structural principle and an organizing theme, helping to spur the transition from one legend of virtue to the next and ensuring that its questing knights never quite arrive at their destinations. Taking its cues from the poem's own volatile structure, this book charts a similarly errant and erratic course across what we blandly call its reception history—which, on closer and more curious inspection, turns out to be a record of ongoing tension between *The Faerie Queene*'s designs on readers and readers' designs on *The Faerie Queene*. What results is neither a reading nor a reception history in the usual senses of those terms but a dynamic hybrid of the two: a series of illuminating case studies of reading in extremity, avidly, obsessively, idly, and doggedly, at great length and in sudden bursts of diligent intensity, under duress and in defiance of the rules, in the unlikeliest of circumstances, for the strangest of reasons, and to no apparent end at all.

As a letter sent to the editors of the London daily paper the *Spectator* in July 1712 poignantly attests, reading *The Faerie Queene* can make not reading an increasingly attractive, even necessary-seeming, proposition. "I am now in the country, and reading in Spencer's fairy-queen," it begins. "Pray what is the matter with me?"[14] The problem wasn't that the poem proved uninteresting—or rather, that wasn't the only problem. Instead, immersion in it had produced a bewildering array of psychosomatic reactions, from wild enthusiasm to a stultifying dullness: "when the poet is sublime my heart burns, when he is compassionate my heart faints, when he is sedate my soul is becalmed." Alternately exhilarated and enervated, thoroughly discombobulated, and uncertain how or if to proceed, the letter writer—who signs him- or herself "M.R."—ends by imploring the *Spectator*'s editors to devote a portion of each upcoming Saturday issue to glossing the poem's opening book one stanza at a time, in a manner "short but compendious": "I long to have the Spectator upon Spencer bound in my pocket together."[15] That request was, unsurprisingly, denied: a stanza-by-stanza commentary on book 1 of *The Faerie Queene* would have taken nearly a dozen years of Saturday *Spectator*s to complete, and its dimensions would strain even the roomiest pocket. But a single issue of the paper, published November 19, 1712, did offer "loose Hints" for coming to grips with Spenser's poem: "it requires explication."

The plea of the *Spectator*'s hapless correspondent sounds with endearing frankness a note of consternation that echoes across *The Faerie Queene*'s reception history. Those who address themselves earnestly to the poem frequently come away baffled: "Of the persons who read the first Canto, not one in ten reaches the end of the First Book, and not one in a hundred perseveres to the end of the poem," Thomas MacCauley dryly observed. "Very few and very weary are those who are in at the death of the Blatant Beast."[16] Others, however, pick it up on impulse and find themselves helplessly enthralled, spurred by a devotion at once unsustainable and impossible to shake. As C. S. Lewis put it, "I never meet a man who says that he *used to* like the *Faerie Queene*."[17] For its part, the *Spectator*'s response to M.R.'s letter neatly summarizes generations of critical counsel, to the disaffected and devoted alike: *The Faerie Queene* models holiness, temperance, chastity, friendship, justice, and courtesy; it induces unmanageable extremes of passion and aversion; it requires explication. From the beginning, however, the relation of commentary to text has been vexed by the immensity and internal heterogeneity of the poem itself, which makes any effort at supplementation seem at once extraneous and inadequate to need. As is frequently the case for *The Faerie Queene*'s questing knights, such help as readers receive along the way is inevitably either intrusive and overwhelming or too little, too late.

The 1590 "Letter of the Authors," in which Spenser vowed to "discouer vnto [readers] the general intention and meaning, which in the whole course thereof I haue fashioned," is an exemplary case in point.[18] Placed at the back of the first print edition, the "Letter" offers a partial and distorted retrospect on what precedes it, a description not of the poem we have just read but of some longer, better organized, and perhaps less interesting work. Neither as thorough nor as comprehensive as promised, but containing a good deal of irrelevance, it offers something closer to what the *Spectator*'s editors termed "loose hints." Some of those are misleading—for instance, the account of the origins of Guyon's adventure flatly contradicts what we read in book 2—and all are at least partly conjectural, since the three books printed in 1590 were supposed to be the first of a projected dozen. That unfulfilled ambition for the poem—the vision of what James Nohrnberg calls the "duodecimal" *Faerie Queene*—is telegraphed on the title pages of both editions printed in Spenser's lifetime as well, which advertise it as being "Disposed into twelue books, Fashioning XII. Morall vertues," despite the fact that one edition contains just a quarter and the other only half as many books.[19] Even before turning to the opening lines, then, readers of *The Faerie Queene* were coaxed into sharing an unattainable vision of the poem's capacities and their own. To put it another way, the poem primes readers for disappointment; what the *Spectator*'s correspondent experiences as a bewildering lapse of readerly competence and confidence is a sensation Spenser's text elicits literally by design.

Indeed, the mere prospect of *The Faerie Queene* may carry an intolerable weight of expectation: the dream of the different and better self who would read it. A century and a half after the letter to the *Spectator* was written, a fictional would-be reader, Anthony Trollope's Lady Lizzie Eustace, undertook a similar course in Spenserian self-improvement with still more dispiriting results. Retreating to Scotland with a well-curated selection of morally improving books, *The Faerie Queene* chief among them, Lady Eustace finds herself unable to read anything but her paid companion's cheap romances:

> She had intended during this vacant time to master the "Faery Queen," but the "Faery Queen" fared even worse than "Queen Mab." . . . For poor Mcnulty, if she could only be left alone, this was well enough. To have her meals, and her daily walk, and her fill of novels, and to be left alone, was all that she asked of the gods. But it was not so with Lady Eustace. She asked much more than that, and was now thoroughly discontented with her own idleness. She was sure that she could have read Spenser from sunrise to sundown, with no other break than an hour or two given to Shelley,—if only there had been some one to sympathise with her in her readings. But there was no one, and she was very cross.[20]

Crossness, compounded in equal parts of frustration with the poem and frustration with oneself, is very often the result of an attempt to read *The Faerie Queene*. Hence the need for what the *Spectator* calls "explication" and Lady

Eustace "someone to sympathize with"—and the likelihood of its failure to satisfy.

Such failures are, of course, generative in their way; the 1590 "Letter of the Authors" was only the beginning. In the centuries that followed, *The Faerie Queene* has nurtured a vast and spreading ecosystem of explanatory supplements, from footnotes, endnotes, and marginal glosses to prefaces and appendices, concordances, encyclopedias, and readers' guides. In time, such supplements have come to seem more like scaffolding, an indispensible support to poem and readers alike. But they function as protective fencing, too, warning away the uninitiated and ill-equipped: like the textual equivalent of an endangered species, *The Faerie Queene* now lives almost exclusively in the secure environs of the classroom. Trollope's novel and the letter to the *Spectator* suggest that this was not always the case: there was a time, centuries even, when a lone lay reader might encounter *The Faerie Queene* in the wild—or, at least, on a country estate. But the novel and the letter also suggest that such encounters were nonetheless fraught with anxiety and informed by an inchoate sense of duty. For the vast majority of readers, past and present, it is a book we read not because we want to but because we have to, or feel we should.

Inevitably, the atmosphere of obligation that surrounds *The Faerie Queene* shapes readers' responses to it, typically for the worse. Those who love poetry frequently fail to love this particular poem, and those who love this particular poem must learn to do so, usually with some initial difficulty. Exceptions merely prove the general rule: recalling the story told by John Keats's boyhood tutor, who claimed that the young Keats raced through *The Faerie Queene* "as a young horse would through a spring meadow—ramping!"[21] Henry A. Beers, an eminent scholar of British and American literature at the end of the nineteenth century, ruefully observed,

> It must be confessed that nowadays we do not greatly romp through "The Faëry Queene." There even runs a story of a professor of literature at an American college who, being consulted about Spenser by one of his scholars, exclaimed impatiently, "Oh, damn Spenser!" Still, it is worthwhile to have him in the literature, if only as a starter for young poets.[22]

Of course, young poets themselves have not always proved grateful for the start. Studying English at Oxford in the early 1940s, Philip Larkin left a resentful note in his college library copy of the poem: "First I thought *Troilus and Criseyde* was the most *boring* poem in the English language. Then I thought it was *Paradise Lost*. Now I *know* that *The Faerie Queene* is the *dullest thing out. Blast it.*"[23]

Such judgments are less distinctively characteristic of what Beers calls "nowadays" than he (or we) might suppose. In fact, it is hard to say which came first: *The Faerie Queene*'s reputation as a poem for studious dullards or its function as a foundation for the academic study of English. Even in the early seventeenth century, when John Milton was a pupil at St. Paul's, his schoolmaster Alexander Gill incorporated extracts from *The Faerie Queene* into a pioneering textbook on English rhetoric and orthography, and a hint of Larkin's schoolboy churlishness is palpable in Milton's qualified approbation in *Areopagitica* for the poet he terms "our sage and serious . . . Spenser" and deems "a better teacher than *Scotus* or *Aquinas*."[24] For having invoked Spenser as teacher, Milton promptly proceeds to forget his text, offering a notoriously inaccurate summary of the Cave of Mammon episode in book 2 of *The Faerie Queene*. (Milton's association of *The Faerie Queene* with the classroom might also account for the fact that in *Paradise Lost* Spenserian allegory, in the personified figures of Sin and Death, is pointedly confined to Hell.) The impulse both to laud the didactic content of Spenser's poem and to purge it from memory persists across the eighteenth century. As *The Faerie Queene* secured a place in the classrooms of Eton, Winchester, Westminster, and other elite grammar schools, the pedagogical structure of the classroom increasingly made its way inside the text, in the form of ever more elaborate glossaries, annotations, and editorial apparatuses.[25] An entry in an anonymous commonplace book from the early eighteenth century hints at the stultifying consequences for readers: "Spenser was a great genius," it dutifully begins. "[He] endeavoured . . . to make instruction instead of story the object of an epic poem. His execution was excellent, and his flights of fancy very noble and high, but his design was poor and his morality lay so bare that it lost its effect."[26]

In reaction against such damningly faint praise, later eighteenth- and nineteenth-century proponents of *The Faerie Queene*—the so-called Romantics—found it increasingly necessary to warn potential readers against taking the poem too seriously, lest they lose all will to begin. "If they do not meddle with the allegory," William Hazlitt famously advised the timid, "the allegory will not meddle with them."[27] And yet, as David Hume confessed, without a certain self-punishing instinct, readers of Spenser's "peculiarly tiresome" poem were unlikely to persevere. "This poet contains great beauties," he declares,

> yet does the perusal of his work become so tedious that one never finishes it from the mere pleasure which it affords. It soon becomes a kind of task reading, and it requires some effort and resolution to carry us to the end. . . . Upon the whole, Spenser maintains his place upon the shelves of our English classics; but he is seldom seen on the table.[28]

That "but" might equally be a "because": *The Faerie Queene*'s place on the shelves of English classics was guaranteed in part by the rarity of its appearances on the tables and in the hands of readers. By the same token, the poem's sterling reputation did as much to repel readers as to attract them.

Indeed, by the twentieth century, it seemed to Virginia Woolf that the chief obstacle facing a would-be admirer of *The Faerie Queene* was the cloud of irreproachable virtue in which the enterprise of reading it was shrouded. "Dare we then at this time of day come out with the remark that *The Faery Queen* is a great poem?" she wonders at the start of her wry, witty, and ultimately appreciative essay on the poem. "So one might say early rising, cold bathing, abstention from wine and tobacco are good; and if one said it, a blank look would steal over the company as they made haste to agree and then to lower the tone of the conversation." Hence her paradoxical counsel to those eager to develop a taste for Spenser's poem: "The first essential is, of course, not to read *The Faery Queene*."[29]

Woolf wrote from experience. After deliberately avoiding all contact with the poem for more than five decades, she took it up shortly before her fifty-third birthday and was startled to find herself liking it: "I am reading the *Faery Queen*—with delight," reads her diary entry for January 23, 1935. "I shall write about it."[30] But for all the pleasure she took in her belated discovery of the poem, she had no regrets about the belatedness. On the contrary, the gratifications of reading it were in her view necessarily delayed. "Put it off as long as possible," she urges:

> Grind out politics; absorb science; wallow in fiction; walk about London; observe the crowds; calculate the loss of life and limb; rub shoulders with the poor in markets; buy and sell; fix the mind firmly on the financial columns of the newspapers, weather; on the crops; on the fashions. At the mere mention of chivalry shiver and snigger; detest allegory; and then, when the whole being is red and brittle as sandstone in the sun, make a dash for *The Faery Queen* and give yourself up to it.[31]

As the rhythms of her prose elegantly suggest, putting something off can be a way of heightening its appeal as well as holding it at bay. And in practice, not reading *The Faerie Queene* served Woolf as both prelude to and prophylactic against the otherwise too absorbing experience, at once captivating and claustrophobic, of reading it. In Spenser's Faerie Land, she observes, "we are confined in one continuous consciousness," "liv[ing] in a great bubble blown from the poet's brain." And a habit of ironic detachment proved a useful stay against "the indistinctness which leads, as undoubtedly it does lead, to monotony."[32] Within weeks of beginning the poem, she was plotting her escape from it: "I now feel a strong desire to stop reading *F.Q.*," reads a diary entry for February 27, 1935. "As far as I can see, this is the natural swing of the pendulum."[33]

Indeed, the contradictory extremes of Woolf's encounter with *The Faerie Queene*—attraction and repulsion; eagerness and exhaustion; delight and a strong desire to stop—are poles between which Spenser's readers have continually ranged. "I am almost afraid I must go and read Spenser, and wade through his allegories and drawling stanzas, to get at a picture," Horace Walpole wrote to a friend when planning the gardens at his country estate.[34] "Spenser I could have read forever," countered Sir Walter Scott, recalling his youthful obsession with a poem he "devoured rather than perused": "I could repeat whole Cantos . . . and woe to the unlucky wight who undertook to be my auditor, for in the height of my enthusiasm I was apt to disregard all hints that my recitations became tedious."[35] Another teenage devotee, Robert Southey, devised a plan to complete the poem's six missing books and, even late in life, spoke with regret of his failure to follow through. "Without being insensible to the defects of the Fairy Queen," he wrote to Walter Savage Landor, "I am never weary of reading it."[36] For his part, Landor termed Spenser's poetry "a Jargon" and classed him "among the most inelegant of our Writers."[37] Such diversities of opinion are not simply the result of changing tastes; all of the examples above are drawn from the late eighteenth and early nineteenth centuries, and almost any period would afford a similar range. Unreasoning animus and passionate attachment are the twin hallmarks of *The Faerie Queene*'s reception history. The two can hardly be thought separately, as Woolf helps us to see, for the resistance the poem engenders in readers is often merely the obverse of the diligence it demands and the devotion it threatens to inspire. As a result, wild enthusiasm can give way to weariness and distaste in the space of a single encounter with the poem, much to the bemusement of the reader himself. "I don't wonder that you are in such raptures with Spenser! What an imagination! What an invention! What painting! What colouring displayed throughout the works of that admirable author!" Samuel Richardson wrote to Susanna Highmore in 1750. "[A]nd yet," he adds, "for want of time, or opportunity, I have not read his *Fairy Queen* through in series, or at a heat, as I may call it."[38]

Want of time and opportunity are trusty excuses for Spenser's reluctant admirers, and far from being a modern innovation, "putting it off" is a venerable—indeed, the very oldest—technique for accommodating oneself to his poem. The first mention of *The Faerie Queene*'s existence comes in a letter Spenser wrote in the spring of 1580 to his friend and former college tutor Gabriel Harvey, then reader in rhetoric at Cambridge University. In the letter the young writer, whose first book had been published pseudonymously a year earlier, pleads for the return of his fledgling manuscript. It had evidently been in Harvey's possession for some time: "I praye you hartily send me it with al expedition," Spenser writes, "and your frendly Letters and long expected Iudgement wythal, whyche let not be shorte, but in all pointes suche, as you ordinarilye vse, and I extraordinarily desire."[39] But Harvey's reply, when it came, merely prolonged the wait: the answering letter ranges across several pages and a host of unrelated topics before finally, reluctantly arriving at the object of Spenser's extraordinary desire: "In good faith I had once again nigh forgotten your *Fairie Queene*. And must you of necessity haue my Iudgement of hir in deede?" In a now notorious passage, Harvey proceeds to dismiss the poem as a travesty of its author's talent— "Hobgoblin run away with Apollo"—and ends by suggesting that Spenser write something, or anything, else instead. He then bids his friend farewell, "till God or some good Aungell putte you in a better minde."[40]

This unsympathetic response earned Harvey the scorn of critics in his own time and after, helping to secure his reputation as a self-regarding pedant. But the plea that "God or some good Aungell" put Spenser "in a better mind" prefigures many subsequent responses to *The Faerie Queene*: awe at the poet's abundant gifts is nearly always touched with irritation, bemusement, or anxiety at the extravagant uses to which he put them. In the decades that followed its appearance in print, Thomas Nashe chastised Harvey for failing to appreciate the music of its "stately tuned verse" but admitted to being daunted himself by its "strange contents": "perusing [it] with idle eyes," he confesses, "I streight leapt over to the latter end."[41] Ben Jonson reportedly complained that, "in affecting the Ancients, [Spenser] writ no language" but added that he would "have him read for his Matter."[42] In his *Orlando Furioso* John Harington deemed *The Faerie Queene* an "excellent Poem" but hinted in his *Epigrams* that the meaning of its allegory escaped him, terming that "a question fit for higher skils."[43] In his sonnet sequence *Delia*, Samuel Daniel celebrated Spenser's achievement but politely declined to imitate it, writing, "Let others sing of Knights and Palladines, / In aged accents, and vntimely words."[44] Eager to distinguish his epic and historiographical undertaking in *Poly-Olbion* from *The Faerie Queene*'s "Elfin Story," Michael Drayton urged readers to treat the earlier work as "a Poeticall authority only," not seeking for truth in its myths, legends, and "too fabulously mixt stories."[45]

Within a century, the idea that *The Faerie Queene* itself was a too fabulous mixture of folly and genius—Hobgoblin and Apollo, as Harvey names them— had become a formula, and readers of the poem were repeatedly cautioned to take care in disentangling one from the other. Even proponents conceded that reading it required certain defensive measures. John Hughes, who produced the first annotated edition in 1715, counseled readers to focus on a single book at a time, confessing that "the whole frame of it wou'd appear monstrous." Thomas Warton, author of the first scholarly commentary, noted that the episodic structure lent itself to reading selectively—and warned that those who tried to read it straight through would discover it did not "constitute one legitimate poem."[46] Hazlitt's advice not to meddle with the allegory was echoed and intensified by James Russell Lowell, who judged that the poem's "true use" was not as an incitement to thinking but a temporary respite from it: "as a gallery of pictures which we visit as the mood takes us, and where we spend an hour or two at a time, long enough to sweeten the perceptions, not so long as to cloy them."[47] Even an avowed Spenser completist like Alexander Grosart, whose ten-volume 1882–84 edition of the poet's *Works* aimed at countering the circulation of his verse in anthologized extracts, admitted that "[t]he novice must read him wisely" and "in our 'fast' days . . . commonly has not time to do so" and proposed a careful study of the House of Holiness and the Cave of Mammon episodes as a reasonable substitute for reading *The Faerie Queene* as a whole.[48]

Woolf's joking dictum that the first essential for enjoying *The Faerie Queene* is not to read *The Faerie Queene* was thus the reductio ad absurdum of a critical tradition as old as the poem itself—and a surprisingly effective one at that. From the late sixteenth century through the end of the nineteenth, not reading *The Faerie Queene* wasn't the opposite of reading it, but reading's indispensible adjunct; acquiring a taste, or merely a tolerance, for Spenser's poem was very much a matter of learning what to disregard, how to select or skim, and when to stop. But even as Woolf's essay brilliantly synthesizes this tradition of counsel, it also marks its terminus. For at the moment she took up Spenser's poem, the paradoxical ideal of reading with which it had long been identified—at once sophisticated and naive, learned and playful, admiring and ironically detached— fell prey to a fierce, two-stage conflict within the young field of literary study, first between what Chris Baldick terms "professional Knowledge" and "amateur Taste" and then between the scholarly specialists in philology and literary history and a new breed of critics eager to popularize the techniques of what came to be known as "close reading."[49] In the long run, that conflict helped to birth the modern English department. Along the way, however, it thoroughly upset the delicate balance of attraction and avoidance that had enabled so many readers' relationships to *The Faerie Queene*. Indeed, by the time Woolf's essay appeared in print, a decade after it was written, reading and not reading had altered from complementary strategies of engagement with Spenser's poem to defiantly assumed postures of allegiance to rival conceptions of the practice and purpose of literary criticism.

In the contest between amateurs and professionals, scholars and critics, that shaped English as a discipline in the first half of the twentieth century, *The Faerie Queene* was firmly enlisted on the side of expertise.[50] The association was in many ways mutually beneficial: "In the first three decades of the twentieth century," David Hill Radcliffe points out, "more was written about Spenser than in the previous three hundred years," while "in the decades prior to 1965, more dissertations were written on Spenser than any other writer save Shakespeare."[51] Both facts bespeak the more general shift of poetry from popular cultural forms and institutions like the anthology and the lecture tour to the exclusive domain of academic specialists.[52] But they also attest to the special sympathy that seemed to obtain between *The Faerie Queene*'s educative ambitions and the aspirations of those who longed to establish British and—more often—American college and university programs in English on the same rigorous footing as the doctoral degree courses imported from Germany at the end of the nineteenth century. The remoteness of the poem's language, the density of its allusions, the abundance of sources to be traced and identified, the intricate obscurity of its allegory, the wealth of topical references and historical trivia: everything in the poem that had once been seen as an obstacle to readerly interest conspired to make it an ideal object of academic research. As Radcliffe writes, "The classic problems in Spenser studies were exactly the kinds of problems that philological scholarship was best able to address," and the very interpretive difficulties that earlier generations of critics sought to ameliorate or ignore were prized by scholars who saw them as validations of their training and effort.[53]

To a significant extent, however, *The Faerie Queene*'s status as a rite of disciplinary passage was due to the influence of a single scholar—who, for his part, believed that literary scholarship owed a great deal to *The Faerie Queene*. In *The Province of Literary History*, his 1931 defense of academic scholarship against what he saw as an encroaching critical amateurism, Edwin F. Greenlaw hailed Spenser as a literary historian avant la lettre, "an antiquary who delved in the old documents and records," "compiled ... sources," and "studied folk customs, old etymologies, monuments and tapestries," and he traced the origins of a properly rigorous tradition of English literary historicism to Warton's 1854 *Observations on the Faerie Queene of Spenser*. "[S]cholarship and poetic imagination united to produce [Spenser's] epic," he declared, "[and] scholarship, and not criticism, whether in Elizabethan days or ours, produces readers of the poet, which is the end and aim of literary investigation."[54] In addition to being a Spenserian, Greenlaw was also, as Graff describes him, "one of the imposing figures of early twentieth-century scholarship": a staunch proponent of historicism and philology, a highly successful builder of institutions, a committed teacher and mentor, and an influential presence in the growing business of academic publishing.[55] What one contemporary resentfully dubbed "the Greenlaw trust"—an expansive network of former students, advisees, colleagues, and collaborators cultivated over the course of his career as editor of *Studies in Philology* and

Modern Language Notes, dean of the Graduate School at the University of North Carolina, professor of English at Johns Hopkins University, and founding editor of the Johns Hopkins University Press series of Monographs in Literary History—was in many ways a *Faerie Queene* trust, kept afloat on a steady stream of graduate theses, doctoral dissertations, journal articles, editions, bibliographies, and monograph-length studies of the poem, culminating a year after Greenlaw's death with the appearance of the first two thickly researched and painstakingly annotated volumes of the Spenser *Variorum*.[56]

For all his professionalizing genius, however, Greenlaw was wont to idealize literary study, treating it as a quasi-spiritual vocation. In this respect, too, *The Faerie Queene* was well suited to his vision: the preface to his and James Holly Hanford's 1919 *The Great Tradition* cites its ambition "to fashion a gentleman or noble person in gentle and vertuous discipline" as an apt summation of their own scholarly and pedagogical aims.[57] Indeed, in taking Spenser's poem as both object and exemplar of disciplinary rigor, Greenlaw and his acolytes could understand their piecemeal labors on it as part of a vast and venerable intellectual project. Thus the conclusion to Jewel Wurtsbaugh's 1936 survey of eighteenth- and nineteenth-century scholarship on *The Faerie Queene*, published as part of the new Hopkins series, identifies the poem's early editorial history as a crucial inflection point in the "history of scholarship at large":

> The fumbling, but increasingly successful efforts of [editors and scholars such as] Hughes, Jortin, Birch, Church, Upton, and Todd towards greater accuracy of the text represent the slow process by which scholars came to have a regard for careful, painstaking research [and] the breaking down of an old canonical rigidity and narrow dogmatism that judged a work of art by standards of a later time rather than by such criteria as had originally inspired it.... Thus slowly reaching out, weighing evidence pro and con, learning by error, and more and more carefully scrutinizing fact, Spenserian scholars were drifting towards something more vital than meaningless parallels and minute matters of diction.... [I]t was not merely the question as to whether Spenser borrowed from Chaucer or Ariosto in a particular instance, but rather that Jortin, Upton, Warton, and Todd were painfully and laboriously struggling toward "the truth that sets men free."[58]

With its application of the words of Christ in the Gospel of St. John to the editorial history of a sixteenth-century poem, this is a startlingly grand, even grandiose, rendering of the advance of literary scholarship—a rendering, indeed, that bears more than a casual resemblance to the plot of *The Faerie Queene*'s opening book: a quest for enlightenment proceeds painfully and laboriously, through error and out of bad old dogmas, toward a glorious revelation of truth. However strained the parallel, it suggests that scholars like Wurtsbaugh and

Greenlaw found more in Spenser's poem than a seemingly bottomless trove of textual cruxes, bibliographic puzzles, and historical arcana; they discovered a powerfully appealing myth for their own academic labor, a way of imbuing the deskbound drudgery of scholarship with the spirit of an epic romance.

Needless to say, this is not how many of their contemporaries saw either literary scholarship or *The Faerie Queene*. A year after *The Province of Literary History* appeared in print, T. S. Eliot professed doubt as to whether Spenser's poem had value to anyone but literary historians: "Who except scholars, and except the eccentric few who are born with a sympathy for such work, or others who have deliberately studied themselves into the right appreciation, can now read through the whole of *The Faerie Queene* with delight?"[59] The mocking query inverts the proud conviction that reading Spenser was a badge of scholarly achievement: *The Faerie Queene*, Eliot implies, was a poem only a PhD could love. W. L. Renwick offered a similarly dry take on the heroic labors of Greenlaw and his colleagues in a 1933 review of the new Spenser *Variorum*, observing that the poet had "long engaged the fealty of American scholars—was, indeed, all but abandoned to them."[60] But among those eager to rescue English literature from the dry and instrumentalizing touch of scholars (or the vulgar clutches of Americans), *The Faerie Queene* was rapidly becoming anathema: outdated, overrated, and inessential to both literary history and the practice of literary criticism.

Although he offers a brilliant and appreciative analysis of the workings of Spenser's stanza in *Seven Types of Ambiguity* (1931), William Empson therefore forecloses the necessity of any further critical engagement with the poem on the grounds that, "having said that every use of the stanza includes all these uses in the reader's apprehension of it, I may have said enough."[61] And even a single stanza was more Empson's influential younger colleague, F. R. Leavis, could bear: "We don't read Spenser anymore," Leavis announced to students in his poetry seminars at Cambridge University—"as if," one later wrote, "reading Spenser were some kind of vice."[62] In Leavis's characteristically intemperate view, it more or less was. A brief approving mention of *The Faerie Queene* by I. A. Richards in his study of Coleridge was, for Leavis, "comment enough" on the weakness of that entire book; E.M.W. Tillyard's admiration for the poem as a foundational English epic struck Leavis as an egregious instance of that scholar's "tendency to find new burdens for the literary student"; even Eliot's grudging willingness to class *The Faerie Queene* among "long poems . . . in the first rank" was indicted by Leavis as a mark of his unregenerate "conventionality."[63] The fact that in the same essay Eliot described Spenser as one of those poets "who are very important, but whom we don't like" was hardly sufficient: in Leavis's sharply revised canon of English poetry, a contemporary observed, "Spenser was not so much attacked as dismissed."[64] Attacked *and* dismissed was better yet: writing in *Scrutiny*, the journal Leavis founded and for many years edited, Derek Traversi accused Spenser of having "crush[ed] the true poetic genius of English," describing the moralizing vision of *The Faerie Queene* as "a disembodied and destructive intellect preying on the body to kill the soul."[65]

As admiration for the techniques and style of the Cambridge critics spread to the United States, so too did their prejudice against Spenser.[66] In American colleges and universities in the 1940s and '50s, dislike for *The Faerie Queene* served as a calling card among partisans of what came to be known as the New Criticism. Such critics had their own notions of professional exclusivity: "It is not anyone who can do criticism," John Crowe Ransom declared in his 1937 polemic "Criticism, Inc.," and the sort of learning painstakingly acquired in the service of understanding a poem like *The Faerie Queene* was the most likely disqualification for doing it: "the more eminent (as historical scholar) the professor of English, the less apt he is to be able to write decent criticism."[67] Ransom couldn't wholly escape Spenser: first at Vanderbilt and then at Kenyon College, he "grimly taught *The Faerie Queene*" as the curriculum required but made his dislike of it widely known; "though he found Spenser's allegory without intellectual meat," his student Robert Lowell later recalled, "it amused him like a crossword puzzle or a blueprint for his garden."[68] His Kenyon colleague and fellow New Critic Allen Tate concurred, complaining that its "art . . . oversimplifies experience," its characters "remain homogeneous throughout," and "the action has no meaning apart from the preconceived abstractions."[69] At Yale, another bastion of New Criticism, the task of teaching Spenser was delegated to the department Anglo-Saxonist, while Cleanth Brooks, another of Ransom's former students, mocked members of what he called "the *Faerie Queene* club": the "small minority of pedants" who had managed to read it all the way through.[70] To Brooks, the poem was merely a primitive (and failed) attempt "to unite the intellect and the emotions when they begin to fall apart."[71] When a colleague gamely attempted to persuade him of its interest as a formal failure, the author of *The Well-Wrought Urn* (1947) is said to have retorted, "I like forms that work."[72]

The jibe is revealing. Although critics on both sides of the Atlantic cast their objections to *The Faerie Queene* in terms of aesthetic principles—the poem was too loosely organized, too crudely didactic, and too hard to understand without reference to the taboo subjects of history and biography—those objections were also, at bottom, pragmatic: it was simply too long to fit neatly with the confines of the interpretive forms, the seminar and the essay, that secured the closeness of close reading. For the Leavisites, the New Critics, and their fellow travelers, the great achievement of the English Renaissance was the lyric poem, a form made for seminar-length discussion and essay-length analysis. Spenser was discarded in favor of hitherto lesser contemporaries: *The Well-Wrought Urn* invokes a single stanza from *The Faerie Queene* in a postscript to underscore a point about a poem by Robert Herrick, while Yvor Winters's history of sixteenth-century verse champions the poems of Fulke Greville and George Gascoigne as exemplars of the period, dismissing *The Faerie Queene* as an "elaborately decorative" dead end by a poet "concerned largely with the pleasures of rhetoric for its own sake."[73] Even Mark van Doren, who included *The Faerie Queene* among the "ten great poems" in *The Noble Voice*, his 1946 study of epic tradition—a genre that would seem to license, if not necessitate, a certain sprawl—struggled to suppress his impatience with its size. "[M]any, indeed, have found it monotonous in its variety and therefore, since it is endless, dull," van Doren admits. What sparks of genius it contained could not save it from irrelevance: "there [is] too much bulk to rescue."[74]

"The grounds of our aversion [to Spenser] lie deeper in our contemporary culture than we can dig," observed Merritt Hughes in an essay written to mark the four-hundredth anniversary of the poet's birth in 1552.[75] But as the twentieth century reached its midpoint, that ground began to yield unexpected fruit. A generation "brought up," in Hayden Carruth's words, "to regard *The Faerie Queene* with disdain ... and hence to suspect its readers of callowness, pedantry or worse," turned to the poem in reaction against their teachers. Seizing gleefully on the very qualities in it that those teachers most deplored—"the longest poem in English! that allegorical bore! what interminable rhymes! what ghastly pseudo-diction!"—the new generation of Spenserians rejected both the orthodoxies of traditional historicism and the New Critics' iconoclasm, taking the poem's resistance to the protocols of scholarship and close reading alike as an incitement to reading otherwise.[76] Indeed, without meaning to, in making *The Faerie Queene* a limit case of readerly capacity—for good or ill—traditionalists like Greenlaw and renegades like Leavis and Ransom had combined to invest the poem with a power to undermine their own totalizing claims, revising disciplinary norms well beyond the confines of Spenser studies itself. As Northrop Frye explains in the preface to *The Anatomy of Criticism* (1957), his groundbreaking attempt at a "synoptic account of the scope, theory, principles, and techniques of literary criticism ... began [as] a study of Spenser's *Faerie Queene*." But reading the poem as it both allowed and required rapidly exceeded the affordances of criticism as Frye had been taught to understand it: "The introduction to Spenser became an introduction to the theory of allegory, and that theory obstinately adhered to a much larger theoretical structure"—the structure of "the whole work of scholarship and taste concerned with literature which is a part of what is variously called liberal education, culture, or the study of the humanities."[77]

Frye wasn't alone in sensing both a challenge and an opportunity in *The Faerie Queene*, particularly in its most unfashionable and unrewarding aspects. The same year that *The Anatomy of Criticism* was published, Harry Berger Jr.'s *The Allegorical Temper* made a case for the revelatory potential of Spenser's elaborate style, which, he revealed, far from being merely ornamental, was rich with the very ambiguities of meaning prized by Empson and the New Critics.[78] In the decade that followed, Angus Fletcher and Rosamund Tuve produced accounts of Spenserian allegory that reclaimed that much-maligned feature as an engine of speculative argument, formal ingenuity, and readerly engagement.[79] In 1976, Paul Alpers's *The Poetry of "The Faerie Queene"* made a paradoxically profound case for dwelling on what he called "the surface of the poem," allowing its apparent inconsistencies to modify, complicate, and enrich readers' responses.[80] That same year, Nohrnberg's nine-hundred-page-long *Analogy of "The Faerie Queene"* embraced the immensity of the poem and "the conspicuous heterogeneity of its matter" as occasions for dazzling excursions across the whole of classical, medieval, and early modern culture.[81] Spenser's investment in romance—which most twentieth-century critics, with the signal exception of Lewis, either ignored or deplored—was reclaimed, too, in Patricia Parker's *Inescapable Romance* (1979) and Jonathan Goldberg's *Endlesse Worke* (1981), each of which married the poem's errant, error-filled plotting to the open-endedness of deconstructive analysis.[82] Inspired by feminist and Marxist theories, Maureen Quilligan and Louis Montrose found in Gloriana, the absent center around which *The Faerie Queene* revolves, a supremely rich case study in the history and politics of gender, sexuality, and authorship.[83] And a single, seminal chapter in Stephen Greenblatt's *Renaissance Self-Fashioning* (1980) made Guyon's wasting of the Bower of Bliss—a crux on which countless prior readings had foundered—a touchstone of the New Historicism and a signal trace of "the early, tentative, conflict-ridden fashioning of modern consciousness."[84]

By the early 1980s, when studies by Goldberg, Greenblatt, Montrose, and Quilligan appeared in print, it was clear that the pendulum of reading and not reading *The Faerie Queene* had swung back in favor of reading it. Those who had deemed it unreadable hadn't simply gotten the poem wrong; they had gotten the discipline wrong, too. "I went to work on Spenser, partly because the New Critics thought Spenser was bad," Harry Berger Jr. later recalled. "So I figured, well, I'd show 'em."[85] But as the remark suggests, *The Faerie Queene* maintained a paradoxically oppositional relation to the field of academic study it helped to establish: reading it was both an assertion of mastery and a declaration of independence, a way of fitting in and acting out all at once. *Reading and Not Reading "The Faerie Queene"* channels both aspects of this relation. It owes an obvious debt to those who claimed (and reclaimed) *The Faerie Queene* as an object of study and a locus of theoretical and methodological innovation. But it is equally indebted to those who tried to read the poem and failed, or went astray, and to those who refused to read it at all. Indeed, in the chapters that follow, even as I work to generate new insights from Spenser's poem, I often do so by aligning myself with readers short on understanding, skill, objectivity, patience, learning, curiosity, broadmindedness, sophistication, and all of the other intellectual virtues with which we tend to associate literature in general and *The Faerie Queene* in particular. Such limited, resistant types make up an unusually large proportion of Spenser's readers, and their responses to his poem can be as telling as those of their more successful or pliant counterparts.

My aim is not necessarily to endorse their perspectives on the poem, but to adopt them as clarifying, usefully distorting, or prismatic lenses on the experience of reading it, enlisting their impulses and assumptions against the complacencies of my own critical and scholarly formation. For from the late sixteenth century on, readers of Spenser's poem have met its challenges and expectations with their own peculiar demands, refashioning both its language and and its material form in conformity with the dictates of circumstance, necessity, and desire. As a result, the poem has been repeatedly and at times radically revised, including by the poet himself: depending on where, when, or who is reading it, *The Faerie Queene* might consist of one book, three books, six books, or more; it might contain learned annotations or no gloss at all, elaborate editorial apparatuses or fanciful illustrations. Some versions of the poem purport to be comprehensive, while others cheerfully carve it into pieces; some burden it with additional meanings and some try to get rid of allegory altogether; one is in rhyming couplets and quite a few are in prose. Such transformations have influenced how *The Faerie Queene* has been received, but they are also products of that reception, traces of the efforts publishers, editors, critics, scholars, and assorted amateurs have made to render an unusually rich and recalcitrant text legible to themselves and others.

Not all of their efforts succeeded: no one adopted Gill's 1621 effort to render the poem in a made-up alphabet of Anglo-Saxon letter forms, and Bronson Alcott's attempt to teach the poem to five-year-olds in his nineteenth-century Massachusetts school went swiftly and predictably awry. And those that did can now seem woefully misguided: despite its canonical prestige, *The Faerie Queene* has long flourished in what Michael Warner calls "the enormous shadow of *uncritical* reading."[86] Where critical reading is alert, informed, and attentive, detached, reasonable and self-reflective, uncritical reading is everything else: "identification, self-forgetfulness, reverie, sentimentality, enthusiasm, literalism, aversion, distraction." As it happens, these are all modes of engagement that *The Faerie Queene* not only permits but at times solicits or even requires. Indeed, the list of prohibited identities Warner cites as foundational to the scholarly critic—"Don't read like children, like vacation readers on the beach, like escapists, like fundamentalists, like nationalists, like antiquarians, like consumers, like ideologues, like sexists, like tourists, like yourselves"—is a concise accounting of the kinds of readers who predominate in the poem's reception history and the pages that follow.[87] Their misdeeds in relation to the text are many: they change its spellings; ignore, or overemphasize, the allegory; take images, phrases, and entire stanzas out of context; fixate on the fates of particular characters; indulge in unpersuasive, anachronistic, and self-serving analogies; pick fights with other readers; deface the margins of their books; and—bored, distracted, or otherwise occupied—give up on the poem altogether.

Rather than seeking to exclude or amend their wrongheaded responses, this book cherishes them, as an index of the poem's own ambivalently mixed signals, a sensitive barometer of shifts in literary culture, and an indispensable archive of repressed or forgotten episodes in the history of reading itself. In doing so, it seeks to capitalize on a mode of interference that *The Faerie Queene*'s own history makes inevitable, for whether we are conscious of their influence or not, readers of Spenser's poem encounter the text through the mediation of other readers. Competing ideals, ambitions, and methods of reading thus inform and interact with one another in the course of any single encounter with it, turning the text from neutral ground into a plain on which historical and fictive readers meet, form alliances, quarrel, and fight the occasional pitched battle. Present to us in the guise of editorial apparatuses and critical commentaries, adaptations and appropriations, scribbled marginalia and (what is more difficult to perceive) our own unexamined assumptions, former readings of *The Faerie Queene* are like Guyon's reading of the *Antiquitee of Faerie Lond*: both in the past and not yet ended. Indeed, as I have learned repeatedly in the course of researching and writing this book, old readerly habits die hard or not at all, and their effects extend into the present, even—perhaps especially—when they have been vehemently repudiated. In crafting my arguments about Spenser's poem and its place in the history of reading, I have therefore worked from the assumption that my own reading of the poem is necessarily shaped, and can be usefully enriched, by association with the habits of readers past. A willingness to recognize their readings at work in my own is both an essential form of disciplinary humility and a valuable source of disciplinary insight. It is also, I hope, a stimulus to disciplinary creativity: *Reading and Not Reading "The Faerie Queene"* claims reception history not simply as a record of how reading used to happen but as a still vital matrix for the ways we read now.

For instance, for all their blunt insensitivity to the rewards of reading *The Faerie Queene*, the Leavisites and the New Critics were keenly attuned to an aspect of reading it that the poem's critical champions have tended to underrate or, worse, ascribe to the defects of its readers: the problem of time. The fact that it is impossible to complete *The Faerie Queene* in a single sitting, that one looks up from it to discover the light has changed or one's coffee gone cold; the fact that periods of immersion in it are necessarily broken by intervals of inattention, and that when we return to it, it can seem an altogether different work: these inconvenient realities are the basis of some of the poem's most salient insights into the nature of readerly experience, but they are also genuine obstacles to understanding and enjoying it. As Christina Lupton argues, the question of "when we read"—along with the fantasy of a time in which there was enough time to do so properly—is inseparable from the phenomenon of literacy itself: "ever since people like us have had access to books, the time we've spent with them has been defined as fragile, hard to come by, and good to hope for."[88] But for Spenser's readers, the problem of time has another dimension as well: for as long as people have had access to *The Faerie Queene*, the time they've spent with it has seemed dauntingly expansive, hard to justify, and potentially good for nothing. The question it persistently poses is not just "When do we read?" but "When will we do anything else?"

Acknowledging that problem as real—not an excuse or admission of failure, or even a challenge for pedagogy and criticism to surmount, but the challenging condition of reading itself—puts us in a better position to appreciate the significance of the fact that the book Guyon reads in book 2, canto 10 is both extremely (perhaps interminably) long and conspicuously dull. If we could comprehend the motive for Guyon's absorption in the *Antiquitee of Faerie Lond*, or set some reasonable limit on it, that absorption would not be nearly so arresting, or so provocatively at odds with the legend in which it appears. Of all the virtues in *The Faerie Queene*, temperance is the least suited to reading the poem itself, and the one that draws closest to our anxieties about the future of reading in an era of limited attention and proliferating content. As Ann Blair has shown, these are anxieties Spenser and his contemporaries shared, and in the face of which they invented or refined a host of time- and labor-saving devices, from the alphabetical index to the genre of the reference book.[89] Modern literary scholars, by contrast, although we rely on such devices every bit as much as our early modern precursors, have tended to embrace the expenditure of time as a mark of readerly distinction, valorizing our own reading practices as a synthesis of concentration, understanding, and pleasure: what Stanley Fish calls "the paying of a certain kind of attention."[90] Amid ongoing debates about the ideal aims, methods, and objects of critical reading—close versus distant, surface versus depth, suspicious versus reparative or "just"—there remains a broad consensus about the value of attention itself.[91] But because *The Faerie Queene* makes such extreme and incommensurate demands on the attention of its readers, it cannot easily be enlisted on any particular side in those debates. Rather, it illuminates their reflexively oppositional character: the "versus" that implicitly or explicitly structures any bid for a new and better way of reading, and the alternatives that are thereby sacrificed.

At the end of book 2, canto 10, Guyon has to put aside the *Antiquitee of Faerie Lond* for an unexpectedly homely reason: the owner of the castle in which he is staying appears to tell him that dinner is waiting. In its blithe dispensation of readerly discipline, the episode anticipates a scene in *Lionel Asbo: State of England*, Martin Amis's 2012 satire of British cultural decline, in which the novel's proudly antisocial title character discovers his nephew, Des, immersed in writing something:

> "What are you doing with that there pen? What's that you writing? Guiss it."
> Des thought fast. "Uh, it's about poetry, Uncle Li."
> "*Poetry?*" said Lionel and started back.
> "Yeah. Poem called *The Faerie Queene*."
> "The *what*? . . . I despair of you sometimes, Des. Why aren't you out smashing windows? It's not healthy."[92]

Amis's satire is aimed squarely—perhaps too squarely—at the sort of reader who worries about the future of literature in an age of reality TV and perpetual online entertainment. Its humor often relies on the unsubtle contrast between thuggish Lionel and polite, bookish Des, who, as one reviewer noted, is a thinly veiled stand-in for his creator: "We know that he has full authorial approval, not least because—not unlike Amis—he is an etymology pedant and a usage bore, with a near-religious reverence for the *Concise Oxford Dictionary*."[93] But the humor of this particular scene is more layered. For one thing, we know Des is lying: he's not writing about poetry, he's writing a letter to a local advice columnist confessing that he has begun a sexual affair with an older woman, who happens to be his grandmother and Lionel's mother. As has so often been the case in its reception history, *The Faerie Queene*, which Des may not have read at all, serves merely as a badge of readerly virtue—and a reliable conversation-stopper. But, of course, Lionel does have a response, and that response gives the joke a further, unpredictable spin, for even readers won over by the general thrust of Amis's moralizing critique might be struck with momentary horror at the prospect of an afternoon spent reading, writing, or merely thinking about *The Faerie Queene*: Why not smash windows instead?

It is a perspective for which the poem itself has the occasional spasm of sympathy: one way of understanding Guyon's destruction of the Bower of Bliss in book 2, canto 12 is as a window-smashing correction to the profligate stillness of his reading in canto 10. Obviously, if the choice is between reading and vandalism, reading looks to most of us like the right thing to do. But if the choice is between reading one way and reading another, between reading this book and reading something else, or between reading and going to dinner or reading and saving a life—which is another, equally valid way of understanding what Guyon does in the Bower of Bliss—the calculus gets harder. This as much as anything seems to be what Spenser means by discipline: the making of hard choices among rival goods, without expectation of any ultimate confirmation that we have chosen well. The sequential structure of *The Faerie Queene* promises progress toward perfection, but that progress never accrues. Instead, the commencement of a new quest entails the abandonment of already proven modes of interpretation, and within each book—sometimes, within a single canto or stanza—readers are forced to unlearn one kind of reading in order to perform another. And although the poem treats this learning and unlearning as a life's work, it pauses now and then to consider if it might not also be an unconscionable waste of time. Not reading is an option *The Faerie Queene* never allows us to foreclose—reading's first essential, its inevitable endpoint, and a possibility all the way through.

1

"The Falsest Twoo"

FORGING THE SCHOLARLY READER

WITHIN THE cache of Shakespearean manuscripts, documents, and letters nineteen-year-old William Henry Ireland claimed to have discovered in 1794, in the home of an anonymous country gentleman, was a pair of quarto volumes, printed in 1596 and filled with marginalia. Rebound in handsome green morocco by Ireland's father, Samuel, a London bookseller and amateur antiquarian, and supplemented with neat italic transcriptions of an almost illegible secretary hand, the volumes were exhibited in Samuel's shop on Norfolk Street as the crown jewel of the so-called Shakespeare Library: Shakespeare's *Faerie Queene*, sixteenth-century England's most celebrated poem as read by its most celebrated playwright. In reality, of course, William Henry was responsible for every bit of the marginalia, which he crafted with an eye to eighteenth-century readers' longing for a Shakespeare whose tastes complemented (and complimented) their own. "Upon the margins of this poem, I was most particular in my comments," he recalls in his memoir of the hoax, published a decade later, "well aware that a writer of such celebrity as Spenser must have attracted the notice of Shakespeare; and I was fully convinced that such notes would be regarded with the strictest scrutiny by every visitant in Norfolk Street."[1] Indeed, the forged annotations—many helpfully signed "Wm. Shakspere" or initialed "W.S."—went well beyond establishing that Shakespeare had read *The Faerie Queene*; they suggested he had revered and even imitated it. Spenser's poem puts Ireland's "Shakspere" into ecstasies of admiration: "Innedeeede goode Spencerre whenne thourte praysedde tis notte vayne Flatterye butte thatte whyche thou doste trewly merytt"; "the language in thys canto is worthye mye great masterre Spencerre"; "Thye Genyus O Spencerre is greaterre / Thanne language canne paynte / In trothe thourte morre thanne mortalle"—and so on.[2] The leaf following the end of book 1 contains an acrostic on Spenser's name, which Ireland claims in his memoir was hailed as equal to any of Shakespeare's published verse. Most daring of all is the note scrawled in the margins of canto 2, next to Spenser's description of the Redcrosse Knight's horrified response to Fradubio and—in an irony probably lost on Ireland—across from the description of Duessa's "forged beauty": a draft of Hamlet's horrified reaction to his father's ghost.

Shakespeare's *Faerie Queene* was a sensation; according to Ireland, a visitor to the Norfolk Street exhibit offered his father sixty pounds for the pair of volumes, an extravagant sum Samuel rejected as unworthy (*Confessions*, 196). But Shakespeare's *Faerie Queene* also contained the germ of Ireland's undoing, for it was spelling—his own and Edmund Spenser's—that gave the game away. The orthography of the Shakespeare Papers attracted suspicion from the start. Irelandisms like *innedeede*, *innevennecyonne*, and *innetennecyonne* "set at defiance the spelling of all periods," James Boaden complained in a letter to George Steevens:

> Look at the authors from whose orthography the poet must have derived his knowledge of language, and from whose pages we can form alone any guess of the orthography of his times, how decide they? Look at Hollinshead and the poets from whose records and tales he has drawn the materials of his dramas, is there in all or one of these or any other writers, a single example of language so idle in its literal form, so clogged, so confounded by unnecessary letters?[3]

"Shakespeare's spelling" became a cause célèbre, disputed in the pages of the *Gentleman's Magazine*—where an anonymous correspondent argued that "no such mode of spelling prevailed at the latter end of the sixteenth century, nor indeed at any period of our literary history, anterior or posterior"[4]—and played for laughs in the *Telegraph*, which printed an invitation from "Williamme Shaekspere" to "MISSTEERREE BEENJAAMMINNEE JOOHNNSSONN," to "dinnee wythee meee onn Fridaye nextte, attt twoo off theee clockee, too eattee sommee muttonne choppes andd somme poottattoooeesse."[5]

Despite such ridicule, the Shakespeare Papers had their adherents, prominent literary men among them, and it fell to the distinguished Shakespeare scholar and editor Edmund Malone to put an end to the debate—indeed, in February 1796, *Gentleman's Magazine* printed a letter from "Anna Hatherrewaye" to "Dearesste Masterre Edmonne," begging him to do so.[6] Malone's response, a five-hundred-page *Inquiry into the Authenticity of Certain Miscellaneous Papers and Legal Instruments*, published in December 1795, was extreme in severity and length. Like everyone else, he began with Ireland's spelling, which he exposed over the course of seventy pages as unexampled in the writings of any known Elizabethan, including the queen herself. He saved Spenser for the end, comparing an extract from the Shakespeare Papers with the opening stanzas of "THE FAERY QUEENE of Spenser, whose orthography is at least as ancient as that of any of his contemporaries."⁷ When even *The Faerie Queene* could not match the "laboured and capricious deformity of spelling" in the letter, Malone pronounced it "an entire forgery": "the spelling of no time" (68–69, 126).

Malone's use of *The Faerie Queene* to strip the pseudoantique varnish from Ireland's forgeries proved effective, but it entailed an irony of which the scholar himself was only partly aware. Spenser's spelling revealed the spuriousness of Ireland's not because it was known to be typical of late sixteenth-century usage, but because it famously wasn't, being, in Malone's paradoxical formulation, "at least as ancient as any of his contemporaries." In other words, if Ireland had only read *The Faerie Queene* more attentively, he might have discovered in it both a prophetic allegory of truth's triumph over fraud and a guide to the artful and convincing fabrication of old spelling. But the very faith Malone invests in Spenser's poem as a limit case of orthographic antiquation rests on a pair of assumptions—that the spelling of *The Faerie Queene* is notably archaic by sixteenth-century standards and that it is Spenser's own—with almost no foundation in textual, bibliographic, or historical evidence. Both beliefs were in fact of relatively recent vintage, fetishistic attachments rebranded as articles of scholarly faith and badges of editorial rigor. Malone's seeming textual conservatism thus betrays his anachronistic relationship to *The Faerie Queene* no less than Ireland's flagrant imposture of Shakespeare reading it. Taken together, they deliver an illuminating instance of the entanglement of discipline and desire at the roots of literary scholarship. Moreover, they cast productive doubt on the peculiar fashion in which we continue to read *The Faerie Queene* today: not simply line by line but letter by letter.

Old Spelling, Modern Usage

The question of how to represent the orthography of *The Faerie Queene* in modern texts is both settled and unsettled, entrenched as an editorial convention but increasingly shaky as a matter of editorial conviction. Unlike modern editions of Donne's love lyrics or Shakespeare's sonnets, which routinely update the orthography of their print or manuscript copy-texts, editions of Spenser's poem nearly always preserve the late sixteenth-century spellings: it's *The Faerie Queene*, not *The Fairy Queen*. Orthographic purism is not always matched with typographic purism—an ampersand may be replaced with "and," or long-s with its modern equivalent—but despite such concessions, justifications of the practice tend to be categorical. As the editors of the Penguin Classics *Faerie Queene* explain, the old spellings "are so integral to the meaning that we are not willing to submit them to the regularities of modern usage."⁸ The editors of the Norton Critical Edition of *The Poetry of Edmund Spenser* and the textual editors of the Longman *Faerie Queene* concur: modern spellings "would diminish the impression [of archaism] Spenser wanted to give" and efface the most important of the poem's "generally accepted Spenserian characteristics."[9] When scholars working on the forthcoming Oxford edition of Spenser's works proposed normalizing a further handful of typographic conventions, such as the use of "u" for "v" and "i" for "j," readers for the press objected, feeling that a version of Spenser's *Faerie Queene* in which "highest *Ioue*" appeared as "highest *Jove*" would be neither Spenser's nor *The Faerie Queene*.[10]

The reproduction of old spellings communicates a set of seemingly irreproachable editorial commitments: to textual fidelity, to philological precision, to the material and cultural contexts of poetic composition, and, above all, to authorial intent. Ironically, however, the effects of old spelling on Spenser's modern readers are hard to justify in such terms. As Robert Kellogg and Oliver Steele argue in the introduction to the only available modern-spelling version of *The Faerie Queene*, a 1965 Odyssey Press edition of books 1 and 2, the antiquated appearance of the poem's orthography today far exceeds what a contemporary reader would have seen as archaic or strange; moreover, and more seriously, the preservation of all those odd variant spellings in a modern edition confers the impression of poetic intent on what may well be "the inconsistent and idiosyncratic orthography of individual sixteenth-century typesetters." There is, they conclude, "little of literary value in them."[11] There is, indeed, considerable risk—warnings against which have generally gone unheeded. As Emma Field Pope argued in 1922, the singular treatment of Spenser's verse by modern editors has contributed to "certain misapprehensions as regards to his language": "the diction of *The Faerie Queene* is by no means so antiquated as is often supposed," she writes, and "many Spenserian words cited as archaisms are not really archaisms since they are also found in the writings of his contemporaries."[12] Amplifying and extending Pope's argument six years later, with the assistance of the newly completed *Oxford English Dictionary*, Bruce McElderry observed that "[t]he loose use of the word archaism has ... been particularly misleading in regard to Spenser, for so much has been said of his archaisms that even the informed reader tends constantly to overestimate [them]," classing as "Spenserian" terms that, if they appeared in the work of a contemporary, would simply register as "Elizabethan."[13]

Neither Pope nor McElderry blamed old spelling in particular for the misperception of archaism by Spenser's readers—Pope describes Elizabethan orthography as "thin ice, whence retreat is the best course"—but orthographic antiquation played a leading role in establishing Spenser's reputation for archaism in the eighteenth century. And, as is increasingly clear, it has little relevance to the period in which *The Faerie Queene* was written. Partly in response to the failure of the campaign to selectively modernize the Oxford Spenser, Anupam Basu, Joseph Loewenstein, and Stephen Pentecost at Washington University developed the EEBO-TCP N-gram browser, which allows users to track clusters of orthographic variants across a digital corpus of some 60,000 English books printed between 1473 and 1700.[14] Using the EEBO-TCP N-gram browser and an array of statistical modeling techniques, Basu and Loewenstein have embarked on a thoroughgoing analysis of what they call "the impression of the linguistic distinctiveness of Spenser's poetry," starting with its spellings: "in general," they found, "Spenser's corpus is not orthographically distinctive" from the rest of the EEBO-TCP corpus. On the contrary, the spellings in both the 1590 and 1596 editions of *The Faerie Queene* "conform very closely to those of other texts printed at or around the same time" and "would not have struck early readers" as either old or odd.[15] That finding confirms what Kellogg and Steele suspected: although it aims at preserving the text as Spenser wrote it and early readers read it, the so-called old-spelling *Faerie Queene* is largely an artifact of the poem's "modern usage."

In particular, as the case of Ireland suggests, it is an artifact of its role in securing the distinction between experts and impostors, scholars and charlatans. In part for that reason, even the authority of "big data" may not be sufficient to overcome our attachment to the old-spelling *Faerie Queene*, which is the version of the poem on which scholarly readers have long staked their identities. Nor is it clear that it should: despite what Kellogg and Steele imply, literary value need not be restricted to what we know to be authorial, or even what we know to be genuinely old. Editorial traditions may be worth preserving even if they are founded on a mistaken basis. And accidents, whether editorial or linguistic, can be extraordinarily difficult to distinguish from intentions, authorial and otherwise. From one perspective, the tradition of reading that has insisted on the significance of each individual letter in *The Faerie Queene* is an embarrassing shared delusion; from another, it is an ingenious response to the poem's own surplus of signification, a fantastic and (literally) literal way of localizing the pervasive potential of allegory on the page.

As I argue in what follows, the orthography of *The Faerie Queene* is well worth our attention, though not necessarily the sort we are accustomed to giving it. Although the "old-spelling" *Faerie Queene* encodes much less of Spenser's meaning than most modern editions of the poem imply, it retains more of what the poem has meant to readers, and to the tradition of literary scholarship. What one of the founders of that tradition, Thomas Warton, called "the charm of old spelling" is a multitemporal effect, compounded of an unstable mix of poetic artifice, editorial intervention, scholarly ambition, and readerly desire. Hence the double irony of Malone's invocation of the orthography of *The Faerie Queene*: Malone may deem Ireland's faux-antiquated orthography "the spelling of no time," but the evidence to which he turned was itself the spelling of at least two times: the 1590s, when the earliest editions of the poem appeared in print, and the 1750s, when the first scholarly editions were made. For us, it is the spelling of three times: the 1590s, the 1750s, and the latter half of the twentieth century, when Spenser scholars labored to redeem the poem from the charge that it was inimical to readerly pleasure or critical interest. As a result of their efforts, the poem's antiquated orthography, which had a genetic relationship to the emergence of literary historicism, acquired an equally powerful kinship with close reading.

For although the preservation of old spellings by modern editors of *The Faerie Queene* no doubt contributed to the Leavisites' and New Critics' distaste for the poem, it supplied Spenser's champions with an extended hermeneutic warrant: each variant spelling opens at least a potential aperture onto the shadowy whole. And as anyone who has taught the poem can attest, although the antiquated orthography creates an initial obstacle to comprehension, it also enables a thrillingly attentive variety of interpretation. Because the surface of the text is so pervasively defamiliarized—and because both allegorical form and narrative content so insistently call us to suspect outward shows—typographic features one would ordinarily read past or through present themselves as worthy and even necessary objects of scrutiny. The returns on such scrutiny can be spectacular: as Martha Craig pointed out in an influential 1967 essay titled "The Secret Wit of Spenser's Language," the spirit of the poem does on occasion inhere in a letter.[16] Thus, in canto 7 of book 1, the Redcrosse Knight encounters and is defeated by the monstrous Orgoglio, described as a "Geaunt." A canto later, Prince Arthur defeats Orgoglio, now described as a "Gyaunt," and restores Redcrosse to freedom. The spelling in canto 7 isn't simply older and rarer than the spelling in canto 8; it conveys a crucial etymological and theological truth. Calling Orgoglio a "geaunt" highlights his parentage—giants are sons of Gaea, the earth—and the genealogy he shares with the Redcrosse Knight, whose given name is George. Both giant and knight are sons of earth and also, by punning extension, of Adam. It's because of this that Redcrosse requires Arthur's assistance: to Arthur, child of grace, Orgoglio is merely a monster, but to Redcrosse he is something more intimate and perilous—a brother, or alter ego, whose destruction entails the hero's own. The shift from "Geaunt" to "Gyaunt" is thus a compact allegory of grace, which alone redeems mankind from the inheritance of Adam.

The publication of Craig's essay coincided with two broad movements in the field of English literature: a discipline-wide turn toward close reading as the essence of literary professionalism and a concerted effort by Spenserians to prove *The Faerie Queene* not only amenable but richly responsive to such treatment.[17] As Paul Alpers, who brought Craig's then-unpublished work to wide attention in *The Poetry of "The Faerie Queene,"* put it, "our experience [of the poem] is specifically an experience of words and is modulated and developed in the very act of reading."[18] Old spelling was regarded as essential to that experience, and sensitivity to orthographic wit as the mark of a qualified reader both in and of *The Faerie Queene*: the ability to glimpse the pun "hidden" in a word like "pourtra*hed*" is, for David Miller, what "sets Arthur apart from Ignaro," good reader from bad; for Leigh Deneef, the poem's status as a "wise rede" depends on our noticing the pun "on the Anglo-Saxon *ræd* and Middle English *rede*"; Jonathan Goldberg's deconstruction of book 4 begins with an orthographic anatomy of the phrase "perfect hole"; Andrew Hadfield and Willy Maley identify the word "salvage" (used throughout *The Faerie Queene* where a modern author would write "savage") as one of the poem's "foundational puns . . . simultaneously expressing the hope of salvation and religious purity, and the fear of disintegration and damnation."[19] Such readings demand critical ingenuity as well as attentiveness, but they rest on a residual faith in poetic intentionality. Alpers is explicit on this point: "the treatment of poetic language as if meaning were inherent in it" demands "passivity" from readers, and Craig's "microscopic analyses" of Spenser's spelling "are valuable less for telling us how to read [particular passages] than for revealing a feeling for or use of language" at work in the poem as a whole.[20] As Angus Fletcher observes, the sometimes stilted quality of Spenser's wordplay—he cites the spelling of "christal" as an example—only heightens its power: "'Badness' in punning seems to mark a special kind of verbal accident; it seems to prove coherence where there is no 'reason' to expect it. This 'badness' of punning is marvelous, a source of wonder, a fairly miraculous proof of providential order."[21]

Alternatively, of course, one could argue that the pun registers the triumph of orthographical and acoustical accident over writerly intent; the pun, as Catherine Bates puts it, is a "worthless liability," a "leaky element in the structure of language."[22] This essential ambiguity makes puns vulnerable, Margaret Ferguson observes: easily effaced by shifts in usage, spelling, and pronunciation and—in the case of early modern texts—uniquely susceptible to editorial correction.[23] Spenser's modern editors have, perhaps, been too conscious of this latter peril: in their eagerness to avoid the Scylla of hypercorrection, they risk plunging us into the Charybdis of overreading, tempting us (as Fletcher's repeated use of the word "seems" may register) to mistake the application of critical intelligence for an inlay of authorial wit. But in doing so, they have also been responsive to *The Faerie Queene*'s repeated injunctions *not* to confuse one similar-seeming figure for another, to remain perpetually alert to the possibility of meaningful difference within apparent likeness.

Consider, for instance, the unsettling effect of an extra "o" on a pair of stanzas that appear midway through the opening canto of the 1590 poem. Una and the Redcrosse Knight have fallen asleep in the hovel of a kindly hermit, who descends to his study and reveals himself as the wicked magician Archimago:

Then choosing out few words most horrible,
   (Let none them read) thereof did verses frame,
   With which and other spelles like terrible,
   He bad awake blacke *Plutoes* griesly Dame,
   And cursed heuen, and spake reprochful shame
   Of highest God, the Lord of life and light,
   A bold bad man, that dar'd to call by name
   Great *Gorgon*, prince of darknes and dead night,
At which *Cocytus* quakes and *Styx* is put to flight.

And forth he cald out of deepe darknes dredd
   Legions of Sprights, the which like litle flyes
   Fluttring about his euerdamned hedd,
   A waite whereto their seruice he applyes,
   To aide his friendes, or fray his enimies:
   Of those he chose out two, the falsest twoo,
   And fittest for to forge true-seeming lyes;
   The one of them he gaue a message too,
The other by himselfe staide other worke to doo.[24]

From this parodic scene of poetic creativity stems the whole of Archimago's duplicitous plot: the forging of the false Una, Redcrosse's plunge into doubt, his seduction by Duessa, and his displacement at Una's side by a cunning simulacrum that leads Truth herself astray. The catastrophic effect of those doublings and re-pairings is telegraphed here in the description of Archimago's hellish associates, those "two, the falsest twoo." The gratuitous "o" in "twoo" throws the phrase off-balance, exposing a lurking gap between the written word and the stable, self-similar meaning it is pledged to represent. Spenser's reader and his poem teeter on the brink of the extra letter, whose silent, senseless departure from its original anticipates the Redcrosse Knight's unthinking lapse from holiness to hypocrisy, truth to counterfeit, Una to Duessa.

But the phrase "the falsest twoo" may also herald the comeuppance of the poem's attentive close reader. After all, a keyword search of *Early English Books Online* (EEBO) confirms that "two" and "twoo" were semantically interchangeable in sixteenth-century usage, although by 1590 the former spelling was considerably more common than the latter. Patterns of orthographic standardization were broadly consistent over time, as Basu and Loewenstein have found, but particular variants could prove stubborn: thirty years after Spenser's poem appeared in print, the Scottish author of a 1620 manuscript treatise *Of the Orthographie and Congruitie of the Britan Tongue* still lamented the fact there was "sik uncertentie in our mens wryting, as if a man wald indyte one letter to tuentie of our best wryteres, nae tuae of the tuentie, without conference, wald agree."²⁵ Ignoring the difference between "two" and "twoo" might be a capitulation to Archimago's double-dealing, but assigning meaning to that difference risks burdening the poem with an anachronistic expectation of orthographic regularity. The same caution applies to "christal," "hole," and "salvage": in sixteenth-century printed texts, a keyword search reveals, "christal" and "christall" are more common spellings than "crystal"; "hole" appears instead of "whole" in hundreds of instances, in medical treatises, chronicle histories, and devotional handbooks; and "salvage," a widely attested variant of "savage," seems to have had no association with saving or redeeming until the mid-seventeenth century. Such findings don't rule out the possibility of punning associations, of course, but they make it considerably less obvious such associations were intended—or would have occurred to the poem's contemporary readers.

Paradoxically, then, if we want to retain the privilege of close reading *The Faerie Queene*'s spelling, we may have to subject the poem to an unusually concentrated sort of distant reading. As Franco Moretti describes it, distant reading scales attention up or down, "focus[ing] on units that are much smaller or much larger than the text," and as N. Katherine Hayles argues, there is no reason why close readers shouldn't capitalize on its affordances.²⁶ For Spenserians, certainly, online databases like EEBO can make our orthographically inflected readings more plausible and precise. Thanks to Basu, Loewenstein, and Pentecost, it will soon be possible to measure how peculiar any given spelling in *The Faerie Queene* would have appeared in the late sixteenth century, relative to other texts from the period, thus salvaging genuinely idiosyncratic, artful, or antiquated spellings—real Spenserianisms—from what Loewenstein terms "an accidental wash of archaism."²⁷ As the results of their preliminary statistical analysis indicate, such investigation is likely to demystify many—indeed, most—spellings in *The Faerie Queene*, revealing them as strange to us but not to Spenser or his contemporaries. But digital database analysis may also confirm critical hunches: for instance, using the EEBO-TCP N-gram browser to compare "geaunt" and "gyaunt" shows that, although "gyaunt" was one of a handful of more or less equally current spellings in the latter half of the sixteenth century (along with "gyant," "giaunt," and the now-standard "giant"), "geaunt" was genuinely idiosyncratic—of the nine instances in which the spelling appears between 1540 and 1590, six are in texts by Spenser. In the 1590 *Faerie Queene*, three of four occur in the context of Redcrosse's defeat by Orgoglio. Of course, a modern reader of the poem might well miss this fact, distracted by so many other seemingly idiosyncratic spellings. The EEBO-TCP N-gram browser reveals the hidden cost of editorial conservatism: an occasional feature of Spenser's allegorical conceit has become the hallmark of his style in *The Faerie Queene*, distributed across the poem in a way that both exaggerates and dilutes its effect on readers. If we wish to use spelling as an index of poetic meaning, it may well be time for a far more selective approach: perhaps one that tests each variant against a predetermined and statistically rigorous "threshold standard of orthographic rarity," as Basu and Loewenstein suggest.[28]

What would such a test make of those "two, the falsest twoo"? It is hard to guess. A late sixteenth-century reader of *The Faerie Queene* might well have been struck by the appearance of the extra "o" in "twoo": as the EEBO-TCP N-gram browser reveals, "two" is far more common than "twoo" both in the corpus of texts printed between 1580 and 1590 and in the 1590 *Faerie Queene* itself, where it appears in just one other place—a line in book 1, canto 2 that also refers to Archimago's sprites. On the other hand, "twoo" isn't unique to *The Faerie Queene* or to Spenser—although it remained much less common than "two" throughout the sixteenth century, it had a burst of relative popularity from 1540 through the early 1570s—and Spenser's readers would quite possibly have encountered it elsewhere. Less common is the use of "two" and "twoo" in close proximity, but here, too, the EEBO-TCP N-gram browser retrieves a range of instances, including a 1477 edition of Chaucer's "Knight's Tale," a 1570 edition of Euclid's *Elements*, and a 1585 commentary on the Song of Solomon. In the vast majority of the ninety-one texts printed between 1473 and 1600 in which "twoo" and "two" appear within six words of each other, the orthographic variation seems wholly irrelevant to the context in which it appears; it's just something that (very) occasionally happened.

As this example suggests, the orthography of *The Faerie Queene* offers an ideal object for what Daniel Shore calls "plural reading" or the "systematic study of local forms."[29] But it is also an instance of how digital reading necessarily enfolds and returns to acts of interpretive judgment—our own, and those of other readers. As Shore points out, database analysis can only identify patterns of commonality; it cannot tell us what to make of the differences. This is precisely the challenge of those "two, the falsest, twoo": what gives the pairing of "two" and "twoo" its uncanny charge is the narrative content of book 1, canto 1, the fact that the difficulty of reckoning the difference, if any, between "two" and "twoo" so closely mimics the trap that Archimago is setting for Redcrosse in fashioning the false Una. This doubling of the perils and pleasures of interpretation—the sense that we, as readers of *The Faerie Queene*, share in the errors and epiphanies of readers in *The Faerie Queene*—is one of the poem's chief attractions, and if the preservation of old spelling heightens the effect, that is no small argument in its favor. On the other hand, an old-spelling modern edition can efface our awareness of interpretative agency, creating the illusion of submission to a remote authorial intelligence—and, as Randall McLeod has argued, it can prompt us to see eye rhymes, pronunciation cues, and orthographic variation where a compositor meant only to justify a line or avoid damaging a piece of type.[30] But for readers of *The Faerie Queene*, orthography also has an intimate and vexing relationship to reception history: whether old or new, idiosyncratic or regularized, spelling constitutes a crucial and largely unrecognized point of contact between readers, past and present. What we think of "Spenser's spelling" is the product of an editorial and critical tradition that began over a century after the poet's death. And even if sifting the poem's Spenserian variants from their accidental doubles brings us closer to the intentions of the author, it can't help estranging us from other readers, those to whom such distinctions were immaterial and those to whom they have been unthinkable.

Before "Old Spelling"

Even without the benefit of digital databases, we would have good reason to question the current editorial approach to the orthography of *The Faerie Queene*—and good reasons to wish to preserve it. Ben Jonson's well-known remark that "Spenser ... writ no Language" has been taken as evidence that the poet's English was as strange to contemporary readers as it is to us, but given the idiosyncrasies of Jonson's own orthography, spelling likely played no role in that judgment.[31] Moreover, Jonson's copy of *The Faerie Queene* was the 1617 folio edition, which alters many spellings from 1590: now Archimago's sprights are "two, the falsest two."[32] Indeed, for the first hundred and fifty years that *The Faerie Queene* was in print, beginning in Spenser's lifetime and continuing for more than a century after his death, its orthography was in continual flux—and no one appears to have cared. Transformations that seem disfiguring now went without question among Spenser's earliest readers; impulses understood as conservative or antiquarian today once appeared cutting-edge. The poem's old spellings became "Spenser's spelling" only in the eighteenth century, christened by a new breed of editors and critics proving the legitimacy of their professional identities, not their close-reading chops. The archaic orthography they restored to *The Faerie Queene* might not have been strictly authorial, but neither was it accidental; rather, it was an adjunct of the poem's assimilation from the realm of critical taste to a regime of scholarly practice. But it was also—paradoxically—the outward sign of a thoroughly sentimental and highly romanticized attachment to the ghost of Edmund Spenser.

Communing with Spenser's ghost is, in fact, a key affordance of the old-spelling *Faerie Queene*, for the impulse to interpret the poem's orthography rests on a fantasy of near-superhuman authorial presence in the text. Like Archimago, we imagine, Spenser chose his "spelles ... terrible," and it is up to us to discover their significance. Since no authorial manuscript of *The Faerie Queene* (or any of Spenser's poems) survives, that presumption depends on the further supposition that the poet was unusually closely involved in the printing of either or both of the two editions produced in his lifetime, books 1–3 in 1590 and books

1–6 in 1596. The external evidence for this is slight. We know that Spenser traveled from Ireland to England in 1589–90 and again in 1595–96, and it's reasonable to suppose that his purpose on both occasions was to hand-deliver the manuscript of *The Faerie Queene* to his publisher, William Ponsonby. In order to justify a wholesale adherence to the early spellings, however, one must go a good deal further—as A. C. Hamilton, editor of the Longman edition, does, claiming that "both editions were guided through the press by the poet himself."[33]

But if Spenser was present in John Wolfe's print shop in 1590, or in Richard Field's in 1596, he seems to have had other things than spelling on his mind. The three-book version of the poem printed by Wolfe is notoriously confused: much of what would normally appear as prefatory material—dedicatory verses to various potential patrons, the "Letter of the Authors"—comes at the back; some copies have fewer dedicatory poems than others; and, in a few copies, the opening dedication to Queen Elizabeth is entirely missing. Various theories have been advanced to account for these anomalies, but the overall impression is of an expeditious, if not hasty, print process.[34] Andrew Zurcher argues that Spenser intervened at several points to reconfigure politically sensitive parts of the text—the dedication to Elizabeth; Merlin's prophecy in book 3—but since multiple presses and skeleton formes were in use simultaneously, he can't have kept a close eye on individual spellings.[35] Those were the purview of Wolfe's typesetters, and as textual analysis has shown, the internal patterns of orthographic variation seem to mirror the division of labor between three men, each responsible for a different section of each gathering: "Else," "forrest," "foorth," "little," "whyles," and "whylome" are the favored spellings of Compositor X, while "els," "forest," "forth," "litle," "whiles," and "whilome" are the spellings of Compositor Y; Compositor Y prefers "daies," "eies," "guide," and "noise," but Compositor Z favors "dayes," "eyes," "guyde," and "noyse."[36] What appear to a modern eye as artful estrangements of the poem's language from itself may well be, in many cases, the variant preferences of Compositors X, Y, and Z.[37]

The only positive sign of concern for the poem's orthography in 1590 comes in the brief list of "Faults escaped in the Print" at the back of the volume, which includes among more substantive corrections a handful of spelling changes: "renowmed" for "renouned," "talants" for "talents," "diapase" for "Dyapase," "tonge" for "tongue" (606). But, with the exception of "renowmed," these emendations escaped the notice of the poem's next printer, Richard Field, whose compositors reset the text of books 1–3, making frequent changes to its spelling. According to the editors of the Spenser *Variorum*, book 1 of the 1596 poem contains "approximately 2,250" orthographic changes, "or about one to every two and one-half lines." These changes are "so frequent and so generally distributed throughout the book that they constitute almost a line by line alteration of the spelling," but are also "so inconsistent and haphazard that we cannot suppose a systematic editing by Spenser or some other person."[38] Investing any particular orthographic variant in the poem with authorial intent is thus doubly risky: no single, uniform "old-spelling" text of *The Faerie Queene* ever existed in print, and the orthography of the two editions produced in Spenser's lifetime was the result of multiple minds and hands.

If spelling did matter in a peculiar way to Spenser, its significance would have been hard for *The Faerie Queene*'s early readers to access, since no sixteenth- or seventeenth-century publisher of the poem attempted to preserve the orthography of earlier printed editions. The spelling of the title itself was unfixed: in a 1579 letter to Gabriel Harvey, published in 1580, Spenser refers to "my *Faery Queene*";[39] in 1590 and 1596, the poem appeared as *The Faerie Queene*; in the 1611 edition of Spenser's *Works*, it became *The Faerie Queen* and in 1679 *The Faery Queen*. The same process was at work in all Spenser's printed works, whose spelling changed with each new edition. The word "aeglogues," which appears on the title page to the 1579 *Shepheardes Calender*, is the exception that proves the rule: because E.K. insists on the pseudoetymological spelling—instead of the more usual "eclogues"—in his preface to the poem, printers retained it.[40] Absent such a pointed directive, Spenser's spelling was slowly standardized along with the rest of English print.

Readers thus had little reason to attend to *The Faerie Queene*'s orthography. And if they did, Alexander Gill's 1619 *Logonomia Anglica* suggests, they were free to improve it. In addition to demonstrating the beauties of rhetoric to English schoolboys, *Logonomia Anglica* serves as a brief for schoolmaster Gill's reformed orthography, a hybrid of Anglo-Saxon, Greek, and Latin letter forms meant to restore the vernacular to its true pronunciation and etymology. Spenser was Gill's favorite poet, and his catalog of schemes and tropes is packed with extracts from the poem he calls "Ðε Fäerj Qujn."[41] Thus, to illustrate the figure of division, or *regressio*, Gill cites Archimago's selection of his pair of hellish associates:

Of ðøz hj ćɷz out tv, ðε fålsεst tv,
And fitεst for tu forg trv-sïmig ljz:
Ðe ɷn of ðεm hj gɑv a mεssɑg tu;
Ðε oðεr bj himsεlf staid oðεr wurk tu dv. (114; fig. 5)

In Gill's eyes, Spenser's spelling was bad, but typically—not willfully—so; when he quotes passages from Philip Sidney, Samuel Daniel, James Harrington, and Richard Stanyhurst, he fixes their spelling, too.

Changing Spenser's spelling was for Gill an act of service, a way of making his meaning more legible and his artfulness more apparent. In this respect Gill is typical of *The Faerie Queene*'s seventeenth-century admirers, who frequently sought to amend and emend Spenser's work. Ralph Knevett's *Supplement of "The Faerie Queene"* (ca. 1635) adds three books to the poem, extending its political allegory through the reign of Charles I; *The Faerie Leveller* of 1648 interprets the Egalitarian Giant's assault on Artegall as a prophetic allegory of Parliament's villainous treatment of Charles and "a lively representation of our times"; Edward Howard's 1687 *Spencer Redivivus* recasts book 1 in heroic couplets, the poet's "Essential Design preserv'd, but his obsolete Language and manner of Verse totally laid aside" and his matter "improv'd by my Thoughts."[42] The 1679 edition of Spenser's *Works* not only printed his poems in up-to-date orthography, it included Theodore Bathurst's translation of *The Shepheardes Calender* into elegant Latin verse. To the extent that such revisionists considered Spenser's intentions at all, they regarded them as impulses awaiting perfection: as Howard boasts in the preface to *Spencer Redivivus*, "he is render'd what he ought to have been instead of what is to be found in himself" (A4r).

"Spenser's own spelling"

The belief that *The Faerie Queene*'s spelling was Spenser's own, and worth preserving as such, first appeared in 1715, in John Hughes's six-volume edition of *The Works of Mr. Edmund Spenser*. Hughes was no textual conservative in the modern sense, but he draws a firm distinction between explicating a poet's words—as his "Glossary of Old and Obsolete Words" promises to do—and updating them. "An Editor of the Works of a dead Author," Hughes writes, "ought to consider himself as a kind of Executor of his Will; which he should endeavour to perform with the same Care, and, in every Circumstance, after the same manner he believes the Author himself wou'd have done, if living."[43] In Spenser's case those circumstances include spelling: "Care has been taken, not only to collect every thing of this Author which has appear'd before, and to preserve the Text entire, but to follow likewise, for the most part, the old Spelling." Acknowledging that some will regard this as "too strict and precise," Hughes defends it as essential "not only to shew the true State of our Language, as *Spenser* wrote it, but to keep the exact Sense, which wou'd sometimes be chang'd by the Variation of a Syllable or a Letter" (1:cxi).

There is a crucial equivocation here, poised on the fulcrum of the phrase "as *Spenser* wrote it." If the justification for recovering *The Faerie Queene*'s old spellings is "to shew the true State of our Language," as not only Spenser but any Elizabethan wrote it, then the poem's orthography is a historical artifact. But if orthography acts as custodian of the poet's peculiar intentions—keeper of his "exact Sense"—then it is, precisely, unrepresentative: not Elizabethan but Spenser's own. Hughes embraces the contradiction, insisting that where "*Spenser* himself is irregular"—for instance, in fudging the orthography of his end rhymes—he adheres to "the Practice of that Age" (1:cxi): peculiarity is the property of the period. In practice, this leaves Hughes free to choose among orthographic variants, assigning meaning to some and not to others. The "old Editions," he explains, "are not every where follow'd; but when the Sense is render'd obscure by such Alterations, the Words are restor'd to their proper Orthography" (1:cxi). The estimation of propriety rests with Hughes himself, and although he sometimes reverts to a variant from 1590 or 1596, he largely follows the modernized text of 1679—and occasionally contributes an updated spelling of his own. In 1590, when Archimago prepares to summon the "twoo" false sprights, he "bad awake blacke *Plutoes* griesly Dame"; in 1679, he "bad awake black *Plutoe's* grisly Dame" (4); in Hughes's edition, he "bad awake black *Pluto's* griesly Dame": "griesly" is restored, but "*Pluto's*" is further modernized (1:32; fig. 6).

It's unfair, perhaps, to take Hughes to task for inconsistency. For all his talk of the poem's "exact Sense," his motives for reverting to the old spellings are less sensible than sentimental. "[O]wing to an extraordinary native Strength," he writes, Spenser's poems "have been able thus far to survive ... and seem rather likely, among the Curious at least, to preserve the Knowledg of our Antient Language, than to be in danger of being destroy'd with it, and bury'd under its Ruins" (1:xxvi). Ruination is central to Hughes's appreciation for *The Faerie Queene*, whose design he famously likens to a decaying work of "Gothick Architecture" (1:lx), and to his attachment to Spenser, whose biography he narrates as a series of unmerited catastrophes, culminating in the loss of the final six books of *The Faerie Queene* in the poet's flight from Ireland to England. There is no historical basis for the story, which Hughes adapts from James Ware's 1633 preface to *A View of the Present State of Ireland*, but it helps to explain the editor's puzzling lack of deference to the early printed editions. As far as Hughes is concerned, the only truly authoritative text of *The Faerie Queene* was lost at sea or in the London streets in 1599. What remains is not "the Text entire" but a poem in pieces: the haunted ruin of Spenser's ambitions.

By the end of the eighteenth century, however, Hughes's editorial approach had come to seem too partial altogether. Anachronism displaced indecorum as criticism's cardinal sin: in 1735 William Duncombe praised Hughes as a reader of "superior Judgment," but in 1779 Samuel Johnson dismissed him as merely tasteful, a connoisseur of elegant images who "wanted an antiquary's knowledge."[44] Far from crediting Hughes for drawing attention to *The Faerie Queene*'s sixteenth-century orthography, later critics accused him of paying it too little mind. "We who live in the days of writing by rule, are apt to try every composition by those laws which we have been taught to think the sole criterion of excellence," notes Thomas Warton in his 1762 *Observations on the Faerie Queene of Spenser*, "and we require the same order and design which every modern performance is expected to have, in poems where they were never regarded or intended."[45] Hughes's handling of Spenser's spelling appeared to Warton an egregious instance of this misguided approach: "that editor, among other examples of his exactness," he wryly observes, "has reduced Spenser's text to modern orthography with great accuracy" (1:121).

A different sort of accuracy was promised by Thomas Birch's 1751 edition of *The Faerie Queene*, based, as the title page announced, on "an exact Collation of the Two ORIGINAL EDITIONS, Published by Himself at London in Quarto." Birch was the first modern editor to consult the 1590 text, and although the existence of two "original editions" of books 1–3 complicated Birch's task, it also allowed him to advertise his own edition as a triumphant synthesis of novelty and antiquity: "a just Representation of the genuine Text, not hitherto given in any single Edition," not even those printed in Spenser's lifetime.[46] Even as the quest for a "genuine text" begins, it is still imagined as an improvement on the past. The restoration of the poem's sixteenth-century spellings was part of this effort at constructing an ideal text but not, for Birch, the most important part. His collation takes no notice of orthographic variation between 1590 and 1596 and, like Thomas Warton, he habitually refers to the poem as the "*Fairy Queen.*"

John Upton's 1751 *Letter concerning a new edition of Spenser's "Faerie Queene,"* by contrast, makes "keep[ing] to *Spenser's spelling*" the hallmark of a reformed editorial practice and a stay against "the incroaching spirit of criticism."[47] "If transcribers and printers, or editors, will be perpetually varying from the spelling of their author," he observes, "we shall necessarily have a constant source of corruption" (36). Like Warton, who complained that *The Faerie Queene* contained "numberless ... instances of orthography destroyed for the sake of rhyme" (1:118), Upton characterizes Spenser's "bad spelling" as a symptom of the author's unfortunate addiction to end rhyme: "the rock which *Spenser* split on" (27). But Upton's embarrassment at the poem's spelling only intensified his desire that it be recognized as Spenser's own. Indeed, there is something defensive in his insistence on this point in his 1758 two-volume edition: "The reader will be pleased to remember," he writes in the preface, "that the spelling is not the editor's, but the poet's"—a point reiterated throughout the notes, and with particular vehemence in the note on the stanza describing "the falsest twoo."[48] Upton doesn't see the extra "o" in "twoo" as encoding any particular meaning; rather, he assumes that Spenser needed it to emphasize his meter and his rhyme, a crutch Upton deplores (2:349). But critical distaste only confirms the necessity of editorial conservatism: for Upton, spelling marks a necessary boundary between critic and editor, taste and accuracy, poet and reader, past and present: to improve even a single letter, as John Hughes did, would be "not only misleading, but unscholarlike" (1:xlii).

Ralph Church's edition of *The Faerie Queene*, also published in 1758, offers a different rationale for reverting to the old spellings. Like Thomas Birch, Church produced his edition through a scrupulous collation of the early printed texts—but not because he shared Birch's confidence that these editions were "published by [Spenser] Himself." Noting the various states of the 1590 poem and the "gross blunders" in arrangement, Church concluded that "our *Poet* could have had no concern in correcting that impression."[49] The 1596 edition seemed worse—"still we are to lament that neither *Spenser* nor any judicious Friend was concerned in the care of that *second* Impression" (1:iv)—and the 1609 folio worse yet, "clogged and perplexed" by unartful emendations (1:v). Convinced that each subsequent edition must be "less valuable . . . in proportion as it is farther removed from the Fountain-head" (1:v–vi), Church founds his own editorial practice on a negative determination to do as little further damage as possible. "[I]f the Poem is not now placed in a fairer and more advantageous light than in any former edition," he writes, "at least it has received no real injury" (1:x).

On the face of it, this is a weak rationale: if orthographic variants are as likely to originate with the poem's careless compositors as with its ill-served author, why keep them? Church skirts the issue in his preface, confronting it instead in a lengthy footnote to canto 8 of book 1, in which the rhetoric of injury recurs to startling effect. The note is appended to a stanza in which "almightie Ioue" is described, in apparently ludicrous terms, as "hurl[ing] forth his thundring dart with deadly food, / Enrold in flames" (1:141 [*FQ* 1.8.9.1]). Church borrows Hughes's explanation that "food" means "feud"—Jove is taking vengeance, not hurling rotten tomatoes—but objects strenuously to his emendation of the spelling. Citing Hughes's own observation that "the exact sense . . . would sometimes be *chang'd* by the variation of *a Syllable* or *a Letter*," he writes,

> Of this *Change* there are numberless Instances in Mr. *H*'s Edition. In the present Copy care has been taken to retain *altogether* the antiquated spelling of the Editions published in *Spenser*'s Life-time: and, if I mistake not, it gives a venerable air to the Poem. And I freely own, my Ear is as unwilling to consent to an alteration of our Poet's *Spelling*, as my Eye is to an alteration of the *Drapery* in his *Picture*. Reduce either of them to the *Fashion* and *Standard* of the present times, and the *agreeable features* in the one, and the *venerable Aspect* in the other, will in my opinion, be much injur'd and disfigur'd. (1:143)

Despite his reference to "our Poet's *Spelling*," Church doesn't stake his editorial practice on the ground of authorial propriety. On the contrary, what he "freely owns" is a readerly privilege, the taste of an individual eye or ear. There is little reason, in his view, to suppose Spenser's spellings his own: Elizabethan spelling, he observes, "was in general, equally at least as irregular and improper, as unfixt and strange" (1:xlvii). Nor do those spellings clarify the poem's meaning—Church admits that Hughes's emendation makes good sense of an otherwise nonsensical line. What sustains his unwillingness to alter the poem's "antiquated spelling," absent any faith in its intelligibility or its authorial provenance, is a quasi-religious, aesthetic power: "the *Venerable aspect*."

Venerability is the property of a relic: for all Church's insistence on avoiding injury or disfiguration, it's clear that for him the value of Spenser's spelling, like the value of his poem, accrues in and through temporal estrangement. Anachronism isn't a problem of reading *The Faerie Queene*; it's the pleasurable point. Upton's 1751 *Letter* suggests that he partly shared this view. Orthographic modernization changes more than a poem's spelling, he writes, "for by this alteration, which insensibly goes on from smaller to greater things, that antique cast is lost, which of itself carries so venerable an aspect":

> [O]ur modern editors, in this respect, resemble the officious servant of the late learned antiquary Dr. Woodward, who in scowering off the rust from an old shield, which his master had just purchased, made it more resemble the new scowered cover of an old kettle, than the shield of an ancient heroe. Such kind of scowerers were Mr. Urry and Mr. Hughes; who by endeavouring to reduce the spelling of their authors to modern use, have shamefully, in many instances, blundered, as well as grievously erred, in their first entrance. (36)

Upton includes Shakespeare and even Milton among the authors "served in this manner," but by pairing John Hughes with John Urry, editor of the 1721 edition of Chaucer's *Works*, he assimilates *The Faerie Queene* to a much earlier moment in literary history—this is not historicism but willful anachronism, authorized by Spenser's own example. It was Chaucer, Upton declares, "whose footsteps with deference *Spenser* always followed," and it is Chaucer's Middle English to which Upton appeals as the ground of his own approach to Spenser's spelling. Objecting to Hughes's emendation of the end rhyme "downe"/"sowne" to "down"/"sound," Upton looks not to the 1590 and 1596 editions but to *The Book of the Duchess*, in which the same end rhyme appears. Hughes's emendation "is neither *Spenser*'s spelling nor *Spenser*'s rhime," he concludes, because it is not *Chaucer*'s spelling or *Chaucer*'s rhyme: Spenser "wrote *downe sowne*, as Chaucer did before him" (11).

Even for Upton then, at least in 1751, the value of *The Faerie Queene*'s old spellings had as much to do with an indeterminate sense of pastness—call it literary tradition—as it did with historical precision. That sense of pastness helped revive Spenser's reputation in the mid-eighteenth century, imbuing literary studies with a feeling of heroic opposition to modern culture. Thanks to what

Jonathan Kramnick terms "the romance of scholarship," readers could encounter both Spenser and an idealized version of themselves in *The Faerie Queene*'s old spellings.[50] Consciousness of that self-pleasing motive is evident in Upton's *Letter* and Church's edition, but it was subsumed in subsequent editions by a rhetoric of necessity. In 1778, when John Bell included Spenser in his 109-volume series of "Poets of Great Britain from Chaucer to Churchill," he made sure to follow Upton's text of *The Faerie Queene*, noting that "attention to Spenser's own spelling seems indispensably necessary."[51] Henry John Todd's 1805 edition of Spenser's *Works* extended the old-spelling treatment to the minor poems as well, now "unadulterated," free from "innovation and errour," on the grounds that the poet ought not to be "unjustly presented in a piebald suit."[52] Readerly taste was recast as scholarly rigor and authorial privilege.

Conclusion: Unrepressed Antecedents

In retrospect, the eighteenth-century debate over Spenser's spelling is legible in terms of the nascent contest between scholars and critics, philology and belles lettres. In the nineteenth century scholarship won out, though belles lettres remained, as John Guillory argues, "an unsuccessfully repressed antecedent."[53] The old spelling of *The Faerie Queene* is one such remainder, an object of aesthetic desire refashioned as a badge of historicist precision, and the primary ambition of this chapter has been to bring its repressed antecedents back in view, as a step toward recognizing and reckoning with their continued influence on how we read the poem now. For, despite the rhetoric of conservatism with which it was identified, the restoration of "Spenser's own spelling" transformed the object it promised to preserve, estranging *The Faerie Queene* not only from the present but from its sixteenth-century contemporaries, locating it instead alongside the works of Geoffrey Chaucer. The association between Spenser and Chaucer was not, of course, new—it goes back to E.K.'s preface to *The Shepheardes Calender*, which invokes the "olde famous Poete Chaucer" in its opening line[54]—but it was given a new aura of inevitability by a shared editorial insistence on textual and, especially, orthographic precision. The editorial history of *The Canterbury Tales* is complicated by numerous issues that did not affect the editing of Spenser's poems—above all, by the existence of multiple, often substantively different, manuscript sources—but the broad outlines of the story in the eighteenth century are strikingly similar to the treatment of *The Faerie Queene*: like Upton's *Spenser*, Thomas Tyrwhitt's 1775 edition of Chaucer announces itself as the first "to draw a line between the imperfections that be supposed to have been left in it by the author, and those which have crept into since," and maligns John Urry's 1721 *Canterbury Tales*, like Hughes's 1715 *Faerie Queene*, as the nadir of editorial self-indulgence, its "strange license . . .

lengthening and shortening Chaucer's words" making it "by far the worst that was ever published."[55]

Even as old spelling was rendered indispensible to editions of Chaucer and Spenser, it was rejected as a medium for the works of Shakespeare. In the preface to his 1790 edition of Shakespeare, Malone reports that Tyrwhitt tried to persuade him to follow the example of his Chaucer, being convinced "that in printing these plays the original spelling should be adhered to, and that we never could be sure of a perfectly faithful edition, unless the first folio copy was made the standard." In Malone's view, however, a scrupulously sourced and carefully annotated modern-spelling Shakespeare would "obtain all the advantages which would have resulted from Mr. Tyrwhitt's plan, without any of its inconveniences."[56] The only Shakespearean spelling on which Malone did insist was that of the poet's name, "Shakspeare," as written in several surviving manuscript documents, including the poet's will:

> Much has lately been said in various publications about the proper mode of spelling Shakspeare's name. It is hoped we shall hear no more idle babble upon this subject. He spelt his name himself as I have just now written it, without the middle *e*. Let this therefore forever decide the question. (1:192)

The question was not, of course, so decided, but Malone's insistence on the point helps to illuminate the impact of the decision to preserve all of the old spellings in Spenser's verse. For Malone, Shakespeare's proper name is the only word for which an authorial spelling is both certain and significant: "he wrote his name himself as I have just now written it." In the case of *The Faerie Queene*, by contrast, that emphatic coupling of orthography and identity was distributed over thousands of variant forms, whose component letters were granted the authenticating power of a signature.[57]

In 1795 Malone wielded this power to devastating effect against Ireland, enlisting the old spelling of *The Faerie Queene* in his effort to redeem the protocols of the new textual scholarship from the taint of fraud. Malone shared Ireland's investment in *The Faerie Queene* as an authenticating talisman, but his use of the poem highlights a crucial shift in the understanding of Spenser's spelling: it was now assumed to be recognizably different from that of other Elizabethan writers, and recognizing that difference became a test of scholarly acumen. And scholarly acumen, far more than authorial propriety, was the issue in the case of the Shakespeare Papers: Ireland's forgeries might not have been convincing imitations of Shakespearean art, but they were uncomfortable approximations of Malone-like expertise.[58] As Anthony Grafton has shown, the history of textual scholarship is uneasily twinned to the history of forgery—and in Ireland's case the resemblance was calculated: in his memoirs, he boasts of modeling his paper and ink on real bibliographic specimens but confesses that he relied on documents reproduced by eighteenth-century editors for his rendition of Shakespeare's signature, "keeping the transcript of his original autograph before me" (47).[59] It is this dangerous doubling that Spenser's spelling helps Malone to undo, proving Ireland not only a fake sixteenth-century poet, but also, more importantly, an unworthy imitator of Malone: as Upton would say, "not only misleading, but unscholarlike."

Ireland's spelling did remind Malone of one other earlier writer: Thomas Chatterton, forger of the poems of "Thomas Rowley," a supposed fifteenth-century monk. As Malone acknowledges, his methods of orthographic authentication are borrowed from the *Enquiry into the Authenticity* of Rowley's poems published a decade earlier by Thomas Warton, for whom Spenser's language and spelling likewise serve as constant reference points. Warton's *Enquiry* makes explicit the double-edged character of old spelling, as both a proof of textual antiquity and a tell-tale sign of fabrication. To those who regarded the Rowley poems as genuine, the fact that they were "all authenticated by specimens of the most obsolete spelling" was an unanswerable point in their favor, but in Warton's expert view, "the artificial sprinklings of obsolete spelling ... detect what they should disguise": "In the pseudo-Rowley, we are imposed upon by the charm of old spelling," he concludes.[60] That such a charm might impose also—albeit in a less calculated way—on eighteenth-century readers of Spenser's verse Warton does not consider: like Malone, he needs Spenser's spelling as a limit case of orthographic artifice, the true archaism by which mere anachronism could be discerned. Only an archpoet could detect an archforger.

As the uses Malone and Warton made of old spelling suggest, the restoration of *The Faerie Queene*'s sixteenth-century orthography changed the standards of readerly competence for early literature, and for Spenser's verse in particular. As Marjorie Garber has shown, amateurism retains certain privileges in the world of Shakespeare studies, where it (rhetorically, at least) can appear as the aesthetically superior alternative to rank professionalism.[61] *The Faerie Queene*, by contrast, became the preserve of specialists: in a figurative transposition Spenser might have admired, but could not have anticipated, the distinctive character of scholarly reading was encoded in the distinctive character of his spelling. Thus, in a 1960 essay arguing vehemently against the use of old spelling in modern editions of Renaissance texts, on the grounds that they mislead ordinary readers, John Russell Brown leaves a loophole for Spenser, "who took special care to ensure an individual form of spelling"; Spenser, he allows, was "exceptional."[62] Since Brown's overall argument has less to do with authorial intent than with readerly capacity, however, the halo of exceptionality radiates outward: in effect, every reader of *The Faerie Queene* must become an expert.

Over the course of the twentieth century, Spenser's orthographic exceptionality became an article of faith, impervious to the expertise it was meant to confirm. Occasionally a dissenting voice is heard: in his three-volume study of Chaucer, Thomas Raynesford Lounsbury, a historian of spelling and pronunciation, observes in passing that "there has never been the slightest pretext for continuing to reproduce Spenser's works as they were originally printed."[63] More commonly, one finds otherwise scrupulous scholars laboring to evade the implications of their own textual discoveries. When the editors of the 1932 *Variorum* edition of book 1 compared a wide range of original printed texts, they found that Church was more or less right in his perception of the 1590 and 1596 editions: orthographically, these texts strongly resemble others produced by John Wolfe and Richard Field and are thus unlikely to preserve in any systematic or easily discernible way the traces of Spenser's own hand.[64] Even so, they signal their wholehearted commitment to old spelling on the title page, which refers to the poem as *The Faerie Qveene*. Hiroshi Yamashita conducted the digital analysis of the 1590 *Faerie Queene* that confirmed the compositorial origins of many of that text's spellings—but in his textual introduction to the 2007 Longman edition of the poem, he justifies using the 1590 edition as a copy-text for books 1–3 on the grounds that it preserves the poet's own spellings, as "established through studies of extant documents written by his hand" (21). The study in question—there is just one—was written in 1958 by Roland M. Smith and arrives at precisely the opposite conclusion. On the basis of letters Spenser wrote in his role as secretary to Lord Grey in Ireland, Smith determines, his orthographic preferences (in prose, at least) were simple and decidedly up-to-date: in Smith's view, "neither 1590 nor 1596 reflects Spenser's spelling."[65]

Smith, who believed modern scholars exaggerated the archaism of Spenser's language, disregards the possibility that the poet deliberately altered his orthographic habits in *The Faerie Queene*, antiquating or estranging his spelling in service to his allegorical conceit. It's an important oversight, since that is precisely what most modern advocates of the old spellings believe: that is, that even if the majority of the poem's orthographic variants are historically unremarkable, nonauthorial, or both, a crucial few are stamped, as it were, by Spenser's own hand. The difficulty, of course, is that no modern reader of *The Faerie Queene* can tell one from the other. The paradox of the old-spelling edition is that it frustrates the very desire for scholarly precision it appears to gratify, tempting readers to mistake accidents for intentions and ordinary usage for secret wit. There is a way in which this paradox suits Spenser's poem, especially in book 1: the alienating, enticing, and misleading quality of the orthography replicates the challenges faced by the Redcrosse Knight as he strives to tell truth from error and outward seeming from hidden intent. And as Margreta de Grazia and Peter Stallybrass have noted of the contested spelling of Shakespeare's description of the "weyard" or "weyward" sisters in *Macbeth*—modern editors have typically rendered it as "weird," or supernatural, although early modern readers would just as likely have read it as "wayward," or unruly—editorial judgment in such matters is inevitably shaped by interpretive desire: we straiten the waywardness we fear; we invent the weirdness we crave.[66]

Digital tools are a valuable adjunct to such judgments, and they may well help future editors of *The Faerie Queene* to clarify and even quantify the difference between deliberate Spenserian archaisms and accidentally outmoded variants, whether authorial or compositorial. But those editors will be left with a no less difficult set of decisions about whether and how to represent such differences in print—or, as is more likely the case, on the screen. In the conclusion to their statistical study of Spenser's spelling, Basu and Loewenstein envision a radically individualized approach to editing *The Faerie Queene*, in which the responsibility for determining orthographic and typographic salience devolves largely on readers. "By committing [the poem] to the screen," they write, "we can offer a toggled edition in which the reader can systematically and incrementally reduce (or augment) the alterity of Spenser's text":

> For the skilled reader who seeks minimal editorial intervention, we can display page images of individual witnesses. For the skilled reader habituated to early modern orthography, we can present a conservatively corrected text that suppresses a few textual signals agreed to be of very low salience, replacing drop-caps, substituting s for long-s, w for double-v, expanding words abbreviated by means of macron and tilde, and dissevering consonantal ligatures. And for the somewhat less skilled, we can add another thin layer of modernizations and normalizations, by adding a set of transformations customary in editions of many non-Spenserian early modern texts: the modernizing swap of i/j and u/v, the standardization of other abbreviations ("&c," "S.", ".xii."). The serious question is whether to thicken the layer of orthographic (and perhaps other) normalizations offered to the unskilled reader and, if we decide to do thicken it, how to do so without the obtrusion of too much editorial caprice.

In other words, there will be no escape from the hazards of individual judgment: statistical analysis "enables us to identify the few spellings in any given Spenserian text that depart by some measure of significance from the normal spellings of a given moment," and it can bolster our confidence in whatever numerical value we choose to assign to that indeterminate "some," but even the "statistically assisted editor" or reader will have to decide what to do with variants that hover just at or above their "threshold standard of orthographic rarity."[67]

Absent the discovery of a holograph manuscript of *The Faerie Queene*, then, the salience of an orthographic anomaly like those "two, the falsest twoo" seems destined to remain at least partly in doubt, Archimago's to the last. But not only Archimago's: as with any artifact of literary history, the spell it casts is of readers' making, too. That is one essential lesson of the odd, overdetermined history of Spenser's spelling. Another—perhaps harder to assimilate—is that we should be wary of our tendency to equate readerly skill with a capacity or willingness to reckon with linguistic alterity: that, after all, is how we ended up with the old-spelling *Faerie Queene* in the first place. As the Redcrosse Knight learns over the painful course of his career in book 1, difficulty and strangeness are no more reliable metrics of authenticity than obviousness and ease; sometimes the truth is staring us full in the face, however strenuously we labor to disguise it.

2

Una's Line

CHILD READERS AND THE
AFTERLIFE OF FICTION

C. S. LEWIS'S account of *The Faerie Queene* in *The Allegory of Love* (1936) begins with the declaration that "allegory is no afterthought in Spenser's poem": "When it is allegorical at all, it is radically and momentously allegorical."[1] The force of the main clause makes it easy to overlook the qualifying introduction, which hints at the possibility that what Spenser termed the poem's "continued Allegory" is in fact intermittent: What, one wonders, might *The Faerie Queene* be up to in the meantime?[2] That question is at the heart of this chapter, which accesses the lapsed middle of Spenser's allegory in book 1 of *The Faerie Queene* by reanimating a prolonged and now highly disreputable interval in the poem's reception history, when allegory was indeed an afterthought, and readers were advised to cultivate a blithe disregard for its intrusions on the plot. "The dullest and most defective parts of Spenser are those in which we are compelled to think of his agents as allegories," sighs Samuel Taylor Coleridge—who for that reason ranked the opening book of *The Faerie Queene* below the first part of Bunyan's *Pilgrim's Progress*, in which "the interest is so great that [in] spite of all the writer's attempts to force the allegoric purpose on the reader's mind by his strange names," readers could persist "with the same illusion as we read any tale known to be fictitious, as a novel, [and] go on with his characters as real persons, who had been nicknamed by their neighbors."[3] This is an approach to allegorical narrative—and especially to book 1 of *The Faerie Queene*—that critics following in Lewis's wake have tended to deem irresponsible in the extreme: with its relentless suspicion of surfaces and seeming, its dense web of classical and biblical allusions, its apocalyptic intimations, and, yes, its carefully chosen repertoire of names, the Legend of Holiness "denies recourse to characterological realism," as Judith H. Anderson writes. Although we may insist, as Isabel MacCaffrey does, that "no element of the verbal surface in *The Faerie Queene* bears more than a tangential, oblique, or parabolical relation to what is called the 'allegorical sense,'" we cannot condone readings that deny that relation altogether—to do so would be tantamount to affirming Archimago's proposition that a false Una is just as good as the true.[4] Read allegorically—valued as she deserves—Una is one of *The Faerie Queene*'s richest symbolic nodes, a figure for truth, fidelity, unity, God's covenant with his chosen people, the Church Militant, and the Bride of Christ. Read "autonomously, psychologically, novelistically," Anderson observes, "Una becomes merely baffling."[5]

For much of the eighteenth and nineteenth centuries, however, Una was at the epicenter of *The Faerie Queene*, and the poem's ideal reader—the reader to whom her qualities were supposed to appeal most intensely and successfully—was one naturally impervious to any moralizing pretensions: a child, usually but not always a boy, old enough to read independently but not so grown as to have lost a taste for imaginary play or developed a sensitivity to allegory. Today, when nearly all readers of *The Faerie Queene* encounter the poem in the confines of a classroom or a footnoted scholarly edition, it is hard to appreciate the influence such actual and imagined young readers once had on its critical and popular reception. Far from requiring or fostering the hyperliteracy with which Spenser is now associated, *The Faerie Queene* was characterized by both admirers and detractors as quintessential children's fare: an almost too effective engine of readerly enchantment, a gateway to the more demanding (but also more rewarding) poetry of Milton, and a rich repository of adventures and images, ripe for anthologizing and adaptation. Although this approach to *The Faerie Queene* ignored or occluded much of what scholarly readers now consider essential—Spenser's language, for instance, or his religious, political, and ethical commitments—it attended with useful closeness to parts of the poem that now get short shrift: its richly detailed fictive landscape and the characters who populate it, without necessarily having much to do with its meaning. Paradoxically, the most important of these characters was the symbol-laden heroine of book 1—not, however, in her allegorical function as the avatar of Truth, Fidelity, and Christian Unity, but as the endearing protagonist of a series of adventures occupying the book's middle cantos. Figured in a host of paintings and engravings, placed on the covers of illustrated editions and adaptations, and invariably accompanied by animals or surrounded by romping satyrs, Una represented *The Faerie Queene* not because she signified eternal truth but because she embodied a transitory fiction, a pleasure fated to give way to more serious and lasting pursuits. Indeed, as the most cherishable and vulnerable of Spenserian fictions, Una stood not only for *The Faerie Queene*, with all its minor virtues, but for the imagined or recollected idyll of childhood reading itself, a realm of infantile satisfactions whose appeal was inextricable from the awareness that they would one day be outgrown.

By fixing the poem's moral allegory (especially, and not coincidentally, its idealization of marital sexuality) as the horizon of readerly engagement, Lewis's account of *The Faerie Queene* worked to counter this earlier reception history, but as a reader he was hardly immune to its influence. Lewis, of course, wrote books for children as well as literary criticism for adults, and in an essay published five years after *The Allegory of Love*, he argued that childish or childlike reading was not the antithesis of a mature appreciation for *The Faerie Queene* but its indispensible foundation:

> Beyond all doubt it is best to have made one's first acquaintance with Spenser in a very large—and, preferably, illustrated—edition of *The Faerie Queene*, on a wet day, between the ages of twelve and sixteen; and if, even at that age, certain of the names aroused unidentified memories of some still earlier, some almost prehistoric, commerce with a selection of "Stories from Spenser," heard before we could read, so much the better.[6]

Why "so much the better"? Such vague, preliterate, almost prelinguistic impressions as Lewis's imaginary child reader retains, more sound than sense, seem remote from and even antagonistic to the allegorical sensitivity his criticism sought to foster. Surprisingly, however, Lewis suggests that the reverse is true: allegorical awareness approximates in its effects the faded recollections of childhood. The reader whose first encounter with the poem occurred in infancy returns to it with the uncanny feeling of having "met all these knights and ladies, all these monsters and enchanters, somewhere before," he explains. "What corresponds to this in the experience of the mature reader is the consciousness of Spenser's moral allegory"—not, however, the clear-sighted apprehension of its meaning but "the sense of some dim significance in the background" (43). By this account, appreciation of the poem's moral meaning is not the end or antithesis of childish reading but a relic or simulacrum of it: an afterthought in an entirely different sense.

The intuition that understanding, once achieved, might feel like the remnant of something more fragmentary but also more fulfilling haunts a key scene in Lewis's own allegorical epic for child readers, *The Chronicles of Narnia*, in which Lucy Pevensie learns from the lion Aslan that she and her brother Edmund will soon outgrow the world of their fantastical adventures:

> "Dearest," said Aslan very gently, "you and your brother will never come back to Narnia."
>
> "Oh, Aslan!" said Edmund and Lucy both together in despairing voices.
>
> "You are too old, children," said Aslan, "and you must begin to come close to your own world now."
>
> "It isn't Narnia, you know," sobbed Lucy. "It's *you*. We shan't meet *you* there. And how can we live, never meeting you?"

"But you shall meet me, dear one," said Aslan.

"Are—are you there too, Sir?" said Edmund.

"I am," said Aslan. "But there I have another name. You must learn to know me by that name. This was the very reason why you were brought to Narnia, that by knowing me here for a little, you may know me better there."[7]

Here Lewis's earnest proselytizing, as Kevin Pask observes, "has the unintended effect of making Christian revelation seem like a substitute for a more powerful experience of childhood fantasy." Pask attributes the strain to the tension between Christian ideals of spiritual maturity, grounded in the Epistles of Paul, and "the Victorian cult of the child,"[8] but it might equally be seen as a legacy of Lewis's Spenserianism, for the pairing of girl and lion evokes the most famous icon of *The Faerie Queene* in eighteenth- and nineteenth-century culture, Una and her lion. The lion enters book 1 at the moment it lapses from high-allegorical purposiveness into the entanglements of romance, just after the Redcrosse Knight has been tricked into abandoning Una for Duessa, and the content of the conversation between Lucy and Aslan reworks the scene in which that lapse is finally both reversed and transcended: the mountaintop encounter between Redcrosse and Contemplation, in which Spenser's Knight of Holiness learns that the poem he inhabits is itself a childish fiction, and will one day "vanish into nought." It is a scene to which the poem's scholarly readers have given abundant notice, marking as it does the acme of Spenser's self-reflexive allegorical practice, his habit of marking the representational limits of his own poetic figurations. But a childish perspective on the scene, such as Lewis offers in the passage above, highlights something else—an unexpected resistance to relinquishing allegory's fictive trappings, even in exchange for the better knowledge of Christian revelation. For granted an apocalyptic foretaste of heaven, Redcrosse's first instinct, like Lucy's, is to mourn for all heaven can't and won't contain: "But deeds of armes must I at last be faine, / And Ladies loue to leaue so dearely bought?" As the first stanza of the entire poem informed us, "fierce warres and faithfull loues" are the very substance of Spenser's song: what Redcrosse laments is the supersession of *The Faerie Queene* by the truth to which it gestures.

The expanse of poem between the appearance of Una's lion and the sanctification of the Redcrosse Knight—the eventful but allegorically underdetermined middle of the Legend of Holiness—is the focus of my attention here. It is a part of *The Faerie Queene* that assumed peculiar, seemingly outsized importance to Spenser's eighteenth- and nineteenth-century critics (the so-called Romantics) and to the authors of the dozens of adaptations of *The Faerie Queene* written specifically for children in the nineteenth and early twentieth centuries. One aim of this chapter is to show the common origins and shared assumptions of these seemingly disparate strands of reception history. Romantic critics and the authors of juvenile adaptations evinced very different—indeed, nearly opposite—attitudes toward Spenser's moral allegory: critics almost universally scorned it and urged readers to pay it no mind, while the authors of adaptations were uniformly respectful of it, though no less willing for reasons of their own to set it aside. But they arrived at these positions by way of a shared perception of the poem as childish reading: for critics, memories of childhood pleasure in *The Faerie Queene* motivated and authorized the effort to rescue it from allegorical pedantry; for the authors of children's adaptations, assumptions about the limited capacity and immature tastes of their intended audience licensed departures, both subtle and striking, from their original, which was reimagined as the perfected telos to which childish reading might one day lead.

The history of *The Faerie Queene*'s child readers here intersects in complicated ways with the history of childhood itself. When critics like Leigh Hunt and James Russell Lowell urged readers to approach *The Faerie Queene* as a gallery of beautiful pictures, basking in its loveliness without troubling themselves with its meaning, they drew on theories about the benign atmospheric influence of art that, as Douglas Mao has shown, emerged in the nineteenth century in concert with a faith in the radical impressibility of childhood. Children, declares Oscar Wilde, "are pretty much what their surroundings make them," and the beauty of those surroundings could inculcate virtue even while bypassing the intellect: those raised among lovely things "will love what is beautiful and good, and hate what is evil and ugly, long before they know the reason why."[9] Indeed, the object of such youthful exposure to art was, as Mao observes, "a developed *inattention* to beauty—a taking of graciousness for granted, a becoming 'accustomed' to the comely—that somehow improves our very selves."[10] Such cultivated inattention is, as we shall see, precisely the kind of reading to which nineteenth-century critics believed *The Faerie Queene* best suited; the poem was not a lesson to be studied but a garden or gallery in which to wander.

But Spenser's didacticism, so strenuously repressed by critics like Hunt and Lowell, made *The Faerie Queene* equally amenable to a different understanding of childhood, as an allegory in its own right: a usefully simplified emblem of questions and conflicts that became complicated and murky in adulthood. As Carolyn Steedman has shown, childhood offered eighteenth- and nineteenth-century philosophers and political theorists a powerful frame for thinking about the relationship between moral abstraction and embodied particularity, with the figure of the child flickering between personification and personhood.[11] And as the work of scholars like Samuel Pickering and Karen Sánchez-Eppler attests, that quasi-allegorical notion of childhood was nowhere more evident or more ambivalent than in the nascent field of children's literature. "Although much early fiction warned children against the dangers of the imagination," Pickering notes, "it did so in imaginative stories," relying on allegory as "a staple" for converting imaginative pleasure into instruction. But allegory was understood to bear risks of its own, for the more subtle and inventive its deployment in fictional narratives, the greater the risk "that children would be so attracted by the surface of allegory that they would miss the lessons conveyed."[12] By the nineteenth century, Sánchez-Eppler argues, childhood reading had been enlisted in support of two seemingly incommensurate ideals of literacy and citizenship: on the one hand, the figure of the reading child functioned as an emblem of books' civilizing power, their capacity to shape unruly subjects into social and political conformity; on the other, it stood for subjectivity's resistant core, for the imaginative freedom of literature and the indelible self-possession of readers.[13]

Even as the experiences of child readers supply a point of historical access to and a theoretical frame for a crucial interval in *The Faerie Queene*'s reception history, the poem itself affords an illuminating perspective on the simultaneous rise of children's literature and the realist novel, a perspective from which the charged relations between children and their books—relations of possessive affection, stubborn resistance, confusion, pleasure, and understanding—take on heightened significance. As we shall see, the real, recollected, or imagined scene of a child reading *The Faerie Queene* offered a particularly concentrated version of the contradictions Pickering and Sánchez-Eppler describe, since the poem itself seemed split between allegorical instruction and narrative wildness: reader and text thus inhabited the same shifting margin between transparent idealism and dense corporeality, moral understanding and sheer sensory pleasure. If we peer closer at the many recurrences of and variations on that scene throughout the eighteenth and nineteenth centuries, what it reveals is the depth of the observing, remembering, or imagining adult's ambivalence toward a kind of reading at once inferior and vastly preferable to his or her own. Such ambivalence was germinal to the emergence of the novel as a literary form. As Michael McKeon argues, techniques of novelistic representation have their roots in childish misreadings of allegorical romance, readings that substituted pleasure in narrative detail for anxiety about understanding, turning the "problem of mediation" into a recipe for successful fiction.[14] But as novels grew in popularity and prestige, practitioners and critics alike sought to disavow its affinity with childhood reading by fashioning ever stricter distinctions between mere fantasy and novelistic fiction: fairy tales were relegated to the tastes of childhood, while mature readers were taught to appreciate realist fiction as the acme of serious art.[15] Spenser's poem was caught in the middle, suspect both as moral allegory and as fairy fantasy.

The condescension with which critics treated *The Faerie Queene* was more than a reaction to the increasing prestige of the realist novel; it was also a legitimate response to the poem's own mixed signals, reflecting and refracting Spenser's unease about its fantastic trappings and the kinds of reading they might solicit—readings that failed to register what was ultimately at stake, absorbed instead with things of passing or illusory value. The tension between otherworldly significance and worldly event that helped to produce the realist novel, as well as the distinction between childish fantasy and mature perception that lent it authority, are both already present within *The Faerie Queene*, in the fraught interplay of narrative figure and allegorical referent. The key difference is that within Spenser's poem, attachment to what is present before one's eyes never loses the character of an error; realist reading remains essentially childish. Redcrosse's impulsive outburst to Contemplation marks one such instance of childish reading, but it is preceded by a number of others, each with Una at its center. The charismatic non- or quasi-human companions who, for obvious reasons, assume such a visible place in versions of book 1 written and illustrated for children are no less necessary to the original text: Una's lamb and dwarf, her lion and the troop of satyrs who succor her in canto 6 are all agents and figures of immature understanding—indeed, of an intimacy and an appreciation predicated on defects in understanding. Like Una herself, they are destined to vanish at the instant of revelation, giving way to higher and more ultimate realities. To cling to them would be childish, but it is a childishness to which Spenser himself seems intermittently prone.

Eunuchs and Satyrs: Versions of Childish Reading

Nothing in the contents or the presentation of the earliest editions of *The Faerie Queene* suggests that either Spenser or his publishers imagined children as an audience for the poem. Indeed, the very category of children's literature could hardly be said to exist in sixteenth-century England, outside of texts produced for schoolroom use or religious catechesis. Although children undoubtedly read for amusement, the books to which they turned were rarely designed for their use.[16] In many ways, it is precisely the absence of children's literature that made childhood reading of *The Faerie Queene* possible, if not exactly common, in the century and a half after its initial publication. As Katie Trumpener has argued, before the commercialization of children's literature by John Newbery in the 1740s, and continuing to some extent well into the nineteenth century, "highly literate children grew up reading not contemporary juvenile literature, but a rather random hodgepodge of recent, older, and even ancient books that happened to fall into their hands."[17] That is precisely the situation described by Abraham Cowley in an extraordinary passage in his 1668 essay "Of Myself," in which Cowley attributes the precocious fashioning of his poetic sensibility to an inadvertent encounter with *The Faerie Queene*:

I believe I can tell the particular little chance that filled my head with such Chimes of Verse, as have never since left ringing there: For I remember when I began to read, and to take some pleasure in it, there was wont to lie in my Mothers Parlour (I know not by what accident, for she herself never in her life read any Book but of Devotion) but there was wont to lie *Spencers* Works; this I happened to fall upon, and was infinitely delighted with the Stories of the Knights, and Giants, and Monsters, and brave Houses, which I found every where there: (Though my understanding had little to do with all this) and by degrees with the tinckling of the Rhyme and Dance of the Numbers, so that I think I had read him all over before I was twelve years old, and was thus made a Poet as irremediably as a Child is made an Eunuch.[18]

The charm of the anecdote inheres in the unlikely pairing of heedless young reader, swaddled in an atmosphere (or a naive impression of?) maternal devotion, and hypersophisticated text—"That indeed is a Poem fitter for the examination of men than the consideration of a Child," marveled Cowley's contemporary Thomas Sprat[19]—although the startlingly brutal image with which it concludes highlights a darker undercurrent of haplessness and helplessness. Indeed, for all its shaping influence on Cowley's future, his youthful encounter with Spenser's poem is curiously devoid of intentionality. Like the castration to which it is compared, the child reader's initiation into a life of verse takes the form of an eroticized passivity: the book "was wont to lie" in his mother's parlor by some inexplicable "accident," the boy "happened to fall upon" it, and his reading of it passes in an episodic rush of "Knights, and Giants, and Monsters, and brave Houses," "all over before I was twelve years old." Stripped of moral significance, or meaning of any kind—"my understanding," Cowley assures us, "had little to do with all this"—*The Faerie Queene* itself is reconstituted as a kind of eunuch text, productive of a delight that is both infinite and to no apparent end. Cowley experiences the poem not as a "continued Allegory," as Spenser terms it in "Letter of the Authors" annexed to the 1590 edition (714), but as a loose concatenation of images, acoustic effects, and events, *adventures* in the etymological sense of happenings or befallings: "Knights, and Giants, and Monsters, and brave Houses." What meaning there is, either in the poem itself or in the experience of reading it, is legible only in retrospect: the adult writer interprets his reading of *The Faerie Queene* as a fall in the biblical sense, from innocence and ignorance to poetic experience, but the child undergoes it as sheer accident, a vertiginous tumble into a world of sensory impressions and fantastic eventualities.

But even as it neglects—or neuters—much of what mature readers of Spenser's poem, then and now, would consider its primary purposes, Cowley's anecdote points out a feature of *The Faerie Queene*'s composition Spenser himself acknowledges as essential. The subtitle of the "Letter of the Authors" at the back of the 1590 edition tells us it is provided "For the Better Understanding" of Spenser's readers, to whom it supplies both a key to the poem's allegorical subtext and an account of the poet's "generall intention" in writing it. That intention, famously, is "to fashion a gentleman"—which is to say, to usher readers out of the indeterminate pleasures of youth into a mature self-understanding (714). Spenser's "Letter" thus purports to tell us not only what the poem means but also (and again: purportedly) how the poet means for us to read it. To evade one kind of meaning is, by implication, to frustrate the other. Lapses of allegorical understanding are defects in gentlemanly self-discipline, and readers like the young Abraham Cowley fail on both counts: to read *The Faerie Queene* for the "infinite pleasure" of it is to opt for life as a eunuch. But despite its heading, the "Letter" at the close of the 1590 poem is not wholly devoted to the author's intentions or the gentlemanly fashioning of readers, and neither, it suggests, is the poem itself. On the contrary, in the penultimate paragraph Spenser acknowledges that a significant fraction of the text has little or no relation to its didactic intent: "But by occasion hereof, many other adventures are intermedled, but rather as accidents then intendments." The examples Spenser supplies—"the love of Britomart, the overthrow of Marinell, the misery of Florimell, the vertuousnes of Belphœbe, the lasciviousnes of Hellenora, and many the like"— are not comprehensive, but they suggest a distinct pattern: allegorical intendment seems to loosen its grasp on the poem whenever its female characters assume the lead (718). This admission, relegated within the "Letter" to the status of an aside or afterthought, suggests that the effeminating and accidental character of Abraham Cowley's childhood encounter with *The Faerie Queene* is itself not entirely accidental. Rather, Cowley's memory of reading registers a fault line within the poem, an uneven and gendered dichotomy between adventure and intention that belies the author's pretense to singleness of purpose.

Gordon Teskey argues that this hybrid design is key to Spenser's representation of the deep mythical past as imminent and unfolding: the poem "entangles past and present in the signifying procedures of allegory and the randomizing patterns of narrative romance," an entanglement that enlivens historical subjectivity while unsettling the past's moral authority.[20] One advantage of approaching the poem from the perspective of child readers is that the difficulty such readers have (or are assumed to have) in prioritizing intendment over accident can put into relief the tension between history as lesson and history as happening. This, certainly, was the effect of Bronson Alcott's use of *The Faerie Queene* as a read-aloud text in his experimental Temple School in Boston, Massachusetts, from 1834 to 1841. The curriculum at the Temple School covered little in the way of reading, writing, and arithmetic, at least in the usual sense, being oriented instead around the communal exegesis of a handful of literary works, *Pilgrim's Progress* and *The Faerie Queene* chief among them (see fig. 1). The primary object, as Alcott's assistant teacher Elizabeth Palmer Peabody explains in her 1835 *Record of a School*, was not to teach the children how to read, per se, but "how to use a book": "to consider how words bodied forth thoughts, signing external objects, and suggesting internal facts of spirit."[21] *Pilgrim's Progress*, with its clearly labeled allegorical figures and its end-oriented (if accident-ridden) progress toward revelation, was a natural fit with Alcott's interest in what he termed the "spiritual culture" of childhood (iv). But *The Faerie Queene*, with its wayward knights and distractingly lovely ladies, required more concerted classroom management, lest use lapse into abuse, as the following description by Peabody reveals:

> He then said he was going to read some pictures of what goes on in the mind during the period of its development on earth, by means of the duties of life; but if one boy or girl interrupts me, said he, I shall stop; and that boy or girl shall bring a deprivation upon the whole school; those who are innocent being obliged to suffer, as the good are always willing to do, for the instruction of the guilty. This remark elicited some doubts, which were settled by reference to Christ, and all martyrs, and self-sacrificing philanthropists, who make it their vocation on earth, to seek and to save that which was lost, to suffer and die to bring life and immortality to light.
>
> At last, the Fairy Queen was opened, and Mr. Alcott began. (100)

It is hard to imagine a scene of childhood reading more different from the one described by Abraham Cowley: Alcott's rigidly disciplined, interpretively straitened reading of *The Faerie Queene* to the children in his classroom seems orchestrated to forestall any idle, haphazard, merely delighted response to Spenser's poem. Peabody insists that the children were enraptured by what they heard—"They listened with the most intense interest, and could not help exclaiming, as they sympathized," and when Alcott paused, "they all exclaimed, go on, go on" (100–101)—but their sympathetic absorption in the story is not the point, and Alcott makes some effort to thwart it, pausing at intervals to ask questions or to provide a moral commentary on the characters and their actions.

For instance, rather than read the stanzas describing Una outright, Alcott "paraphrases" them, telling the children that Una "represented Truth"; "she 'inly mourned' because Wickedness and Error existed; she was 'in white,' because truth is pure, bright, and innocent" (100). Each aspect of her adventure with the Redcrosse Knight in the poem's opening canto is glossed in this fashion, up to but not—for obvious reasons—including the creation of the false Una and her attempted seduction of the Redcrosse Knight. Halting there, Alcott

FIGURE 1. "View of Mr. Alcott and the children conversing," Bronson Alcott, *Conversations with Children on the Gospels*, 1836. Beinecke Rare Book and Manuscript Library, Yale University.

quizzes the children on what they have learned. "To avoid evil," replies one young scholar. "Mr. Alcott then went on to speak of the conduct of good and evil within themselves," Peabody reports, "and made individual applications which brought the subject home to each one's own experience" (101). But such efforts were not always sufficient: even as it attests to the merits of *The Faerie Queene* as a primer in allegorical reading and being, Peabody's *Record* hints at the ways the poem and its childish audience conspired against Alcott's moralizing ambitions. Thus, on one occasion, Alcott reads the story of Arthur's encounter with Ignaro as a pointed lesson in the perils of laziness and inattention, but the force of the lesson is diluted by a boy ("a lately entered scholar," Peabody is careful to note) who eagerly persists in asking "if that story was true?" What he means is "did it really happen?"—not, as Alcott would hope, "does it communicate some higher truth?" Frustrated, Alcott exclaims, "There are some boys who do not understand that there are realities in the mind; and when I shape out the realities of the mind by means of outward things that represent them, these boys say that is not true" (60).

Like Cowley's eunuch, Alcott's threatening invocation of the boys who do not and will not understand hints at a hidden peril of childish reading in *The Faerie Queene*: the possibility that interest and sympathy will not give way to deeper forms of engagement but will, by their very intensity, preclude them. Some boys never do understand. Of course, this anxiety is largely palpable from the outside, from the perspective of the remembering or supervising adult. As Karen Sánchez-Eppler observes, the cultural meaning of childhood—that is, its meaning to adults—inheres in the weird temporality of anticipatory nostalgia: "For adults, childhood is not only teleological, pointing toward unknown futures, but also archeological and nostalgic, recovering a lost past."[22] In her dazzling account of Spenserian romance, Patricia Parker identifies the narrative expanses of *The Faerie Queene* with a similarly bracketed yet elastic temporality— the *dilatio*, or meantime, of salvation history between the Incarnation and the Second Coming—in which moral judgment may be suspended, vitiated, or beside the point: "what seems more important is the romance experience of not knowing where lines are until they have been violated or crossed."[23] It is precisely this experience of belated recognition that brings childish reading into view as such—and that marks its end. Children's reading becomes childish reading with the retrospective realization of its provisional and partial character. Immersive and absorbing in the moment, childish reading is reading one grows out of, in all senses of the phrase.

Unless, that is, one doesn't. In its potential to arrest the very development it is meant to foster, childish reading impinges on the central problem of poetic representation in *The Faerie Queene*, the danger that Spenser's delightful accidents will overwhelm his serious intendments, and that the appeal of fiction will prove more durable than the claims of understanding. Within book 1 that possibility is figured by Ignaro—an obviously negative exemplar—but also, more ambivalently, by the satyrs who rescue Una in canto 6. Smitten with Una's beauty, the satyrs prove cheerfully impervious to her efforts to catechize them; when she forbids their worship of her, they content themselves with worshipping her ass. Although the satyrs can themselves be allegorized as Jews, unconverted Gentiles, Roman Catholics, and other unregenerate types—"the category of souls for whom there can be no excuse ... and also no hope of salvation," in Darryl J. Gless's formulation—the poem treats their blunders more gently than such a judgment might lead us to expect: "even as theological perspectives predict for Una's rescuers an eternal exclusion from grace, the pastoral and romance modulations of the episode solicit a combination of sympathy and nostalgia."[24] Gless identifies this as a tension "between the characteristic values of idyllic pastoral" and those of Reformed theology, which is no doubt how sixteenth-century readers would have perceived it, but in their misguided devotion to Una's outward form, the satyrs manifest a tension implicit in childish reading, between the imperative to grow in understanding and the yearning to cling to a partial but beloved incarnation of truth. As we shall see, the fondness with which Spenser regards his goat-men is echoed and amplified in the attitudes of many former child readers of *The Faerie Queene* toward the poem they once adored. But childish reading need not give way to sophisticated indulgence, and its persistence has an ethical force of its own, transforming the leisurely errancy of romance into a concentrated investment in the present. Like Alcott's literal-minded questioner, Spenser's satyrs hint at the possibility of an attachment to fiction characterized neither by goatish obstinacy nor by witty dalliance but by earnest absorption.

In this respect, childish reading might help us recognize and value one of *The Faerie Queene*'s most distinctive and elusive qualities: its occasional passages of what Jeff Dolven calls "ordinariness." What is ordinary in the poem, Dolven suggests, is what remains outside of and somehow immune to narrative development or allegorical intendment. Even as it gestures at a critique of allegorical incompetence, Una's uneventful, unproductive, and ultimately harmless stay with the satyrs in book 1 is ordinariness incarnate, right down to the description of how men with goats' legs kneel: backward—which is to say, in stubborn opposition to educative discipline but also in innocent conformity with anatomical fact. Such ordinariness besets Una from the moment of her separation from the Redcrosse Knight: when Spenser's Truth awakens to her abandonment by the Knight of Holiness at the start of book 1's second canto, she undergoes a rapid fall from allegorical coherence to narrative contingency. Deprived of the relationship that defines her meaning in the poem, which is to say, both her identity and her purpose, Una errs, wandering in and out of a series of more casual affiliations, with beastly humans and humane beasts, none equal to interpreting her. Readers, of course, can take satisfaction in recognizing meanings that escape characters—we can see where the satyrs go wrong and why, parting company with their incompetence—but doing so puts us at strange odds with Una's own inclinations. For even as accident imperils understanding, it makes room in the poem, and in Una herself, for less exalted readerly virtues: for dogged persistence, patient incomprehension, and what we might call kindness, the fellow feeling of one fallen creature for another. These are not the perfected forms of holiness at which book 1 finally aims, but they are accommodations it is willing to treat as indispensible for a time.

The willingness to set aside, if only temporarily, a concern for what ultimately matters is the version of childishness I seek to emulate in my own account of Una's accidental adventures. Doing so allows me to pay more attention than is usual, or perhaps even warranted, to incidental details in Spenser's narrative, without striving to put them in service of any larger interpretive or literary historical end. In his study of *Renaissance Realism*, Alastair Fowler cautions explicitly against the temptation to read into the intermittent realism of *The*

Faerie Queene: Spenser's poem is not devoid of naturalized events and interactions, Fowler allows, but "such fleeting resemblances to novelistic mimesis have a way of leading the interpreter nowhere."[25] But going nowhere is precisely the point. The assumption that realist representation must serve the larger progress of the poem is itself anachronistic, as is Fowler's unstated implication that narrative realism is noteworthy to criticism only insofar as it prefigures or tends toward the novel. Spenser's realism escapes notice—and differs from its novelistic successors—by being ancillary to both his allegorical and his narrative aims, accruing instead to seemingly random fragments of description and plot. As Rosemond Tuve notes, almost as an aside in her study of allegorical imagery, Spenser's reading of medieval romances gave him a "flair for ordinary realism in its simplest sense": "for situations drawn from daily life, natural rather than contrived conversation, unadorned reportage of a matter-of-fact presentation of what we instead isolate and call 'the marvellous,' [and] credible and unelaborated motivations." Indeed, although romance is associated in the critical imagination with an estrangement from reality, "one might claim with justice that the romance-like portions of *The Faerie Queene* are the portions where we retire comfortably from the exotic and the thoroughly incredible into the plain affairs of serious but ordinary daily life." The forests and fields in which Una wanders in the middle cantos of book 1 offer just such a respite: not an escape from reality, as romance is often characterized, but an escape to it. And it is this homeliness, rather than any supernatural flourishes, that allows Spenser to achieve, in Tuve's phrase, "an *interesting* romance," one whose milieu is not merely generic but particular, lush and rough with gratuitous and plausible detail.[26]

What would it mean to admit the interest of such details while accepting Fowler's judgment that they "lead . . . nowhere"? Spenser offers one possible answer to this question at the very end of book 1, in the form of a literal—and literal-minded—child. His entrance into the poem is purely accidental and, in Dolven's terms, ordinary: he appears only after both the allegory and the plot of book 1 have more or less been resolved; grace has triumphed over sin, and Una restored to her parents' loving arms. Indeed, he appears just as Una is revealed, for the first time, in her true form: "in her self-resemblance well beseene" and "seem[ing] such, as she was, a goodly maiden Queene" (1.12.8.8–9). But the drama of this revelation makes no impact on him, for it is undercut by a rival spectacle: the corpse of the dragon slain by Redcrosse, which remains sprawled across the foreground of this final canto, "stretcht on the ground in monstrous large extent" (1.12.9.7). A crowd of people, inhabitants of the Edenic countryside, gather around the corpse to wonder at it, and among them is this little boy—perhaps as young as the four- and five-year-olds in Alcott's classroom and certainly no older than Cowley's twelve—whom we see through the eyes of his exasperated parent:

> One mother, when as her foolehardie chyld
> Did come too neare, and with his talants play,
> Halfe dead through feare, her little babe revyld,
> And to her gossips gan in counsell say;
> How can I tell, but that his talants may
> Yet scratch my sonne, or rend his tender hand?
> So diversly themselves in vaine they fray.... (1.12.11.1–7)

The narrator's condescending aside invites us to dismiss the boy, his mother, and her friends as bad readers; even here, on the threshold of salvation, it seems that some people will find a way to distract themselves with vanities. But the boy and his mother might also be seen as having (almost literally) stumbled upon one of the major unresolved and unresolvable preoccupations of *The Faerie Queene*: What is the status of an allegorical body that has ceased to mean but not to be? Or: How do we reckon with fictive attachments we recognize as erroneous or unproductive but fail to outgrow? This is the problem of childish reading; for many eighteenth- and nineteenth-century critics, it was the problem of *The Faerie Queene*; within book 1 of the poem itself, it is the problem of Una.

Perplexing Una

As James Kearney has argued, the opening book of *The Faerie Queene* can be read as a reflection on the perilous method of the poem as a whole. For Spenser's reader, the progress of the Redcrosse Knight serves as a model of what Kearney terms "an iconoclastic hermeneutics that distinguishes between a properly transcendent reading and an idolatrous tarrying with letters and things."[27] That progress culminates on Contemplation's Mount, with the discovery of the knight's true, predestined identity as St. George and the revelation that all outward appearance, including the substance of the poem he inhabits, is a pale and passing dream. In this reading, defeating the dragon is a kind of afterthought: a necessary but also trivial enactment of Redcrosse's triumph over the trappings of his own heroic selfhood. If we find the battle between them somewhat wearisomely prolonged, so much the better; it shows our own progress from idle and idolatrous enjoyment to reverence—in Augustinian terms, from *cupiditas* to *caritas*. As we have just noted, however, the dragon doesn't vanish into naught, and his corpse distracts some inhabitants of book 1 from recognizing the Truth that stands before them. This bizarre displacement of attention from Una's revelatory appearance in canto 12 to the monstrous body of her foe is a parodic exaggeration of a pattern that runs throughout book 1, in which animal bodies serve to highlight Una's status as a corporeal fiction—in Kearney's terms, an "incarnate text" (2)—and obscure her function as an allegorical signifier. The effect of that obscuration is an intensification of interest and, even, of intimacy: like the child who rushes forward to prod the dead dragon's body with his tender hand, readers who respond to Una's outward form often make up in feeling what they lack in understanding.

Such readers proliferate within the poem as soon as Una is parted from the Redcrosse Knight at the start of canto 2, and their idle, even idolatrous perceptions of her gradually reshape her self-understanding. Indeed, the course of Una's solitary misadventures suggests an exception to what Susanne Wofford calls "one of the fundamental 'rules' of *The Faerie Queene*," that "the characters do not know they are in an allegory."[28] This is emphatically true of the Redcrosse Knight (at least, until his meeting with Contemplation in canto 10), but it doesn't hold for Una, whose difficulties navigating the book's middle cantos stem in part from her lack of any other kind of knowledge. That is, if the Redcrosse Knight must learn to read himself allegorically, as the temporary embodiment of an elect eternal soul, Una is forced over the middle cantos of book 1 to come to terms with the here and now—which is to say, with the persistence of original sin and the primacy of plot. What Wofford terms "the epistemology of errantry" (220)—a limited, literal-minded processing of events as happenings and as they happen—is for Una not a default mode but a hard-won achievement. Along the way, Spenser's readers are made to reckon with both the perils and the advantages of reading childishly: with an eye fixed on the present, willfully or helplessly blind to the world to come.

It is worth recalling how Una herself enters *The Faerie Queene*. Her name suggests singularity and self-containment, but Una arrives in the Legend of Holiness in remarkably scattered fashion, riding on a white donkey, accompanied by a lamb on a leash, and trailed by a dwarf who is loaded with her baggage:

> A louely Ladie rode him faire beside,
> Vpon a lowly Asse more white then snow,
> Yet she much whiter, but the same did hide
> Vnder a vele, that wimpled was full low,
> And ouer all a blacke stole she did throw,
> As one that inly mournd: so was she sad,
> And heauie sat vpon her palfrey slow:
> Seemed in heart some hidden care she had,
> And by her in a line a milke white lambe she lad.

> So pure and innocent, as that same lambe,
> She was in life and euery vertuous lore,
> And by descent from Royall lynage came
> Of ancient Kings and Queenes, that had of yore
> Their scepters stretcht from East to Westerne shore,
> And all the world in their subiection held;
> Till that infernall feend with foule vprore
> Forwasted all their land, and them expeld:
> Whom to auenge, she had this Knight from far compeld.
>
> Behind her farre away a Dwarfe did lag,
> That lasie seemd in being euer last,
> Or wearied with bearing of her bag
> Of needments at his backe.... (1.1.4–6)

This description can, of course, be read as an iconographic tableau, in which each element—donkey, lamb, dwarf—figures some aspect of Una's psychology: her humility, her innocence, her steadfast patience. But the complex syntax of the three stanzas works against such straightforward analysis, presenting readers instead with a loose network of conjunctions and dependencies: beside, upon, yet, but, under, over, as, and, by, in, from, of, till, behind. And the narrator himself seems hesitant to read too deeply into these connections. The black stole marks the maiden "*as* one that inly mourned"; her "heavie" posture "seemed" to tender some "hidden care," and the dwarf who lags "behind her farre away ... lasie seemd"—but may, after all, be merely tired. According to Paul Alpers, the characterization of Una throughout book 1 exemplifies the poem's delicate balance of assertion and qualification: "the hallmark of Spenserian narration is confidence in locutions which are at the same time understood to be provisional." Alpers insists, however, that such provisionality is only accidental, in the Spenserian sense of the word: the meanings for which Una stands "are ultimately one," and the uncertainties that cloud them "attend not Una herself, but her story."[29]

In this opening description, however, uncertainties literally attend Una— are, in fact, tethered to her—in the form of her mysterious allegorical entourage. It's only in the middle of the three stanzas that the narrator speaks with conviction: Una is "so pure and innocent, as that same lamb, / ... in life and euery uertuous lore, / And by descent from Royall linage came." But the "and" that blandly links these two assertions at the start of line 3 masks the tension between them. Una's innocence guarantees her function in the allegory of book 1, as the Truth on which Holiness depends, but it contradicts her role in its plot, as the heir to an Eden despoiled by the Fall. The "Royall linage" that connects Una to her parents implicates her in the universal corruption that descends from them, "from East to Westerne shore," turning humanity's royal dominion—"all the world in their subjection held"—into a common legacy of guilt: all the world held in the subjection of Adam and Eve. The calculated indeterminacy of Una's relationship to those around her in this opening tableau reflects her double meaning: on the one hand, sanctity, and on the other, the suffering incurred as a consequence of original sin.

That innocence and guilt should coexist is both impossible and the axiomatic premise of Christian moral teaching: as John Calvin puts it, the doctrine of original sin means that "even infants themselves carry their condemnation along with them from their mother's womb."[30] Spenser's opening description of Una mitigates that harsh doctrine just a bit; Una carries her condemnation with her, but at a distance and in the arms of a helpful dwarf. Fallenness becomes immanent and material to Una only after she awakens to find her knight has abandoned her—taking the dwarf with him. Redcrosse's departure has disastrous consequences for the knight, but it alters Una's existence no less, dispersing her allegorical entourage and initiating her into the facticity of plot. The lamb who was the sign of Una's innocence simply vanishes from the poem, and although the donkey remains, he seems to have changed from an iconographic figure to a real beast. In the opening tableau, the plodding feet of a "palfrey slow" keep pace with the pricking of the knight's eager horse: the physics of allegory are non-Newtonian. The same trick no longer works in canto 2, when "after him she rode with so much speede, / As her slow beast could make; but all in vaine"; the donkey is no longer a match for the "light-foot steede" (1.2.8.1–3). The realities of fallen human existence have always been Una's "by descent," and figured in her mourning robes, but now they descend on her with literal force: she bears her own bag, and her limbs are "wear[ied]" by it (1.2.8.6).

Spenser offers scant assistance to his heroine; on the contrary, he seems to take a certain satisfaction in her confusion. Immediately after the stanza describing her departure from Archimago's hovel, the narrative assumes the gleeful perspective of the magician himself, who rejoices at her suffering, "th'end of his drift": "For her he hated as the hissing snake, / And in her many troubles did most pleasure take" (1.2.9.4, 8–9). The reference to the snake confirms Una's identity in this section of the poem as a daughter of Eve, heir to the enmity God puts between serpent and woman in Genesis 3 and to the "increase[d] ... sorrows" that ensue: no longer granted any distance, spiritual or physical, from the effects of original sin, Una now inhabits the world of human error.[31] Her first attempt at interaction in this world is with "the rude wench" Abessa, who "her answerd not at all," for "[s]he could not hear, nor speake, nor vnderstand" (1.3.11.3–4). Between Abessa and Archimago, unfeeling disregard and prurient satisfaction, is surely a virtuous medium, but it is one the poem's narrator conspicuously struggles to locate, veering instead between detached matter-of-factness (as in the comic bloodbath at Abessa's cottage, from which Una emerges not merely unscathed but oblivious) and maudlin outbursts of sentiment. Canto 3 begins with such an outburst:

> Nought is there vnder heau'ns wilde hollownesse,
> That moues more deare compassion of mind,
> Then beautie brought t'vnworthy wretchednesse
> Through enuies snares or fortunes freakes vnkind:
> I, whether lately through her brightnesse blind,
> Or through alleageance and fast fealtie,
> Which I do owe vnto all woman kind,
> Feele my heart perst with so great agonie,
> When such I see, that all for pittie I could die. (1.3.1)

The hesitance in the middle of the canto, as to whether this feeling of compassion is specific to Una or general to her sex, is a red herring: the real question is whether it exists at all.[32] Certainly what the narrator feels at the spectacle of Una's wretchedness several stanzas later, when a greedy lion "with gaping mouth at her ran greedily, / To haue attonce deuoured her tender corse," is something less than perfect sympathy (1.3.5.5–6). Overcome by the beauty of Una's unveiled "angel face," the lion "forgat his furious force" and fawns over her (1.3.4.6, 5.9). The narrator is delighted by the picture, and the moral it contains—"O how can beautie maister the most strong, / And simple truth subdue auenging wrong?" he exclaims (1.3.6.4–5)—but Una, understandably, takes a bit longer to calm down. "Still dreading death," she assumes the lion is licking her because he plans to eat her and does not recognize the signs of his submission until "she had marked long" (1.3.6.7). The delay between our realization that Una is safe and her own occupies just nine lines, but it is an important one. There is, Spenser recognizes, a particularly piquant pleasure to be had from the gap between a character's sense of peril and a reader's: once we know Una is safe, we are free to enjoy the spectacle of her innocent terror.

Such enjoyment is one of the chief attractions of cantos 3 and 6, and with it comes the temptation to know Una not only better than the various incompetent readers with whom she is surrounded but better than she knows herself: to accept her as the temporary heroine (and ourselves as the temporary readers) of a romance, resting content with the knowledge that her confusion will mean nothing in the end. As Joe Moshenska suggests, the figure in book 1 who most clearly embodies this childish impulse to treat moral conflict as a kind of play is, again, Archimago, whose pleasure in impersonating the Redcrosse Knight comes almost fatally unmoored from his purpose in doing so.

Archimago's bizarre decision at the end of canto 3 to do battle with Sansloy—his allegorical ally in evil—suggests a kind of infantile absorption in his own charade: Why else would an elderly wizard risk life and limb defending the honor of a lady he despises?[33] I would locate the onset of Archimago's "second childhood" a bit earlier, in the stanza just before he encounters Sansloy, when he listens eagerly to the story of Una's recent adventures and asks her, in all seeming earnestness, "what the Lyon ment" (1.3.32.8). It isn't allegorical significance that Archimago is after here; he's frankly curious—even pleased—to discover that the story he was writing has a bit in it he didn't script.

The lion's relation to Una is, in fact, worth pausing over. Given his behavior at the start of canto 3, he appears to be that rarest of beings in *The Faerie Queene*: an ideal reader. His glimpse of the unveiled Una begets in him both tenderness and an unparalleled capacity for understanding: "From her fayre eyes he tooke commandement, / And euer by her lookes conceiued her intent" (1.3.9.8–9). But as a defender of truth, the lion proves sadly inadequate: when he springs to Una's defense at the end of canto 3, he is promptly run through by Sansloy's iron spear. His perfect intuition of Truth counts for nothing against an enemy who "feates of armes did wisely understand" (1.3.425). The lion's bloody death marks the end, in book 1 and perhaps in the poem as a whole, of a certain kind of faith in the efficacy of right reading. No one comprehends Una more fully and fluently than the lion; no one is more helpless to protect her. Indeed, it's worse than that: having killed the lion and seized Una, Sansloy becomes his dreadful double. He too sees Una unveiled at the start of canto 6, but his encounter with unmediated truth only inflames his impulse to destroy it: "Then gan her beautie shyne, as brightest skye, / And burnt his beastly hart t'efforce her chastitie" (1.6.4.8–9). If this, too, is an allegory of reading, it is one that suggests texts do not survive encounters with readers intact; interpretation invariably ends in violence.

The lion's failure to defend Una from Sansloy is only legible, I think, in light of Una's own incapacitation in canto 3—an incapacity born not of guilt but of innocence. To begin with, however, the poem tempts us to treat Una's misjudgments as lapses, or even contradictions, in her identity as Truth. The distance between Una and the reader begins in the middle of canto 3, when she glimpses a familiar figure riding atop a nearby hill:

>from whence when she him spyde,
>By his like seeming shield her knight by name
>Shee weend it was, and towards him gan ride:
>Approching nigh she wist, it was the same,
>And with faire feareful humblesse towards him she came. (1.3.26.5–9)

For readers, these lines are heavy with unsubtle ironies: we know, because the narrator has told us two stanzas before, that the mounted figure is not the Redcrosse Knight but his false double, the duplicitous Archimago; for us, the phrase "his like seeming shield" is burdened with the full weight of the poem's skepticism toward semblance and resemblance. But it isn't only Archimago who is ironized in our view: the progress Una makes from supposition to certainty— "she weend" and then "she wist"—is for us a specious slip from a wish that knows itself as such to a wish disguised as knowledge. The three stanzas that follow record the conversation between Una and her supposed knight—her anguished reproaches, his smooth self-justification—and Spenser allows us to feel both the intensity of Una's righteous anger and the inadequacy of Archimago's excuses: "Ah, my long lacked Lord, / Where haue ye bene thus long out of my sight?" she demands, and he replies, "[S]ooth to say, why I lefte you so long, / Was for to seeke aduenture in strange place" (1.3.27.1–2, 1.3.29.1–2).

When Archimago urges Una, "Now then your plaint appease" (1.3.29.9), she acquiesces with distressing eagerness, in a stanza that offers what Alpers terms "the most extraordinary deployment of aphorisms in the entire poem" (28):

> His louely words her seemd due recompence
> Of all her passed paines: one louing howre
> For many yeares of sorrow can dispence:
> A dram of sweete is worth a pound of sowre:
> Shee has forgott, how many, a woeful stowre
> For him she late endured; she speakes no more
> Of past: true is, that true loue hath no powre
> To looken backe; his eies be fixt before.
> Before her stands her knight, for whom she toyled so sore. (1.3.30)

What is extraordinary about the stanza, Alpers suggests, is the narrator's "complete absorption" in the "dilemmas and truths of human love" that claim his heroine's attention (28). Indeed, the voice of the poem approaches something like free indirect discourse in this stanza, the declarative verbs gradually increasing in confidence and giving rhetorical fixity, if not logical force, to Una's faltering faith: his lovely words her *seemed*; one loving hour *can* dispense; a dram of sweet *is* worth; true *is*, that true love *hath* no power to looken back; his eyes *be fixed* before. The insistent rhythm of the accumulating platitudes, emphasized by the absence of conjunctions between clauses, urges Una toward what seems like an inarguable truth: before her stands her knight.

For Alpers, Una's confidence in the false Redcrosse is a paradigmatic instance of narrative provisionality: her experience in the moment is "true, but incomplete" (30), a mirror of the reader's own gradual progress toward understanding. But the eagerness of Una's thought encounters resistance from Spenser's narration; the fit between her perception and ours is not exact. Thus, even as the closing lines proclaim true love's inability to look back, the second half of the alexandrine does just that, and invites readers to do so as well: "before her stands her knight, for whom she toyled so sore." Indeed, the very form of the stanza—its dense enjambments—force the reader's eye to engage in the back-and-forth shuttling between past and present, before and after, of which Una is incapable. If we resist the enjambment between lines 6 and 7, or lines 7 and 8, we see how Una's fidelity, the truth to which she clings, might incapacitate her: "She speakes no more"; "true loue hath no power." We see on the page the disjuncture between the word "before" at the end of line 8 and the same word at the beginning of line 9; we feel how, in movement from right to left—in the traversal of blank space that is the dumb counterpart of reading left to right—the word's telescopic vision narrows to a focus so obsessive it verges on blindness. The slippage in tense, from "seemd" in line 1 to "stands" in line 9, coerces us into sharing Una's limited view, so that the final line of the stanza possesses both an unanswerable authority and a conspicuous illogic, for it makes Una's suffering—all she forgets at the stanza's midpoint—into the justification for her continued faith: *her knight, for whom she toyld so sore.*

Una's misperception redeems suffering tautologically: the more she has suffered, the more worthwhile that suffering must have been. In short, Una appeals to her own narrative experience as the ground of faith. The weakness of that rationale is made cruelly manifest ten stanzas later, after Sansloy defeats Archimago in battle and Una begs for mercy for "one the truest knight aliue" (1.3.37.6). The pagan knight ignores her, unhelms his opponent, and Archimago is revealed. The revelation unsettles Sansloy himself, who suffers an access of shame his name would seem to forbid, and wonders, "Or thine the fault, or mine the error is, / In stead of foe to wound my friend amis?" (1.3.39.4–5). As for Una, she "Amased stands, her selfe so mockt to see / By him that has the guerdon of his guile, / For so misfeigning her true knight to bee" (1.3.40.2–4). Una has literally been mocked by Archimago, of course, in his fashioning of the false Una in canto 1, but here the other Una that floats before her eyes is the specter of her own self of ten stanzas earlier, embracing the man she believed to be her own dear knight, eagerly effacing the memory of his failure. That moment is retrospectively infected for her, as it always was for the reader, with irony. Una has suffered the physical consequences of the Fall—weariness, toil, pain, and the threat of death—from the moment of her abandonment by the Redcrosse Knight, but here, for the first time, she feels the epistemological consequences of original sin: the belated and mortifying consciousness of one's own naked self—necessarily, but without compulsion, in error.

For Spenser's readers, I propose, the challenges of this episode are not epistemological but ethical: the question isn't what to think but how to feel. And it is possible, perhaps necessary, to resist the undertow of ironic detachment. Read in isolation, apart from our knowledge of the false Redcrosse Knight's real identity, Una's response in stanza 30 offers a moving account of faith in action, transforming doubt into belief; read with full knowledge of the preceding stanzas, however, it's a woefully, willfully, worrisomely poor performance of discernment. But if we move too quickly in judgment of Una, we lose more than the example of her deliberate self-forgetfulness, her single-minded attention to what's before her; we also, paradoxically, risk forgetting something of our own. At the beginning of canto 2, when Archimago adopted the guise of the Redcrosse Knight, the narrator implicated us in the imposture: "Full iolly knight he seemde, and wel addrest, / And when he sate vppon his courser free, / *Saint George* himselfe ye would haue deemed him to be" (1.2.11.9). It is because we've read this stanza that we know Una is wrong when "she wist, it was the same" knight, her own dear George, in canto 3. But it's only by forgetting this stanza that we can abstract ourselves from her conviction; if we remember what the narrator has told us, that we ourselves would have been deceived, then Una's conviction becomes ours, too: "Before her stands her knight, for whom she toyld so sore." To forget what we were told in canto 2 flatters us as readers—*we* aren't taken in by this shallow impostor—but it also tempts us into repeating the Redcrosse Knight's own original sin: like Redcrosse, we abandon Una to Archimago's wiles, preferring to believe her in error rather than reckon with the constraints of our own guilty sight. Reading stanza 30 as Una reads Archimago, full of naive admiration for the virtue of true love, is a failure of sophistication but also, Spenser suggests, an act of kindness.

What remains to Una by the end of canto 3 is only the mute and uncomprehending sympathy of her donkey, who still "followes her far off": "ne ought he feares, / To be partaker of her wandering woe, / More mild in beastly kind, then that her beastly foe" (1.3.44.7–9). Kindness is gentleness rooted in commonality; it partakes of the suffering, erring nature of others because that nature is its own. Such creaturely kindness is by no means proof against deceit, but its very shallowness affords Una a kind of respite in canto 6, where we find her still in the clutches of the rapacious Sansloy:

> So when he saw his flatt'ring arts to fayle,
> And subtile engines bet from batteree,
> With greedy force he gan the fort assayle,
> Whereof he weend possessed soone to bee,
> And win rich spoile of ransackt chastetee.
> Ah heauens, that do this hideous act behold,
> And heauenly virgin thus outraged see,
> How can ye vengeance iust so long withhold,
> And hurle not flashing flames vpon that Paynim bold?

> The pitteous maiden carefull comfortlesse,
> Does throw out thrilling shriekes, & shrieking cryes,
> The last vaine helpe of womens great distresse,
> And with loud plaints importuneth the skyes,
> That molten starres do drop like weeping eyes;
> And *Phoebus* flying so most shamefull sight,
> His blushing face in foggy cloud implyes,
> And hides for shame. What wit of mortall wight
> Can now deuise to quit a thrall from such a plight? (1.6.5–6)

Once again, the narrator's protestations of horror prolong Una's agony and readers' suspense, lingering on the prospect of her violation, and, once again, we perceive her rescue before she does. It arrives at the start of the next stanza in startling form: "a rude, misshapen, monstrous rabblement" (1.6.8.7) of fauns and satyrs who put the terrified Sansloy to flight. As William Oram acutely observes, the satyrs make for an "unlikely rescue force," since we have already seen Sansloy face down the lion and the false Redcrosse Knight; he speculates that the satyrs oppose Sansloy as an embodiment of unperverted bodily desire.[34] Given that Sansloy has just torn off Una's veil, however, they also seem to figure a retreat from the assumed virtues of revelation; the desire to see truth plain has become indistinguishable from rape.

The immediate result of the satyrs' rescue of Una is, in fact, the further befuddlement of Spenser's Truth. The satyrs are instantly sympathetic to Una, but she regards them as yet another threat and "more amaz'd, in double dread doth dwell" (1.6.10.1). In a remarkable reversal of allegorical expectation, while the satyrs achieve instantaneous understanding of Una's innocence, "read[ing] her sorrow in her countenance sad" (1.6.11.4), they must labor to persuade her of "their barbarous truth" (1.6.12.2):

> Their frowning forheads with rough hornes yclad,
> And rusticke horror all a side doe lay,
> And gently grenning, shew a semblance glad
> To comfort her, and feare to put away,
> Their backward bent knees teach her humbly to obay. (1.6.11.5–9)

The syntax of the final line is suggestively unclear: perhaps it is the satyrs who, unaccustomed to obedience or to kneeling, must teach the backward-bending joints of their knees to fold. But the gesture, affecting in its awkward anatomical precision, is also meant to instruct Una in her humiliation: no longer guarded by a lion or a lionhearted knight, she must content herself with the dubious chaperonage of goat-men. The lesson takes, gradually and tentatively: "Their harts she ghesseth by their humble guise, / And yieldes her to extremitie of time"

(1.6.13.1–2). The humbling that began for Una with the discovery of Redcrosse's abandonment is now complete, Truth reduced by circumstance to a wild guess.

As a self-reflexive account of allegorical instruction, Una's stay with the satyrs provides a dismal gloss on Spenser's own moralizing ambitions. All her efforts to instruct them in Christian doctrine are confounded by their determination that she is the ultimate object of devotion: "And henceforth nothing faire, but her on earth they find" (1.6.18.9). Once again, Spenser's syntax allows for two readings. In the most immediate sense, the line follows from the revelation that the satyrs now scorn their former lovers, the nymphs and hamadryads of "their woody kind" (1.6.18.8): no other earthly being is fair compared to Una. But there is also the suggestion that Una's presence blinds the satyrs to heavenly matters, restricting their devotion to "her on earth." The following stanza confirms that hint, for however much "her gentle wit she plyes, / To teach them truth," the satyrs "worshipt her in vaine,"

> And made her th'Image of Idolatryes;
>   But when their bootlesse zeale she did restraine
> From her own worship, they her Asse would worship fayn. (1.6.19.5–9)

The turn from Una to her ass is humorous proof of the satyrs' obstinate attachment to the material world, but it also underscores the reality of Una's own existence in the poem: worshipping Una's ass is no better than worshipping Una, which is the joke on the satyrs, but neither is it worse, which is the joke on Spenser's readers. In a sense, this moment marks the necessary end of the "linage" traced in book 1's opening stanzas, connecting Una to her fallen parents. There the donkey served as an emblem of Una's humility, but it is no longer required for that function; Una herself does just as well. As a daughter of Adam and Eve, she too is a child of earth, the humus that is humility's root cause.

Una's stay with the satyrs, which occupies most of canto 6, is the nadir of Truth's hapless errancy, but it is also a rare interval of calm, a deliberate and unrebuked pause in book 1's progress toward allegorical fulfillment. For once, neither idleness nor idolatry manifests as a moral catastrophe. Una herself assents to the intermeddling of accident in her intended course with grace, and even gratitude:

> Glad of such lucke, the luckelesse lucky maid,
> Did her content to please their feeble eyes,
> And long time with that saluage people staid,
> To gather breath in many miseries. (1.6.19.1–4)

Luck and lucklessness are accidents, not intendments; neither says anything about Una's virtue or lack thereof. Nor, surprisingly, does her inclination "to gather breath": rest, even more than lust, is stigmatized in the Legend of

Holiness, the ultimate lapse in fidelity, but here Una is allowed, for a "long time" even, to content herself with what she knows are lesser beings and lesser truths. The poem reflects Una's gentleness toward the satyrs. When she finally leaves, secretly and with the assistance of the half-satyr knight Satyrane, the narrator makes clear that they have missed their chance for revelation—"Too late it was, to Satyres to be told, / Or euer hope recouer her againe: / In vaine he seekes that hauing cannot hold" (1.6.33.5–7)—but the observation is more rueful than severe. Readers are left with the odd sense that benign misreading has a vital, even redemptive place in the poem's system of hermeneutic value. It is not where Truth permanently resides, or where Holiness is meant to seek her, but it is where she sometimes—occasionally and accidentally—catches her breath.

She may even learn something. For what ultimately redeems Una from the contradictions of her story, allowing her to read her errant experience without being unmade by it, is not understanding but its opposite: an accommodation with uncertainty, a willingness to accept accident as the operation of grace in a fallen world. Aptly enough, this redemption begins with Una's reunion in canto 7 with her dwarf, whose departure in canto 2 precipitated her fall into accident. Before redemption, however, comes a near-death, death by allegorical interpretation. Spying the dwarf's new burden, the empty armor, idle shield, and discarded spear of the defeated Redcrosse Knight, Una draws a fatal conclusion: seeing "the signes, that deadly tydinges spake, / She fell to ground for sorrowfull regret, / And liuely breath her sad breast did forsake" (1.7.20.6–9). She is revived by narrative: by her willingness, strengthened by his ministrations, to listen to the story of what she believes she already knows. "Tell on (quoth she) the wofull Tragedy, / The which these reliques sad present vnto mine eye" (1.7.24.8–9). That narrative, the story of the poem we have been reading, ends in a crucial uncertainty—"of [Redcrosse's] life or death he stood in doubt" (1.7.26.9)—and it is that measure of ambiguity that brings Una back to her feet, "resoluing him to find / Aliue or dead" (1.7.28.2–3).

Several stanzas later, she "chaunce[s], by good hap" (1.7.29.1) to meet Prince Arthur: narrative accident is again the agent of Una's redemption. It also becomes the mechanism of her self-understanding. Telling the "story sad" of her parents' oppression and her knight's failure leads Una to a wonderfully equivocal profession of faith: "Be iudge ye heauens, that all things right esteeme, / How I him lou'd, and loue with all my might, / So thought I eke of him, and think I thought aright" (1.7.49.7–9). This is a very different sort of faith than the true love that greeted Archimago in canto 3, which had "no powre / To looken back"; "I think I thought aright" *is* the mind looking back on its own past judgments, not in perfect confidence but with a rueful sense of its capacity for misjudgment. Una acquires something like narrative self-consciousness here:

an identity divided but also constituted by its capacity for reflection. The text she asks heaven to interpret—how she loved and loves, thought and thinks—is joined by conjunctions that now traverse the gap between past and present selves. The scattered Una of canto 1—a self made coherent by allegorical understanding—has given way to a self bound by the line of its accident-prone, error-ridden plotting.

Una's trajectory in the middle cantos of book 1 mirrors and inverts the Redcrosse Knight's progress from doubt to faith and from narrative error to allegorical understanding. The climax of that story, as I noted earlier, occurs at the end of canto 10, on Contemplation's Mount, when the regenerate knight is given a vision of the New Jerusalem, the true glory of which his earthly achievements—and the substance of Spenser's poem—are mere temporary reflections. The vision rattles Redcrosse, as does the revelation that the heroic identity he has so painfully assumed must one day pass away: "But deedes of armes must I at last be faine," he asks, "And Ladies loue to leaue so dearely bought?" "What need of armes, where peace doth ay remain, / . . . and bitter battailes all are fought?" Contemplation replies. "As for loose loues they are vaine, and vanish into nought" (1.10.62.5–9). The phrase "loose loues" here, astonishingly and heartbreakingly, includes Redcrosse's bond with Una; that, too, will vanish in the New Jerusalem, where, as Christ tells the apostles, "they neither marry nor are given in marriage." That verse—Matthew 22:30—lurks in the background of Contemplation's speech to Redcrosse, but its more immediate biblical source is 1 Corinthians 13:9–12, in which Paul anticipates the passing away of his own prophetic words in the moment of their fulfillment, assimilating Scripture itself to the category of "childish things":

> For we know in part, and we prophesy in part. But when that which is perfect, is come, then that which is in part shall be abolished. When I was a child, I spake as a child: I understood as a child, I thought as a child: but when I became a man, I put away childish things. For now we see through a glass darkly: but then *shall we see* face to face. Now I know in part: but then shall I know even as I am known.

For the Redcrosse Knight, childish things include his love for Una; for Spenser's readers, they include *The Faerie Queene* itself. To understand the poem is, in the end, to stop reading it: in the clear light of apocalypse, all reading is childish reading and must be put away.

But the poem doesn't end with this revelation, although Redcrosse seems to expect it will:

> O let me not (quoth he) then turn againe
> Backe to the world, whose ioyes so fruitlesse are,

> But let me heare for aie in peace remaine,
> Or streight way on that last voyage fare,
> That nothing may my present hope empare. (1.10.63.1–5)

To which Contemplation simply replies, "That may not be" (1.10.63.6). He then reminds Redcrosse of his promise to accompany Una: in a surprising inversion, Una is identified not with the "streight way" of salvation but with the world's perplexity. To remain faithful to "that royal maides bequeathed care" (1.10.63.8), as Contemplation urges Redcrosse to do, is perhaps to embrace the love Paul calls *agape* and the Vulgate translation of the Bible terms *caritas*, the one human virtue Paul says will "never fall away, though that prophesyings be abolished, or the tongues cease, or knowledge vanish away" (1 Corinthians 13:8). But "care" is only punningly associated with *caritas*; it is more directly descended from the Old English *cearu*: suffering, sorrow, trouble, or preoccupation.[35] Una is Redcrosse's beloved, but she is also a burden he will one day be permitted to set down, an attachment he will outgrow. Even so, Spenser asks readers not to disdain such care: it rescues Una from the contradictions of her experience in the middle cantos of book 1, and it rescues Spenser himself from the need to disavow poetry altogether at the end of book 1. Una's ultimate, apocalyptic meaning may be Oneness and Truth, but within *The Faerie Queene*, she is cherished as a remnant—as a childish, but surprisingly tenacious, fiction.

Fancying Una

When eighteenth- and nineteenth-century critics struggled to account for their persistent attachment to *The Faerie Queene*, it was Una, and childhood, they remembered. The overwhelming emphasis such critics tended to place on the poem's sensual pictorialism and episodic interest, rather than its moral didacticism and allegorical coherence, has led modern scholars to dismiss them as willfully inattentive readers, at best revisionary and at worst ignorant of Spenser's stated intentions for his poem.[36] But the so-called Romantic Spenserians—the designation "Romantic" here includes Augustan and Victorian critics, too—weren't wholly inattentive: they gave a good deal more attention to the middle cantos of book 1 than many recent critics. Indeed, precisely because of their relative lack of allegorical significance, Una's wanderings served such critics as an epitome of *The Faerie Queene*'s essentially narrative and distinctively feminine appeal, to which they responded with an eroticized, half-guilty affection. "Spenser has ever been a favourite poet with me," Alexander Pope observed in a letter to John Hughes; "he is like a mistress, whose faults we see, but love her with 'em all"; comparing Spenser to Chaucer, Shakespeare, and Milton, Coleridge perceives in him "a mind constitutionally tender, delicate, and, in contrast to his three compeers, I had almost said, *effeminate*."[37] Una emerged as an excuse for this faintly indecorous attachment to a poet and a poem that could not easily be excused on critical terms. Her wayward career in the middle cantos of book 1 might exemplify the gothic imperfection of Spenser's design, but it also created a space in which undisciplined and aimless reading—reading for pleasure—could flourish.

Thus, in his otherwise rueful account of Spenser's disorganized plotting in his preface to the 1715 edition of *The Faerie Queene*, John Hughes singles out "the Adventures which befal Una" for particular praise, both as "very fine emblems"— episodes with the neatly modular and eminently pictorial quality of an emblem book—and as expressions of imaginative freedom, marked "with an agreeable Wildness of Fancy."[38] "Fancy" is a signal term in the reception history of *The Faerie Queene*, and a vexed one, too, with a particularly close relation to both childishness and effeminacy. The association was sometimes a positive one: in 1647 Henry More expressed gratitude to his father for "having from my childhood tuned my ears to Spencers rhymes, entertaining us on winter nights, with that incomparable Piece of his, *The Fairy Queen*, a Poem as richly fraught with divine Morality as Phansy."[39] Two decades later, Thomas Sprat invoked fancy as the reason for young Abraham Cowley's delight in a poem so manifestly not written for children: "in him it met with a Fancy, whose strength was not to be judged by the number of his years" (sig. A2r). Within *The Faerie Queene*, however, fancy is identified not with precocity but with an artificially arrested development. It appears at the head of the allegorical pageant in Busyrane's palace, "like a louely Boy, / Matchable . . . to that ympe of *Troy*, / Whom *Ioue* did loue, and chose his cup to beare" (3.12.7.1–4). A "daintie lad" clad in feathers, "like the sunburnt *Indians* do aray / Their tawney bodies, in their proudest plight," this Ganymede-like figure is, precisely, eunuch-like, his exotic appeal spiced with a hint of savagery (3.12.7.5, 8.1–3). In the proem to book 4, moreover, fancy is explicitly named as the motive of bad youthful readers, who, in the ventriloquized complaint of an unsympathetic critic, "better were in vertues discipled, / Then with vaine poemes weeds to haue their fancies fed" (4.proem.1.8–9). Spenser voices this judgment in order to discount it, but over the course of the seventeenth century, as neoclassical notions of poetic decorum cast the writing of early authors into increasing disfavor, it assumed a more prophetic and normative cast in relation to *The Faerie Queene*: Spenser's poem was increasingly seen—for better and for worse— not as an instrument of virtuous discipline but as "pleasing baite" for "fraile youth" (4.proem.1.6–7).

Even as *The Faerie Queene* became identified with fancy, the fantastic—partly by way of association with *The Faerie Queene*—was increasingly identified with an immature phase in the development of English literature. By the end of the nineteenth century, the equation of the fantastic with childhood and childish reading was a critical (and commercial) commonplace, but in the eighteenth century, as David Sandner notes, that equation was "secondary to the relationship of the fantastic to the primitive and superstitious cultural past."[40] Thus Thomas Rymer declares in the preface to his 1674 translation of a treatise on Aristotle's *Poetics*, "*Spenser*, I think, may be reckon'd the first of our *Heroick Poets*"—"first" here denoting primitivity rather than primacy. Within *The Faerie Queene*, Rymer continues, "all is fanciful and chimerical, without any uniformity, without any foundation in truth; his Poem is perfect *Fairy-land*. They who can love *Ariosto*, will be ravish'd with *Spenser*; whilst men of juster thoughts lament that such great Wits have miscarried in their Travels for want of direction to set them in the right way."[41] Rymer's judgment set the patronizing tone for two centuries of Spenser criticism to follow. In his 1694 verse history of English poetry, Joseph Addison's praise for *The Faerie Queene*, which he termed an "admirable work," is drenched in condescension toward the humors of an antique and antic age. For Addison, *The Faerie Queene* stands at an adolescent midpoint between the "unpolish'd strain" of Chaucer and Milton's "high and haughty" sublimity:

> Old *Spencer* next, warm'd with Poetick Rage,
> In Antick Tale amus'd a Barb'rous Age;
> An Age that yet uncultivate and Rude,
> Wher-e'er the Poet's Fancy led, pursu'd
> Through pathless Fields, and unfrequented Floods,
> To Dens of Dragons, and Enchanted Woods.
> But now the Mystick Tale, that pleas'd of Yore,
> Can Charm an understanding Age no more.[42]

Uniquely among the authors who form Addison's rudimentary canon of English poets, Spenser is both a poetic forefather and a reminder (or remainder) of vernacular literature's awkward youth. To be made a poet on the model of Spenser, as Cowley claimed to have been, was therefore both an initiation into literary maturity ("I ... was thus made a Poet") and an arresting of that development ("as a Child is made an Eunuch"), a failure to rise to the expectations of "an understanding Age."

Stories of boyhood encounters with *The Faerie Queene* proliferated in the eighteenth and nineteenth centuries, becoming almost a cliché of literary memoir, and testifying to what many critics saw as a natural sympathy between Spenser's fantastic imagery and the unregulated imagination of childhood. "I read the Faerie Queene, when I was about twelve, with infinite delight," Pope recalls in Joseph Spence's *Anecdotes*, his phrasing almost exactly replicating that of Cowley fifty years before.[43] "Spenser I could have read forever," writes

Walter Scott. "Too young to trouble myself about the allegory, I considered all the knights and ladies and dragons and giants in their outward and exoteric sense; and God only knows how delighted I was to find myself in such society." Like Cowley before him, Scott happens upon Spenser by "chance," in the miscellaneous reading he conducted "in the intervals of my school hours ... unregulated and undirected," away from the censorious eyes of his tutor and his mother.[44] For Robert Southey, the transformative encounter occurs in a local lending library, and Scott's own historical romances served as the obvious analogue:

> No young lady of the present generation falls to a new novel of Sir Walter Scott's with keener relish than I did that morning to the Faery Queen.... The delicious landscapes which he luxuriates in describing brought every thing before my eyes. I could fancy such scenes as his lakes and forests, gardens and fountains, presented; and I felt, though I did not understand, the truth and purity of his feelings, and that love of the beautiful and the good which pervades his poetry.[45]

The hallmarks of such anecdotes of *The Faerie Queene* are a sympathetic and sensual identification with the poem's fantastic images and a near total disregard for their allegorical correlatives. "I was infinitely delighted ... [t]hough my understanding had little to do with all this," Cowley writes; "I felt, though I did not understand, the truth and purity of his feelings," says Southey, and where each poet writes "though," we might put "because": to read without comprehending or even noticing a deeper meaning, "[t]oo young to trouble ... about the allegory," as Scott puts it, seems essential to the fascination *The Faerie Queene* exerts on its child readers. Among the poem's notable child readers, only John Dryden reported having liked it better as an adult, ruefully observing, "I remember, when I was a Boy, I thought inimitable *Spenser* a mean Poet, in comparison of *Sylvester's Dubartas*."[46]

With the exception of Dryden, early reading of *The Faerie Queene* seems not only to have endeared Spenser to his youthful admirers but to have inoculated them against the judgment they later felt, or recognized they ought to feel, as adults. The increasing commonness of stories about reading Spenser as a child corresponds to a downward shift in the author's reputation, from literary exemplar to minor poet—which is to say, a poet only minors truly love. To persist in an untroubled fascination with *The Faerie Queene* was to risk infantilization and emasculation, a risk that could be managed only by being transferred to Spenser himself. What the mature critic feels for Spenser in the eighteenth and nineteenth centuries is, very often, the patronizing fondness one feels for a younger self. "[W]ithout being insensible to the defects of the Fairy Queen," says Southey, "I am never weary of reading it."[47] If "to the reader of riper years" the design of *The Faerie Queene* appears "somewhat tedious and involved," Scott writes, "it must be allowed, on the other hand, that, from Cowley downwards, every youth of imagination has been enchanted with the splendid legends of the Faery Queen."[48]

The matrix of childish reading had a determining effect on criticism of *The Faerie Queene*. As the poem's allegorical design came to seem increasingly confused, its language increasingly strange, and its political commitments increasingly dubious, the key to retaining an unembarrassed admiration for it was to cultivate an ironic detachment from Spenser's express aims, emphasizing instead the poem's luxuriant imagery and sensual atmosphere—to insist, in effect, that the way one read as a child was right after all. The most famous, and also the most paradoxical, instance of this logic appears in William Hazlitt's 1818 *Lectures on the English Poets*. "Of all the poets," Hazlitt claimed, Spenser "is the most poetical":

> In Spenser, we wander in an ideal world, among ideal beings. The poet takes and lays us in the lap of a lovelier nature, by the sound of softer streams, among greener hills and fairer valleys. He paints nature, not as we find it, but as we expected to find it; and fulfils the delightful promise of our youth.[49]

According to Hazlitt, "the love of beauty . . . and not of truth" was "the moving principle of his mind," and he particularly celebrates "the character of Una"—the lady herself, that is, and not her allegorical referent—as one of "the finest things in Spenser" (69, 73). It is immediately after his praise of Una that Hazlitt offers his notorious advice to those who claim "they cannot understand [*The Faerie Queene*] on account of the allegory":

> They are afraid of the allegory, as if they thought it would bite them: they look at it as a child looks at a painted dragon, and think it will strangle them in its shining folds. This is very idle. If they do not meddle with the allegory, the allegory will not meddle with them. (74)

The child who fears the dragon who can do him no harm is, of course, drawn directly from the pages of *The Faerie Queene* itself, but Hazlitt inverts the meaning of Spenser's figure: the childish or "idle" reader is now precisely the reader who keeps the poem's allegorical sense too much in mind, allowing it to interfere with his enjoyment; the stigma of immaturity has been transferred from fancy to morality. Consciously or not, Hazlitt's use of the word "meddle" hearkens back to Spenser's description of his poem's accidents as "intermedled," but with a precisely opposite force: what obtrude themselves, occasionally and inconveniently, on the poem's pleasing unity are, for Hazlitt, its intendments.

Understanding isn't the mechanism or medium by which one appreciates *The Faerie Queene* but an obstacle to enjoying it.

Spenser's affiliation with fancy came to define his place in the English canon as the supposed "poet's poet." It is worth pointing out that the poet and critic who is our only recorded source of that oft-cited phrase—Leigh Hunt—might well have been imagining the poet-reader of Spenser as a child reader. Hunt first encountered Spenser at the same age as Cowley and Pope, as a boy of twelve. As he recalls in his autobiography, the purchasing of a cheap pocketbook edition of English verse was the highlight of his week during his time at Christ's Hospital, an antidote to the grammar schoolboy's forced march through the classics:

> When the master tormented me, when I used to hate and loathe the sight of Homer, and Demosthenes, and Cicero, I would comfort myself with thinking of the sixpence in my pocket, with which I should go out to Pater-noster Row, when school was over, and buy another number of an English Poet.[50]

It is in this fashion that Hunt came into possession of "an odd volume of Spenser," whose *Faerie Queene* he "adored," devoting himself to a hundred-stanza continuation of it: "the *Fairy King*, which was to be in emulation of Spenser!" The tone of amused condescension with which Hunt recalls this juvenile effort, and the affection with which he regards the material book itself—"How I loved those little sixpenny numbers containing whole poets! I doated on their size; I doated on their type, on their ornaments, on their wrappers containing lists of other poets, and on the engravings . . . !" (373)—flavor his adult criticism of *The Faerie Queene*, which he cherished all the more for the limitations he perceived in it. In *Imagination and Fancy* (1860), Hunt hails "luxuriant, remote Spenser" as poetry's "immortal child": [51]

> he is not so great a poet as Shakspeare or Dante;—he has less imagination, though more fancy, than Milton. . . . But when you are over-informed with thought or passion in Shakspeare, when Milton's mighty grandeurs oppress you, or are found mixed with painful absurdities, or when the world is vexatious and tiresome, and you have had enough of your own vanities or struggles in it, . . . then Spenser is most excellent. (68)

This evaluation culminates in Hunt's citation—the only written source for the phrase—of Charles Lamb's praise of Spenser as "the Poet's Poet" (66). In context it's clear that, whatever Lamb meant by it, for Hunt the phrase is as much a fond diminutive as a reverent superlative: Spenser, Hunt observes, "has had more idolatry and imitation from his brethren than all the rest put together" (66). Unlike the drama of Shakespeare or Milton's *Paradise Lost*, whose perfection defied mimicry, *The Faerie Queene* solicited imitation, offering aspiring poets a model they could first emulate and then outgrow, progressing from idol to ideal.

That progress is precisely what the satyrs of canto 6 fail to achieve, when they insist on worshipping Una instead of the Truth for which she stands—and then, when rebuked, on worshipping her ass. To a critic like Hunt, however, the satyrs understood the poem better than its creator did: "[L]et no evil reports of his allegory deter you," Hunt urged would-be readers of *The Faerie Queene*, for "his allegory itself is but one part allegory and nine parts beauty and enjoyment" (64). Writing a decade later for an American audience, James Russell Lowell concurred: "Undoubtedly Spenser wished to be useful, but he could not escape from his genius, which, if it led him as a philosopher to the abstract contemplation of the beautiful, left him as a poet open to every impression of sensual delight."[52] Una is the purest embodiment of this delight; like "the visionary Helen of Dr. Faustus," she possesses "every charm of womanhood except that of being alive" (339). Lowell claims to find "this glamour of fancy . . . admirable," calling it Spenser's "quality, not his defect" (340), but even so, he recommends enjoying it in limited doses: "The true use of *The Faerie Queene* is as a gallery of pictures which we visit as the mood takes us, and where we spend an hour or two at a time, long enough to sweeten our perceptions, not so long as to cloy them" (326).

The Faerie Queene was, in fact, a frequent source of inspiration for eighteenth- and nineteenth-century painters, illustrators, and engravers, and Una, accompanied by a lion or surrounded by satyrs, was by far the most popular subject, appearing as the theme of portraits of wealthy young girls painted by Benjamin West, Joshua Reynolds, and George Stubbs (figs. 2, 3, and 4) (Horace Walpole termed Reynolds's depiction of fourteen-year-old Elizabeth Beauclerc as Una "very sweet"[53]); in images by William Edward Frost and William Hilton the Younger (figs. 5, 6, and 7); and, in 1839, on the reverse of the five-pound gold coin issued to commemorate the beginning of Queen Victoria's reign (fig. 8). Such visual representations draw on Una's symbolic and sentimental power as a figure of chaste English womanhood, but they also capitalize on her physical appeal—and, especially in Frost's depiction of her among the satyrs, on her capacity to arouse dangerous erotic interest. Indeed, the most revealing artifact of the period's aesthetic investment in Una—literally and figuratively speaking—is the Parian ware statuette designed by Joseph Pitts in the 1850s as part of a set of four collectible pieces, recently included in a museum exhibit on Victorian-era pornography (fig. 9). The inscription on the statue's base reads "The Vision of the Red Cross Knight," and it shows the knight, lolling, mouth agape, in the instant of his "guiltie sight" at the end of canto 1: the object of the vision, it takes a scandalized moment to realize, is Una—or, at least, her false double,

FIGURE 2. Benjamin West, *Una and the Lion (Mary Hall in the Character of Una)*, 1771. Oil on canvas, 66¼ × 86⅛ in. Wadsworth Atheneum Museum of Art, Hartford, Connecticut. The Ella Gallup Sumner and Mary Catlin Sumner Collection Fund 1941.591. Photography credit: Allen Phillips / Wadsworth Atheneum.

sent by Archimago, barely clad in a gauzy garment, which she is in the process of removing.

Pitts's reduction of the scene from an allegory of lost faith to an elegant striptease is an extreme but also representative instance of the way *The Faerie Queene* was read throughout the eighteenth and nineteenth centuries, not as part of the cultivation of moral understanding but as an indulgent escape from the pressures of thought, a return to childish freedoms and pleasures, and an endlessly excerptable repository of images, with no necessary relation to their larger allegorical context. The veil of plausible deniability that (thinly) shrouds Pitts's statue—she isn't quite naked, yet, and she isn't actually Una—is characteristic of the way otherwise serious and sophisticated readers justified their attachment to a poem they couldn't fully respect. As Lowell puts it, "Spenser's world, real to him, is real enough for us to take a holiday in." This is just what

FIGURE 3. Thomas Watson, print, 1897, after Joshua Reynolds, *Una and the Lion (Portrait of Elizabeth Beauclerc)*, 1782. © The Trustees of the British Museum.

John Chilton Scammell, editor of *The Library of Entertainment: A Thousand Hours of Enjoyment with the World's Great Writers* (1910–18), urged readers of his multivolume anthology to do with his highly truncated version of *The Faerie Queene*. Scammell's anthology was designed to furnish "Johnny and his sister Molly" with "enjoyment in a simple, clean-cut manner," and to allow their weary

FIGURE 4. George Stubbs, *Una and the Lion (Portrait of Isabella Saltonstall)*, 1782. © The Fitzwilliam Museum, Cambridge.

FIGURE 5. Etching after William Hilton II, *Una Entering the Cottage*, 1832. © The Trustees of the British Museum.

FIGURE 6. Lithograph after William Edward Frost, *Una Alarmed*, 1843. © The Trustees of the British Museum.

FIGURE 7. William Edward Frost, *Una among the Fauns*, 1848. Royal Collection Trust / © Her Majesty Queen Elizabeth II, 2019.

FIGURE 8. Gold coin, "Una and the Lion," 1839. Image courtesy of The Royal Mint Museum, United Kingdom.

parents to recover "those days of sunshine and delight . . . on which the friendly pages of some treasured author were first opened."[54] Scammell's *Faerie Queene* includes just three extracts from the poem, each starring Una: he begins with the opening stanzas of canto 1, titled "Una and the Redcrosse Knight," skips to the beginning of canto 3 ("Una and the Lion"), and concludes with a long extract from canto 6 ("Una, Rescued from Sansloy by the Wood-Gods, Dwells with Them").[55] A young reader whose experience of the poem came only from this volume would know it as a series of exciting, if random, adventures featuring a footloose young woman who, initially sad when caught in a rainstorm with a gallant knight, ends by leading a happy life in a community of goat-men. It isn't a poem that could teach you very much, but it is one you might well enjoy.

FIGURE 9. Joseph Pitts, *The Vision of the Red Cross Knight*, statuary porcelain, produced by John Rose, ca. 1850. Image courtesy of the Witt Library, Courtauld Institute of Art, London.

Adapting Una

The line of criticism that grew out of Cowley's anecdote about reading Spenser for pleasure, and that came to dominate the poet's reputation in the eighteenth and nineteenth centuries, constitutes one crucial afterlife of *The Faerie Queene*'s childish reading: an anti-allegorical, almost anti-interpretive approach to the poem that—satyr-like—salvaged its pictorial and narrative pleasures at the expense of its moral meaning. But this is not the only story that can be told about child readers and *The Faerie Queene*. Hazlitt's claim that only a child would be frightened by Spenser's allegory is meant in jest, but it conveys an ironic truth: in the nineteenth and early twentieth centuries the burden of caring about the poem's moral, shrugged off by its learned critics, was shouldered by the authors of adaptations specifically for children. Unlike adults, who were encouraged not to let allegory meddle with their enjoyment, child readers were encouraged to treat their attraction to *The Faerie Queene*'s exciting story and rich imagery as a point of departure for the worthier, if less exciting, work of allegorical understanding. In this sense, too, childish reading engages with the figure of Una: not as an object of erotic attachment but as a model of self-canceling spiritual and intellectual growth.

The opening scene of Eliza Bradburn Weaver's 1829 *Legends from Spenser's "Faerie Queene," for the Children*, the first published version of the poem for young people, seems deliberately to echo the outlines of Abraham Cowley's anecdote about reading *The Faerie Queene* by accident in his mother's parlor—but Weaver transforms the story into a parable about the value of maternal oversight. Weaver's book is structured as a dialogue, which begins when three children happen upon a painting or illustration of Una and her lion. At first, they seem destined to reproduce young Cowley's uncomprehending delight: "Here is a picture I like very much," exclaims the eldest, a girl named Eliza, to her younger sister and brother. Unlike the young Cowley, however, Eliza and her siblings possess a kind of instinct for allegory, and their discussion of the picture turns immediately to a consideration of its meaning. "How mild and good this beautiful lady looks," Eliza observes. "She does not appear in the least degree afraid of the lion that is gazing at her; and I think his countenance seems to say, 'I have a great reverence for you, pretty Lady; I will defend you even with my life.'" Her sister Emily responds, "I should like to know her history. Very likely she lost her way in that forest, and God preserved her from being devoured by the lion, because she was a good woman." At this point their little brother William intervenes: "Mamma is coming, and I dare say she can tell us her name and all about her."[56]

Indeed she can: unlike Cowley's mother, who is the unwitting occasion of her son's encounter with *The Faerie Queene*, Bradburn's "Mamma" is both gatekeeper of the poem's contents and guide to its significance. She and her children had already appeared a year earlier in Bradburn's *The Story of "Paradise Lost," for Children*, an adaptation whose significance, Julie Pfeiffer observes, "lies in Bradburn's insistence that the poem be framed and even translated rather than simply abridged for children."[57] In the case of *Paradise Lost*, Mamma's (and Bradburn's) anxiety is largely theological: how to present Milton's exciting, inspiring, but occasionally heretical version of Genesis without allowing it to displace the biblical original in the children's minds. But as Jonathan Sircy notes, the accommodations to which Mamma subjects Milton's text eventually extend to the Bible's own confusions, so that the ultimate, apocalyptic goal of her instruction is "a moment where readings are *completely* unnecessary, when the text is internalized to such an extent that the suitable reader and tale are indistinguishable": a *Paradise Lost* within thee, happier far.[58] When she comes to *The Faerie Queene*, Spenser's own allegorical method both anticipates Mamma's aims and, in its sophistication, impedes them. Although she willingly identifies the lady in the picture as "UNA, whose adventures, with those of the RED-CROSS KNIGHT, are recounted in the 'Fairy Queen,'" she declines to read the poem aloud, saying, "there are other reasons why this work ought not to be put into your hands now" (4). "The 'Fairy Queen,'" she explains, "is a kind of allegory, which, I have told you before, is a fable, or story, in which one thing is related and another thing is understood"; the goal of her retelling is to ensure that the gap between "*literal* sense" and "*spiritual* meaning" remains much smaller than it does in the poem itself (5). Even before readers begin the book, they are alerted to its moralizing aims by two quotations inscribed on its title page. The first, from Plutarch, is a compressed allegory of allegorical method: "As grapes on a vine are covered by the leaves which grow about them; so, under the pleasant narratives and fictions of the poets, are couched many useful morals and doctrines." The second, from the Old Testament book of Hosea, is still more direct: "I have used similitudes."

The children in Bradburn's book prove themselves diligent allegorists; the only time they express frustration with their mother's story is when it fails to yield a clear moral lesson. "Pray what is the meaning of the lady's name?" Emily asks Mamma, who answers, "Una is the feminine Latin for ONE, and is emblematical of *Truth*, or True Religion" (8). The children then wonder why Spenser permits this singular Truth to become so embroiled in confusion and conclude, with evident disappointment, that "Spenser did not intend everything that was done signify something else, though it was an allegory" (11). Nonetheless, it is the allegory that interests them: "I think it entertains me more than it would if there were no meaning to be found out," William says. "And that is the case with me, William," Emily replies, "I am thinking what every thing signifies" (14–15). Emily does retain a residue of her initial, emotional response to the picture of Una in peril—"Though I know it is only an allegory, I feel so sorry for Una!" she exclaims (19)—but is relieved when her mother translates this feeling into theological terms, as an experience of spiritual conviction. "Now I understand the picture," she says with satisfaction, "and I think this part of the story is to teach us the power religion often has in softening hard and savage hearts; and that the very worst people may become good, and experience as great a change as that lion did." "You are right, my love," Mamma replies (23).

Subsequent adaptations of *The Faerie Queene* for children—twenty-six were published between 1829 and 1929—can be neatly divided between those in which, as in Bradburn's *Legends*, every incident is wrung for a moral and those in which, by contrast, no moral is sought at all.[59] The earnest extreme of the first type is reached, perhaps, in John S. Hart's 1847 *Special Exposition of "The Fairy Queen,"* a school text that enlists Spenser into the Temperance movement, among other worthy causes, by interpreting the phantasmatic monsters Guyon encounters near the Wandering Islands at the end of book 2 as "the after-horrors . . . of Delirium Tremens" that "cause the poor inebriate, intent on reform, to falter in his course."[60] Sophia L. MacLehose's popular 1896 collection of *Tales from Spenser* is representative of the latter, more easygoing approach, which dispenses with the allegory up front and out of hand. "Intended for children, the stories are related simply as stories, and therefore only those episodes in the poem most interesting and complete in themselves have been chosen," MacLehose explains in her preface. "In no case do the Tales pretend to relate to the whole that Spenser tells."[61] But even such a disclaimer grants to *The Faerie Queene*'s moral allegory a far more integral role than most contemporary critics did: without it, MacLehose is clear, she cannot pretend to have communicated the whole.

The distance between Bradburn's and Hart's heavy-handed allegoresis and MacLehose's narrative free-for-all measures the range of attitudes toward children's reading in the nineteenth century, when children's literature first flourished as a conceptual category and a commercial enterprise. On the one hand, as Karen Sánchez-Eppler writes, "literacy claim[ed] to change the behavior of children," exerting a socializing and civilizing influence on them, but at the same time, "childhood [was] increasingly praised for embodying what is best about the literary—imaginative freedom" (xxi). The same could be said of *The Faerie Queene*: reading Spenser's poem was at once a remedy for childishness and the nostalgic epitome of it. Una in particular could assume both functions; she was an allegorical ideal and a sentimental fiction, a figure for spiritual maturity and a figure of innocent fun, surrounded by a host of charismatic animal companions. It's for this reason, in part, that Una features so prominently in children's versions of the poem. For Spenser, book 1 is "The Legend of the Knight of the Red Crosse, *or* Of Holinesse," but nearly every children's adaptation of the poem gives Una equal or top billing: she, as much or more than Redcrosse, was the figure with whom children were expected to identify.[62]

But Una is also a figure for the self-consciously limited ambitions of children's adaptations—ambitions that bring them paradoxically closer to Spenser's own sense of poetic vocation than many eighteenth- or nineteenth-century critics were willing to come. As Contemplation reveals to Redcrosse at the end of canto 10, Una herself is not the Redcrosse Knight's heavenly destiny but his earthly love, a temporary placeholder for a more ultimate, eternal devotion. In this respect, Una is the object of Spenser's own deepest ambivalence about the transitory nature of allegorical images. When the publishers of children's versions of *The Faerie Queene* placed her on the covers and frontispieces of their volumes, as they often did (see figs. 10, 11, 12, 13, 14, and 15), they did so for aesthetic and commercial reasons: to attract readers, as the children in Bradburn's story are attracted, by "a picture [they] like very much." But the task of the successful adaptation was to make the child reader dissatisfied with mere liking, to instill a desire for understanding, too, and, eventually, a desire for the poem itself. As M. H. Towry writes in the preface to *Spenser for Children* in 1878,

> The volume can only give a most imperfect foretaste of the pleasure to be afterwards enjoyed from the original work, and is designed to serve as an incitement to turn to it. Children read on account of the interest of the narrative; beautiful thoughts and artistic excellence of composition are not perceived until a riper age, when the Poems themselves can be enjoyed.[63]

Of course, children who did outgrow their childhood versions of *The Faerie Queene* would find in the poem itself merely an elaboration of this pattern: not the fulfillment of their desire but an extension of it into eternity, where all images and idols vanish into nought. By giving Una such prominence in their retellings of *The Faerie Queene*, the authors of children's adaptations help to illuminate, perhaps unwittingly, both the self-canceling premises of the new genre in which they wrote and the self-canceling character of Spenser's own supreme fiction, with her simultaneous and irreconcilable obligations to materiality and its transcendence, the real and the ideal.

At least one author of a children's version of book 1 seems to have registered the tension. Eliza Palmer Peabody's *Holiness; or The Legend of St. George: A Tale from Spencer's Faerie Queene, by a Mother*, was published in Boston in 1836—a year after her daughter Elizabeth's account of Bronson Alcott's use of *The Faerie Queene* at the Temple School and three years before the first full-fledged American edition of Spenser's poem, edited by George S. Hillard. Eliza Peabody herself was a schoolteacher, and she claims to have produced her version of book 1 for the enjoyment of her own children and the girls she taught. In her preface she writes that she has provided explanatory notes "to aid the

FIGURE 10. Frontispiece, M. H. Towry, *Spenser for Children*, illustrations by Walter Jenks Morgan, 1885. Houghton Library, Harvard University.

FIGURE 11. Cover image, *Spenser's Faerie Queene*, illustrated by Walter Crane, 1897. Beinecke Rare Book and Manuscript Library, Yale University.

development of the allegory," but adds that these notes are "not intended to explain the allegory fully; this would require as many pages as the Tale itself."⁶⁴ Moreover, it would deprive young readers of what Peabody regards as the "peculiar charm" of *The Faerie Queene*: that a reader might, in effect, grow up with it. The incidents of Spenser's poem, she observes, appeal "to the youngest" children, to whom "a Tale of Chivalry is always delightful," but "a profound philosophy of life pervades it, which gradually dawns upon the reader . . . and this again and again, at the successive stages of experience" (iii).

FIGURE 12. Frontispiece, N. G. Royde-Smith, *Una and the Red Cross Knight*, illustrated by T. H. Robinson, 1905. Houghton Library, Harvard University.

This slow-dawning appreciation that what one has enjoyed is, in fact, an "exhaustless mine of thought"—that it need not be abandoned but may be cherished anew—is the primary object of Peabody's arrangement of her text, whose notes are confined to the end so they do not intrude on the story. But it also accounts, in a paradoxical and probably unconscious fashion, for the

FIGURE 13. Title page, N. G. Royde-Smith, *Una and the Red Cross Knight*, illustrated by T. H. Robinson, 1905. Houghton Library, Harvard University.

FIGURE 14. "Una and the Lion," in Andrew Lang, *Red Romance Book*, 1905. Beinecke Rare Book and Manuscript Library, Yale University.

rare occasions on which Peabody intervenes in the narrative, offering a gloss on an episode as it unfolds.

She does so only twice, and on both occasions rather forcefully: first, at the start of canto 4, when Spenser laments in passing the "lightnesse and inconstancie" of the Redcrosse Knight in abandoning Una (1.4.1.8), and again in canto 10, when Contemplation tells Redcrosse that he must return to Una. Redcrosse's inconstancy piques Peabody to an indignant tirade:

> When Archimago impeached the loyalty of Una, did St. George stop to inquire or reason? Did he bid her plead her own cause, or even stop to ascertain the certainty of what he had witnessed? No; he listened, and at one hasty glance, believed; he never called on Una to explain; but allowed the vile magician to accuse the lady of his love of infidelity to his vows, and raging in jealous fury, left her whom he had sworn to protect, alone among strangers, in a desert place, exposed to lawless passion, to dungeons and to death. (56)

In her vehemence on Una's behalf, Peabody departs not only from her text in canto 4, but from Spenser's plot—it is Redcrosse, after all, and not Una, who is exposed to dungeons and death in book 1. But for Peabody, the story of book 1 is the story of Una, whose perfection matters intensely to her.[65] Commenting in a note on the lion's submission to Una in canto 3, she notes that Spenser's

FIGURE 15. Cover image, Jeanie Lang, *Stories from "The Faerie Queen" Told to the Children*, illustrated by Rose Le Quesne, 1906. Houghton Library, Harvard University.

Una is "still nobler" than Milton's Eve, of whom Adam says, "what she wills to do / Seems wisest, virtuousest, discreetest, best." "Spenser knows not '*seems*,'" Peabody scoffs: "Una is more than Eve. Innocence and truth melt into one, to form ideal woman, before whom bow the Lionhearted, in the service that elevates the very quality of their nature" (177).

To say that Spenser "knows not 'seems,'" however, is to efface allegory altogether—to read Una and the poem in which she appears not as the preternaturally intuitive lion does, "ever by her looks conceiv[ing] her intent" (1.3.9.9), but as the stubbornly literal-minded satyrs do: refusing to consider any intent beyond the looks themselves. Bradburn, determined allegorist that she is, compresses the episode of the satyrs to a single sentence and gives the impression that Una's teaching of them is in fact successful: "She dwelt a long while in the woods, instructing these people, who would not part with her, in the truths of religion" (39). Peabody's version of canto 6, by contrast, gives full scope to its pastoral pleasures; it is joyful in tone, lavishly descriptive, and presents the satyrs as virtuous exemplars of the fidelity Redcrosse fails to display. Of their persistence in treating Una as a goddess, Peabody writes, "they continued faithful to the object of their worship, and thought no one else on earth was lovely." Una, for her part, is "glad of finding safety among these honest wood-gods" and "content to remain a long time with them" (98).

Indeed, there is nothing to suggest the scene is not an ideal situation for Peabody's Una except the fact that she leaves it, with the assistance of Satyrane. Spenser's Una is gracious to Satyrane, grateful for his help even if she cannot return his affection, but Peabody's Una is almost churlish: she "took little pleasure in her new acquaintance" (100). Peabody herself seems to regard Satyrane as an irritating puzzle. In a lengthy note on canto 6, she patiently unfolds the meaning of Una's time with the satyrs:

> When Truth had lost her Christian champion, who was taken to the House of Pride by the gilded falsehood of Romish trappings; and Manliness, lion heart though he was, had yielded her, with his life, to lawlessness—what could she do but flee from the courts of degenerate Civilization, and seek retreat with the rustics of the wild woods, who in their simplicity worshipped without understanding her, and whom she taught her heavenly lore. But who is Satyrane? (178)

Who, indeed, is Satyrane? In Eliza Weaver Bradburn's version of the poem, he is the "remarkably brave knight" who, having "gladly learned truth and faith from her lips," rescues Una from her unhappy plight among beings Bradburn calls "savages" (39). In Spenser's version, he is something more ambivalent: Una's escort away from the kind but inadequate ministrations of the satyrs, and back to the world of allegorical intendment. But Peabody has depicted the satyrs as ideal readers of Una's self-referential truth, faithful to her precisely because of their simplicity, which makes Satyrane's arrival on the scene an intrusion on a mutually satisfying idyll of incomprehension.

A similar defensiveness against allegorical translation motivates Peabody's gloss on Contemplation's response to Redcrosse's desire to proceed immediately to the New Jerusalem. Where Spenser has Contemplation simply and starkly say, "That may not be" (1.10.63.6), Peabody's Contemplation explains why: "We must not leave the path of duty, if we wish to find the path to heaven" (153). This is less an expansion of Contemplation's argument, however, than a reversal of it. Spenser makes no pretense that Redcrosse's love for Una is the path to heaven; on the contrary, Contemplation explicitly cautions that love, however "dearely bought" (1.10.62.6), is an earthly vanity that must fall away in the pursuit of true holiness. His admonition to Redcrosse—"ne maist thou yit / Forgo that royall maides bequeathed care, / . . . Till from her cursed foe thou haue her freely quit" (1.10.63.6–9)—makes clear that care has a temporal limit, and that outside that limit the obligation is void. For Peabody, by contrast, marriage to Una is the ultimate telos of the Legend of Holiness. Her Redcrosse, unlike Spenser's, is not merely betrothed at book's end: he is "peaceful at heart, in the full possession of a divine and faithful wife, secured forever in the paradise regained of virtuous home," as she writes in her final note on the poem (182). Both this misleading account of the actual ending of book 1—in which Una is "left to mourne" (1.12.41.9)—and the reframing of Contemplation's advice can be traced to Peabody's insistence that, when it comes to Una, "Spenser knows not '*seems*'": the meaning for which Una stands is Una. Peabody's identification with Una motivates her disgust at Redcrosse's infidelity, her editorial finessing of Contemplation's judgment, and her subtle reworking of the story's end into one more suited to a novelistic marriage plot. But it also gestures to Una's function as a figure for fiction itself, and particularly for the fictions of childhood. Peabody's characterization of *The Faerie Queene* as an "exhaustless mine of thought" reflects a desire—both Spenserian and anti-Spenserian—that the partial revelations of poetry need not give way to an apocalypse of understanding, that the affective and aesthetic pleasures of childish reading might persist into maturity and after.

Coda: Naming Una

It is no accident that both critics and the authors of children's adaptations turned to Una as an emblem of how *The Faerie Queene* should be read; after all, as Bradburn's Mamma points out, she "is emblematical of *Truth*." What is surprising, however, is their frequent resistance to understanding her in those terms. As Truth, Una is a figure for the immutable, eternal reality to which poetry and human existence can only gesture: an allegory of allegory itself. But like the child who runs into the poem in canto 12, most eighteenth- and nineteenth-century readers had little regard for this Una, "in her self-resemblance well beseene" (1.12.8.8). Instead, their attention and affections were fixed on a prior incarnation, the frail, fleshly Una who wanders through the middle cantos of book 1, subject to the same accidents as any mortal being or fictive creation. It is certainly possible to indict this fixation as childish: that is, as immature, hedonistic, and unworthy of the aspirations of Spenser's moral allegory in the Legend of Holiness. But the persistent fascination with Una in the eighteenth and nineteenth centuries can also be understood as a remnant or residue of the poem's own mixed feelings about her, and about the project of allegorical transcendence for which she ultimately (but only ultimately) stands.

A remnant or residue may be all that survives of childhood reading in adulthood. C. S. Lewis is precise about what his imaginary child reader of "Stories from Spenser" is likely to recall later on: not the allegory or even the plot, but the mere sound of "certain of the names." Just what meaning might echo in the music of a Spenserian name is a question Eliza Palmer Peabody's middle daughter, Sophia, and her husband, Nathaniel Hawthorne, confronted in March 1844, when they announced the birth of their first child, a little girl named Una. The choice of name was anything but accidental: "Many months before she was born," Sophia reports in her journal, "we anticipated a daughter, & named her Una."[66] The name perfectly expressed the idealizing expectations of the baby's parents, to whom she appeared—in Nathaniel's words—"the symbol of the one true union in the world, and of our love in Paradise."[67] Others, however, were more skeptical: "Nearly everyone has had something to say about it," Hawthorne wrote irritably to his sister Louisa (*CE*, 16:20). Among those who expressed doubts was an old and trusted friend: George Hillard, Hawthorne's former landlord and the editor of the first American edition of Spenser's poems, published in Boston in 1839. Hillard congratulated Hawthorne on the baby's arrival, but "as to the name of Una," he confessed, "I hardly know what to say":

> The great objection to names of that class is that they are too imaginative. They are rather to be kept and hallowed in the holy crypts of the mind, than to be brought into the garish light of common day. If your little girl could pass her life playing on a green lawn, with a snow white lamb, with a blue ribbon round its neck, all things would be in a "concatenation accordingly"; but imagine Sophia saying, "Una, my love, I am ashamed to see you with so dirty a face," or "Una, my dear, you should not sit down to dinner without your apron." Think of all this, before you finally decide.[68]

Such reservations are striking, given how emphatically Hillard champions Una in the preface to his edition of *The Faerie Queene*, not as an allegorical abstraction but as the object of readers' "warm flesh-and-blood interest." "It is Una—the trembling, tearful woman—for whom our hearts are moved with pity, and not forsaken Truth," he writes. "We may fairly doff the allegory aside, and let it pass."[69] As his letter to Hawthorne suggests, however, in practice Hillard found

Una's allegorical significance harder to dismiss—and impossible to assimilate to the experiences of a living, breathing, accident-prone child.

In his reply to Hillard, Hawthorne insists, rather defensively, that he *had* thought of all this:

> Perhaps the first impression may not be altogether agreeable, for the name has never before been warmed with human life, and therefore may not seem appropriate to real flesh and blood. But for us, our child has already given it a natural warmth; and when she has worn it through her lifetime, and perhaps transmitted it to descendants of her own, this beautiful name will have become naturalized on earth;—whereby we shall have done a good deed in first bringing it out of the realm of Faery. (CE, 16:22)

Hawthorne himself was a child reader of *The Faerie Queene* (according to family lore, it was the first book he purchased with his own money as a boy), and in this defense of Una's name, "naturalized on earth" by association with a succession of real little girls, whose sensual, sensuous forms override its moral significance, we can see one version of what such reading is and ought to be. Understanding has little to do with it. After all, Hawthorne continues, "I like the name, not so much for any associations with Spenser's heroine, as for its simple self—it is as simple as a name can be—as simple as a breath—it is merely inhaling a breath into one's heart, and emitting it again, and the name is spoken" (CE, 16:20).

A pleasure as simple—and as involuntary—as breathing: this is what child readers since Abraham Cowley have claimed to find in Spenser's poem, and it is what numerous eighteenth- and nineteenth-century critics, including Hillard, urged them to find in it, "doff[ing] the allegory aside." But the figure of Una Hawthorne—an embodied reading of *The Faerie Queene* if ever one existed—does not necessarily equate the future of Spenser's poetry with an escape from its allegory. On the contrary, the records Nathaniel and Sophia kept of their daughter's childhood show just how tenaciously allegorical intendment clings to a pair of Spenserian syllables, however thoroughly domesticated. Little Una, Sophia vowed in her diary, "will be rightly named—a most delicate spirit, impatient of wrong & ugliness—demanding beauty of all things and persons—& like the 'heavenly Una' of Spenser." As if conscious that this might be a bit much, she adds, "At the same she will know the Real" (148). In fact, the impulse to narrate the child's daily existence through Spenser's allegorical fiction proved irresistible. When two-month-old Una received a Newfoundland puppy from her godfather, the dog was promptly christened "Leo": "so the lady Una already has her Lion," Sophia noted with satisfaction, "to guard her from all peril, & to crouch at her feet & kiss her lily white hand.... Her little soul shines brighter and brighter out of her eyes" (149). At seven months, little Una was "a book baby—an ideal child" (150), and as she grew (and was joined by a younger brother, Julian, and a baby sister, Rose), Sophia made sure she knew the book that had given her her name. "I read from Spenser to the children, in the morning, of St. George and Una, Una and the Lion, and Prince Arthur," she wrote to her mother. "They made an exquisite picture with the hobby-horse," she adds, Julian astride the horse and Una, like her namesake, "at his side."[70]

Nathaniel Hawthorne was somewhat less prone to idealize his children, especially Una—of her going to bed one evening after a bout of particular naughtiness, he writes, "she ... departs with the blessedness and kindliness of a euthanasia" (*CE*, 8:409)—but he too was attached to the allegory of her name, far more so than he was willing to let on to Hillard. In the diary he kept of Una's childhood, he labors to reconcile her imaginary nature with her material existence. "She has a scratch on her face ... and her cheeks are somewhat swollen with cold," he notes of her, dressed in Sunday finery one morning in 1848, "so that my description, or rather affirmation, of the grace of her little phiz, must be taken as referring to her general appearance, rather than to the passing moment" (*CE*, 8:400). His tone is humorous, but such vicissitudes evidently troubled him: "Her beauty," he reports, "is the most flitting, transitory, uncertain and unaccountable affair," and so was her mood, having "no settled level" (*CE*, 8:421). She didn't merely smudge her face or forget her apron, as Hillard predicted she might; she threw burrs in her little brother's hair and romped through the house half-naked, "prostrating herself on all fours, and thrusting up her little bum as a spectacle to men and angels" (*CE*, 8:417). "There is," Hawthorne confesses, "something that almost frightens me about the child—I know not whether elfish or angelic ..., a spirit strangely mingled with good and evil, haunting the house where I live" (*CE*, 8:430–31). Even the doting Sophia could be taken aback by the child's crude vigor. In one of the final entries of the family journal, she describes Una pretending to be a country boy to amuse her little brother:

> The voice, & manner & phrases & pronunciation were of the most uncivilized, barbarous clodhopper ... Where was the grace, the softness, the order of my little Una? Utterly gone—No changeling could have been a greater change. What an Elfish element there is in her—What a tract of untameable wilderness, whither she rushes to dens and morasses, to air herself as it were. I never knew such a combination of the highest refinement & the rudest boorishness—one lies at the door of the other—When she was a little infant, in one position as she lay asleep, she reminded us of Pan ... & in another the most sweet, angelical, etherial—spiritual aspect beamed forth—. (166)

She was, in short, a child: a vigorously embodied being containing a tract of untameable wilderness, and an allegorical screen for the projection of adult longings and fantasies. Rude and refined, Pan-like and angelical, she was satyr and Una both.

Such uncanny girl-children recur throughout Hawthorne's fiction, most famously in the guise of little Pearl in *The Scarlet Letter*. Pearl, F. O. Matthiessen claimed, is "the purest type of Spenserian characterization, which starts with abstract principles and hunts for their proper embodiment."[71] A "living hieroglyphic" of her parents' sin and the outward sign of "the oneness of their being," she is also a relic of the romance tradition, described with disapproval by the pious Mr. Wilson as "one of those naughty elfs or fairies, whom we thought to have left behind us . . . in merry old England."[72] But Pearl is also a child reader, of the letter "A" on her mother's breast, and her responses to that brief text illuminate and complicate the familiar trajectory of childhood reading, from delight to understanding. The letter, Hawthorne writes, "was the first object of which Pearl seemed to become aware" and evokes her first infant smile (67); as the child grows older, however, she torments her mother with questions about it: "What does the letter mean, mother? . . . what does the scarlet letter mean?" (123–24). Pearl's fixation on the letter culminates with the encounter between Hester and Dimmesdale in the forest, during which Pearl goes off to play and the letter is (briefly) cast away. As Sacvan Bercovitch has argued, it is the determining force of meaning itself Hester rejects in throwing the letter to the ground and plotting her escape with Dimmesdale back to Europe, and it is meaning to which she submits in putting the letter back on. But, he points out, meaning doesn't simply vanish from a discarded signifier. The temporarily abandoned A has a meaning of its own:

> Never does the A more vibrantly represent the imperatives of whim, free will, defiance, and abandonment, and never does it more sternly recall us to the fact that its office has not yet been done. It stands for the paradox of autonomy preserved, precariously yet decisively, and all the more decisively for its precariousness within the bounds of culture.[73]

What Bercovitch calls "the paradox of autonomy preserved" is, in effect, the structure of Una's existence in the middle cantos of book 1: a compound of "whim, free will, defiance, and abandonment"—of what Spenser terms "accident"—contained precariously within an allegorical intendment whose office has not yet been done.

Bercovitch, of course, does not need Spenser in order to make this point, but it is possible Hawthorne did. Hawthorne describes the idyllic encounter in the woods between Hester and Dimmesdale as "a mystery of joy," sanctioned by "the sympathy of nature—that wild heathen Nature of the forest, never subjugated by human law, nor illuminated by higher truth" (138): these are Spenser's woods, not the allegorical woods of Error, but the tract of untamable wilderness in which Una is permitted to catch her breath among the satyrs. To sharpen the association, Pearl returns from her romp in the woods, looking like "a nymph child, or an infant-dryad, or whatever else was in closest sympathy with the antique wood" (139)—"It is as if one of the fairies, whom we left in our dear old England, had decked her out to meet us," her mother exclaims (140)—but the resemblance is misleading: the child demands that her mother restore the letter to her breast, resubmitting herself to its signifying power. In the end, Dimmesdale dies, and Hester leaves New England only to return; this brief interval is all they are given of life together. Even so, Hester thinks to herself, "she had drawn an hour's free breath!" (143).

The scene inverts a more familiar pattern in Hawthorne's fiction, in which children provide a respite from the punitive necessity of meaning. "I delight to let my mind go hand in hand with the mind of a sinless child," says the narrator of "Little Annie's Ramble" to his young companion. "So come Annie; but if I moralize as we go, do not listen to me; only look about you and be merry!"[74] Such cheerful imperviousness to moral instruction has long been the privilege of the child reader and so, too, is the capacity to "revive the . . . moral nature" of adulthood, as the narrator says Little Annie has done for him, with "free and simple thoughts," "native feeling," "airy mirth, for little cause or none" (182). The sketch concludes with an injunction to "spend an hour or two with children" and then "return into the crowd . . . to struggle onward" (182): the aimless, causeless existence of children, accident untouched by intendment, remains the object of a temporary fancy, not an enduring commitment. But as Hawthorne's more subtle and darkly shaded depiction of Pearl suggests, it isn't only adults—parents or schoolmasters or the authors of didactic storybooks—who insist on conscripting childhood into a textual regime; children cling just as fiercely (more fiercely, even) to the texts they imprint themselves upon.

I began by saying that childish reading is reading one grows out of, but childish reading is also reading that refuses to let go, reading that clings to what it ought to outgrow. Twice during his stay in Hillard's home in the summer of 1840, while he was courting Sophia Peabody, Hawthorne wrote letters to her in which he describes taking *The Faerie Queene* to bed on a lazy afternoon and falling asleep with the book in his hand (*CE*, 15:473, 477). Such contact—at once intimate and evasive—seems to have been Hawthorne's preferred way of negotiating the poem's stubborn grasp on his imagination: "After I awoke," he says, "I did not take up the Faery Queen again" (473). Napping is also, it is worth remembering, how Una accommodates herself to an existence at a temporary remove from allegory. Exhausted by her solitary wanderings, at the start of canto 3 she takes off her veil, lays it to one side, and falls asleep:

> One day nigh wearie of the yrkesome way,
> From her vnhastie beast she did alight,
> And on the grasse her daintie limbes did lay
> In secret shadow, farre from all mens sight:
> From her faire head her fillet she vndight,
> And laid her stole aside. Her angels face
> As the great eye of heauen shyned bright,
> And made a sunshine in the shadie place;
> Did neuer mortall eye behold such heauenly grace. (1.3.4)

It is a scene that recurred to Hawthorne's mind while writing his letter to Hillard after the birth of little Una. Writing stories, he complains, is "the most unprofitable business in the world," and fatherhood has forced him to take such mundane considerations seriously: perhaps he will have to "write for bread," a humiliating prospect. "If I alone were concerned, I had rather starve," he declares, "but in that case, poor little Una would have to take refuge in the almshouse—which, here in Concord, is a most gloomy mansion. Her 'angel face' would hardly make a sunshine there" (*CE*, 16:23). The contrast with Spenser's Una is implicit, and embittered: allegorical abstractions don't need bread, and they don't dwell in almshouses. But the remarkable thing about the middle cantos of the Legend of Holiness is that Una *is* required to confront the needy realities of her fallen existence—for a time, at least—and that Spenser asks us to regard that confrontation as an enhancement, not a privation, of her function as Truth. Hawthorne inherits allegorical romance from Spenser, but he inherits a kind of realism, too: the awareness that donkeys are not as fast as horses; that wandering is weary, irksome work; and that if satyrs did exist, and knelt to an allegorical embodiment of a transcendental truth, their knees would bend backward—in the direction of childhood, myth, and romance, and as they simply happen to do.

3

Load Every Rift

AVID READERS IN THE LEGEND
OF TEMPERANCE

IN AUGUST 1820, six months before his death from tuberculosis, John Keats wrote to Percy Shelley, thanking the elder poet for an invitation to convalesce at his home in Pisa and acknowledging receipt of Shelley's recently published verse tragedy, *The Cenci*. He proceeds to offer his view of the work, in a tone that shades rapidly from self-deprecation to oracular pronouncement:

> There is only one part of it I am judge of; the Poetry, and dramatic effect, which by many spirits nowadays is considered the Mammon. A modern work it is said must have a purpose, which may be the God—an artist must serve Mammon—he must have "self-concentration," selfishness perhaps. You I am sure will forgive me for sincerely remarking that you might curb your magnanimity and be more of an artist, and "load every rift" of your subject with ore.[1]

In Keats's compressed allegory of poetic "self-concentration," the biblical money-god Mammon takes on the unexpected role of muse: a figure for the supposedly ornamental attributes—"Poetry, and dramatic effect"—that the artist recognizes as constitutive of his work's essential value. To be "more of an artist" in this respect is to disregard any "purpose" beyond the accumulation and refinement of whatever accords with one's own sense of beauty—to care less, in other words, for readers, the desires of even the most sympathetic of whom clash with the necessary solipsism of art. In enjoining Shelley to "curb [his] magnanimity," Keats hints that his friend should guard his manuscripts more closely, lavishing greater care in revising them and resisting the temptation to publish too quickly. Bedbound and starved for amusement, he writes that he is "in expectation of *Prometheus*"—Shelley's latest play, then in press— "any day," but adds, "[c]ould I have my own wish for its interest effected you would have it still in manuscript—or be but now putting an end to the second act." Impishly inverting the usual association of Mammon with material wealth (for as he confesses, he understands full well that both he and Shelley have "published... from a hope of gain"), Keats claims the greedy god as the deity of an absolute aesthetic idealism, equally at odds with the demands of the marketplace and the appetites of readers.

But for those who recognize the source of his stirring injunction to "'load every rift'... with ore," Keats's parable in praise of poetic selfishness has a further resonance, for it betrays his light-fingered and grasping approach to the poetry of *The Faerie Queene*. The figure of the loaded rift has become an emblem of Keats's own opulent style, as Marjorie Garber notes, shedding its internal quotation marks along the way, but as William A. Read first pointed out in 1897, it is borrowed from the central episode of Spenser's Legend of Temperance, Guyon's visit to the Cave of Mammon.[2] In canto 7 of book 2, the Knight of Temperance finds Mammon crouched on the ground, surrounded by heaps of gold and fondling a lapful of old coins, and accepts an invitation to "come... and see" his subterranean lair (2.7.20.5). Hard by the entrance to Hell, a door opens onto a massive and dimly glittering space:

> From whose rough vaut the ragged breaches hong,
> Embost with massy gold of glorious gift,
> And with rich metall loaded euery rift,
> That heauy ruine they did seeme to threat. (2.7.28.3–6)

It is this hidden vault from which Keats mines his metaphor of poetic "self-concentration," in a gesture Miriam Allott calls "ironic" but that might better be regarded as both shameless and wittily self-deprecating.[3] Extracted from the gloomy confines of Mammon's cave, the loaded rift sheds its ominous weight, becoming a figure of desirable linguistic richness. Even so, the inverted commas hold the phrase at a cautious remove; somewhere in the background of Keats's unacknowledged allusion to Guyon's adventure lurks an awareness that he is willfully misinterpreting its moral, which identifies the instinct to accumulate with the threat of "heauy ruine." Recalled to its dark and dangerous origins, the loaded rift becomes a far more ambivalent figure for the acquisitive tendencies of readers, from which no poet or poem is secure.

The instability of the image reflects Keats's relationship to *The Faerie Queene*, to which he responded with a mix of delicacy and voracity. Like Abraham Cowley, Walter Scott, Robert Southey, and Nathaniel Hawthorne, he first encountered Spenser as a boy, introduced to the poet by his tutor, Charles Cowden Clarke. He "took away with him that night the first volume of the 'Faerie Queene'" and "went through it," Clarke later recalled, "as a young horse would through a spring meadow—ramping!"[4] But even as he devoured Spenser's story and marveled at his allegorical inventions, what captivated the "true poet" in Keats, Clarke insisted, was the lavishness of the poem's descriptions and the brilliance of its style:

[H]e had whole passages by heart, which he would repeat; and he would dwell with an ecstasy of delight on fine particular phrases. He especially singled out epithets, for that felicity and power in which Spenser is so eminent. He *hoisted* himself up, and looked burly and dominant as he said, "What an image that is—*sea-shouldering whales!*"[5]

Such youthful appetite gave way to a lifelong habit of appropriation. Both the first and the last poems Keats wrote were imitations of Spenser, leading Matthew Arnold to dub him "the one modern inheritor of Spenser's beautiful gift," while late nineteenth-century critics combed through his verse, cataloging numerous words, phrases, and images taken from Spenser.[6] And yet, as Allott observes, his attachment to Spenser remained "instinctively selective": *The Faerie Queene* was a mine to which the poet-reader returned again and again, emerging from each time with a clutch of fresh inspirations, but "it was Spenser's richness of language, imagery, and stanzaic skills, not his moral themes," on which he invariably seized.[7] The allusive detour through Mammon's cave in the letter to Shelley exemplifies this "selective" approach—its precisely tailored focus and its willful imprecision. Raiding the episode's descriptive resources, Keats also slyly inverts its moral content, treating as gospel the demonic counsel Guyon receives from Mammon: "Take what thou please of all this surplusage" (2.7.18.6–7). Within *The Faerie Queene*, that counsel is roundly rebuked by Guyon, who answers, "All that I need I haue, what needeth mee / To couet more, then I haue cause to vse?" (2.7.39.3–4); in the letter to Shelley, no such rebuke is heard. And this is perhaps Keats's point, for as he urges Shelley to remember, any argument from "use" alone—the "purpose" that others take as their God—misses the mark where poetry is concerned: the loaded rift may be turned to any number of figurative uses, but it is also a sign of the useless opulence and gorgeous inutility of figuration as such.

It wasn't just nineteenth-century critics and theorists who worried about the purposelessness of poetic ornament; critics and theorists in Spenser's time did, too. For as the authors of sixteenth-century arts of rhetoric frequently noted, figurative language—like gold, jewels, cosmetics, silks, spices, flowers, or any other luxury in excess of bare human necessity—has little to do with necessity. On the contrary, coveting more than one has cause to use is the entire motive and justification for eloquence, as well as the most damning argument against it. "[T]here is nothing more admirable or more splendid than a speech with a rich abundance of thoughts and words overflowing in a golden stream," reads the opening of Erasmus's 1521 *De Copia*, the foundational text of the sixteenth-century grammar-school curriculum in rhetoric.[8] Contemporary vernacular treatises on eloquence echoed Erasmus's theme: "Brauerie of speech ... was first inuented of necessitie for want of words, but afterwards continued and frequented by reason of the delight and pleasant grace thereof," explains Abraham Fraunce in his *Arcadian Rhetorike* of 1588, one of the earliest English arts of rhetoric and the first to illustrate its precepts with extracts from vernacular poets, including Spenser.[9] "[F]igures and figuratiue speaches ... be the flowers as it were and coulours that a Poet setteth vpon his language by arte, as the embroderer doth his stone and perle, or passements of gold vpon the stuffe of a Princely garment," declares George Puttenham in his 1589 *Arte of English Poesie*, "delight[ing] and allur[ing] as well the mynde as the eare of the hearers with a certaine noueltie and strange maner of conueyance, disguising it no litle from the ordinary and accustomed."[10] The appetite for novelty and excess sustains the market for poetry as for any other luxury good, and—as Keats's letter reminds us—that same appetite keeps poetic language in circulation, thanks to a secondhand economy of excerption, imitation, adaptation, and allusion.

Keats's raid on the Cave of Mammon thus makes a potentially rich contribution to our understanding of book 2 of *The Faerie Queene*. For the trials of temperance—getting and spending, hunting and gathering, cultivating, preserving, hoarding, thieving, using, misusing, and laying waste—are the trials of a particular breed of reader: not the errant or bewildered reader with whom the Legend of Holiness is so anxiously preoccupied, but the *avid* reader, practitioner of the self-interested art Michael de Certeau termed "reading as poaching":

> Far from being writers—founders of their own place, heirs of the peasants of earlier ages now working on the soil of language, diggers of wells and builders of houses—readers are travellers; they move across lands belonging to someone else, like nomads poaching their way across fields they did not write, despoiling the wealth of Egypt to enjoy it themselves.[11]

Insofar as it is an allegory, *The Faerie Queene* prohibits such vagrant uses, but in virtually every other respect, from its richly figurative language to its formal disposition into discrete stanzas and end-stopped lines of verse, it is an environment ripe for exploitation. The invitation Mammon extends to Guyon—to come and see, and to take what pleases him—is an invitation Spenser's poem makes to readers at every turn. And to one schooled in the humanist culture of extraction and imitation, reading with pen in hand and commonplace book at the ready, the great obstacle to progress through it might lie not in confusion, boredom, or exhaustion, but in an excess of interest: a force of distraction emanating from the poem's own superabundant descriptive resources.

Of course, the impulse to annotate, extract, copy, quote, or imitate is not necessarily at odds with the mandate to keep reading. On the contrary, as we shall see, such diversions can be a powerful mechanism for sustaining readerly engagement in the absence of more seemingly essential factors like narrative absorption or the desire for understanding. This can be true for entire generations of readers: as Hazel Wilkinson argues, periods in which interest in *The Faerie Queene* has seemed scanty or superficial to modern critics—the first half of the eighteenth century, for instance, or the whole of the nineteenth—are often those in which a market for what she calls "miscellaneous Spenser" has flourished, in anthologies, imitations, illustrations, popular adaptations, and collections of extracts.[12] By the same token, however, the aims of the avid reader are liable to diverge from the aims of both the poet and the poem itself; reading like a commonplacer, collector, or curator is often reading that goes nowhere, narratively and allegorically speaking, content to dwell on the cherished objects of a private fascination. As Certeau says, such reading "takes no measures against the erosion of time"; "it does not keep what it acquires, or it does so poorly."[13] Like Mammon's horde, its spoils can seem both excessive and spendthrift, a heap of arduously culled trinkets.

One cannot serve God and Mammon, says Christ in the Sermon on the Mount, a text Spenser himself unapologetically pillages in book 2, and faced with the choice, readers of *The Faerie Queene* have very often preferred the latter to the former, privileging what was excellent, exemplary, or interesting in their own eyes over what Keats calls "the purpose." Self-concentration isn't only the prerogative of the poet, in other words; it is also the privilege of readers, whose idiosyncratic interests and appetites can create new economies of poetic value. Keats's cheeky appropriation of Spenser's loaded rift is an apt illustration of this truth, an almost literal enactment of Certeau's metaphor of reading that "frees itself from the soil that determined it."[14] The fruits of such excavations do not resemble what we commonly call "readings" of the poem: instead, they result in catalogs of favorite features, running commentaries on one obsessive theme, gatherings of seemingly trivial observations, or hyperelaborate analyses of a single stanza. Scattered in emphasis, limited in scope, marked by peculiar fixations, and largely oblivious to such basic critical concerns as character or context, they offer myopic and oddly blinkered perspectives on its expanse. Attending to them doesn't necessarily enlarge our conception of what *The Faerie Queene* means, but it shows just how variously the poem is capable of mattering to individual readers—those who have an important role to play in its reception history, like John Keats, and those who decidedly don't.

Unsummable Parts: In Defense of Irrelevance

"'Irrelevance' is a strange word to use in speaking of *The Faerie Queene*," Jeff Dolven notes, "for we tend to assume the overdetermined mattering of each of the poem's parts to all the others"—indeed, such pervasive and continuous mattering is an essential aspect of what we mean when we call the poem an allegory.[15] And yet the fear of irrelevance might be termed the founding anxiety of criticism on *The Faerie Queene*. The origins of that anxiety are embedded in book 2—ironically, because the virtue of temperance is at odds with excess of all kinds, but also unavoidably, because the very existence of a second book, following on the apocalyptic climax of book 1, raises problems of redundancy that then haunt *The Faerie Queene* as a whole, or, rather, haunt our conception of it *as* a whole. In 1754, when Thomas Warton published volume 1 of his *Observations on the Faerie Queene of Spenser*, the first comprehensive critical study of the poem by a literary scholar, the mere fact of book 2 threatened to doom the project altogether. Like many of his contemporaries, Warton was troubled by the variety and disunity of *The Faerie Queene*'s several books, which impinged on the even greater problem of the poem's genre. The worrying question, as Jonathan Kramnick writes, was "whether to assign it to the class of the epic—and so see its formal unity as particularly flawed or, as Spenser himself seemed to suggest, simply dispersed over twelve adventures under the unifying aegis of Arthur—or to assign it a version of the romance shorn of its relation to the novel and nostalgically revalued as an enchanted and sublime contrast to the secular and rational present."[16] Almost the whole opening section of the *Observations* is devoted to this conundrum, to which Warton arrives at no satisfactory solution. "Upon the whole, and in general," he confesses, "it must be observed, that Spenser's adventures, which are the subject of each single book, have no mutual dependence upon each other, and consequently do not contribute to constitute one legitimate poem."[17]

Character should have solved the problem of poetic unity but didn't: if the magnanimity of Arthur were *The Faerie Queene*'s continued focus, "shin[ing] in every part with a superior and steady lustre," Warton writes, "our author would stand acquitted." But as it is, "it bursts forth but seldom, in obscure and interrupted flashes" (1:7). And the very completeness-in-itself of book 1, which John Hughes, *The Faerie Queene*'s 1715 editor, had noted in mitigation of its digressiveness elsewhere, struck Warton rather as a kind of original sin, necessitating the extraneous and fragmentary character of all that followed. For, he declares,

> As the heroic poem is required to be one WHOLE, compounded of many various parts depending upon, and relative to each other; so it is expedient, that not one of those parts should be so regularly contriv'd, and so completely finished, as to become a WHOLE of itself. For the mind being thus once satisfied in arriving at the completion of an orderly series of events, acquiesces in that satisfaction, and its attention and curiosity are diverted from pursuing, with due vigour, the final and general catastrophe; whereas while each part is left imperfect, I mean, incomplete, if disjoined or separated from the rest, the mind still desirous and, eager of gratifying its expectations, is

irresistibly and imperceptibly drawn on from part to part, till it receives a full and ultimate satisfaction from the accomplishment of one great event, which all those parts, following and illustrating each other, contributed to produce. (1:8–9)

In the end, as Kramnick argues, Warton could only free Spenser from the dictates of epic form by rediscovering "romance as the textual tradition subtending the poem"—although even that rediscovery could not account for all of the poem's "beautiful and sublime representations" (1:225).[18] In place of orderly links and steady luster, what Warton saw in *The Faerie Queene* was a concatenation of detached and glittering fragments, the very fascination of which—unconnected to any central plan or purpose—exerted a centrifugal force on readerly "attention and curiosity." Rather than being "irresistibly and imperceptibly drawn on," the mind of Spenser's reader was scattered across the text, ceaselessly and pointlessly diverted.

Romantic critics redefined this defect as a virtue, urging readers not to ruin the pleasure of the poem by striving to connect its allegorical dots—or by spending more than a few hours with it at a time. But in the twentieth century, the dominance of the New Criticism, with its preference for tightly crafted lyric forms, raised the charge of irrelevance to a new pitch: not only did *The Faerie Queene*'s various parts matter too little to each other; the poem itself mattered too little to English literary tradition, its influence either negligible, regrettable, or both. Relegated to the volume on "The Age of Chaucer" in the popular 1954 *Pelican Guide to English Literature* on the grounds that it was "curiously rootless," "the work of a poet of genius who has the grave disadvantage of really belonging to no particular country," "as different as can possibly be from Chaucer . . . but also essentially different from his own contemporary Elizabethan[s]," *The Faerie Queene* was treated as a freakish and blessedly inconsequential departure from what Derek Traversi calls "the main line of English poetic development."[19] Indeed, Traversi's essay on *The Faerie Queene* for the volume characterizes the poem in relentlessly negative terms: "limited," "narrowed," and "neglect[ful] of certain imagistic and emotional resources that had formerly been the natural heritage of English poetry," full of characters and situations that "fail to cohere into a recognizable hierarchy of significances . . . but remain isolated and finally meaningless," its very stanzaic form "tend[ing] irresistibly to become an instrument of disintegration, furthering the dissolution of the declared moral intention" until "the pretense of allegorical structure collapses almost entirely."[20] Internally incoherent and mutely unresponsive to precursors, contemporaries, and successors alike, *The Faerie Queene* seemed destined to remain both a part and apart—an anomaly at best and an aberration at worst.

It was to this entrenched strain of skepticism, shared in some measure even by the poem's ostensible champions, that Harry Berger Jr. addressed his 1957 study of the Legend of Temperance, *The Allegorical Temper*. Berger begins by observing that book 2 of *The Faerie Queene* poses in particularly concentrated form the question that had so long troubled critics: "Precisely how is it a poem? How is it *one*?"[21] This was in part because it followed on, and thus undid, the seeming completeness of book 1 but also, Berger noted, because it was laden from start to finish with what he terms "conspicuous irrelevance": descriptive passages, ornamental stanzas, and entire cantos whose appeal to readers exceeds any apparent moral lesson or narrative point.[22] Berger coins the phrase in explicit homage to Thorsten Veblen's theory of "conspicuous consumption," the ostentatious expenditure of wealth or acquisition of luxury goods as a public display of social status, whether actual or imagined. For readers of *The Faerie Queene*, he suggests, attention is the currency and understanding the sanctioned commodity; conspicuous irrelevance characterizes any element of the poem that tempts readers into less profitable expenditures of interest. The phenomenon—or, as Berger terms it, "the technique" (123)—of conspicuous irrelevance is not unique to book 2, but he argues that it intensifies there, coming to a spectacular head in the Cave of Mammon. He interprets Guyon's sojourn in the cave as *The Faerie Queene*'s metapoetic commentary on the very perils of distraction and digression to which so many critics had seen it as falling prey. In its apparent superfluity to the quest on which Guyon is bound and in the peculiar form of temptation it presents to knight and reader alike, Mammon's cave epitomizes the risks of attending to what doesn't matter: it is Spenser's anticipatory rebuke to those who would accuse either him or his poem of irrelevance.

For if Guyon is unmoved by Mammon's invitation to take the riches in his horde, responding that he has no use for them, Berger notes that this is partly because the gold itself is of no possible use: it "could never be spent, not merely because there was so much, but because there was no legitimate currency, only unminted metal and coins for the numismatist—'straunge and rare'" (21). Rather than Guyon's greed—of which, in any case, he has none—it is the rarified tastes of the collector, the curator, or the connoisseur to which Mammon's horde appeals, he argues, not only through the impulse to acquire but also, more dangerously, through the subtler pleasure of self-denial:

> It is the hero's curiosity, his desire of novelty on which the tempter plays. Guyon has no inclination to touch, to taste, or to possess. He enjoys resisting insofar as he takes pleasure in his virtues; he is also there to see.... The narrator never lets us forget that the Cave's appeal is chiefly to Guyon's eye, and that the secrecy and rarity of the spectacle constitute that appeal. (20)

All of this builds to a notorious anticlimax: having steadfastly resisted all of Mammon's supernatural lures, Guyon leaves the cave after three days only to collapse in a faint induced by the pedestrian causes of hunger and lack of sleep. The seeming remoteness of this physical collapse from any moral significance is precisely the point: led through Mammon's cave by "an idle and consuming curiosity," Guyon is punished not for indulging his appetites but for denying them, "feed[ing] his eyes at the expense of sustaining nature" (26, 23). For the truly remarkable (and dangerous) thing about the treasure in Mammon's cave, as Berger shows, is that it isn't good for anything except its own splendid display. The reader of canto 7 is left with the uneasy suspicion that we have fallen into the same trap: If Guyon was never tempted to take Mammon's gold, what have we been reading this canto for? The same anxious question returns with a vengeance at the end of book 2, in the Bower of Bliss, where the longest canto of the entire *Faerie Queene*—eighty-seven stanzas—is filled with lavish descriptions of a place that holds no apparent interest for Guyon, and that, at canto's end, he rapidly and remorselessly destroys. As Berger helps us to see, every conspicuously irrelevant detail in Mammon's Cave or the Bower of Bliss, as well as the delightfully and unduly protracted episodes themselves, are challenges to our confidence in the purposefulness of our own readerly interest, and thus incitements to confront "the general problem of poetic unity" that *The Faerie Queene* "raises in a special and pressing manner": "How do its diverse parts and elements contribute to an impression at once intricate and simple, complex and unified?" (121).

Like Thomas Warton before him, Berger assumes that the critic's task is to solve this difficulty, to shore up through his own interpretive efforts not only the impression but the reality of poetic unity, to discover by wit and erudition the chain of metaphorical associations, the source text, or the metapoetic frame that secures the relation of part to whole. Unlike Warton, Berger finds the task eminently surmountable, and his analysis of book 2's relation to *The Faerie Queene* as a whole is frequently dazzling; again and again he demonstrates that what to the casual reader might seem like superfluous ornament or "untranslatable detail" is in fact a densely encoded argument. In a pointed riposte to those New Critics who had dismissed the poem as unreadable, he insists that the failure to perceive poetic coherence is in the eye of the beholder: "Certain passages"—and certain poems—"demand closer reading than others." The challenge was not to look away from digressions and distractions but to make looking at them worthwhile, to convert the useless horde of local beauties and textual curiosities into "nodal points of meaning, moments in which the larger significance of the narrative is compressed, illuminated, altered" (133). The paradoxical result of such concentrated analysis is a perfectly uniform distribution of potential interest: a poem in which "nothing," as Dolven writes, "is really irrelevant."[23]

Dolven wonders whether that assumption really accounts for every moment in *The Faerie Queene*, whether some episodes—he cites Britomart's blank staring at the tapestries in Busyrane's palace as an example—might not invite "an unreconstructed indifference ... when the habits of reading that allow us to fulfill the poem's ambitions for totality and wholeness might properly be suspended" (170). We might also wonder whether it accounts for every instance or interval in its reception history. For where Warton saw obstacles to critical appreciation and Berger provocations to critical enterprise, other readers—John Keats, for instance—might see opportunity: the opportunity to notice, delight in, puzzle over, memorize, or cite a passage without regard—or, in Keats's case, with an impish disregard—for either the intended meaning or the context in which it appears. It is such readers with whom the rest of this chapter is primarily concerned. For the most part, they encountered the poem before the advent of literary scholarship and professional criticism, and so they do not share what Dolven calls "the habits of reading" that prompt scholars and critics to search for meaningful links between seemingly disparate textual parts. Instead, they were amateurs in every sense of the word, dilettantes, devotees, and occasional readers for whom *The Faerie Queene*'s conspicuous irrelevances were not defects requiring interpretive remediation but incitements to annotation, excerption, and obsession.

Keats's injunction to "load every rift" is an exemplary case in point: mined by critics, essayists, and the compilers of Internet quoteboards, it has been embraced as a motto of the Romantic cult of poetic genius, shedding any association with *The Faerie Queene* or with temperance. It is tempting to identify this process with the dispersal—that is, both the widening and the attenuation—of Spenser's influence in modern literary culture: in the wake of its revival as a Romantic touchstone, *The Faerie Queene* became a poem that many people had heard of and increasingly few people had read in anything close to its entirety. But this is to misrepresent, even invert, both the poem's reception history and the history of reading: the partial, glancing, second- or third-hand exposure to *The Faerie Queene* that seems so characteristic of its modern afterlife was a significant factor in its circulation and consumption from the start. Indeed, Spenser's contemporaries could quote *The Faerie Queene* before they could properly read it, and many early encounters with the poem would have taken the form of brief or concentrated attention to an isolated fragment: a stanza of verse, a neat turn of phrase, a flower or jewel of eloquence.

In some respects, then, what follows offers a historicist revision of Berger's still influential approach to the poem and of the eighteenth-century critical tradition to which that approach is indebted. As Adam Smyth and others have shown, early modern readers saw texts differently than we do, treating the printed book (or the poetic work) "not as a coherent stable whole but as a collection of potentially applicable parts."[24] At the time Spenser wrote *The Faerie Queene* and for well over a century after, then, determining which parts of a text were worth attending to and which might be ignored was not an evasion of readerly responsibility but the chief exercise of it. But the traces of deep and cursory engagement left by *The Faerie Queene*'s early readers—collected in commonplace books, sampled in miscellanies, digested into new literary and nonliterary forms, or picked out by underlinings and annotations in the margins of printed editions—frequently defy synthesis, as much as the poem's own glittering fragments and distracting episodes tend to do. They, too, are conspicuous irrelevances: monuments to the interests and appetites of *particular* readers, individuals who resist assimilation into any broader collectivity of readers. Some, indeed, have strenuously resisted incorporation into this chapter, and my reluctance to relinquish them may be taken as evidence of my own intemperate impulses and unregenerate attachments.

Mine and Garden: The Quotable *Faerie Queene*

Given the fraught relation between temperance and readerly interest, it is no coincidence that the two great arenas of Guyon's temptation—the mine and the garden, the Cave of Mammon and the Bower of Bliss—are also the exemplary metaphorical spaces in which early modern reading was supposed to transpire. The mine and the garden supplied early modern pedagogical theorists with models for the necessary and virtuous character of readerly appetite, and they lent their names to the textual repositories in which the fruits of reading were collected—the treasury, the thesaurus, and the anthology, the storehouse and the florilegium. As the etymologies of such terms remind us, the aim of reading in Spenser's time was frankly acquisitive: an increase not simply of pleasure or understanding but of a personal stock of witty sayings, wise sentences, apt proverbs, and striking figures of speech, to be underlined in passing, jotted down in margins, or—ideally—transcribed and ordered by topic in the pages of a specially purposed commonplace book. The great exponent of such acquisitive reading in the early modern period was Erasmus himself, whose ever-multiplying, ever-expanding editions of the *Adagia*—a commonplace book of proverbs and wise sayings gathered from antiquity—provided a material record of the avidity of his own readerly appetite. For Erasmus, mine and garden were indispensible figures for literary tradition: sites for the accretion of cultural value, the exercise of readerly judgment, and the transfer of intellectual and poetic authority.

The two metaphors weren't precisely interchangeable, however, and in the gap between them we can begin to perceive one of the fundamental tensions of avid reading, between the impulse to accumulate and the mandate to exercise judgment and selectivity. Reading as flower-gathering was an expansive affair: Erasmus begins *De Copia* by repeating Horace's dictum that the reader ought to "flit like a busy bee through the entire garden of literature," sipping nectar from the works of other poets and transmuting it into the honey of his own eloquence; indeed, he insists, the well-educated reader ought to "cover the whole field of literature . . . at least once in his life."[25] But the dedicatory epistle to his 1516 *Parabolae sive similia* casts the work of extracting parallels and similitudes as a more rarified endeavor, describing the resulting collection as "no common present . . . but many jewels in one small book":

> Jewels I may well call them, these parallels selected from the richly furnished world of the greatest authors of antiquity. . . . I have not chosen what was ready to hand, nor picked up pebbles on the beach; I have brought forth precious stones from the inner treasure-house of the Muses. The barber's shop, the tawdry conversation of the marketplace are no source for what is to be worth the attention of the ears and eyes of educated men. Such things must be unearthed.[26]

Indeed, Erasmus insists on the "twofold difficulty, and double praise" of this endeavor, both the discovery and the arrangement of "what is really good," for "it is something to have found a precious jewel in the first place, but there is credit to be won from its skilful mounting in a sceptre or ring" (23:131). Far from covering the vast expanse of potential sources—"I am well aware," he writes, "what an ocean of parallels might be got together from the whole realm of nature, from all the fields of knowledge, all the poets, the historians, the orators"— he has deliberately restricted himself to a select few, chiefly Plutarch and Seneca: "an attempt to pursue the infinite would be madness" (23:134). Copia demands continence, and continence, as the narrator of book 2 reminds us, is "[a] Harder lesson to learne . . . / In ioyous pleasure than in grieuous paine" (2.6.1.1–2).

Even as it tested readers' capacities for selectivity and self-discipline, however, the treasury or anthology could also be seen as a vehicle for the more equitable redistribution of literary goods—as the term "commonplacing" itself suggests. This was especially true as the anthology made its way into print: the preface to Richard Tottel's 1557 *Songes and Sonnets, written by the right honorable Lorde Henry Haward late Earle of Surrey, and other*—commonly known as Tottel's Miscellany—urges the reader "y^t thou thinke it not euil don, to publishe, to ye honor of the english tong, and for profit of the studious of Englishe eloquence, those workes which the vngentle horders vp of such tresure haue heretofore enuied the."[27] The readerly reflex that prompts the keeping of a commonplace book, the compiling of a poetic miscellany, or simply the marking of a phrase or line of verse is thus at once greedy and openhanded. Extraction, citation, adaptation, and allusion are mechanisms for sharing language as well as for appropriating it, and, as Tottel insists, they can dramatically extend the reach of a work's influence—though only by sacrificing claims of authorial intention, originality, and textual coherence.

The early reception history of *The Faerie Queene* is thus linked, both directly and indirectly, to the emergent discourse of English rhetoric and poetics and to the growing conviction, among poets, pedagogues, and literary theorists, that vernacular writing was a worthy field for cultivation and imitation. In 1588, two years before the first edition of *The Faerie Queene* appeared in print, a single stanza from the Legend of Temperance appeared in the twenty-fifth chapter of Fraunce's *Arcadian Rhetorike*. There, as a supplement to his descriptive catalog of tropes and figures, Fraunce offered a gallery of examples from classical and contemporary poets, "conceited verses" whose "grace & delicacie proceedeth from the figures aforenamed."[28] Alongside extracts from Homer, Virgil, Tasso, du Bellay, Philip Sidney, and others, appear nine lines from "Spencer in his Fairie Queene. 2. booke. cant. 4":

> Wrath, iealousie, griefe, loue, doo thus expell:
> Wrath is a fire, and iealousie a weede,
> Griefe is a floud, and loue a monster fell:
> The fire of sparkes, the weede of little seede,
> The floud of drops, the monster filth did breed:
> But sparkes, seede, drops, and filth doo thus delay,
> The sparks soon quench, the springing seed outweed,
> The drops drie vp, and filth wipe cleane away.
> So shall wrath, iealosie, griefe, loue, die and decay.[29]

There is no way of knowing whether Fraunce chose this particular stanza from a longer manuscript to which he had access or whether the stanza was already circulating on its own, copied into the commonplace book of some other reader—in either case, the passage's appeal is a function of its detachability and self-containment. Indeed, in 1588, the attribution prefixed to the stanza, anchoring it to a particular author and work, was surely of limited value: the vast majority of Fraunce's readers would have had no way of knowing what Spenser's "Fairie Queene" was, much less of identifying the fourth canto of its second book. Certainly they could not have guessed the dramatic context in which this particular stanza occurs, as part of an address by the wise Palmer to a young man whose jealous rage has prompted him to kill his betrothed and his best friend. But the inaccessibility of that knowledge is hardly a problem for Fraunce: although he diligently references its source in Spenser's poem, the passage serves his needs precisely because it requires no larger context; it is a perfectly portable lesson in poetic control, a master class in formal and ethical self-containment.

Fraunce calls his extracts "conceited verses," and the phrase speaks both to the artfulness and to the compactness he must have sought in making his selections. A "conceit" can be an idea or device—typically an ingenious one—but it can also be a trinket, ornament, dainty, or trifle. His quotations must be both: wittily crafted and easily excised, not only from their textual sources but also from their immediate context in *The Arcadian Rhetorike*. These are extracts designed for re-extraction, to be copied into the commonplace books of admiring readers and imitated by aspiring poets and rhetoricians. And in this sense, the prepublication appearance of *The Faerie Queene* in *The Arcadian Rhetoric* illuminates an aspect of the poem liable to recede from the view of scholarly readers, whose task it is to anchor the meanings of particular textual details in larger motivating and explanatory contexts—narrative, allegorical, historical, political, cultural, bibliographic, and so on. The task of a reader like Fraunce is just the opposite, to single out those parts of a poem that retain value and interest apart from any such context, extracts whose appeal inheres simply in their status as literary artifacts.

For all its length and intricacy, *The Faerie Queene* is well suited to such treatment, thanks in part to its regular division and subdivision into book, canto, stanza, and line. And Fraunce was by no means the only reader to see in Spenser's poem a potentially valuable trove of illustrative material (though he was notably quick off the block). In the years immediately after its initial publication, the genre of the printed poetic miscellany—curated collections of verse by contemporary English authors—emerged as a crucial secondary vehicle for the circulation of Spenser's poetry, *The Faerie Queene* included. Extracts from Spenser, both attributed and not, appeared in *The Phoenix Nest* in 1593 and in three different miscellanies published in 1600: *Bel-vedére, or, The Garden of the Muses*; *Englands Helicon*; and *Englands Parnassus*.[30] This last, compiled by Robert Allott and published by Cuthbert Burby, Thomas Hayes, and Nicholas Ling (himself the compiler of *Englands Helicon*), is a particularly dense tissue of Spenserian extracts: Dora Anna Scribner counts 377 passages from Spenser (as against 210 from Michael Drayton, 162 from William Warner, 128 from Samuel Daniel, and 91 from William Shakespeare), 343 of which come from *The Faerie Queene*.[31]

So frequent and so varied are these extracts that to peruse *Englands Parnassus* is to see *The Faerie Queene* anew, through the eye of the curator or collector. For what Allott regards as worth extracting rarely corresponds to the poem's stated project of gentlemanly fashioning—or, indeed, to the didactic aims of earlier English quotation books, like Thomas Elyot's *The Bankette of Sapience* (1539) and William Baldwin's *The Treatise of Moral Philosophy containing the Sayings of the Wise* (1547).[32] Instead of staking its value on the moral substance of its extracts, the title page of *Englands Parnassus* advertises their aesthetic appeal:

"The choysest Flowers of our Moderne Poets, with their Poeticall comparisons. Descriptions of Bewties, Personages, Castles, Pallaces, Mountaines, Groues, Seas, Springs, Riuers, &c." For Allott, as this expansive catalog suggests, the metaphors of anthology and treasury have literal force: the flower and the ornament, natural beauty and manmade luxury, are not simply figures for poetic value but constitutive of it. More telling still is the tension between the title page's emphasis on selectivity—"The *choysest* Flowers"—and the indeterminacy of its final "&c." That tension between rarity and abundance is, as I have already suggested, endemic to the culture of commonplacing and encoded in its governing metaphors of mine and garden, jewel and flower. Here those metaphors exert literal sway over Allott's selections from *The Faerie Queene*, which he reproduces for readers as both a cabinet of curiosities—filled with quaint figures, beautiful maidens, and monstrous creatures—and a panoramic landscape of scenic charms.

The effect on the poem is wildly destabilizing: scrubbed of any identifying markers beyond those supplied in Allott's generic topic headings, the people and places of *The Faerie Queene* float free of their allegorical referents. Vice masquerades successfully as virtue: the villainous Archimago, in disguise as a holy man, appears to Allott's reader simply as "A Palmer" (352), while the Redcrosse Knight's ignominious flight from the House of Pride is rebranded as an instance of "Courage" (442). Crucial distinctions of character and motive are effaced by superficial resemblances: the heroic Arthur appears alongside the monstrous giantess Argante, a hapless knight named Diamond, and an evil sultan as emblematic figures "Of Rage" (435–39), while a section titled "Hope" features both the divine Speranza of the House of Holiness and her debased counterpart in the masque at Busyrane's palace (136–37). Densely metaphorical images shed their spiritual significance: the figure of Redcrosse consumed by sin becomes merely a description "Of a starved man" (383–84), while the "harmfull fowles" and "hellish Harpies" that attack Guyon on his passage to the Bower of Bliss are placed under the bland heading "Of Birdes" (488). Occasionally, a passage seems simply misplaced—"Fresh Hyacinthus," "Foolish Narcisse," and "Sad Amaranthus," the flower boys of the Garden of Adonis, are gathered under the heading "Of Hounds" (489)—but more often the chapter headings are accurate enough; they simply disregard the moral shadings and figurative depths that distinguish one lovely or striking thing from another and that guide, or are meant to guide, our responses to them in the poem.

Allott's plundering of *The Faerie Queene*'s descriptive resources is thus at conspicuous and even comic odds with the poem's didactic aims. Or, rather, it foregrounds the degree to which the poem is at odds with itself: thanks to its disregard for allegorical content and narrative context, Allott's catalogs of images can also expose unresolved tensions within the design of *The Faerie Queene*. For instance, one of the lengthiest sections in *Englands Parnassus*, "Descriptions of Beautie & Personage" (385–420), includes descriptions of five of the poem's female characters, from the divine Charissa to the wicked Acrasia, alongside seductive blazons of Shakespeare's Lucrece, Sidney's Stella, Marlowe's Hero, and the mistresses of more than a dozen other contemporary lyricists. The resulting spectacle of female flesh—a buffet of rosy cheeks, ruby lips, snowy breasts, and silken limbs—mounts a devastating critique of Spenser's claim to distinguish lust from love and appetite from awe: set side by sensual side, all of *The Faerie Queene*'s beauties look more or less the same. Careful readers of Allott's catalog, it is true, might note that Charissa's breasts are bared to nurse her hungry babes, while Acrasia's are "bare to ready spoyle / Of hungry eyes," but the extract that follows levels even that distinction, presenting us with the hapless Serena of book 6, whose "paps . . . like white silken pillowes" are stripped to feed both the literal hunger of her cannibal captors and the hungry eyes of Spenser's (and Allott's) readers (403, 407–8). Within the confines of the allegory, such resemblances might be marshaled to a morally instructive end—see how cannily vice imitates virtue!—but abstracted from that context, they hint at a more basic and troubling lack of discrimination on the part of poet and reader alike.

The paradoxical effect of *Englands Parnassus*, and perhaps of anthologies in general, is that the very extracts singled out as "choicest" prove indistinguishable en masse. In the end, all those vivid and striking images—"Descriptions of Bewties, Personages, Castles, Pallaces, Mountaines, Groues, Seas, Springs, Riuers, &c.," as the title page promises—collapse into the vagueness of the final et cetera. This spreading sameness is a danger to which *The Faerie Queene* is itself highly vulnerable, as Allott's hodgepodge reassembly of its component parts reveals. Like the anthology, the allegorical poem justifies its tendency to excess by an appeal to exemplarity. In the "Letter of the Authors" appended to the 1590 edition of *The Faerie Queene*, Spenser explains that the moral content of his poem is "coloured with an historicall"—that is, narrative—"fiction, the which the most part of men delight to read, rather for variety of matter, than for profite of the ensample, . . . so much more profitable and gratious is doctrine by ensample, then by rule" (715–16). In theory, delight yields insensibly to doctrine, and variety of matter submits to the straightness of moral precept. In practice, however, one can easily persist in placing pleasure above profit, and a taste for variety may terminate only in a feeling of aesthetic surfeit; what readers take from *The Faerie Queene* may be "choicest," Allott's anthology suggests, simply in the circular sense of having been chosen. *Englands Parnassus* helps us see this impulse to extract not as an abuse of the poem's methods but an application of them, for what is learning by example if not the capacity to extrapolate, to read out of and beyond some original context?

The anthologized *Faerie Queene* may not preserve any of the poem's didactic content, but it provides shrewd if unintended commentary on its didactic technique, with its reliance on a highly portable, necessarily transferable stock of words and images. And on occasion the poem returns the favor, an extract from it speaking sharply to its new anthological context. Thus, near the end of *Englands Parnassus*, following a whirlwind tour of Spenserian gardens and great houses, Allott returns to book 2, closing his chapter of "Pallaces, Castles, &c." with a description of the island to which Phaedria ferries Guyon in canto 6:

> It was a chosen plot of fertile land
> Amongst the wild waues set like a litle nest,
> As if it had by natures cunning hand
> Bene choicely picked out from all the rest,
> And laid forth for ensample of the best:
> No daintie flower nor hearbe that growes on ground,
> No arboret with painted blossomes drest,
> And smelling sweete, but there it might be found
> To bud out faire, & her sweet smels throw all around.
> No tree whose braunches did not brauely spring,
> No braunch wherein a fine bird did not sit,
> No bird but did her shrill notes euer sing,
> No song but did containe a louely dit.
> Trees, braunches, birds, and songs were framed fit,
> For to allure fraile minds to carelesse ease. (Allott, 475; FQ 2.6.12, 13.1–6[33])

The first four lines of the passage offer an approving metatextual gloss on Allott's own anthological labors—his cunning "pick[ing] out" of isolated passages and "chosen plot[s]," "laid forth" to readers "for ensample of the best"—while the next nine restate the promise of his title page: like *Englands Parnassus*, Phaedria's island miraculously weds the pleasures of superabundance to the promise of exacting judgment. But the belated caution in the extract's final line pulls the anthological reader up short, indicting our progress through Allott's collection as a weak-minded indulgence in obvious and easy pleasures—not a refinement but a vulgarization of reading. Unlike the audience of *Englands Parnassus*, readers of *The Faerie Queene* are given advance warning not to trust Phaedria or her island: the argument to canto 6 tells us that "immodest Mirth" will lead Guyon "into loose desyre," hinting that what might appear as abundance is in fact incontinence (2.6.argument.1–2). The reward of reading the passage in context, then, is the opportunity to distinguish oneself from the feeble types who might confuse the island's pastiche of beauty with a genuine poetic paradise.

Indeed, the whole encounter with Phaedria in canto 6 can be read as a Spenserian satire of the promises of Erasmian *copia* and the rewards of acquisitive reading. "Abound[ing]" in "pleasaunt purpose" and possessed of "a storehouse" of "merry tales," Phaedria is an embodied treasury of wit, and her island, drifting on the surface of an idle lake, is an anthology of sensory delights and poetic allusions (2.6.6.3–5). The song she sings to lull her captive visitors to sleep is, fittingly, a tissue of borrowed words and images, modeled both on the Siren's song in canto 14 of *Gerusalemme Liberata* and—more daringly, not to say blasphemously—on the words of Christ in the Sermon on the Mount. But it can be hard to distinguish the learning of a lesson from its misapplication: Christ's message, as Phaedria reminds us, was already founded on the virtues of imitation and ease. "Learn how the lilies of the field do grow: they are not wearied, neither spin," he enjoins his disciples (Matt. 6:28); "Behold, O man, that toilesome paines doest take, / The flowers, the fields, and all that pleasaunt growes, / How them selues doe thine ensample make," Phaedria echoes (2.6.15.1–3). The very act of culling ornament from Scripture might be taken as an enactment of this ethos: Why labor over a fresh image when a perfectly good one is ready to hand?

Of course, Phaedria's version of the analogy brazenly dispenses with the injunction that follows in the Gospel, to "seek ye first the Kingdom of God" (Matt. 6:33), replacing it with an invitation to "Refuse such fruitless toile, and present pleasures chuse" (2.6.17.9). And it may be that this repressed injunction and its replacement hold the key to the entire episode: as in Mammon's cave, Guyon shows no signs of susceptibility to Phaedria's shallow charms, but he does allow her to detain him on his way; as readers, we have no choice but to dally with them as well. Even if Phaedria's wandering island serves as a cautionary example of the waywardness of textual appropriation, then, the episode also points out the looseness of the ties that bind citation to source, the pleasurable ease with which a well-crafted image, phrase, or passage can slip its contextual moorings. Indeed, *Englands Parnassus* wasn't even the first stop on the island's post-Spenserian itinerary: seven years earlier, in Thomas Watson's 1593 sonnet sequence *The Tears of Fancie, or Loue Disdained*, the six lines beginning "No tree whose branches..." appear—uncited—in the middle of Sonnet 51, where they provide a metaphorical backdrop to the speaker's barren hopes.[34] To accuse Watson of plagiarism would surely be to miss the point: choicely picked out and laid forth for example, the wandering island isn't a place so much as a topos, a rhetorical convention designed to travel across and among texts. Like the garden and the mine, it serves as a figure for a culture of imitation and citation in which the part might well exceed the value of the whole.

Jonson, Hoby, Warton: Reading in Pieces

Volumes like the *Arcadian Rhetorike* and *Englands Parnassus* disseminated the language and imagery of *The Faerie Queene* well beyond the confines of the poem, with little or no reference to the narrative or allegorical contexts from which they were taken. In this respect, I have argued, they were merely representative of the literary culture from which the poem itself emerged. But memorable episodes and striking passages were at odds with the poem as a whole in a different sense, too: cunningly wrought, ingeniously witty, allusively dense, or richly ornamented, they invited readers who encountered them within the text to defer, abandon, or simply ignore the work of comprehending the whole. Phaedria's aimless paddling on the Lake of Idleness—and her equally idle appropriation of the imagery of the Sermon on the Mount—threaten to strand Guyon in the midst of book 2, and the frequency with which her canto was chosen for extraction, imitation, and anthologization suggests that Spenser's readers were no less susceptible to her charms. But print anthologies weren't the only vehicles for such aimless pleasure; hand-annotated editions of *The Faerie Queene* from the sixteenth, seventeenth, and eighteenth centuries also testify to the essential ungovernability and miscellaneity of readerly interest and taste. Indeed, attending to the bits of the poem such readers noted—or ignored—doesn't produce a new, synthetic account of early reading practices in relation to *The Faerie Queene* so much as reveal the folly of that ambition: there are as many ways of reading as there are readers. In the section that follows, I consider three strikingly different but equally self-willed such readers: the poet and playwright Ben Jonson, the puritanical magistrate Thomas Posthumus Hoby, and a college-aged Thomas Warton, for whom *The Faerie Queene* was not yet a scholarly project but a youthful pastime.

As the modern editors of Jonson's annotated 1617 folio edition of Spenser's *Works* observe, both the abundance and the tenor of the markings throughout Jonson's text belie the critical commonplace that he disliked Spenser's poetry (typically reinforced by citing his dictum that Spenser "writ no language") and forged his own verse practice in opposition to the elder poet's example.[35] In the case of book 2, we might go further and say that Jonson seems to have read Spenser specifically for his style—and that he valued the Legend of Temperance precisely for its willingness to transgress its ostensible ethos of restraint. For in contrast to his annotations in book 1, which chart his decoding of the spiritual allegory, Jonson's notes on book 2 largely register his pleasure in the poem's figurative language, especially its epic similes and its elaborate descriptions.[36] "An excellent D<escr.> of a butifull La<dy>," he writes alongside the blazon of Belphoebe beginning at 2.3.22 and, a few pages later, next to the description of Braggadochio at 2.3.36, "An excell. Simile to express cowardnesse." Although he dutifully notes the poem's skepticism toward its own luxuriant idylls—the depiction of Cymochles "poured out . . . In daintie delices, and lauish ioyes" (2.5.28) prompts the moralizing gloss "excesse of pleasur enervats the body and exanimates the strongest"—he nonetheless delights in its figurative riches, adding, "An excellent Description of a man drownd in pleasures." When Phaedria enters the poem in canto 6, he correctly identifies her as "V<aine> delight," which "extinguishes our godliest and best resolutions," but adds just below, "An Exce. Descr. Of a pleasant Iland," and writes "Reminisce"—"Remember" or "Memorize"—beside her seductive song.

The tension between Jonson's approval of book 2's ethic of restraint and his attraction to its aesthetic of excess is most marked in his dense glossing of canto 12, the Bower of Bliss. He begins well, writing "the misery of prodigality" and "Memento"—"Remember"—by the stanzas describing the Gulf of Greediness and the Rock of Reproach, as if in obedience to the Palmer's stern injunction to "Behold th'ensamples . . . Of lustfull luxurie and thriftlesse wast" (2.12.9.1–2)—but he can't help noting that the very next stanza contains "An excellent Des<cr.> of Rowinge" (2.12.10). In the pages that follow his eye is repeatedly caught by ornamental details: "the Descrp: of certaine monsterous fishes" (2.12.23–24), "the Desr. Of the ill bod<ing> Birds" (2.12.36), "Desrp. Of the bouer of Blisse" (2.12.42), "the Desrp: of mans good genius" (2.12.47), "An excellent D<esrp.> of a most pleasant <place>" (2.12.58), "Admirable Desr. Of a melodious sound" (2.12.71), and, finally, at the long-delayed revelation of Acrasia herself, "the Des. Of a f[a]ire woman" (2.12.78)—a gloss that renders the evil Acrasia more or less indistinguishable from her polar opposite, Belphoebe.

That inattention to moral judgment is characteristic of how Jonson encounters the Bower of Bliss, especially at its most conspicuously ornamental. The arbored grapevine that grows in Acrasia's bower, in which real fruits mingle with jeweled counterfeits, for instance, is one of the poem's most striking figures for the dangerous alignment of ornament and abuse: the false grapes were "So made by art, to beautify the rest," observes the narrator, but "the weake boughes, with so rich loade opprest, / Did bow adowne, as ouerburdened" (2.12.55.2, 5–6). But, with recourse to his favorite adjective, Jonson transfigures the excess into excellence: "A excellent Derp: of a vine" (at 2.12.54–55). Most telling of all is Jonson's gloss of the book's climactic final stanzas. Of Guyon's capture of Acrasia, his rescue of Verdant, and his destruction of the Bower of Bliss, he makes no remark, but he pauses to write a relatively long note on the "lovely lay" (2.12.74.1) that echoes through the bower just before Guyon attacks, describing it as "A song shewing the shortnesse of pleasures and the Life of man, and therefore enviting to the enjoyinge of it" (on 2.12.74). That decidedly intemperate invitation is allowed to stand as Jonson's final comment on the Legend of Temperance, and it decisively aligns enjoyment with the most transitory pleasures of the text, even those on the brink of imminent destruction.

Against such a rarified aesthetic appreciation, we might set the more pragmatic, but no less willful approach taken to the Legend of Temperance by Jonson's contemporary Sir Thomas Posthumus Hoby (or Hobby). Born into a well-connected family of diplomats and scholars, Hoby was a long-term member of Parliament and a protégé of William Cecil, Lord Burghley—Elizabeth's secretary of state and, by general consensus, the target of Spenser's complaint, in the opening stanzas of book 4 of *The Faerie Queene*, against those "Stoicke censours" (4.proem.3.9) who had criticized his work, insensible to the charms of love and poetry. Like his mentor, Hoby was known as a stern and censorious man: a Puritan in religious matters and the agent of multiple lawsuits against acquaintances he believed had insulted him, he has been cited as a possible inspiration for Shakespeare's Malvolio and is described by one historian as the "most overbearing, touchy, and resentful of Yorkshire magistrates" (another, more charitable account characterizes him simply as "exceptionally conscientious").[37] At some point in the late sixteenth or early seventeenth century, Hoby acquired a 1590 edition of books 1–3 of *The Faerie Queene*, now part of the Bodleian Library rare books collection at Oxford, which he proceeded to annotate.[38] How did this legalistic and self-serious man read Spenser's lavish and improvident poem?

Unsurprisingly, perhaps, given his abstemious tendencies, Hoby gravitated to the Legend of Temperance: his marginal annotations commence at the very end of book 1 and continue through book 2, canto 9, after which they abruptly cease. But Hoby shows little interest in the moral content of book 2, beyond bracketing the occasional sententious passage; instead, he is wholly preoccupied with the particularities of plot: names and places, entrances and exits, encounters and exchanges, and, especially, the distribution of objects. This focus causes his attention to alight in peculiar places, and on details that have proved of little interest to most scholarly readers. In canto 3, for instance, Hoby takes scant notice of the famously and extravagantly sensual blazon of Belphoebe, whom he identifies simply as the "lady that made Braggadochyo soe much afearde" (224), but he pays close attention to an expository stanza early in the canto, in which we learn that it was Braggadochio who stole Guyon's horse in the canto before. Next to 2.3.2.2, which reminds us that Guyon is now forced to fare on foot, "Sith his good steed is lately from him gone," Hoby wrote "Looke fol: 208" (219). Turning back to folio page 208, in canto 2, we find the narrator's teasingly incomplete account of the moment at which Guyon, distracted by his encounter with the dying Amavia, discovers that his horse has vanished:

> And turning to that place, in which whyleare
> He left his loftie steed with golden fell,
> And goodly gorgeous barbes, him found not theare.
> By other accident that earst befell,
> He is conuaide, but how or where, here fits not to tell. (2.2.11.8–9)

This playful narrative disclaimer evidently dissatisfied Hoby, who adds a clarifying note in the margin beside it: "Gyons horse stolen by Braggadocchio. fol: 219" (208). What was meant as a witty bit of romance plotting—the sort of loose thread that links otherwise disparate episodes, drawing a reader curiously on—is secured by Hoby with a tight cross-referential loop.

Lacking numbered stanzas, which were not introduced to the text until the 1609 edition, to organize his experience as a reader, Hoby fills his margins with such page references, reminding himself again and again of how book 2 might be made to cohere. Almost none of his notes are interpretive, but many are clarifying: he frequently supplies in advance the names of characters that the narrator temporarily withholds, marks significant shifts in setting, and provides speech tags to track the progress of lengthy dialogues and debates. Indeed, his gloss of canto 7 tracks Guyon's progress through the Cave of Mammon largely by way of such speech tags, transforming the episode's glittering visual appeal into a bland talkiness:

Fol. 271:	"Gyon compared to ye master of a shypp."
Fol. 272:	"Gyon comes to name him. fol: 273." [On "an uncouth, salvage, and uncivile wight"]
Fol. 273:	"Gyons speach to Mammon."
	"Mammon his answer."
Fol. 274:	"Mammon tempteth Gyon."
	"Gyons answer."
Fol. 275:	"Covetousness." [The stanza beginning "Ne thine be kingdomes, ne the scepters thine" is bracketed.]
	"Mammons reply."
	"Gyons reply."
	"Mammons reply."
Fol. 276:	"Gyons answer."
Fol. 277:	"Mammons reply."
	"Mammon leadeth Gyon into a Cave. The dyscriptione of that Cave, and of the way to the house of ryches."
Fol. 278:	"the howse of riches next to hellmouth, on the one syde, and the howse of sleepe on the other syde."
	"Gyon goeth wth Mamon into the howse of ryches."
Fol. 279:	"howe Gyon was attended as soone as he entered the howse."

	"the dyscriptione of the howse."
Fol. 280:	"Mammons proffer to Gyon."
	"Gyons answer"
Fol. 281:	"Mammon devyseth a newe way to entrape Gyon, and leades hy[m] to another roome. the dyscriptione of the room."
Fol. 282:	"Mammones offer to Gyon."
	"Gyons answer."
	"Mammon leadeth Gyon further to another roome."
Fol. 283:	"dysdane yᵉ porter."
	"the porter doth quarrell wᵗ Gyon."
	"they are both appeased by Mamon."
	"the dyscriptione of this roome."
Fol. 284:	"the dyscriptione of Philotime. fol: 285."
Fol. 285:	"Mammons speech to Gyon."
	"Phylotime."
	"Gyons answer."
Fol. 286:	"Mammon carryeth Gyon to a gardyne to tempt hym further."
	"the dyscriptione of yᵉ gardyne and the fruyte."
	"Cypress. Gal. Heben. Poppy. Hellebore. Coloquyntyda. Tetra. Samnitis. Cycuta."
	"this is the garden of Prosperyna."
Fol. 287:	"Cocytus."
	"Tantalus."
Fol. 288:	"Tantalus."
	"Pylate."
	"Mammon tempteth Gyon."
Fol. 289:	"Gyon beguyleth Mammon, and hym that did attend upon hym of theyr pray."
Fol. 290:	"Gyon desyreth to be carryed back agayne wᶜʰ Mammon thogh loth doth yeelde unto."
	"Gyon falleth into swowne, at the delve of Mammon."

Despite, or perhaps because of, Hoby's lack of interest in the episode's moral content, his is a perfectly temperate take on Mammon's cave, scrupulously attentive to what transpires within it while betraying no hint of attraction to its lavish decor. In many places, his commentary hardly rises to the level of paraphrase—"Mammon devyseth a newe way to entrape Gyon" glosses "Him to entrap vnwares another way he wist" (2.7.34.9); "this is the garden of Prosperyna" glosses "The Gardin of Proserpina this hight" (2.7.53.1)—and his only interpretive efforts are taxonomic in kind: the enumeration of names, or the cataloging of plant species. What emerges from Hoby's unemotive annotation is not a reading of the episode so much as an inventory: a detailed accounting of the movement of actors and objects through fictional space.

Oddly enough, this perspective on Guyon's adventures proves illuminating: Hoby's diligent tracking of the *stuff* of book 2, particularly the furniture and accoutrements of battle, highlights the extent to which the trials of temperance are trials of dispossession and misappropriation. The moment that troubles Hoby at the start of canto 2, when Guyon looks for his horse and can't find him, sets a pattern for book 2, as a growing arsenal of equipment and arms is set in motion by forgetfulness, borrowing, and theft. Hoby keeps track of it all: he marks the place in canto 3 where Archimago promises to steal Prince Arthur's sword for Braggadochio (223), and cross-references that page with Archimago's return with stolen sword in hand in canto 8, when he gives the weapon to Pyrrochles instead (296). He further notes that Pyrrochles supplements his misbegotten equipment with a shield taken from the sleeping Guyon's side (296), and that the Palmer himself completes the stripping of Guyon several pages later, when he loans Guyon's sword to Prince Arthur after Pyrocchles breaks Arthur's lance (302). In the ensuing battle, as Hoby points out, the moral consequences of these redistributions of property are murky: Pyrrochles's stolen sword "doeth him little pleasure" (299), he observes—being Arthur's "owne good sword *Morddure*," Spenser tells us, "The faithfull steele such treason nould endure" (2.8.30.7–8)—but he also remarks "the benyfytt Pyrrocles had by Gyons sheylde" (302), which, since it bears the image of the Faerie Queene, Arthur is hesitant to strike. Hoby's final annotations on book 2—and on the poem as a whole—appear in canto 9, where he notes with satisfaction the restoration of Arthur's sword and Guyon's shield to their rightful owners (307); he then proceeds to mark with his usual care the inhabitants and architectural features of Alma's castle, but of what transpires within the castle, or of Arthur's great battle with Maleger, or even of the entire climactic episode of the Bower of Bliss, he writes nothing—and perhaps read nothing, either. For Hoby it is as if the whole work of temperance, and of reading the Legend of Temperance, inhered in the careful management of property.

And so, in some ways, it does. Had Hoby obtained a copy of the six-book 1596 edition of *The Faerie Queene*, one imagines he would have appreciated the seemingly gratuitous interlude in book 5, the Legend of Justice, when Guyon suddenly emerges from the crowd assembled at the wedding of Marinell and Florimell in order to reclaim, at long last, "his owne good steed" from the light-fingered Braggadochio (5.29.5). In the stanzas that follow, book 2 is given a strikingly Hoby-like review: asked by Arthegall, the Knight of Justice and the hero of book 5, to justify his claim, Guyon gives a succinct rehearsal of "all that piteous storie" in which the central event is the theft of his horse, whose identity he proves by describing a hitherto unmentioned "secret marke": "Within his mouth a blacke spot... / Shapt like a horses shoe, who list to seeke it there" (5.3.31.1, 5.3.34.6, 5.3.32.8–9). The discovery of that mark, along with the revelation of his name, Brigadore—also unmentioned in book 2—restores the horse to Guyon, who then exits book 5 as abruptly as he entered. This is a conspicuous irrelevance if ever there was one, but in his dazzlingly synthetic study of *The Faerie Queene*, James Nohrnberg—the modern critic whose eye for detail and capacity for cross-referencing most resembles Hoby's own—argues that the restoration of Guyon's horse is the knot that secures a web of associations between books 2 and 5, linked as "Books of the Governors" by the "analogy of private and public order."[39] Nohrnberg, of course, traces that web through the poem by a dense network of etymological puns, biblical and classical references, and psycho-symbolic imagery—a kind of allegorical and allusive decoding for which Hoby displays neither interest nor aptitude. For Nohrnburg, Guyon's horse is an allusion to Plato's allegory of the soul, as well as a reference to Ariosto's *Orlando Furioso*, a figure for good aristocratic government, and an emblem of integrated self-possession; for Hoby, it is simply a horse.[40] But the earlier reader's methodical tracking of Guyon's possessions suggests an intuitive grasp of Nohrnberg's astonishingly subtle reading of book 2, in which the virtue of temperance is above all about "holding on" and "letting go"—about the essential, if pedestrian, work of knowing where things belong.[41]

In his impulse to catalog, sort, and accumulate, too, Hoby is not as eccentric a reader as he seems: such collector's impulses can be sufficient to sustain readerly engagement with *The Faerie Queene*, even in the apparent absence of any other form of motivating interest. This, at least, is one way of interpreting the unusual markings left in a 1596 two-volume edition of the poem currently held in the British Library.[42] The owner of the edition was not notably invested in either its narrative or its allegorical content, and he or she leaves just a handful of notes in the volume containing books 1–3. But the second volume, containing books 4–6, is littered with dozens of small marginal crosses, placed alongside any stanza containing an epic simile, from the meeting of Blandamour and Paridell at 4.2.16, "As when two warlike Brigandines at sea..." all the way to the subjection of the Blatant Beast by Calidore at 6.12.35, "Like as whylome that strong *Tirynthian* swain..." The breadcrumb-like trail of those crosses records a kind of readerly progress driven almost wholly by the pleasures of recognition and accumulation. It is possible, of course, that whoever made the marks did so while carefully following the interlaced plots of books 4–6 and tracking the allegories of Friendship, Justice, and Courtesy—but it seems equally plausible that he or she simply paged through the poem keeping an eye out for stanzas beginning with "Like" or "As." Or, perhaps, a hybrid approach was at work: a reading of the poem's second half in which the development of allegory and plot ran like background music to the tantalizing recurrence of a favorite figure of speech.

As it happens, evidence of a similar figural obsession can be found in the 1609 edition of Spenser's *Works* owned and annotated by the young Thomas Warton, then a student at Trinity College, Oxford.[43] Warton shared the book with his elder brother Joseph, whose inked annotations have a decidedly scholarly bent, noting sources and allusions, decoding religious, historical, and political references, and even, alongside a passage in book 3, canto 5, in which Belphoebe treats a wounded Timias with herbs, providing a brief account of the introduction of tobacco to England in the late sixteenth century (148). Thomas's lightly penciled marks, however, are the product of more relaxed engagement with the poem: a note scrawled at the start of book 3 in Thomas's hand locates the reader and his book "att Ox on ye bed in my room" (123). Apart from the occasional indexical reference, such as the name of a character, Thomas's annotations mostly take the form of underlinings, scattered regularly across all six books. The well-trained product of a humanist education—and the son and namesake of an Oxford Professor of Poetry—Thomas displays a proper taste for moral sententiae: he proceeds through book 2, for instance, mostly by marking wise sayings by Guyon, the Palmer, and Spenser's narrator. But throughout the poem he also highlights, at seemingly random places, images and phrases that caught his attention: "foole-happy oversight" (1.6.1; 25), "hastie joy" (1.8.42; 37), "snowie cheeke" (3.7.8; 156), "her golden lockes" (4.1.13; 191), "guilefull Goldsmith" (4.5.15; 210), "grudgefull discontent" (4.8.28; 224), "battred ballaunces" (5.2.50; 255), "the lilly hand" (5.11.17; 292), "greedy gripe" (5.11.27; 293). Apart from a predictable adolescent interest in the female form, the only feature unifying the underlined phrases is a strong taste for alliteration—nearly half of the phrases Thomas marks, from "dearest dred" (1.1.4; 1) in the proem to book 1 to "gaped like a gulfe" (5.12.15; 298) at the close of book 5, are alliterative.

Alliteration never comes up in Warton's *Observations on the Faerie Queene of Spenser*, which launched his academic career (and, eventually, helped propel him into his father's place as Professor of Poetry) a decade after his graduation.[44] Indeed, given his scorn for Spenser's "complicated... BONDAGE OF RHYMING," whose "identical cadences" forced the poet "to run into a ridiculous redundancy and repetition of words,"[45] it is unlikely that the mature critic could have confessed how appealing the boy reader found those ridiculous redundancies and repetitions—although one wonders if Warton's own lapse into alliteration here is satire or an unwittingly fond homage. But Warton cannot quite bring himself to repudiate the richly patterned form of Spenser's stanza, confessing that "some advantages arise from it" (*Observations*, 1:114). As illustration he offers, without further comment, a single stanza from book 2, Guyon's binding of Furor:

> With hundred iron chaines he did him bind
> And hundred knots which did him fore constraine
> Yet his great iron teeth he still did grind,
> And grimly gnash, threatening revenge in vaine:
> His burning eyen, whom bloudie strakes did staine,
> Stared full wide, and threw forth sparkes of fire;
> And more for ranke despight, than for great paine,
> Shakt his long locks colour'd like copper wire,
> And bit his tawny beard, to shew his raging ire. (2.4.15; quoted in
> *Observations*, 1:116)

Warton doesn't specify what advantages he finds in this particular stanza, but knowing how he read the poem a decade earlier, in his college room, we can speculate that it is those "great . . . teeth" that "grind, / And grimly gnash," the eyes that "strakes did staine, / Stared full wide, and threw forth sparkes of fire," the "long locks colour'd like copper"—that is, the vivid and densely alliterative phrases that bring Furor to life on the page. Warton doesn't seem to have had a critical vocabulary for valuing such fragments of poetic brilliance, but he never fully renounces their claim on him as a reader. Even the censorious opening chapter on the "Plan and Conduct of *The Faerie Queene*," which Warton finds so wanting in integrity, ends with an admission that he could not wish the poem otherwise:

> If the FAERY QUEEN be destitute of that arrangement and oeconomy which Epic severity requires, yet we scarcely regret the loss of these, while their place is so amply supplied, by something which more powerfully attracts us: something which engages the affections [and] the feelings of the heart, rather than the cold approbation of the head. If there be any poem, whose graces please, because they are situated beyond the reach of art, and where the force and faculties of creative imagination delight, because they are unassisted and unrestrained by those of deliberate judgment, it is this. In reading Spenser if the critic is not satisfied, yet the reader is transported. (*Observations*, 1:16).

Such transport—transport without arrival at any ultimate satisfaction, anchored in idiosyncratic and fleeting objects of enjoyment—is just what Augustine warns against in *De Doctrina Christiana*, and it is strange, indeed, to find Warton, the great advocate of poetic unity, championing it here. But as Warton's youthful annotation of *The Faerie Queene* suggests, the very features of the poem that the mature critic deplored—all of those too-interesting, too-diverting parts and pieces, "the careless exuberance of a warm imagination" in the disposition of whose "bold and striking images . . . little labour or art was applied" (*Observations*, 1:15)—were what fed the appetite of the youthful reader. They may not have added up to a single, unified work, but they were more than sufficient to keep reading going.

The Inexhaustible Stanza: Kenelm Digby in the Castle of Alma

Canto 9 of book 2—where Thomas Posthumus Hoby apparently stops reading—marks a turning point in the Legend of Temperance: rescued by Prince Arthur from the depredations of Pyrrochles and Cymochles and revived from his deadly swoon, Guyon recommits himself to the "hard aduenture" of capturing Acrasia and destroying the Bower of Bliss (2.9.8.8). No sooner has he made this declaration, however, than he is once again diverted, this time by the sight of "a goodly Castle, plac'd / Foreby a River in a pleasant Dale" (2.9.10.3–4). A swarm of "caitive Wretches" armed with clubs, spears, knives, and blazing torches delays their approach to the castle, but by stanza 22 Guyon and Arthur are at leisure to take in its peculiar design:

> The Frame thereof seem'd partly circular,
> And part triangular: O Work Divine!
> Those two the first and last Proportions are,
> The one imperfect, mortal, feminine;
> Th' other immortal, perfect, masculine:
> And 'twixt them both a Quadrate was the Base,
> Proportion'd equally by seven and nine;
> Nine was the Circle set in Heaven's Place;
> All which compacted, made a goodly Diapase. (2.9.22)

As we subsequently learn, the castle belongs to the virtuous maid Alma, and its appearance marks an interval of calm for Arthur and Guyon, who rest, read, and refresh themselves within its oddly shaped walls. Indeed, for Guyon, as I noted in my introduction, the interval never ends: at the end of canto 9, he happens upon the *Antiquitee of Faery Lond*; at the end of canto 10, he remains immersed in the book, "ne yet has ended: for it was a great and ample volume, that doth far excead / My leasure, so long leaues to repeat" (2.10.70.1–3). In fact, of course, the poem and the knight do move on: Guyon leaves the library at the close of canto 10 to eat his dinner, go to bed, and then fare onward to the Bower of Bliss. But grammatically speaking he remains, enthralled by the amplitude of this unimaginably capacious book, too big even for *The Faerie Queene*.

Oddly enough, that fleeting paradox, of a text too vast for the poem in which it is ostensibly contained, also characterizes the fate of the passage quoted above, the description of Alma's castle. More than any other single stanza in the poem, 2.9.22 has attracted the obsessive interest of readers, even—or perhaps especially—of those with little interest in the poem as a whole. In fact, the early reception history of *The Faerie Queene* is in no small part a reception history of these nine lines, which circulated in the seventeenth century well beyond the circle of those who read *The Faerie Queene* itself. Even today, the editors of the Spenser *Variorum* devote an entire appendix to interpretations of 2.9.22, a treatment given no other stanza in the poem but justified, as they say, both by the abundance of commentary on it and by the fact the poem's critical reception history can be said to start with this one "recondite stanza," which "called forth the earliest learned commentary on Spenser, Sir Kenelm Digby's *Observations*."[46]

As myths of origin go, this one has considerable appeal, not least for the dashing light in which it casts the typically sedentary labor of textual analysis. The story begins in January 1628, when the twenty-four-year-old Digby—son of a coconspirator in the Gunpowder Plot, a Cambridge MA, a recent convert to Protestantism, and a newlywed husband to the beautiful Venetia Stanley—set sail from the port of Deal in Kent, aiming for the bloodstained waters of the Mediterranean to make his fortune. Digby was equipped with two ships, a crew of 250 men, 200 barrels of gunpowder, a commission from King Charles to sack any French or Spanish vessel that crossed his path, and a trunk of books that included a 1617 folio edition of *The Works of Edmund Spenser*. The first six months of his two-year-long voyage carried Digby along the North African coastline to Algiers, where he met with the pasha, negotiated better terms for the city's English merchants, banqueted with the Ottoman elite, and bartered for rare Arabic manuscripts; to the coast of Majorca, where he seized a French flyboat; to Scanderoon, at the easternmost point of the Mediterranean, where he engaged a Venetian fleet in pitched battle and earned himself an international reputation as a pirate; and finally to the Currant Islands off the coast of Greece, where he wrote a prose romance titled *Loose Fantasies*, translated Tasso, raided the ancient temple of Apollo at Delos for antiquities, collected specimens of rare botanicals, and also—in an interval of relative calm on the passage from Milos to Zante—produced a dazzling close reading of the castle of Alma, addressed as a letter to his friend Sir Edward Stradling, signed "From aboord my Ship the Eagle the XIII of June, 1628," and published fifteen years later as *Observations on the 22. stanza in the 9th. canto of the 2d. book of Spencers "Faery Queen."*[47]

As Digby's biographer Joe Moshenska wryly notes, "The modern academic, tapping away on his computer screen in an office or library, can only fantasize of writing literary criticism under conditions as swashbuckling as these."[48] But Digby's self-presentation in the *Observations* is calculatedly offhand, a model of Sidneian sprezzatura. Although his undated manuscript *Discourse*

Concerning Edmund Spenser, addressed to his friend Thomas May, suggests a wide and knowing acquaintance with the poet's work, he here presents himself as a curious bystander, the stanza in question having been presented to him by a friend as "an indissoluble Riddle."[49] Rising to the gentlemanly challenge, he proceeds to demolish its obscurities, unpacking the cryptic imagery line by line, phrase by phrase, and word by word. The castle itself, he writes, is evidently an emblem of the human person, framed of spirit and matter both: the mind is a perfect circle in the image of God and the body a lowly triangle, whose sides and angles match the three dimensions of solid space—longitude, latitude, and depth—and the three "great compounded Elements" of alchemy and physiology: salt, sulphur, and mercury (8). These opposites are then gendered—for "as the feminine Sex is imperfect, and receives perfection from the masculine: so doth the Body from the Soul, which to it is in lieu of a male"—and tethered by a mysterious longing: "as there is a mutuall appetence between the Male and the Female, betweene matter and forme; So there is betweene the bodie and the soul of Man, but what ligament they have, our Author defineth not (and it may be Reason is not able to attaine to it)" (14–15). The quadrate that links them is identified with the four humors, and its dimensions of seven and nine traced to the influence of the seven planets and the nine orders of celestial beings; the "goodly Diapase," or harmony, these proportions generate is an emblem of the ideal consonance of body and soul, "when a mans Actions are regular, and directed towards God," figured in the poem by the castle's mistress, "the bright Virgin *Alma*, mans worthiest inhabitant, *Reason*" (22–23). Having run out of text, Digby ends here with a modest apology: "*Her* I feele to speake within me, and chide me for my bold Attempt, warning me to stray no further" (23).

The attempt indeed takes him far afield of book 2, and even of *The Faerie Queene*. Set in print, Digby's exegesis of the nine-line stanza fills twenty-five folio pages and ranges in reference from the Archimedean proof for generating the approximate value of pi and Thomas Aquinas's angelology to the precepts of Galenic medicine and the speculations of astrologers. The gap between the grandness of Digby's insights—in his view, *FQ* 2.9.22 encodes nothing less than a unified field theory of human nature—and the relative scantness of his text is evinced as proof of the poet's genius: "were there nothing else extant of *Spencers* writing," he vows, "yet these few words would make me esteeme him no whit inferiour to the most famous men that ever have been in any age" (3–4). Of course, it is also clearly a mark of Digby's own readerly ingenuity, exercising itself on the narrowest of textual foundations and concluded upon the briefest consideration. "It was Fortune that made me fall upon it, when first this *Stanza* was read to me," he protests to Stradling in closing. "And the same Discourse I made upon it, the first halfe quarter of an houre that I saw it, I send you here, without having reduced it to any better form, or added any thing at all unto it"

(25). For the scholarly reader, this may be the real glamour of the *Observations*—not the fantastical circumstances of its conception but the supposed ease and celerity of its begetting. At once erudite and amateur, Digby's approach to the poem is studiously sportive: this is criticism not as profession but as privateering, a "bold Attempt," risky, rakish, and potentially wildly profitable.

But it is possible to tell a very different story about the *Observations*, and thus, too, about the origins of criticism on *The Faerie Queene*, a story in which piracy is a mask for the seedier and more ordinary crimes of the plagiarist. In their study of Ben Jonson's annotated Spenser—like Digby's, a 1617 folio edition—James A. Riddell and Stanley Stewart point out that in the margins of Jonson's book, alongside canto 9, stanza 22, of book 2, there appears in Jonson's hand a highly compressed version of Digby's celebrated analysis:

> *the circular signe represents th\<e\>
> Soule the Triangular the body \<of\>
> Man.
> The Body is mortall and of it\<selfe\>
> Imperfecte without the Soule \<which\>
> Is in lewe of a maker and actu\<ator of\>
> it*
> By this Quadrat is meant \<the\>
> Principall Humours in man\<s\>
> body.
> *By seven and 9 are ment \<the\>
> Planetes and the Angells which ar\<e\>
> Distributed into a Hierarc\<hy\>
> Which governe the body.[50]

To Riddell and Stewart, the implications of this note, penned at some indeterminate date between 1617 and 1637, the year of Jonson's death, are clear: "the most significant part of the *Observations*—namely, the identification of the details of the allegory—are not Digby's, but Jonson's. . . . Indeed, once one recognizes the ideas for what they are—namely, Jonson's—the most striking quality of the *Observations* becomes the extent of Digby's repetition of them" (100).

As Riddell and Stewart point out, Digby knew Jonson well and was the executor of his literary estate; he no doubt could have accessed Jonson's library as he wished, and the fifteen-year lapse between the supposed date of the *Observations*' composition and the actual date of its publication suggest to them that he almost certainly did, seizing upon the insights he found in Jonson's Spenser, dilating them into a treatise, and then passing it off as a product of his own youthful genius. "Why," they wonder, "would anyone credit the claim that

Digby wrote the *Observations* for a friend? ... It seems more likely that the entire enterprise was a device to get ideas of a greater critic (Jonson) into print" (107). A bit further on, in a less charitable mood, they speculate that what began as "harmless posturing ... extend[ed] into mere fraud," animated by "reasons ... more self-interested than 'worthie and true'" (108). Now the origins of criticism on *The Faerie Queene* appear in a grimmer light, as the careerism of a seventeenth-century social climber.

Riddell and Stewart brush past the possibility that Jonson was among those who read and admired Digby's *Observations* in the 1630s, and that his marginal notes are a digest or epitome of his friend's ample treatise—which to me seems an equally, and perhaps more likely, explanation for the coincidence in their readings of *FQ* 2.9.22. For in their way, the theories Riddell and Stewart propound—that the shipboard composition of the *Observations* was a fiction invented to promote the ideas of Digby's dead friend, or that it was a cover for his own perfidious theft—are as far-fetched as the swashbuckling narrative they aim to displace. At least fifteen manuscript copies of the *Observations* survive, six of which are in miscellanies confidently dated to the 1630s, well before the 1643 print edition and quite possibly before Jonson's death, too; all of them ascribe the treatise to Digby.[51] And although Riddell and Stewart treat the convention of Digby's writing "for a friend" as a gentlemanly cover for authorial ambition, it was this very convention that made the *Observations* worth copying and collecting: of the twelve miscellanies in which manuscript versions of the *Observations* are found, only one contains what we might now call "literary" material; the rest are collections of state letters, addressed from one well-known personage to another. The scribes who copied these texts—or the readers who commissioned them—didn't value Digby because of his reading of *The Faerie Queene*; on the contrary, they valued his reading of *The Faerie Queene* because it was written by Digby and addressed to Sir Edward Stradling.

The motives that would have led the compilers of such political miscellanies to include in them an idiosyncratic treatise on a stanza of *The Faerie Queene* are not so different from those that led Allott to include so many passages from the poem in *Englands Parnassus*. Collecting and compiling, creating new relations between seemingly disparate pieces of text: these are the defining attributes of the culture of commonplacing. But the motives we must ascribe to Digby in order to imagine him as Jonson's plagiarist, including the capacity to see an in-depth analysis of a Spenserian stanza as something worth stealing, are plausible only within a social, professional, and discursive context very different from the one he actually inhabited—though it is one the *Observations* might, in distant retrospect, be credited with helping to invent: that is, the culture of professional literary criticism. But only in distant retrospect: any debate over the direction of interpretive influence—from Jonson to Digby or Digby to

Jonson—may therefore obscure a more consequential point. It isn't that *FQ* 2.9.22 offered early readers of Spenser a foothold in the poem as a whole, a vantage point from which to establish their authority as readers of *The Faerie Queene*. Rather, the stanza itself circulated among friends and acquaintances as the token of a certain kind of gentlemanly refinement and erudition.

And, as it turns out, at least two other figures might claim to have gotten to it first. One of these readers is a relatively recent discovery: the unidentified author of a manuscript note at the back of a 1596 edition of the poem, held since the seventeenth century in the library of Lincoln Minster and found there by A. P. Riemer in 1983.[52] The blank back pages of volume 1 of the edition contain a transcription of 2.9.22, followed by a commentary written in an early seventeenth-century italic hand. The commentary gives substantially the same interpretation of the stanza as in Digby's *Observations* and Jonson's marginalia, but he (or she) treats its meaning as less esoteric than obvious. "It is evident," the commentary begins, "first by the title of the Canto (The *Castle* of Temperance) and secondly by the Lady of the Castle (Alma, w[hi]ch is the Soule) and lastly by the materiall wherewith it was made [e]xpress'd in ye precedent stanza (like to Egyptian slime; and which soone must turne to earth) that this Castle is the frame of man." There follows an itemized list decoding the stanza's key words and phrases:

1. circular: wch is ye soule.
2. triangular: wch is ye Heart, and is taken for ye whole body.
3. ye first proportion: as first made, or Δ. being ye first mathemat[ical] p[ro]portion.
4. ye last: as being afterward infused: or O. being ye last and p[er]fectest p[ro]portion.
5. imperfect; comparatively: mortall: feminine: because weake, and generative.
6. immortal: a created: perfect, masculine; as vigorous, com[m]anding ye body.
7. a Quadrate, ye 4. elements whereof bodyes consist: or ye 4 humours in ye body.
8. proportioned by 7. & 9. Either because the 7 Planets gouerne the Body: / and ye 9 Intelligences ye soule: or alluding to ye climaterick, consisting of 9 times 7.
9. The Circle: the soule; sett to com[m]and ye body: or afterward translatable to Heaven, / where its onely ioy can be.
10. Dyapase. The harmony betwixt ye Body and Soule.[53]

Beneath the list is a pair of initials: "G.T." Whoever G.T. may have been, Riemer says, he or she was not the same reader who annotated the body of the poem:

those relatively scanty notes are in a secretary hand (108). The only surviving trace of G.T.'s engagement with *The Faerie Queene* thus comes from this probing analysis of a single stanza. Such engagement seems less like a reading of the poem, as we typically conceive of it, than it does an act of curation or connoisseurship: as on Digby's privateer vessel, the stanza joins the botanical specimen and the looted antiquity as a curio, a souvenir, an object of isolated fascination. Or, perhaps, as a gift: G.T.'s bequest to the book's less perceptive owner.

Riddell and Scott do discuss at some length the other surviving gloss of *FQ* 2.9.22 from the first half of the seventeenth century, a passage found in William Austin's *Haec Homo, Wherein the Excellencie of the Creation of Woman is Described, By way of an Essay*, published in 1637, the year of Jonson's death.[54] Supplementing his mystical analysis of the "*Geometricall proportion*" of the female body with a series of diagrams, Austin describes the female form as a shifting material allegory of human, earthly, and divine nature: at once "a *perfect Square*," sharing "the form of the *Temple* . . . in the *Revelation*"; a "just *Triangle*: which is a figure of the *Trinitie*"; with legs "*somewhat*" apart, "a just *circle*, which is a *true figure* of the *Earth*"; and, with hands raised and legs wide apart, "a Saint *Andrews Crosse*," sharing the "true form of the *twelve houses* of the *Seven Planets* in Heaven."[55] He secures this esoteric interpretation by reference to *FQ* 2.9.22, noting that his figural analyses

> are very elegantly and briefly contracted, by the *late dead Spencer*, in his *ever-living Fairy Queene*; where, coming to describe the *house of Alma*, (which, indeed, is no *other* but the *body*; the *habitation* of the *Soule*,) he saith. *The frame thereof seem'd partly circular*, and part *triangular, (O worke Divine!)*. (sigs. E4r–E4v)

A poet as well as an essayist, Austin traveled in the same circles as Digby and Jonson in the 1620s and 1630s, as Riddell and Scott note, which makes *FQ* 2.9.22 begin to seem like a collective preoccupation. Intriguingly, one of the early manuscript copies of Digby's *Observations* contains an ownership inscription reading "Tho: Austin," although I cannot find whether Thomas is in any way related to William.[56] Again, however, the point is not to discover, once and for all, who solved the riddle of Alma's Castle—as G.T.'s commentary suggests, it may not have seemed to some readers like much of a riddle at all. Rather, this isolated stanza circulated among seventeenth-century readers, some influential and others anonymous, as a shared locus of interest and pleasure, both curiosity and commonplace.

As the career of *FQ* 2.9.22 suggests, the detachability of a stanza or a line or a phrase from its poetic context can serve as an index of its value as a commodity among readers: what fascinated Digby and the various others who sought to interpret the description of Alma's Castle was a sense of mystery and profundity quite apart from the castle's significance in the Legend of Temperance, or *The Faerie Queene* itself. In contrast to the passages of description that caught the eyes of collectors like Fraunce and Allott, the appeal of 2.9.22 was philosophical rather than aesthetic: an invitation not merely to admire but to ponder and probe, seeking hidden depths. But the appeal of 2.9.22 seems also to have been social: the opportunity to puzzle along with other learned minds over a shared conundrum. In doing so, they may not have aimed at what we would now term a "close reading" of *The Faerie Queene*, but they certainly aimed at closer connections with one another. What Riddell and Stewart treat as a ludicrously implausible motive for Digby's analysis—"Why . . . would anyone credit the claim that Digby wrote the *Observations* for a friend?" (107)—may well be the only explanation that accounts for the apparently inexhaustible interest of this solitary stanza.

In other words, taking a poem to pieces is one way of fashioning more expansive and inclusive networks for its reception. In that respect, cultures of textual accumulation need not be figured as greedy; extraction and annotation can be modes of sociability. Thus it is that in verses surviving in three manuscript commonplace books from the 1730s, the playwright, translator, and would-be poet laureate Thomas May invokes Kenelm Digby's *Observations* on *FQ* 2.9.22 as a model for the forging of strong, sympathetic bonds between poets and patrons, authors and readers, readers and other readers. The poem reads:

> As we esteeme the greatest Princes blest
> To have their worth by ablest penns exprest
> So May wee thinke best poets happy then
> When they are read and fam'd by worthy men
> Such is thy fate brave Spencer thou hast found
> A noble knowing Reader that Can sound
> Thy Mistick depths one that can give thy due
> And make the Age beleeve his Censure true.
> A Sidney died to kil thy bleeding Hart
> A Digby lives to fame thy charming Art
> Brave Sidne's Arts and Spirrit in him are known
> And he no less then Sidney is thyn owne
> Such is thy Digby such thy Sidney was
> I could almost beleeve Pithagoras.[57]

Mindful, perhaps, of the investment of his own hopes in Charles I, to whom he dedicated his translation of Lucan and a pair of English verse histories, May first likens the bond between poet and reader to the mutually beneficial one between prince and poet, and then, more idealistically, to the transmigration of souls propounded by Pythagoras. In the first instance, to be read well is to enjoy the fruits of a kind of patronage relationship; in the second, it is to enjoy a life after death, possessing the reader with an art and spirit not his own. In each case, reading happily blurs the logics of ownership and autonomy: Digby's Spenser is Spenser's Digby, just as Spenser's Sidney was Sidney's Spenser. More to the point, May's Digby is Digby's May, as the transmission of the admiring verses from commonplace book to commonplace book secured each man's place within the close-knit circle orbiting the titanic figure of Ben Jonson—who goes unnamed here, but whose influence breathes in every rhyming line.

To make the point more broadly still: annotation, extraction, allusion, and interpretation are all ways of claiming ownership in a text, but they are also expressions of interest, admiration, affection, and even love, bonds that can generate and sustain associations among readers, across time and after death. As his heavily underlined copies of *The Faerie Queene* and the abundance of Spenserian allusions in his poetry testify, John Keats loved Spenser's poem, devoted to it less for its moral and didactic aims—its God-like "purpose"—than for its superabundant, Mammonesque descriptive horde. But Keats was also a generous reader of Spenser, eager to share the poet's riches with others. In the same summer that he wrote to Percy Shelley, urging him to serve the Mammon of his own selfish genius, he also sent a note to his beloved Fanny Brawne, telling her that he had returned to *The Faerie Queene* once more, for her sake: "For this Week past," he wrote, "I have been employed in marking the most beautiful passages in Spenser, intending it for you, and comforting myself in being somewhat occupied to give you however small a pleasure. It has lightened my time very much."[58]

Regarded as lost for much of the twentieth century, several of the marked volumes were rediscovered in the late 1980s by Greg Kucich, "resting unnoticed . . . at the Keats House Library in Hampstead."[59] As it turns out, the marked books—those that survive are volumes 3–6 of John Bell's 1778 edition—weren't Keats's own to begin with; they were borrowed from, and perhaps never returned to, the poet's friend Charles Brown. And after Keats's death, Fanny sent them on to his sister, also named Fanny, with a letter saying, "you will find the most pleasure in reading as you will find the best parts marked by one who I have heard called the best judge of poetry living—they were marked for me to read and I need not tell you with what pleasure I did so."[60] Here pleasure in reading is indistinguishable from, and enhanced by, the awareness of others'—one particular other's—having read the same thing before, and that economy of shared enjoyment proves touchingly expansive, from friend to lover and lover to sister.

The Faerie Queene "is a poem of moments," writes Gordon Teskey, that "comprise not a plot but an array." Teskey names this array "the field of allegory," adding that what allows this field to seem to be "one and not many . . . are interpretations, which is to say, just the sort of readings that an allegorical poem is designed to elicit."[61] If anything links the idiosyncratic and obsessive-compulsive reading practices tracked in this chapter, however, it is that they are *not* the sort of readings an allegorical poem is designed to elicit; the lenses they supply for Spenser's poem are diffractive and prismatic; they make it many and not one, the better to stash its pieces away. Teskey suggests that this is often the case with our own encounters with *The Faerie Queene*, too, although the synthetic imperatives of scholarly criticism force us to disguise this:

> The experience of reading *The Faerie Queene* is a matter of encountering and storing up moments of wonder. . . . Every competent reader of *The Faerie Queene* knows these moments and remembers them better than the episodes, better than the stories, better than the plan or "foreconceit," and better than the whole. Reading from one moment to the next gives the impression of a poem with no clear outer boundaries, as if it could be extended indefinitely in all directions. Wherever one happens to be in *The Faerie Queene*, one is surrounded on all sides by an array of such moments of wonder. They are like shining persimmons hanging amongst the foliage of the boughs of the tree under which one stands. (221)

One aim of this chapter has been to follow the poem's early readers in counting such abundance as gain and not as loss; to allow both the poem and its reception history to be as diffuse, multiple, and various as they in fact are. For to read like a collector—to annotate and accumulate, quote and copy, extract, imitate, and even plagiarize—is not necessarily to deplete the poem's resources; on the contrary, it may be to replenish them, storing up records of the many ways *The Faerie Queene* has of mattering in the lives of readers.

4

Half-Envying

THE INTERESTED READER AND THE PARTIAL MARRIAGE PLOT

THE ATTACHMENTS readers have developed to *The Faerie Queene*'s images, figures of speech, phrases, lines, and stanzas may enrich our sense of what the poem has to offer, but what of the identifications they make with Spenser's characters? Mindful of what they perceive as the follies of eighteenth- and nineteenth-century critics, who in elevating Una as a feminine ideal often reduced her to a cheaply sentimental trope, present-day scholars tend to be especially stern on this point. As the editors of the most recent Norton Critical Edition remind us in their preface, "Spenserian allegory, to be sure, is not a matter of one-to-one correspondence, but it remains wise to bear in mind the many ways in which *The Faerie Queene* is not a novel."[1] Attempts to read the poem "characterologically" or to relate to its allegorical personages "autonomously, psychologically, or novelistically" top Judith Anderson's list of doomed approaches to *The Faerie Queene*.[2] Such cautions are well founded: anyone who looks to, say, Charissa for a rich depiction of the emotional experience of parenthood will be disappointed, even alarmed, by the briskness with which she wrangles her numerous offspring; Charissa is not a person but an abstraction, and if she deals with her babes rather coldly, that is because they are abstractions, too. But the instinct to treat *The Faerie Queene*'s characters as persons, their existence in some sense akin to our own, is not simply an error of Romantic critics and misguided undergraduates, it is one to which the poem's narrator also occasionally succumbs, especially in the presence of its female figures. And in the case of the poem's most important potential reader, the queen to whom it is dedicated, identifying with those female characters was less an instinct than an invitation, extended repeatedly and at no small risk by the poet himself.

This chapter assesses the surprising degree to which *The Faerie Queene* not only responds to reading "characterologically" but solicits it, as an offering to and claim upon the reader whose interest Spenser was most anxious to secure.

He appeals to her for the first of many times in the proem to book 1, inviting her to join Cupid, Venus, and the Muses in inspiring his song. But Elizabeth has another task, as well:

> And with them eke, O Goddesse heauenly bright,
> Mirrour of grace and Maiestie diuine,
> Great Lady of the greatest Isle, whose light
> Like *Phoebus* lampe throughout the world doth shine,
> Shed thy faire beames into my feeble eyne,
> And raise my thoughts too humble and too vile,
> To thinke of that true glorious type of thine,
> The argument of mine afflicted stile:
> The which to heare, vouchsafe, O dearest dred a while. (1.proem.4)

"The writer's audience is always a fiction," declares Walter Ong, and to read is to submit to that fiction—at least for "a while," as Spenser bids his queen.[3] For Ong, the casting and subjection of an imagined reader constitutes the primary difference between storytellers and authors, oral and literary cultures: "Oral storytelling is a two-way street. Written or printed narrative is not two-way, at least in the short-run. Readers' reactions are remote and initially conjectural, however great their ultimate effects." That remote and conjectural status is in some ways a diminution of power: unlike the audiences of oral narratives, who can communicate their interest, enthusiasm, boredom, or dislike in real time, urging tellers on or forcing them to change course, by the time a reader responds to a written text, whether favorably or unfavorably, it is, in effect, too late. But the remoteness of readers weighs on writers, too, who must cultivate hypothetical interest and enthusiasm and guard against hypothetical boredom and dislike: "we should think more," Ong urges, "about the problems the need to fictionalize audiences creates for writers."[4] In a striking inversion of his initial dictum, he concludes that what we now recognize as fiction—a meaningfully connected sequence of events, populated by a familiar cast of characters—is the formal outgrowth of an exponential rise in readers, and a corresponding intensification of the writer's need to conjure and sustain the presence of their imaginary audience: "Tightly plotted prose narrative is the correlative of the audiences fictionalized for the first time with the aid of print."[5]

The Faerie Queene is not a tightly plotted prose narrative, and its intended reader was no figment of Spenser's imagination; on the contrary, she was a living ruler on whose favor the poet's livelihood depended and to whom, on at least one occasion, he read parts of his uncompleted poem aloud. In what follows, I argue that these well-known facts are related in nonobvious ways: Elizabeth's engrossment in *The Faerie Queene* is the poem's motivating and sustaining fiction, as well as the scene of an imagined catastrophe it must labor to forestall. As the previous chapters have demonstrated, readers of Spenser's poem are perpetually tripping over fictionalized incarnations of themselves; the narrative is studded with scenes in which Spenser anticipates, reflects, ironizes, or attempts to shape his reader's experience of the text. But the primary—and ultimate—audience for *The Faerie Queene* was a singularly potent historical subject: in the words of the dedication to the 1590 edition, "THE MOST MIGHTIE AND MAGNIFICENT EMPRESSE ELIZABETH, BY THE GRACE OF GOD QVEENE OF ENGLAND, FRANCE AND IRELAND DEFENDER OF THE FAITH &c."[6] As Louis Montrose points out, in a society in which power was wholly vested in men except at the very top, the fact of Elizabeth's royal authority required continual and exquisitely careful negotiation, both by the queen herself and by the men who served her.[7] In claiming Elizabeth as inspiration and ideal reader, Spenser's poem participates in a collective fiction of the queen's willing self-subjection to her chastely devoted male subjects, a fiction whose seditious and erotic subtexts were at perpetual risk of contaminating the official narrative. Like the proem to book 1, the dedication thus establishes Elizabeth in a precariously twofold relation to the poem, as its chief subject—"the matter of my song," as the poet puts it in book 3 (3.4.3.8)—and, in Maureen Quilligan's words, its "first reader, in whose place all subsequent readers must, for the moment of the poem's reading, in part fictionalize themselves."[8]

The effects of that double fiction—Elizabeth as poetic subject; reader as queen—extend across the reception history of *The Faerie Queene*, whether or not individual readers are cognizant of them: to read Spenser's poem at any moment in time is to inhabit the imagined perspective of its first and most important audience, to eavesdrop on the poet's solicitations of her, to bask in his praise, and, on occasion, to sense his wary resistance and tentative defiance. But the warping effect of Elizabeth's presence as reader was particularly potent in the years in which she and Spenser were both living, when *The Faerie Queene* was written (and rewritten) to her supposed specifications. Ong regarded sixteenth-century England as a way station on the path from oral to written culture, and the proem to book 1, with its curious mingling of pen and voice—"mine afflicted stile, / The which to heare"—confirms this intuition. In other ways, too, *The Faerie Queene* might be said to constitute both an exemplary instance of Ong's thesis and a qualification of it: as reader, Elizabeth may have been a distant and largely imaginary presence for Spenser, but as queen, she was altogether too close and too real for comfort. Her interest in *The Faerie Queene* is a fantasy toward which the poem yearns, but also a contingency the poet struggles to accommodate, especially at the level of character and plot.

Such accommodations are most obvious and disruptive in its middle books, where the politically fraught theme of marriage comes to the fore and the narrative becomes, as David Miller says, "haunted by an anxiety about the act of address"—an anxiety that, I argue, occasions both the revision of the end of the 1590 version of the poem and the bizarre parsimony of Spenser's plotting in the six-book edition of 1596.[9] Indeed, reading the poem through Elizabeth's eyes, as Spenser repeatedly invites us to do, exposes a crucial exception to the rule—now commonplace among scholarly readers—that *The Faerie Queene*'s narrative plentitude is the ethical and formal antidote to allegorical stringency: when it comes to marriage, Spenser's allegory is far more generous and generative than his plot.[10] Behind the poet's seemingly perverse unwillingness to distribute the goods of marital satisfaction, I suggest, is a principled reckoning with the implications of his dedication, with the sharing of the text between author and royal reader. In the middle books of the 1596 *Faerie Queene*, in an odd inversion of the familiar tropes of poetry as husbandry and marriage as authorial propriety, making room for the interests of readers often means thwarting their desire for narrative closure, by keeping characters single. The necessity of this exchange is by no means obvious. On the face of it, writerly authority, readerly interest, and narrative progress are mutually reinforcing: the writer shapes his text, as Ong argues, to engage and sustain the attention of readers, and readers acknowledge the writer's authority—and the deftness of his plotting—by attending to him. But as a pair of poems written by Spenser in the interval between the first and second editions of *The Faerie Queene* reveal, when the reader in question is also the queen, readerly engagement has a potentially devastating effect on poets and their plots.

In 1595, a year before the six-book *Faerie Queene* appeared in print, William Ponsonby published two small volumes of occasional verse by Spenser. The first, *Colin Clouts Come Home Againe*, is a pastoral narrative written in 1591 and printed along with a collection of (rather belated) elegies for Philip Sidney. The title poem tells the story of Spenser's friendship with Sir Walter Raleigh and of their journey together from Ireland to England in 1589–90. While in London Spenser delivered the manuscript of the first three books of *The Faerie Queene* to Ponsonby, but thanks to Raleigh's influence at court, he also—as his pastoral alter ego Colin Clout reports to his fellow Irish swains—had the opportunity to present the poem in person to its royal dedicatee:

> The shepheard of the Ocean (quoth he)
> Vnto that Goddesse grace me first enhanced,
> And to mine oaten pipe enclin'd her eare,
> That she thenceforth therein gan take delight,
> And it desir'd at timely houres to heare,
> All were my notes but rude and roughly dight;
> For not by measure of her owne great mynd,

> And wondrous worth she mott my simple song,
> But ioyd that country shepheard ought could fynd
> Worth harkening to, emongst the learned throng.[11]

The scene presumably has some basis in historical fact, and Spenser's early biographers made much of the hints it contains about the poet's personal relationship to Elizabeth. But it is also clearly shaped by the pastoral conceit of the poem in which it appears: Raleigh appears as the "shepheard of the Ocean," Elizabeth as Cynthia (Raleigh's epithet for her in his own verse), and Spenser as a piping "country shepheard." Such transformations are conventional, but they have an important consequence for the scene of the poem's reception: reading (either silently or aloud) is refigured as listening, and attention is allowed to be intermittent and partial. A similar transformation occurs in the proem to book 1, in which the poet first invokes Elizabeth as "the argument of mine afflicted stile"—"stile" here meaning both "style" and "stylus," or pen—and then solicits her as an auditor: "The which to heare, vouchsafe, O dearest dred a while." In both cases, the refiguration of writing as song or speech and reading as listening slackens the expectation of undivided, uninterrupted attention: "Heare . . . a while," the poet invites the queen, and she responds in kind, desiring it "at timely houres to heare." Critics are accustomed to describing Spenser's presentation of *The Faerie Queene* in terms of the printed book, commanding in presence and monumental in ambition, but the glimpse we get of its presentation to Elizabeth reveal something looser and more open—a poem one might read in bits and pieces, as time permits, arriving at the end slowly or, perhaps, not at all.

The advantages of this lax dispensation for the reader of such a long and demanding poem are evident, but the advantages for the poet are harder to see. They begin to come clear if we turn to the second volume of Spenser's verse printed in 1595: *Amoretti and Epithalamium*, a collection of love poems written for Spenser's second wife, Elizabeth Boyle, whom he married in the summer of 1594. The *Amoretti*, a sonnet sequence, begins with a declaration that only one reader matters to the poet now: "Leaves, lines, and rhymes seek her to please alone, / Whom if ye please, I care for other none." Thirty-three poems in, however, the speaker explodes that fiction with a sonnet addressed to an entirely different (and hitherto unmentioned) audience, Spenser's friend, neighbor, and fellow poet Lodowick Bryskett. Moreover, *Amoretti* 33 reveals that another reader—indeed, another Elizabeth—has an equal or perhaps greater claim to the poet's devotion, and that while he labors over his sonnets to his beloved, *her* poem remains unfinished:

> Great wrong I doe, I can it not deny,
> to that most sacred Empresse my dear dred,

> not finishing her Queene of faery,
> that mote enlarge her liuing prayses dead:
> But lodwick, this of grace to me aread:
> doe ye not thinck th'accomplishment of it,
> sufficient worke for one mans simple head,
> all were it as the rest but rudely writ.
> How then should I without another wit:
> thinck euer to endure so taedious toyle,
> sins that this one is tost with troublous fit,
> of a proud loue, that doth my spirite spoyle.
> Ceasse then, till she vouchsafe to grawnt me rest,
> or lend you me another liuing brest.[12]

In some respects, the avid royal reader of *Amoretti* 33 is fashioned to flatter the poet's self-image no less than the gracious Cynthia of *Colin Clouts Come Home Againe*: the sonnet's implausible conceit is that the queen has not only read the entirety of the poem Spenser presented to her, but impatiently awaits its conclusion in the promised twelve-book form. But the poet responds to the fantasy of such readerly engagement with an outpouring of anxiety, guilt, and resentment—feelings he channels into comic exasperation with his evidently importunate friend Lodowick Bryskett. Although the poem begins by granting Elizabeth's entitlement to "th'accomplishment" of what the speaker terms "*her* Queene of faery," its tone grows rapidly more aggrieved, building in its final lines to a climax of exhausted patience: "Ceasse then, till she vouchsafe to grawnt me rest, / or lend you me another liuing brest." The pose of harassed genius, subject to his royal patron's whimsical demands and insatiable appetites at any and all hours, is at once self-deprecating and self-aggrandizing—and passive-aggressive to boot. The speaker knows full well that no other "brest" is capable of supplying his place as Elizabeth's poet, and by leaving the referent of the female pronoun suggestively vague, he implies that the queen ought to know it, too: in the amatory context of the *Amoretti*, "she" is Elizabeth Boyle, but the reference to *The Faerie Queene* as "taedious toyle" hints that "she" might just as well be Elizabeth Tudor. If *Colin Clouts Come Home Againe* uses the conventions of pastoral to fashion a setting in which the queen's imperfect or limited attention to Spenser's epic can be finessed, *Amoretti* 33 imagines the royal Elizabeth's interest in "her" poem as a tax on the poet's limited stock of energy and ingenuity.

Setting the two poems alongside each other casts the supposed desideratum of the queen's readerly interest, which the dedication to the 1590 *Faerie Queene* so vigorously solicits, in a far more equivocal light: as reader, it seems, Elizabeth is both dearest and dreaded, and imagining her attending to the poem only at intervals, with one ear or half a mind, may suit the poet better than envisioning her wholehearted, jealous embraces of his verse, her resentfulness at anything that delays or detracts from its completion. The difference between these two types of reader is captured in the two meanings of the word "partial": on the one hand piecemeal and on the other inequitable. In the years that Spenser wrote *Colin Clouts Come Home Againe* and the *Amoretti and Epithalamium*, he also wrote the second installment of *The Faerie Queene*—and transformed the poem from one in which partiality is invariably a shortcoming, both morally and aesthetically, to one in which it is occasionally a solution, a strategy for mediating between equally valid and otherwise incommensurable demands. In order to comprehend this transformation, and its consequences for the poem as a whole—which is to say, its consequential refashioning of the idea of the poem as a whole—it is necessary to do as Quilligan urges, and as Spenser does in *Amoretti* 33: to imaginatively inhabit the fiction of Elizabeth as reader of *The Faerie Queene*, a fiction that motivates and sustains, but also threatens, every other fiction in the poem.

The ultimate result of inhabiting this fiction, as I will show, is a radically altered, deliberately skewed perspective on the poem's interlinked economies of narrative and erotic satisfaction. But the more immediate—and perhaps equally important—effect is to countenance, and even to assign value to, a truth academic criticism of *The Faerie Queene* usually works to suppress: no one reads the poem all at once, and many readers never finish it. Even within the poem's most dedicated professional audience, as Jeff Dolven notes, our habits as readers are almost certainly less scrupulous than our scholarship suggests:

> Among the challenges of many romances, however—certainly the epic romances, with their multiple plots—is to the economies of the understanding. They are delightful, but often tediously delightful. We skip pages, paragraphs, stanzas. We get bored. We get up, do this or that. When we sit down (or lie down) again, the books prove hard, even impossible to remember. They solicit and even mimic the appetitive vagaries of real reading.[13]

Spenser surely anticipated this, and he may even have welcomed it; our experience of *The Faerie Queene* is fragmented by readerly accident and by poetic design. Indeed, what Dolven teasingly terms "real reading" surprisingly coincides with Spenser's depiction of his poem's reception by Elizabeth in *Colin Clouts Come Home Againe*, "at timely houres," and hints at a potential upside to the "economies of the understanding" that limit our ability to read the poem as we think we ought. It may be that partial reading—reading that takes the poem in pieces, allowing interest to wax and wane, or to trail off altogether—is precisely the kind of reading *The Faerie Queene* rewards or even cultivates as an antidote to the more perilous partiality of readerly absorption.

"Something is wrong": Marriage from the Margins

"Something is wrong," reads a handwritten note on book 3, canto 5, stanza 10 in the margins of C. S. Lewis's personal copy of *The Faerie Queene*, "for Florimell was already in flight (III.i.15) before Marinell fell." Lewis makes a similar note on book 4, canto 9, stanza 38: "Why does no one notice Amoret, who was with Arthur in stanzas 19 and 20? Something is wrong."[14] Lewis was a supremely attentive reader of *The Faerie Queene*, and the wrongness he notes at these two instances would seem to inhere in Spenser's (mis)management of the increasingly sprawling, intricately interlaced story lines of the Legends of Chastity and Friendship: the poet, usually so meticulous, simply loses track of his growing cast of virtuous heroines. In the first passage Lewis marks, Prince Arthur receives an eyewitness report that the beautiful maiden Florimell has just departed from Gloriana's court—but he (and we) saw her running into the woods much earlier, in canto 1 of book 3; in the second passage Amoret, who has been carefully guarded and guided by Britomart and Arthur himself through the first two-thirds of book 4, abruptly vanishes from the poem just when she is wanted most. Is Spenser literally losing the plot?

So Lewis seemed to worry—but the wrongness he registers might equally be attributed to a defect in his own reading of the poem's central books, which supply the material for what Colin Burrow describes as "the grand conclusion to *The Allegory of Love*, in which courtly love is banished by domestic affection."[15] Reacting against what he sees as the unwarranted abstraction and fey ethereality of Spenser's modern critics, Lewis argues that *The Faerie Queene* itself is wholeheartedly allied with the earthy "forces of life and health and fecundity": "The poem full of marriages," he declares, committed to the "actual fruition" of desire and "fresh and frank" in its celebration of conjugal pleasure.[16] The difficulty with that reading—a difficulty by which Lewis seems dimly, perhaps unconsciously, troubled in his marginal glosses—is that *The Faerie Queene* is not, in fact, "full of marriages"; rather, it is full of near marriages and near misses: betrothals whose consummation is repeatedly forestalled by the seeming forgetfulness of the poet and the proliferating distractions of his plot. Something is wrong, indeed.

At times, as in the two instances on which Lewis remarks, the poem's failure to arrive at its promised destination seems like the product of an accidental confusion: characters go astray, appearing in two places at once or nowhere at all. But elsewhere it manifests as a more willful resistance to narrative and erotic closure. Lewis, for instance, fails to mention two key facts about an episode he cites as proof of Spenser's commitment to the ideal of wedded bliss, "the rapturous reunion of Scudamore with Amoret" at the end of the Legend of Chastity. First, the episode appears only in the three-book edition of 1590; it is written out of the six-book edition of 1596, replaced by a far less conclusive ending. Second, and perhaps as important, even when the rapturous reunion does occur, at the close of the 1590 version of book 3, the reader's perspective on the scene is mediated through the not entirely benign interest of a third character, the nominal heroine of the Legend of Chastity. As Amoret and Scudamore melt in an ecstatic embrace, the female knight Britomart stands somewhat awkwardly to one side:

> Lightly he clipt her twixt his armes twaine,
> And streightly did embrace her body bright,
> Her body late the prison of sad paine,
> Now the sweet lodge of loue and deare delight:
> But she faire Lady ouercommen quight
> Of huge affection, did in pleasure melt,
> And in sweete ravishment pourd out her spright:
> No word they spake, nor earthly thing they felt,
> But like two senceles stocks in long embracement dwelt.
>
> Had ye them seene, ye would haue surely thought,
> That they had beene that faire Hermaphrodite,
> Which that rich Romane of white marble wrought,
> And in his costly Bath causd to bee site:
> So seemd those two, as growne together quite,
> That Britomart halfe enuying their blesse,
> Was much empassiond in her gentle sprite,
> And to herself ofte wisht like happinese,
> In vaine she wisht, that fate n'ould let her yet possesse. (3.12.45–46 [1590])[17]

As Donald Cheney first noted, the bizarre image of the marble hermaphrodite encapsulates *The Faerie Queene*'s pervasive ambivalence toward marriage, an event it treats simultaneously as miracle, mystery, and monstrosity.[18] Certainly the sight of warm bodies turned to "senceles stockes" seems to give Britomart pause: only "half enuying their blesse," her divided feelings hint at unarticulated doubts about her own marital future.

But Cheney—influenced, no doubt, by Lewis's reading of the poem—insists that such doubts accrue only to the representation or perception of marriage in *The Faerie Queene*, not to marriage itself: whatever unease Britomart (and the reader) may feel at the dehumanizing spectacle of Amoret and Scudamore's union merely testifies to the absolute character of its perfection. "The Hermaphrodite image serves to emphasize the limitations of our understanding of Amoret and Scudamore as lovers," he writes; "we, like Britomart, see them from outside and try to make what we can of the spectacle."[19] By this account, the marital embrace becomes a figure for the poem, and Britomart a stand-in for the puzzled and puzzling reader, whose best efforts at understanding are bound to fall short of the poet's supreme vision. More recent critics have tended to give greater weight to Britomart's inarticulated, half-felt reservations: once hailed as "the greatest marriage poet in English literature," Spenser is now recognized as a perceptive anatomist of heterosexual discontent, his erotic idylls marred by suggestions of coercion, humiliation, and self-loss.[20] Even as a purely allegorical figure of wholeness and completion, marriage has lost much of its luster, for in its premature foreclosure of narrative and hermeneutic possibility, it proves the bane of interesting characters and intelligent readers alike. From the perspective of feminist and queer readings of book 3, Spenser's refusal to marry Britomart to her beloved Artegall at the end of the Legend of Chastity is legible as "a gesture of liberation"—the affective complexity and indeterminacy of the "half enuying" figure permits a strategic evasion of the totalizing embrace of allegorical and narrative closure.[21]

But a more frustrated and frustrating reading of the 1590 conclusion of book 3 is also possible—one that accepts Lewis's judgment of the high value Spenser placed on the delights of heterosexual marriage without ignoring the perverse frequency with which he denies those pleasures to his deserving lovers. The union to which we and Britomart bear witness is, to be sure, a prefiguration of her promised happiness with Artegall, but her presence at the scene is also a reminder of all that book 3 (and the poem in its present, unfinished state) has failed to achieve, the many loose ends left untied by its meandering and multiplying plots. The division and redivision of readerly attention enforced throughout the poem, and especially in the Legend of Chastity, is enacted a final time in the splitting of its climactic image, as the narrator's perspective shifts from Amoret and Scudamore to Britomart. Aligning our view with Britomart's— "Had ye them seene"—the poem subjects the married lovers to a curious change of state, their liquid pleasure hardening into a stony carapace. The meaning of the image changes with this metamorphosis: from an emblem of undifferentiated wholeness—"those two . . . growne together quite"—marriage becomes instead a sign of exclusive and proprietary bliss, its boundaries marked by an emphatic distinction of possessive pronouns: "*their* blesse, which fate nould let *her* yet posesse."

Of course, the making of such invidious comparisons is precisely what the poem's allegorical nature would seem to rule out: to believe that Britomart is injured by the sacrifice of her erotic desires to those of Amoret and Scudamore is to forget that, as Lewis puts it in *The Allegory of Love*, "Britomart is married chastity"; any union of chaste lovers is her triumph. But such forgetfulness of the poem's larger allegorical aims—such unseemly partiality for the interests of one particular character over her virtuous counterparts—is precisely what the ending of the 1590 Legend of Chastity seems to require. "Half-envying" may afford us and Britomart only limited insight into the fullness of marital joy, but seeing marriage "from outside"—from the margins, as it were—also forces us, like Britomart, to recognize the inequity of that joy, the exclusions and negations on which its satisfactions are predicated. Indeed, to see Spenserian marriage only from inside, from the perspective of those who enjoy its exclusive rites—as a symbol, in Kathleen Williams's words, of "the necessary concord of opposites on which the world depends, and individual human welfare also"— is to miss half its meaning. Spenserian marriage secures the welfare of certain individuals at the direct expense of others, *The Faerie Queene*'s first reader and royal dedicatee chief among them.[22]

For as David Quint points out, the half-envious figure of Britomart at the end of the 1590 book 3 can be read as a sinister stand-in for the queen, who was so enraged to discover the secret marriage of Sir James Scudamore and Mary Shelton in 1574 that she beat the bride and broke her finger.[23] Throughout her reign, despite vigorously defending the privilege of determining her own marital affairs (in part by making an example of Hugh Singleton, printer of *The Shepheardes Calender*), Elizabeth claimed a political and personal interest in the matches made among her most prominent subjects.[24] By the time Spenser published the 1596 *Faerie Queene*, the poem's original co-dedicatee, Walter Raleigh, whose intervention had won Spenser his audience with the queen, had spent nearly a year in the Tower of London as punishment for *his* secret wedding to Elizabeth Throckmorton, a disastrous affair that Spenser turns into a major subplot of the poem's second half.[25] Spenser himself never achieved such perilous intimacy with the queen, but—perhaps for that very reason—the specter of her erotic jealousy haunts his poems, serving as a constant reminder of, and figure for, the costs of attracting her interest. To read *The Faerie Queene* as Spenser fantasized and feared Elizabeth would is thus to read its central figure partially: with limited comprehension and uncertain sympathy, through the eyes of those its privileged happiness necessarily excludes. The reading of the poem that emerges from this experiment is itself partial—that is, it foregrounds the poet's seemingly willful reluctance to finish what he starts, but it also takes sides, refusing to abide by the allegorical logic in which all virtuous characters are versions of each other. Partial reading identifies with characters as individual actors and feels their neglect as a slight.

The defects of such reading hardly need enumerating—by definition, partial reading is biased and imperfect—but it offers significant advantages, as well. To begin with, partial reading challenges a number of well-established assumptions about Spenser's poetry and the Protestant, protobourgeois institution of married love it has been understood to exemplify. The eighteenth- and nineteenth-century institution of marriage as an idealized foundation for individual autonomy—Habermas's "intimate domain," the "sphere of the family circle"—is too easily read back into Spenser's more ambivalent figurations of marital intimacy and exclusivity.[26] Britomart's half-envying presence at the end of the 1590 *Faerie Queene* testifies to a less settled moment in the history of private life, when privacy was legible not only as privilege but as the privation of a wider community. The resulting tension between desire and duty is the hallmark of Spenserian marriage: rather than naturalizing marriage as the originary and perfected form of human society, Spenser depicts it as a challenge to friendship, hospitality, and commonality—values that in turn are liable to force departures from its supreme but selfish bliss.

Such forced departures are in fact among the most familiar narrative devices in *The Faerie Queene*. Although we are accustomed to thinking of allegory as the primary constraint on—or even a violent repression of—the poem's otherwise boundless narrative energy, the generous unfolding of character and plot meets a still harder limit in the scarcity of its happy endings. In his groundbreaking study of the poem's narrative method, Paul Alpers insists that the abruptness with which the poem frequently diverts us from one romantic quest to another, although it "must seem clumsy if not meaningless" in fictional terms, serves a higher rhetorical purpose: however sad Redcrosse may be when he is called away from Una at the end of book 1, however frustrated Britomart at the end of book 3, we know that their experiences conform to the poet's "central concern—human experience seen under the aspect of man's relation to God."[27] Readers' feelings matter more than characters'. But the phrase "had ye them seene" seems precisely meant to align our feelings with Britomart's, and to draw our attention to the fundamental inequity of the poem's design. As a trope, marriage proves endlessly generative, but as a much longed-for narrative event, it embeds characters in an economy of lack, coercing them against the cooperative logic of allegory into repeated dramas of rivalry and disappointment.

Marriage has the same ambivalent charge when deployed as a figure for the poet's relationship to his verse. Spenser's career both begins and ends with poems that foreground the hurt feelings of those shut out of love's intimate embrace, adopting their frustration and resentment as metaphors of the recurring conflict between patron and client, poet and reader. *The Shepheardes Calender* (1579) presents Colin Clout as a besotted lover whose infatuation with the unseen Rosalind precludes all prior bonds, to friends, benefactors, and poetry itself. After his sullen debut in the "Januarie" eclogue, he disappears from the poem, "With drawen not onely from him, who moste loued him, but also from all former delightes and studies, aswell in pleasaunt pyping, as conning ryming and singing, and other his laudable exercises," as the Argument to the "Aprill" eclogue explains.[28] "Aprill" features Colin's crowning achievement, his ode to

Eliza, but in his absence the ode must be sung by his forlorn friend Hobbinoll—"him, who moste loued him." It's clear that Hobbinoll isn't the only one defrauded by Colin's singular passion for Rosalind: the exchange of vows at the center of the ode—"Shee is my goddesse plaine, / And I her shepherds Swayne" (ll. 97–98)—celebrates a bond of mutual obligation between Eliza and Colin that has already been breached, its bridal rhetoric ironized by our knowledge of the bridegroom's eventual defection. Spenser's last published poem, the *Prothalamion* of 1596, recasts the story of abandonment with the poet in the role of envious outsider: consumed by "sullein care," "discontent," and "expectation vayne," the poem's gloomy speaker finds beauty but little personal solace in the prospect of the aristocratic double wedding it ostensibly celebrates.[29] On the contrary, arriving at the steps of the "stately place" where the wedding is to occur, he succumbs to self-pity, observing that "oft I gayned giftes and goodly grace / Of that great Lord, which therein wont to dwell, / Whose want too well, now feeles my friendless case" (ll. 138–40). Indeed, the poem's key formal innovation, the invented genre of the "prothalamion," or prewedding song, is a reflection and accommodation of that friendless case: having no invitation to the wedding itself (according to the fiction of the poem, he merely "chaunce[s]" upon the brides on their way to the ceremony [l. 20]), the poet invents a place for himself on its periphery. The precariousness of that place is felt in every iteration of the poem's refrain: "Against the Brydale day, which is not long: / Sweet Themmes runne softly, till I end my song" (ll. 17–18). Driven in equal measure by anticipation ("against the Brydale day") and aggression ("against the Brydale day"), the *Prothalamion* heralds an event in whose joys the poet himself has no share.

The Shepheardes Calender and the *Prothalamion* bracket an oeuvre in which neither sexual propriety nor poetic authority are maintained without cost; both vows and verses are in perpetually short supply, and someone is always left wanting. Critics have noted the frequency with which Spenser's erotic idylls are disrupted by onlookers and intruders, but in doing so, they have tended to assume that the poet's sympathy belongs with his frustrated lovers and bashful brides, whose defensiveness reflects his own "dismay at the necessity of display or spectacle," his impulse to "wrest a fiction of privacy from the facts of book culture," and his longing for a "domain" of poetic autonomy.[30] But Spenser's notion of privacy—or, as he calls it, "privitie"—is more skeptical and evenhanded: as powerfully as he might sometimes feel the longing to retreat from public view into an exclusive inner world, he refuses to discount the interests of those that longing shuts out. From the clownish plaints of Hobbinoll to the disillusioned speaker of the *Prothalamion*, his poetry is keenly sensitive to the privations on which privacy depends; enjoyment never occurs apart from a more general sense of insufficiency. And even when Spenser does assert the right to husband his own creative powers—"Helpe me mine owne loves praises to resound," commands the bridegroom-poet of the *Epithalamion*—he cannot help tacking on an anxious appeal: "Ne let the same of any be enuide" (ll. 14–15). Rivalry and resentment are not the malign forces to which Spenserian marriage is opposed but the inevitable adjuncts of its exclusive bliss. Envy is the uninvited guest at every Spenserian wedding.

The atmosphere of unsatisfied need in which Spenser's consummations take place is related but not identical to what Frances Dolan terms the "marriage economy of scarcity": the fiction of one-flesh union, according to which "marriage only has room for one 'full person,'" and spouses assert their wills at each other's expense.[31] As Richard Mallette and Melissa Sanchez have shown, Spenser's depictions of married love share the anxieties of a larger Reformation culture that regarded all fallen sexuality with profound suspicion: as St. Paul sardonically observes, "It is better to marry than to burn."[32] The Reformed insistence on total depravity gave new force to Paul's equivocal endorsement, and, historical commonplaces about the "Puritan art of love" notwithstanding, sixteenth-century Protestants championed marriage not as a spotless ideal but as a necessary concession to the frailties of the flesh—"brydeling [its] corrupt inclinations ... within the limittes of honestie," as the official state sermon on matrimony in the Elizabethan *Tome of Homilies* declares.[33] As the bridal/bridle pun underscores, marriage merely restrained lust; it could not root it out. "[H]ere are all degrees to be monyshed, whether they be maryed, or vnmaryed, to loue chastitie, and clennes of lyfe," Thomas Cranmer cautioned the audience of a sermon titled "Against Whoredome and Vncleannesse": "For the maryed are bounde by the lawe of God, so purely to loue one an other, that neyther of them seke any straunge loue. The man muste onely cleue to hys wyfe, and the wyfe agayne onely to her husband: they muste so delighte one in an others companye, that none of them couit any other."[34] Given the difficulty of this endeavor, the risks and benefits of marriage could seem almost equally poised: "to him who bears these things in mind," Martin Luther confessed at the end of a 1519 sermon on the subject, "the desire of the flesh may well pass away, and perhaps he could just as well take on chastity [i.e., virginity] as the married state."[35]

Perhaps he—or she—could: Spenser's Knight of Chastity certainly seems to wonder. But given this emphasis on the spreading influence of lust and the binding power of marriage, Spenser's mistrust of marital *privacy* is idiosyncratic, even perverse. Precisely because the doctrine of original sin entailed such a dark view of sexuality, the hiddenness and exclusivity of married love were treated as unquestioned goods: what the *Tome of Homilies* calls the "limittes of honestie" were upheld by an elaborate social, legal, and physical architecture, sheltering sex from the stigma of publicity. In his writings against Pelagius,

Augustine traces the institution of marital privacy to the Garden of Eden, where the new-fallen Adam and Eve hid from the eyes of God:

> This, then, was the reason why the first human pair, on experiencing in the flesh that motion which was indecent because disobedient, and on feeling the shame of their nakedness, covered these offending members with fig-leaves; in order that, at the very least, by the will of the ashamed offenders, a veil might be thrown over that which was put into motion without the will of those who wished it: and since shame arose from what indecently pleased, decency might be attained by concealment.[36]

The same impulse of concealment continues to govern all licit sexuality, Augustine argues: "in all united pairs ever since, however well and lawfully they have used this evil, there has been a permanent necessity of avoiding the sight of man in any work of this kind."[37] In *City of God* he links this necessity to the two parts of the marriage rite, a public exchange of vows followed by a private consummation:

> But what of marital intercourse, the purpose of which, according to the marriage contract, is the procreation of children? This is lawful and honourable, indeed; but does it not still require a private chamber remote from witnesses? Before he even begins to caress the bride, does not the bridegroom first send away all the servants, and even his attendants and all the others who have been permitted to enter because of some tie of kinship? ... This right action desires recognition by the light of the mind, but it nonetheless shuns the light of the eye.[38]

In a less literal sense, too, as its Reformation defenders emphasized, marriage privatized sex by restricting its pleasures to husband and wife. "The whole basis and essence of marriage is that each gives himself or herself to the other, and they promise to remain faithful to each other and not give themselves to any other," Luther declared. "By binding themselves to each other, and surrendering themselves to each other, the way is barred to the body of anyone else, and they content themselves in the marriage bed with their one companion."[39] In the familiar words of the wedding rite in the Book of Common Prayer, marriage enjoins its participants to "keepe thee onely to" each other, "forsakyng all other."[40]

By repeatedly violating this fundamental decorum of marriage, its freedom from the interest and participation of others, Spenser's verse makes readers feel the force of the latter clause, the forsakenness to which marital possession is yoked. The privacy that marriage's orthodox defenders took for granted becomes, especially in the middle books of the 1596 *Faerie Queene*, a difficult and ethically dubious achievement, partial in both senses of the word. And it is this nervous accounting of gain and loss, as much as any vision of balance, wholeness, or hermaphroditic perfection, that motivates the Spenserian analogy between marriage and authorship, thwarted desire and readerly interest. Far from signaling the poet's blissful entitlement to the fruits of his imaginative labors, marriage constellates his anxieties about the disavowals on which sexual fidelity, narrative form, and poetic authority all depend.

Not Yet: *The Faerie Queene*'s Partial Marriage Plot

The word "yet" ("In vaine she wisht, that fate n'ould let her *yet* possesse") implies that the Knight of Chastity must simply learn patience, subduing her longing to the unhurried pace of Spenser's narrative: as the final line of the 1590 poem has it, "to morrow is an holy day" (3.12.47.9 [1590]). As critics have often remarked, *The Faerie Queene* relies on such deferrals as the motor of narrative continuity: avoiding consummation is the mechanism that makes room for more stanzas, more cantos, more books, more poem.[41] But such plenitude has a peculiar, almost hidden cost within the poem: the invidious interchange of gain and loss that structures the movement between its multiplying main plots. For rather than allowing its various lovers to arrive sequentially at their own versions of marital bliss, the expanded six-book poem of 1596 simply repeats the strategy of the truncated 1590 ending: it pairs up Britomart and Artegall by divorcing Amoret and Scudamore and then sends Artegall away in order to marry Florimell and Marinell. None of these yokings and unyokings are logically necessary—as C. S. Lewis notes in the margins of his text, Amoret's forced departure from book 4 is willfully abrupt—but they combine to create an atmosphere of necessity, in which to write one happy ending is necessarily not to write (or even, in the case of the ending of book 3, to unwrite) all others. From the outside looking in, the problem with Spenserian marriage isn't that it condemns its participants to daemonic fixity, but that it abandons everyone else to perpetual irresolution. As the poem's exclusive figure of resolution, marriage transforms allegorical allies into rivals for a store of strictly limited narrative goods: the ministrations of Spenser's narrator and the attention and interest of his reader.

Such consummations as do occur bring this sublimated rivalry to the fore, making it visible to readers and—more strangely—to the characters themselves. In other words: the peculiar thing about the ending of the 1590 poem isn't simply that Britomart only *half* envies Amoret and Scudamore; it's that she half *envies* them. In the pageant of sins at Lucifera's court in book 1 of the poem, Envy stands out as a singularly malignant type, a ravenous, cankered creature who reckons all virtue, pleasure, and beauty as an injury to himself: "So euery good to bad he doth abuse" (1.4.32.1–8). Spenser identifies Envy as particularly inimical to poetic creativity—"And eke the verse of famous Poets witt / He does backebite, and spightfull poison spues, / From leprous mouth on all, that ever writ" (1.4.32.6–8)—an ominous suggestion that is spectacularly fulfilled in the conclusion to the 1596 *Faerie Queene*, when the envious, backbiting Blatant Beast leaps from the allegorical frame to ravage the very poem we are in the process of reading. Compared to the Blatant Beast, Britomart's half-envying gaze is a partial threat indeed, but it nonetheless destabilizes the poem's delicate equilibrium of allegory and plot, which is poised on the cooperation between the various champions of virtue. For as Britomart seems to recognize, the meaning of marital "blesse" has been parceled out with striking inequity: what is bliss and blessing to Amoret and Scudamore is available to her only as the still rankling wound of desire.

Allegorically speaking, this ought not to be a problem. As the "Letter to Raleigh" appended to the 1590 version of *The Faerie Queene* explains, all of the poem's exemplars of virtue are one, summed up in the person of Arthur, whose "magnificence is the perfection of all the rest, and conteineth in it them all."[42] All virtuous desire is one, and all blessings are shared. But within the imaginary world of the poem, characters themselves have only a dim and intermittent awareness of their interrelation: their common virtue makes them likely to cooperate, but they are also frequently in competition—for love, for glory, and, above all, for the attention of narrator and reader. Romance may be a fundamentally expansive and digressive mode, but Spenserian romance treats its expansions and digressions as subtractions from a finite sum of authorial and readerly attention: to tell one story is to leave another languishing in suspense. In this sense, the fiction of the poem is far less generous than its allegorical frame: there is always room for another pair of virtuous lovers, but only one couple can enjoy their virtue's reward. This tension between allegorical elasticity and narrative constraint mars the otherwise joyous conclusion to book 1, as the Redcrosse Knight is forced to sacrifice his relationship with Una to his obligations to Gloriana. As female avatars of virtue, Una and Gloriana are versions of one another, but they function here as rivals; conscious of his vow "Vnto his Faery Queene backe to retourne," Redcrosse cuts short the engagement festivities, postpones the wedding, "and Vna left to mourne" (1.12.41.8–9). It is a pattern repeated everywhere in the poem: fidelity to one beloved, or one narrative thread, invariably requires the abandonment of another.

The Legend of Chastity heightens this tension considerably, first by multiplying the available exemplars of its title virtue and then by treating the objects of their virtuous desire as incommensurate. At the center of the book is the Garden of Adonis, where "all plenty and all pleasure flowes . . . without fell rancor, or fond gealousy," where "franckly each Paramor his leman knows . . . ne any does enuy" (3.6.41.4–8). A similar sense of abundance characterizes book 3's allegorical economy. The proem to book 3 speaks directly to Elizabeth as reader, inviting the queen "in mirrours more than one her selfe to see": "either Gloriana let her chuse, / Or in Belphoebe fashioned to bee" (3.proem.5.6–8). And those options hardly exhaust the possibilities: not only Gloriana and Belphoebe but Britomart, Amoret, and a handful of lesser characters share the task of embodying chastity's multiple forms. The Legend of Chastity thus offers readers a striking range of interpretive options, and the proliferation of benign doubles, twins, and surrogates for the Knight of Chastity makes confusion both inevitable and seemingly innocent: if, in our first reading of canto 7, we assume—as we are virtually certain to do—that the "bold knight" who enters at stanza 37 and is revealed in stanza 52 as a "faire virgin" in disguise must be Britomart, the discovery that in fact she is Palladine, a character who has never been mentioned before and is never mentioned again, has no ramifications for our ability to recognize and understand chastity. On the contrary, Palladine's brief appearance in the poem (underscored, a few stanzas later, by the equally fleeting depiction of the anonymous "Damzell . . . of low degree" [7.59.1]) seems intended precisely to emphasize chastity's transcendence of rivalry, its easy inhabitation of multiple, noncompeting guises. Chastity does not refuse all distinctions—both Palladine and the Damsel of low degree are described as singularly excellent, the former "in deedes of armes" (6.52.4) and the latter in her capacity to resist the advances of the lascivious Squire of Dames—but the singularity of its exemplars is understood to amplify, not imperil, the virtues of their fellows. Thus the narrator can hail Amoret as "th'ensample of true loue alone" (6.52.4) even as he asks us "of faire Britomart ensample take, / That was as trew in loue, as Turtle to her make" (11.2.8–9). Paradoxically, that is, the virtue defined by singlehearted attachment—"trew . . . as Turtle to her make"—can be embraced in multiple guises: both/and, not either/or.

There are, however, exceptions to this generous rule; the most conspicuous of them streaks across the landscape of book 3 in its opening canto, pursued by a "grisly foster" (3.1.17.2). Catching sight of the gorgeous Florimell, Arthur and Guyon promptly abandon their new friend Britomart to join the chase, spurred by "great enuy and fell gealousy" (18.2). Envy and jealousy are odd motives for the champions of magnificence and temperance, but as the narrator explains, Florimell's beauty is not the sort of good that can be shared: "They stayd not to avise who first should bee, / But all spurd after fast, as they mote fly / . . . in hope to win therby / Most goodly meede, the fairest Dame aliue" (18.6–8). The fact that Arthur's virtue includes and perfects his own doesn't make Guyon run any less hastily.

Florimell functions throughout book 3 as a victim of both erotic obsession and narrative neglect. Her beauty makes her an object of continual pursuit, but the poet himself is repeatedly forced to abandon her in order to attend to other characters. "Yt yrkes me, leaue thee in this wofull state, / To tell of Satyrane, where I him left of late" (3.8.43.8–9), protests the narrator to Florimell when he concludes her story at the end of canto 8. Such defensive maneuvers turn plotting from a necessary and uncontroversial authorial function to a fraught assertion of power: "This gentle damsel, whom I write vpon," as the narrator calls Florimell. The contradictory double plot the poem invents for Florimell is perhaps an attempt to evade this burden of authorial imposition, or to allow Florimell herself to evade its consequences. Gordon Teskey describes the sudden apparition of Florimell in flight as a "moment" in *The Faerie Queene*—a static image of beauty that is somehow simultaneously a surge of narrative energy, a propulsive motive force—and it is true that her position in the poem has a Heisenbergian quality of uncertainty: in cantos 1–4 she is presented as on the run long before Britomart wounds Marinell, but in canto 5 Arthur is told by Florimell's dwarf that she only left court after hearing of Marinell's defeat.[43] "Something is wrong," as Lewis notes in the margin of canto 5. But that wrongness may be a calculated effect: when Arthur, giving voice to our own confusion, asks the dwarf to clarify Florimell's predicament—"But can ye read Sir, how I may her finde, or where?" (3.5.6.9)—the dwarf's response suggests that reading in such terms may not be the point. Instead of resolving the contradiction, he urges Arthur simply to act: "Or succor her, or me direct the way, / Do one or other good, I you most humbly pray" (3.5.10.8–9). Unlike so many of the choices in *The Faerie Queene*, this one seems to have no moral stakes: "one, or other" option is equally "good."

But the poem finds it impossible to sustain that open-ended sense of virtuous multiplicity. Marriage coerces all plots into conformity and thus into competition: one *or* other good. The rivalrous tensions Florimell inspires and to which she is subjected are given concrete form in the hag's creation of "another Florimell, in shape and looke / So liuely and so like, that many it mistooke," and "euen Nature's selfe enuide the same, / And grudged to see the counterfeit should shame / The thing it selfe" (8.5.4–6, 8–9). As a "wondrous worke" (8.5.2) that inspires female flesh with a male spirit, the false Florimell is also an uncanny double for the marriage with which the 1590 poem concludes: the description of the hag's son "fast her clipping twixt his armes twayne" (8.10.1) exactly anticipates Scudamore's embrace of Amoret upon her release from the palace of Busyrane, when "lightly he clipt her twixt his armes twaine" (12.45.1 [1590]), and the hermaphroditic automaton has a shadowy afterimage in the spectacle of Amoret and Scudamore "growne together quite," no longer man and woman but "two senceless stocks" (12.45.9, 46.5). The resemblance is more than incidental. In the absolute singularity of her beauty—a quality that, unlike virtue, is subject to the Hag's logic of envy, grudge, and shame—Florimell poses a challenge to the poem's cooperative allegorical ideal akin to the challenge posed in its concluding stanzas by marriage itself, the "happinesse" that "fate"—a convenient alibi for the poem's author—refuses to share between his chaste heroines.

"Drowning in privitie": Marriage at the House of Malbecco

Spenser's parsimonious plotting upends the Christian case for marriage, turning privacy, its saving grace, into a near-occasion of sin. For Augustine and his heirs, marital privacy is the necessary antidote to the shameful consciousness of sin that afflicts fallen human sexuality. But in *The Faerie Queene*, the fundamental exclusivity of the marriage bond aligns it with a different and equally dangerous species of sin—crimes of possession and dispossession, envy and jealousy, hoarding and theft. Perhaps this is why the narrator insists that witnessing the marriage of Amoret and Scudamore would make us think of a "rich Romane," whose "costly Bath" is an arena of purely private pleasures: in treating marriage as a private commodity, the wealthy collector may miss its significance to Amoret and Scudamore, but he exactly captures its significance to Britomart. The 1596 poem offers a similar analogy for the wedding of Marinell and Florimell, inviting us to imagine the married lovers "Spending their ioyous dayes and gladfull nights, / And taking vsurie of time forepast" (5.3.40.2–3): "spending" is fairly innocuous, but "vsurie" makes Marinell and Florimell the beneficiaries of a narrative economy that has lent time and attention to the poem's lovers at vastly unequal rates. Above all, the persistent identification of marriage with the imbalance between allegorical plenitude and narrative constraint may help to explain why *The Faerie Queene*'s only extended description of married life takes place in the house of the miser Malbecco.

When we first arrive at Malbecco's castle in canto 9 of book 3—just after Florimell has been abandoned to Proteus—the narrator hints that the danger lurking within its walls is the familiar evil of lust. Apologizing theatrically for sullying his Legend of Chastity with the story of "a wanton Lady . . . Which with her loose incontinence doth blend / The shyning glory of your soueraigne light" (3.9.1.6–8), he begs readers not to take offense at the spectacular unchastity of Malbecco's wife Hellenore. But there is little danger we would: over the course of her transformation from wedded wife to gleeful nymphomaniac, Hellenore's "loose incontinence" functions as a purely comic device. In retrospect, the narrator's anxiety about her influence on his poem is a feint, for the truly threatening character here is her husband:

> a cancred crabbed Carle . . . ,
> That has no skill of Court nor courtesie,
> Ne cares, what men say of him ill or well;

> For all his dayes he drownes in priuitie,
> Yet has full large to liue, and spend at libertie.
>
> But all his mind is set on mucky pelfe,
> To hoord vp heapes of euill gotten masse,
> For which he others wrongs, and wreckes himself.... (3.5–4.3)

Because "he is old, and withered like hay, / Vnfit faire Ladies seruice to supply" (5.1–2), Malbecco redirects his thwarted passion to the brideling, binding, and barring of others' desires:

> The priuie guilt whereof makes him alway
> Suspect her truth, and keepe continuall spy
> Vpon her with his other blincked eye;
> Ne suffreth he resort of liuing wight
> Approch to her, ne keepe her company,
> But in close bowre her mewes from all mens sight,
> Depriu'd of kindly ioy and naturall delight. (5.3–9)

As the narrator makes plain, Malbecco's failings have literally nothing to do with sex: his jealous suspicion and insistence on "privitie" are "far vnlike conditions" (4.7) to his wife's expansive appetites—and, by the story's grim conclusion, prove much graver evils.

By making Malbecco an impotent miser, free from the rebellions of the flesh but in thrall to the rhetoric of exclusive possession, Spenser mounts an attack on the very edifice erected by Augustine and his heirs as a defense against sexual sin—which is to say, on marriage itself. The narrator's characterization of Malbecco as "drown[ing] in privitie" crucially elides the distinction between several species of possessiveness: the legitimate proprieties of marriage, the unnatural refusal of hospitality, and the cardinal sin of avarice, all of which are subsumed in his "priuie guilt" (5.3), his "haynous sin" (9.7), or, as Satyrane terms it, his "mesprise" (9.9.6). As Spenser's ambiguous syntax in stanza 5 implies, it isn't simply Hellenore but all "living wight[s]" who are impaired by his possessiveness, "depriu'd of kindly joy and natural delight." This conflation of uxoriousness and inhumanity legitimates a shocking degree of aggression against Malbecco. When he refuses entry to the band of knights assembled outside his castle at the start of canto 9, Paridell reacts with what seems like disproportionate rage, proposing to "ransacke all, and him selfe kill" (8.9), but even-tempered Satyrane objects only on practical grounds: "Nay let us first ... entreat / The man by gentle meanes, to let vs in, / And afterwards affray with cruell threat, / Ere that we to efforce it do begin: / Then if all fayle, we will by force it win" (9.1–5). Far from dispelling the general sense of grievance, Britomart's arrival on the scene—in the midst of a sudden, fierce downpour—intensifies it. When Satyrane and Paridell decline to make room for the Knight of Chastity in the shed where they have sought shelter, she responds by nearly killing Paridell; Satyrane persuades her to redirect her vengeful ire to its proper object, "their commune foe" Malbecco (17.8). Ultimately, every one of the seemingly hyperbolic threats bandied about by the irate knights—to "ransack all" (8.9), "flame the gates" (18.2), leaving Malbecco "fowle death to die, or wrap in grieuous woe" (17.9)—is meted out by the plot. Strictly speaking, this is envy at its worst—sad at a neighbor's good and rejoicing in his harm—but weighed against Malbecco's "priuie guilt," it is a variety of envy the poem is willing to indulge. In its pathological grasping, jealousy begets envy as its inevitable, even justifiable counterpart: "dew vengeaunce for his hire" (17.8–9).

The poem's harsh treatment of Malbecco marks a fundamental difference between the modern notion of privacy as an individual right and the sixteenth-century sense of it as an incursion on the common good. Although Elizabethan England has been claimed by social historians as the birthplace of modern privacy, studies of property law, city planning, and domestic space in sixteenth-century London have shown that the boundaries between persons, places, families, and communities remained literally and conceptually porous, and that attempts to shore them up were often met with principled resistance.[44] As Patricia Fumerton demonstrates, even where privacy was understood to exist—in certain parts of the home or city—its effects were unevenly distributed, secured as privilege by some and imposed as privation on others.[45] Consequently, civic officials and ordinary individuals alike regarded the concept of private property with what Lena Orlin terms "an uneasy mixture of desire and distrust."[46]

That distrust was given full voice by Spenser's schoolmaster, Richard Mulcaster. Dismayed by the aristocratic tendency to prefer personal tutors to communal schoolrooms, Mulcaster argues in his influential treatises on pedagogy that the advantages of all forms of privacy must be tallied against their cost to the community at large:

> [T]he verie name [of private] in nature is enemy to publike, as inclosure is to common, and as swelling to much ouerlayeth the common, not onely in *education*, where it both corrupteth by planting to priuate habit, and is corrupted it selfe by a degenerate forme, but also in most thinges else.... Bycause naturally *priuate* is sworne enemy to *publike* in all euentes, ... though *publike* still pretend friendship to [it], as it is plainely seene when the *publike* care doth helpe ech *priuate*, & by cherishing the singuler maintaineth the generall, whereas the priuate letteth the publike drowne, so it selfe may flete aboue.... [T]he one in nature [is] a rowmy *pallace* full of most varietie to content the minde, the other a close *prison*, tedious to be tied to, where

the sense is shakled: the one in her kinde, a *libertie*, a broade *feild*, an open *aire*, the other in the contrarie kinde, a *pinfold*, a *cage*, a *cloister*.

"[T]here can be no worse name than priuate," he concludes, "sauing where the publike doth appoint it."[47] It's possible to discern in Mulcaster's vehemently mixed metaphors the lineaments of the story of Malbecco and Hellenore: degeneracy and drowning, the close prison and the open air, the pretended friend and the common foe. As Paridell and Satyrane see it, Malbecco's attempt to privatize sexual desire is the very worst of his offenses against human nature, and the poem does nothing to distance itself from this view. On the contrary: in our final glimpse of Hellenore, she enjoys the ministrations of an impressively virile satyr and the narrator more or less wishes her well, while Malbecco, consumed by grief and rage at the loss of both his wife and his wealth, "Is woxen so deform'd that he has quight / Forgot he was a man, and Gelosy is hight" (3.10.60.8–9).

This unusually direct application of allegorical logic encourages us to forget Malbecco's humanity as well. Divorced from the poem's human landscape, he dissolves into abstraction, "hagridden out of the poem by his own latent capacity for allegoricalness," as James Nohrnberg writes.[48] Indeed, no sooner is his transformation complete than the narrator denies him altogether: "O let him far be banished away, . . . And of faire Britomart ensample take, / That was in trew in loue as Turtle to her make" (11.2.1, 8–9). Malbecco's emphatically conclusive end satisfies a narrative desire Spenser often leaves unmet, most conspicuously in the two endings to book 3: to know how a story ends for everyone involved. Harry Berger suggests that the narrator's discarding of Malbecco is both an act of "literary wish-fulfillment"—if only the real evil of jealousy could be so neatly isolated and cast off—and part of a "process of condensation" that Spenser at one point intended to apply to all of his poem's lovers, virtuous and vicious alike: in the end the partial and imperfect versions of love figured in Paridell and Hellenore, Florimell and Marinell, Amoret and Scudamore, Timias and Belphoebe, and all the rest would be "discarded and introjected in Artegall and Britomart," whose consummation would include all others.[49] But that isn't the poem Spenser writes. Instead, *The Faerie Queene* in both its 1590 and 1596 versions either defers marital consummation or treats it as an irreplicable singularity, its exclusive nature definitively at odds with the characters' common allegorical functions. When it comes to marriage, Malbecco's miserliness prevails.

Jeff Dolven counters Berger's reading of the poem as evolving to ever higher, more complex, and better organized forms with an account of its constant unmaking of itself, fleeing in panic from its own unresolvable contradictions.[50] For him Malbecco is not a solution to the poem's uncertainties but their agonized embodiment: he "ran away, ran with himself away" (3.10.54.6). We can be precise, I think, about the particular contradiction Malbecco embodies: like Florimell, also suspended in flight from herself, Malbecco turns the poem against itself by laying bare the antagonism between chastity and friendship. In his classic reading of books 3 and 4, Thomas Roche identifies friendship as the intimacy toward which chastity is ordered in and by marriage, but as Lauren Silberman argues, the Legend of Friendship replaces the metaphor of desire as quest with the metaphor of desire as competition: the opposite of losing is no longer finding but winning.[51] Here, too, Malbecco's influence on the poem is unmistakable: from the perspective of the happily married couple, Roche's conciliation of chaste desire and friendly cooperation works, but for those outside of the marital dyad, chastity is maintained at the direct expense of friendship. Orlin identifies this as the central paradox of "companionate marriage": its valuation of spousal relations to the detriment of all other forms of social obligation and attachment.[52] The exclusive intimacy of marriage sacrifices community, friendship, and even kinship on the altar of privacy: as Augustine writes, "the very children that may happen to be born of the process" are as strangers to marriage's central act.[53] It is for this reason, John R. Gillis has argued, that Renaissance wedding ceremonies were such raucous, even violent, affairs, for every marriage was also a divorce from the larger community: a wedding was a "strenuous, often conflicted, social, psychological, and economic process."[54] And no wonder: the guests, as Orlin notes, invariably included "men who here lost the groom to a relationship preeminent to their former friendship as well as men for whom the bride had until then represented [a] potential mate."[55]

The Legend of Friendship begins with an extravagant outburst of all that repressed frustration at the wedding of Amoret and Scudamore:

> For that same vile Enchantour Busyran,
> The very selfe same day that she was wedded,
> Amidst the bridale feast, whilest euery man
> Surcharged with wine, were heedlesse and ill hedded
> All bent to mirth before the bride was bedded,
> Brought in that mask of loue which late was showen:
> And there the Ladie ill of friends bestedded,
> By way of sport, as oft in maskes is knowen,
> Conueyed quite away to liuing wight vnknowen. (4.1.3)

This reconstruction of events transforms the sexual psychodrama of book 3 ("that mask of loue which late was showen") into a scene of social dysfunction: "the Ladie ill of friends bestedded." The implication is that Amoret's friends were too drunk to mount an adequate defense, but the line leaves open the possibility that it is precisely her friends (or Scudamore's) from whom she needed to be defended. Book 4 is full of friendships tested by the privative nature of erotic possession. The only remedy it ever invents for the rivalry between friends over marriage's exclusive rites is to multiply the available number of brides—and that solution only works for minor characters: Cambell and Triamond, Amyas and Placidas. Major couples like Amoret and Scudamore, Britomart and Artegall, and Florimell and Marinell are simply forced to take their pleasures in turn.

The dinner Spenser stages at the house of Malbecco and Hellenore is, on the one hand, another fantasy of resentment unleashed against the privative structure of marriage: a meal grudgingly served up by a jealous husband to guests who reciprocate by seducing his wife and burning down his house. But it also allows Spenser to envision a more subtle means of evading the invidious logic of privacy, by countering it with a virtue he names "courtesy." Courtesy, we are repeatedly told, is a quality alien to Malbecco: he "has no skill of Court nor courtesye" (3.9.3.6); he neglects "gentle courtesyes" in seeking to constrain his wayward wife (7.7); it is his want of "courtesie" for which Britomart accuses him (12.9); and it is in the name of "courtesy" that she and her fellow knights abjure him (25.7). Indeed, the most obvious reason the poem deals more gently with Hellenore than with her husband is because she "shewd her selfe in all a gentle courteous Dame" (26.9). Of course, only in the most cynical and debased sense is it possible to read Hellenore's interactions with Paridell as expressions of courtesy: the secret courtship in which they indulge—their "close messages," "close embassage," and "close signs" (3.9.27.9, 28.2, 31.5)—are more like a parodic double of Malbecco's close-handedness, their "priuy lust" (28.9) the inevitable answer to his "priuie guilt" (5.3). But there is a truer sort of courtesy in the poem's description of her life among the satyrs, where she "milk[s] their gotes, and make[s] them cheese and bredd, / And every one as commune good her handled" (3.10.36.8–9).

Paridell's dinner-table exchange with Britomart demonstrates this same unpretentious virtue, a kind of cheerful openness to the incursions of others. His comically abbreviated retelling of Homer's *Iliad* is, at first, a virtuosic performance of self-absorption, concluding with "I Paridell," who "My natiue soile haue lefte, my dayes to spend / In seewing deeds of armes, my liues and labors end" (37.6–9). Then Britomart cuts in, identifying herself as a "partner of your pain," and asking Paridell gently—"if it should not grieue you"—"backe agayne / To turne your course" (40.2, 5–6) and tell the story *she'd* like to hear, of her own Trojan forebear Aeneas. With unexpected gentility, Paridell obliges her, but, as befits his character, his version of the Virgilian epic becomes a cautionary tale about the discontents of what he calls "wedlock": "constrain'd / To contract wedlock . . . / Wedlocke contract in blood, and eke in blood /

Accomplished, that many deare complaind," Paridell's Aeneas "through the flood / Escaped hardly, hardly praised his wedlock good" (9.42.3–9). When Britomart breaks into the story yet again, eager to drive the narrative to what is, for her, its essential climax, the founding of Troynovant on the banks of the Thames by "the Troian *Brute*" (46.1), the otherwise solipsistic youth is once again gracious about the interruption:

> Ah fairest Lady knight, (said Paridell)
> Pardon I pray my heedlesse ouersight,
> Who had forgot, that whylome I heard tell
> From aged Mnemon; for my wits been light.
> Indeed he said (if I remember right,)
> That of the antique Troian stocke, there grew
> Another plant, that raught to wondrous hight,
> And far abroad his mightie braunches threw,
> Vnto the utmost Angle of the world he knew. (47.1–9)

Paridell's courtesy in allowing Britomart to insert herself into his story, his willingness to "greet [her] well" as "countrey kin," begging her "pardon for the strife, which late befell / Betwixt vs both vnknowne" (51.6–9), is a homely model for the replacement of rivalry and rape with a less violent mode of affiliation with others. In direct contrast to the bloody contract of wedlock, courtesy makes room for others, unto the utmost angle of the world.

Such courtesy is very different than—even opposed to—the virtue that presides over book 6 of the poem, which Nohrnberg defines as "respect accorded to another person's determination upon inward possession" and Michael Schoenfeldt as the capacity "to cross social boundaries without threatening them."[56] No one respects inward possession more than Malbecco, and no one cares less for the preservation of boundaries, material or social, than Paridell. Like Hellenore, Paridell is a character whose flaunting of the apparent rules of virtue the poem sanctions by refusing to take seriously; even in the Legend of Chastity, his appetite for women is a joke. But that is perhaps the point: Paridell's name doesn't just affiliate him with his notorious ancestor, Paris; it also identifies him with a self-consciously minor literary mode, to which Spenser assigns a major ethical function. The etymology of parody—*par-odia* means "side song"—identifies it with the good-humored openness, the willingness to be diverted, that defines courtesy in book 3. It's this same willingness to be diverted that prevails over Britomart's single-mindedness in the final cantos of book 3, when she abandons her search for Artegall in order to assist Scudamore, "a stranger knight" (3.11.13.3), in his quest. Speaking "courtesly" (13.9) to the unknown man, she volunteers her services, urging him to "freely read" the cause of his distress: "Perhaps this hand may helpe to ease your woe, / And wreake your sorrow on your cruell foe" (3.11.4–5). This is as close as Britomart gets in the Legend of Chastity to a plighting of her troth, and the amazed Scudamore recognizes the sacrifice it entails, asking, "what couldst thou more, / If shee were thine, and thou as now I am" (19.3–4)? That is a question that challenges everything we, and Britomart, think we know about chastity, about the absolute singularity and exclusivity of the bond between chaste lovers. Her willingness to embrace such a promiscuous mingling of identities and attachments is a virtue she learns at the house of Malbecco; it makes her the hero of book 3, even as it turns her into a side character in her own Legend.

"Goodly enlarged": Open Marriage, Partial Reading

As an alternative to privacy, the courtesy exemplified by Paridell and Britomart in book 3 accommodates competing demands of exclusivity by refusing to distinguish between persons and properties, sacrificing propriety to what Scudamore calls "magnanimity" (3.11.19.2). In its most rarified form, magnanimity makes it possible to find value—even increase—in concession, as Colin's ambiguous moralizing of the Graces' dance on Mount Acidale suggests: "That good should from vs goe, then come in greater store" (6.10.24.9). On the face of it, the *Epithalamion* Spenser writes to commemorate his own marriage to Elizabeth Boyle in 1594 is an unlikely place to look for such magnanimous concessions. It begins with a striking assertion of authorial and marital privilege, as the bridegroom-poet bids the muses "which have oftentimes / Been to me ayding, others to adorne," to "lay ... aside" such songs and "helpe me mine owne loves prayses to resound" (ll. 1–2, 12, 14). But the speaker displays notable unease about this proprietary gesture: no sooner has he staked his claim to the poem than he anticipates challenges to it, declaring, "Ne let the same of any be envide: / So Orpheus did for his owne bride, / So I unto my selfe alone will singe, / The woods shall to me answer and my Eccho ring" (ll. 15–18). Orpheus, who loses his bride twice over, is an unsettling reference point for a marriage hymn: as Richard Neuse observes, "The poem is born of a sense of privation."[57]

And it ends with one, as well: the enigmatic final stanza addresses the poem as a "Song made in lieu of many ornaments, / With which my loue should duly haue been dect, / Which cutting off through hasty accidents, / Ye would not stay your dew time to expect" (ll. 427–30). The *Epithalamion* must serve as "recompens" (l. 431) for the very ornaments displaced by its untimely arrival— and here it is hard not to recall Orpheus again, his marital bliss cut off by the hasty accident of his own backward glance. Like Neuse, Thomas Greene is struck by the *Epithalamion*'s fearful undercurrents, describing it as "menaced by ... the threat of disaster, the irrational fear of vaguely specified suffering [that] hovers faintly over the poem."[58] By situating Spenser's poem in the long classical tradition of epithalamia, Greene's essay reminds readers of one highly specific motive for that anxiety. As George Puttenham writes in his 1589 *Arte of English Poesie*, the epithalamion was a poem written by "Ciuill Poet[s]," obligated "in conscience and credit" to mark "the chearful day of mariages aswell Princely as others."[59] The epithalamion is, as Puttenham emphasizes, a fully social genre, offered as a wedding gift by civic-minded poets to their patrons (or to those they hoped would become patrons) and shared with all the guests at a wedding. Writing an epithalamion for one's "self alone" is an audacious, even oxymoronic, reworking of the generic convention.

Far from downplaying the risks of that formal innovation, Spenser incorporates them into the progress of his poem. In stanza 21, just as the bridegroom settles into bed to enjoy marriage's most private bliss, a face appears at the window:

> Who is the same, which at my window peepes?
> Or whose is that faire face, that shines so bright?
> Is it not Cinthia, she that neuer sleepes,
> But walkes about high heauen al the night?

The apparition could hardly be less auspicious. Cynthia, after all, is Walter Raleigh's name for the queen, and the appearance of his Elizabeth at the threshold of Spenser's marital bedchamber restages the whole sad—and, in 1595, dangerously recent—drama of secret embraces and furious discovery on which Raleigh's courtly career foundered. Cynthia is the jealous Virgin Queen whose sleepless eye surveys her subjects, prepared to assert her inalienable right to any bridegroom's—or poet's—exclusive favors. At its climactic moment, the circles inscribed by the *Epithalamion*'s ringing, echoing refrains tighten into a noose: shame your bride or lose favor with your queen.

But Spenser's bridegroom-poet suggests a shocking alternative. Rather than decorously drawing the curtains till morning, he greets the moon with a story, and a proposition:

> O fayrest goddesse, do thou not envy
> My love with me to spy:
> For thou likewise didst love, though now unthought,
> And for a fleece of woll, which privily,
> The Latmian shephard once unto thee brought,
> His pleasures with thee wrought.
> Therefore to us be favorable now;
> And sith of wemens labours thou hast charge,
> And generation goodly dost enlarge,

Encline thy will t'effect our wishfull vow,
And the chast wombe informe with timely seed,
That may our comfort breed:
Till which we cease our hopefull hap to sing,
Ne let the woods us answere, nor our Eccho ring. (ll. 372–89)

The first half of the stanza reverses the hierarchy of shame, subjecting Cynthia to a reciprocal violation of privacy by recounting the now forgotten story of her secret affair with Endymion. The residue of that affair is both a possession and a privation: it is that "fleece of woll" brought "privily"—but, apparently, not privily enough—to Cynthia, the tell-tale sign of her own imperfect self-possession. It testifies to what Belphoebe, in a parallel moment of courteous indecorum in book 3 of *The Faerie Queene*, calls the "commun bond of frailtee." Explaining to the wounded Timias why she has brought him, a strange man, into the sanctuary of her virginal retreat, the usually standoffish maid says:

Wee mortall wights, whose liues and fortunes bee
To commun accidents stil open layd,
Are bownd with commun bond of frailtee,
To succor wretched wights, whom we captiued see. (3.5.36.6–9)

In the *Epithalamion*, that common bond licenses an extraordinary openness, for the revelation of Cynthia's indecorous and unchaste affair is not used to banish her from the poem; rather, she is invited more fully in. The envious onlooker is incorporated by the poet as a welcome participant in the act of consummation itself, "enclin[ing]" her "will t'effect" the lovers' "wishfull vow." Even as the possessive pronouns "thy" and "our" trace the boundaries of marital exclusivity, the equipoise of her inclined will and the lovers' wishful vow makes agency impossible to assign: Who is subjected to whom?

The bridegroom's invitation to Cynthia is a flagrant breach of sexual propriety, an extension of courtesy to marriage's most intimate and exclusive space, the "chast wombe" of the virgin bride. It isn't simply the religious stigma of sexual shame that is set aside; it is the whole legal apparatus of legitimate and illegitimate succession, property and inheritance: possessive pronouns vanish from line 386; there is no way of knowing *whose* timely seed informs that chaste womb. Indeed, the offspring imaginatively bred in line 387—the "large posterity" who are envisioned at the poem's end as possessing both an earthly and a heavenly inheritance—belong both to the bridegroom and to Cynthia. Like Paridell and Britomart in the house of Malbecco, the bridegroom-poet and the jealous virgin queen are transformed by courtesy into kin, permitted to share a lineage and a destiny. Thanks to the bridegroom-poet's startlingly unchaste gesture of hospitality, the supposedly private worlds of marriage and poetry are laid open to the common accidents of envy, distaste, and misapprehension—laid open, as it were, to readers. Marriage may be the figure of Spenser's poetic authority, but promiscuity is the sign of his willingness to be read.

Or perhaps of something further: of his willingness to indulge and even capitalize on the vagaries of what Jeff Dolven terms "real reading." I began this chapter by observing that the narrative form of *The Faerie Queen* is intimately shaped (and reshaped) by the living presence of its ideal reader, the queen for whom it was written. But Elizabeth was not the only reader to whom *The Faerie Queene* was opened by Spenser; *Amoretti* 33 proves as much by addressing itself to another expectant reader, the poet's friend Lodowick Bryskett. As it happens, in his 1606 *Discourse of Civill Life*, Bryskett supplies a striking firsthand account of the community of readers to whom *The Faerie Queene* was accessible—at least in parts—as Spenser wrote it. The occasion of the *Discourse*, a philosophical dialogue on the ethics of public and private life addressed to Spenser's Irish employer, Lord Arthur Grey, was a friendly gathering of "certain gentlemen," Spenser among them, at Bryskett's home outside of Dublin, "coming of their curtesie to passe the time with him" in a period of ill health and studious retirement.[60] On that occasion, Bryskett writes, several of his friends teased him, accusing him of using illness as an excuse for idleness, and he turned for his defense to Spenser, as one learned in moral philosophy and capable of distinguishing virtue from vice:

> Therfore (said I) turning my selfe to M. *Spenser*, It is you sir, to whom it pertaineth to shew your selfe courteous now vnto vs all, and to make vs all beholding vnto you for the pleasure and profit which we shall gather from your speeches, if you shall vouchsafe to open vnto vs the goodly cabinet, in which this excellent treasure of vertues lieth locked vp from the vulgar sort. (26)

Spenser demurs, however, on the grounds that he has "already vndertaken a work tending to the same effect, which is in *heroical verse*, vnder the title of a *Faerie Queene*, . . . [w]hich work, as I haue already well entred into, if God shall please to spare me life that I may finish it according to my mind, your wish (M. *Bryskett*) will be in some sort accomplished, though perhaps not so effectually as you could desire" (26–27). Compared to this work, he continues, any speech he could make extemporaneously "would be but simple, and little to your satisfactions" (27). Instead, Spenser urges Bryskett to read aloud the dialogue he himself had composed on the subject, "because thereby it will appeare that he hath not withdrawne himself from seruice of the State, to liue idle or wholy priuate to himselfe, but hath spent some time in doing that which may greatly benefit others" (28). "I must needs fulfill their desires," Bryskett writes, "and so with a courteous force they made me rise from where I sate to go fetch my papers": with that, the *Discourse* commences (28–29).

Bryskett's account does more than offer a rare glimpse into Spenser's daily life and social connections during the years *The Faerie Queene* was written; it also offers a demonstration of the courteous substitutions, and elaborate and mutually beneficial exchanges, that made authorship possible for men like Bryskett and Spenser. As Spenser's response to Bryskett makes clear, for such men readers (or auditors) legitimated the otherwise suspect work of writing: privacy was not the author's privilege, or the necessary condition of his genius, but the charge against which he, by publishing his work or reading it aloud, secured himself. Bryskett's invitation to his friend to open the cabinet of his private thought creates the opportunity—which the poet deftly seizes—for his friend to make the same request of him: the place that might have been filled by an extract from or précis of Spenser's poem is supplied instead by the presentation of Bryskett's dialogue. But Spenser gains something from the elaborate courtesies, too: assurance that his poem, once finished, would have an eager audience. Although "all the company were wel satisfied" with his refusal to speak, Bryskett notes, they also "shewed an extreme longing after his worke of the Faerie Queene, whereof some parcels had bin by some of them seene" (28). The gathering at Bryskett's home likely took place in 1582, years before any version of *The Faerie Queene* appeared in print: the poem, it seems, was never wholly private, never wholly Spenser's own, never necessarily whole at all. The circulation of the unfinished poem in "parcels" to interested readers was the lifeblood of its composition; if such readers occasionally haunted Spenser with the specter of their overinvestment in its completion—as Bryskett and Elizabeth both do in *Amoretti* 33—that was a price the poet was willing to pay.

5

Reading against Time

CRISIS IN *THE FAERIE QUEENE*

NEAR THE end of book 4 of *The Faerie Queene*, one of the poem's recurring minor characters, a sea-nymph known variously as Cymoent or Cymodoce, arrives at a sudden realization about the limits of reading—or, at least, of the kind of reading *The Faerie Queene* itself seems to require: what J. Hillis Miller terms "reading *lento*," "paus[ing] over every key word or phrase, looking circumspectly before and after, walking rather than dancing, anxious not to let the text put anything over on him or her."[1] In book 3 of the poem, Cymoent learns such reading the hard way, through the near-death of her beloved son Marinell. Her text is a prophecy, issued by the sea-god Proteus, bidding her "from womankind to keepe him well: / For of a woman he should haue much ill" (3.4.25.7–8). Cymoent interprets this as a figurative warning against the perils of erotic entanglement—a plausible assumption, given that she and her son inhabit the Legend of Chastity in a densely allegorical poem—and she raises Marinell as a committed bachelor, "warning [him] euery day, / The loue of women not to entertaine" (3.4.26.1–2). But in canto 4 of book 3, the prophecy is fulfilled in gruesomely literal fashion, as the female knight Britomart runs Marinell through with her spear, leaving him "tombled on an heape, and wallowd in his gore" (3.4.16.9). As the narrator wryly observes:

> This was that woman, this that deadly wownd,
> That *Proteus* prophecide should him dismay,
> The which his mother vainely did expownd,
> To be hart-wownding loue, which should assay
> To bring her sonne vnto his last decay.
> So tickle be the termes of mortall state,
> And full of subtile sophismes, which doe play
> With double sences, and with false debate,
> T'approue the vnknowen purpose of eternall fate. (3.4.28)

But Cymoent is not so easily deterred. Finding Marinell in a deathlike swoon, she bears him back to her undersea bower, where she and her fellow nymphs painstakingly nurse him back to health. In canto 11 of book 4, he returns to the poem, hale and hearty, as his mother's escort to the undersea wedding of the Thames and the Medway. There the prophecy strikes again: overhearing the imprisoned Florimell's lament, Marinell falls desperately in love—but, since he is unable to free Florimell, he goes home heartsick. Consumed by desire, unable to eat or sleep, he rapidly wastes away, and his mother finds him once again on the verge of death, "Like ruefull ghost, vnable once to stirre or moue" (4.12.20.9). Confronted with this ghastly apparition, Cymoent applies the lesson she learned in book 3, "read[ing] the roote of his disease" in "that same former fatall wound" (4.12.22.1, 5). But when the old remedies fail, she summons Apollo to the sickbed, and he diagnoses "some inward thought . . . Which loue he red to be" (4.12.25.7, 9).

Cymoent gives herself a single line to "chafe, and grieve" at the cruel double jeopardy to which she and her son have been subjected (4.12.27.9). Then, in a startling reversal, she dismisses both the prophecy and its author as irrelevant:

> Yet since she saw the streight extremitie,
> In which his life vnluckily was layd,
> It was no time to scan the prophecie,
> Whether old Proteus true or false had sayd,
> That his decay should happen by a mayd.
> It's late in death of daunger to aduize. . . . (4.12.28.1–6)

Setting her mind to a more pressing question—"How she that Ladies libertie might enterprize" (4.12.28.9)—Cymoent appeals directly to Neptune himself, arguing for Florimell's release on technical legal grounds. Neptune is convinced by the argument "and streight his warrant made, / Vnder the Sea-gods seale autenticall, / Commaunding *Proteus* straight t'enlarge the mayd." Armed with this new writ, Cymoent "departed straight to *Proteus* therewithall" and "home with her she streight the virgin lad" (4.12.32.7, 4.12.33.8). Two stanzas later, the lovers are united and Marinell is restored to health.

Coming as it does on the threshold of book 5, Cymoent's pivot from the involutions of Protean wit to the straightness of legal judgment heralds the poem's own imminent turn from the erotic, emotional, and narrative entanglements of the Legends of Chastity and Friendship to the more narrowly political aims of the Legend of Justice. But the realization that "it was no time to scan" also hints at an urgency at odds with the slow work of interpretation—and at odds, it would therefore seem, with the entire enterprise of reading an allegorical poem. In the end, Cymoent doesn't reject the prophecy as mistaken, misleading, or poorly worded; her abandonment of it is a sheerly pragmatic calculation, or perhaps an unthinking capitulation to a truth critical reading holds at a necessary distance: reading takes time, and time is running out.

The crucial term is "scan"—and here Spenser's language presents an instructive challenge to the twenty-first-century reader. Since the mid-twentieth-century advent of computer technologies, "scanning" has come to connote speed and superficiality: the gathering of information by the rapid movement of an eye, a beam of light, or an algorithmic code across a text, object, or—as is increasingly the case—the contents of a digitized database. (It also names the ever more rapid and precise process by which such databases are created, as text and images are transformed into code.) But in the sixteenth century, scanning was slow, deep work—reading "lento." Etymologically derived from the Greek word for "climbing," the word entered English in medieval arts of poetry as a name for the painstaking calculus of syllabic measure that organizes language into verse; Renaissance writers extended the term to signify the careful scrutiny, stepwise analysis, or probing interpretation of any ambiguous matter.[2] A line of poetry could be scanned, but so could a logical proposition, a political controversy, the workings of divine Providence, or the suspicious behavior of a wife: "Scan this thing no further" is Iago's disingenuous advice to Othello. In what Jonathan Goldberg, following Roland Barthes, calls the "writerly text" of book 4, scanning is not merely slow but "endlesse worke" (4.12.1.1), as the horizon of meaning is perpetually deferred by the play of hermeneutic possibility.[3] At the very end of the Legend of Friendship, however, Spenser confronts us with a limit to that work, not in language but in the body: reading may be endless, but readers—at least, human readers—aren't. To resolve, as Cymoent does, that "it was no time to scan" isn't to deny the possibility of further and better interpretation, but to recognize that understanding is sometimes too little, too late.

What's needed to keep the poem going is an inhuman reader, and in book 5 of *The Faerie Queene* Spenser gives us one: Artegall's robotic associate, the iron man Talus, "immoueable, resistlesse, without end" (5.1.12.7). In the chapter that follows, I take Talus, by far the least beloved of Spenser's poetic creations, as a guide to the peculiar temporalities of reading in the Legend of Justice, a textual environment whose challenges and opportunities bear a striking, if wholly adventitious, resemblance to reading in the digital age. That admittedly anachronistic analogy is one I press to, and perhaps a bit beyond, its limits in my conclusion, not for the purpose of endowing *The Faerie Queene* with prophetic authority—I am not suggesting that, in Talus, Spenser forecasts the rise of computational technology—but in order to explore the affordances of what I call "reading against time": reading that invokes a pressing sense of necessity in order to license a departure from established readerly norms and values. Book 5 has long frustrated those who look to Spenser's poetry for wit, subtlety, and profound spiritual insight, and who expect to work hard and slowly for such rewards. The obviousness of its topical referents and the bluntness of its moral sensibility have made it, in C. S. Lewis's judgment, "a stumbling-block to poetic readers" and "a bait to unpoetic readers."[4] Inspired in part by sympathy for Cymoent, who reminds us that taking one's time with a text is not only a readerly achievement but a readerly luxury, I make a case for the unpoetic reader, for whom the demands and the insights of the moment supersede the values of patience and diligence on which poetic reading—reading lento—depends. The degree to which such readers have succeeded in extracting value from a part of Spenser's poem that has left more conscientious readers cold suggests that there is something to be said for urgency, haste, brute force, crude approximation, and willful anachronism: for all of the straitening and reductive tendencies of reading in a state of emergency.

To put it another way, it is worth considering the etymological link between criticism and crisis. "Crisis," as it happens, is the technical term for the "streight extremitie" in which Cymoent finds Marinell at the end of book 4. The word entered English just a few decades before *The Faerie Queene* was written, appearing in mid-sixteenth-century medical treatises as a term of art for the decisive juncture in the course of a disease, after which a patient either dies or begins to recover.[5] As the glossary of strange words appended to a 1543 surgical handbook explains, "Crisis sygnifyeth iudgemente, and in thys case, it is vsed for a sodayne chaunge in a disease." Like its lexical cousins "critic" and "criticism," "crisis" derives from the Greek *krinein*, to judge or decide, and it serves as a reminder that judgment itself is both a subjective enterprise and an objective fact, something we do and something we endure. In the original medical sense of the word, passivity predominates, for "crisis" is the interval of maximum helplessness for physician and patient alike; it's the disease that does the deciding. Nonetheless, naming a particular interval as *the* crisis helped mask this reality, allowing the physician to narrate the illness even if he could not determine its course.

Marinell's predicament at the end of book 4 is a crisis in this technical sense, but his mother's reaction to the situation—her determination that "it was no time to scan"—hints at the metaphorical sense of the word that emerged half a century later, particularly in writing about the Civil War: that is, a "decisive stage in the progress" of some action, a time of radical suspense in the wake of which things are permanently altered, for better or for worse.[6] Where the original sense of the word gave physicians a descriptive mastery over diseases whose outcomes remained in doubt, the metaphor of crisis extended that power to the witnesses of historical trauma, giving a name to the feeling that everything was about to change and lending rhetorical force to whatever new course of action that change might arguably require. Spenser shows himself a master of this rhetoric in his 1596 prose treatise, *A View of the Present State of Ireland*, written the same year the six-book edition of *The Faerie Queene* appeared in print and purporting to offer a clear-eyed, hardheaded, on-the-ground account of the political challenges that supply much of the plot of book 5. Scholars continue to debate whether the *View* is a representative expression of Anglo-Irish sentiment in the 1580s or, as Ciaran Brady claims, "unique in its pessimistic determinism."[7] But regardless of how normative or extreme the *View* would have seemed to contemporary readers, there is no question that Spenser cultivates a sense of political extremity in it, justifying the ruthlessness of his recommended policies by characterizing Ireland as a patient on the brink of catastrophic decline. Here, for instance, is how the poet's mouthpiece, Irenius, describes the state of the Irish colonial settlement after the replacement of Spenser's employer, Lord Arthur Grey, as Lord Deputy of Ireland, by Sir John Perrot:

> For it was even as two Physicians should take one sicke body in hand, at two sundry times: Of which the former would minister all things meete to purge and keepe under the Bodie: the other to pamper and strengthen it suddenly againe, whereof what is to bee looked for, but a most daungerous relapse? That which wee now see thorough his rule, and the next after him, happened thereunto, being now more daungerously sicke then ever before. Therefore by all meanes it must bee fore-seene and assured, that after once entering into this course of reformation, there bee afterwardes no remorse nor drawing backe for the sight of any such ruefull objects, as must thereupon followe, nor for compassion of their calamities, seeing that by no other meanes it is possible to cure them, and that these are not of will, but of very urgent necessitie.[8]

As Spenser's application of the metaphor reveals, the rhetorical value of "crisis" is its simultaneous appeal to urgency and inevitability: crisis is the moment at which human judgment is both imperative and superseded; whatever action is taken at such a moment is legitimated in advance as the only possible course.

Etymology itself has a similarly suspect explanatory power, as Paula Blank has argued, conferring an aura of inevitability on the accidents of linguistic history:

> [O]ne of the peculiar pleasures of etymology, now more than ever, is the titillation we feel in the presence of a truth that we, if only for a moment, give ourselves permission to have faith in, trust as real, experience as material signification. The "etymological moment" in contemporary critical practice is not all play: it is also an expression of our desire to be right, our drive to view language as fact, as presence, as identity, as confirmation of who we were and who we still may be, even as we and all such certainties are then undone by it.[9]

The telescopic perspective of etymology "situates the past as if it were always, potentially, with us in the present, whatever else we think," affording readers both the shock of the arcane and unexpected and "the self-gratifying sensation of having known it, ourselves, all along" (122, 119). For all their appeal to the authority of antiquity and erudition, the knowledge etymologies offer, Blank observes, "never seems truer than when they show us something that is at first unrecognizable about ourselves" (122).

By anchoring this chapter in a pair of etymological puns—scan/scan, crisis/criticism—I mean, in part, to signal its embrace of etymology's warped temporality and pseudoscholarly illogic: its opportunistic juxtapositions of past and present, its faith in the secret perdurability of meaning across time, and its reliance on the appeal of the sudden, transformative insight. Etymology, Blank suggests, is closer to crisis than it is to criticism, which makes it kin to the other, equally expeditious and more obviously disreputable strategies of reading book 5 of *The Faerie Queene* models, solicits, and rewards. This is especially true when—as in the brief history of "crisis" I sketch above and, I imagine, in most invocations of etymological origins in recent literary scholarship—lexical inquiry is fueled not by the slow accumulation of scholarly erudition but by the almost instantaneous power of digital search engines. My unpacking of the history of "crisis" took no more than a quarter of an hour: I began with the online *Oxford English Dictionary*, whose dated and hyperlinked entries helped me to locate key instances of the word "crisis" in the digital database of *Early English Books Online*, and from there, I turned to the EEBO-TCP N-gram browser at the website *Early Modern Print*, which generated a graph of the word's usage from the beginning of English print, in 1473, to the end of the seventeenth century. That graph, combined with keyword-in-context searches, provided a clear and striking illustration of the word's transition out of medical terminology and into general usage over the course of the seventeenth century. The transformation Blank charts of the "ancient habit" (111) of etymology into our current "etymological moment" (112) owes much to the affordances of digital databases and computer search algorithms: lexical histories that once required years of reading and language study can now be assembled easily and speedily by anyone with the necessary digital subscriptions.

As scholars, we are habituated to disguise such expediencies—or, at least, to confess them obliquely in footnotes and endnotes—but one of my aims in this chapter is to foreground the shortcuts (of attention, imagination, and sympathy) on which reading lento often relies. In order to do so, I begin by taking a closer look at the kinds of slow, probing analysis the Legend of Justice has seemed to forestall, asking what the frustration of traditional readerly methods in book 5 of *The Faerie Queene* has to do with the value that part of the poem attaches to speed. I then turn to a class of readers, willfully presentist and unabashedly partisan, for whom the bluntness of book 5 has served not as a constraint on interpretation but an incitement to appropriation. The uses to which those readers put Spenser's allegory of justice have less in common with Cymoent's painstaking deconstruction of Proteus's prophecy than with her decisive application of Neptune's warrant; licensed by crisis, they treat the poem as if its meaning and value inhered only in its responsiveness to the present. The defects of such readings are manifest—for one thing, what is timely rapidly goes out of date—but there is something bracing in their refusal to pretend to disinterest. In the final section of the chapter, I ask what an interested and timely reading of book 5 might look like today, a reading that capitalizes on the irony that now inheres in a phrase like "no time to scan," and that looks to our own moment of machine-enhanced (or machine-driven) disciplinary crisis for insight into the various emergencies that constitute Spenser's Legend of Justice.

The Judgment of Talus

For well over a hundred years, the shift from book 4 to book 5 of *The Faerie Queene* has challenged Spenser's critics, who have struggled to accommodate themselves to the poem's sudden lapse from allegorical density and narrative sophistication to a blatantly self-interested and barely fictionalized recounting of recent events. "Much of the narrative in this Book will bear nothing beyond an interpretation by history," complains Kate M. Warren in the preface to her 1898 edition of book 5; "it is impossible to find in it any moral or spiritual meaning":

> The Book calls itself the *Legend of Justice*, but it is not the presentation of the universal principle of Justice, but of Justice as displayed in the British Islands in the 16th century. Artegall, the Knight of Justice, does not often stand for a power of the soul, or a human being fighting for justice in a tangled world of injustice, but most frequently for Lord Grey de Wilton dealing out a more than doubtful sort of justice amidst the bewilderment of Irish difficulties. Here, at once, then, begins the poet's limitation; he links the principle of justice far too closely to a special time, place, and personality.[10]

The time was the early 1580s, the place was colonial Ireland, and the personality was that of Arthur Grey, Spenser's employer and Lord Deputy of Ireland between 1580 and 1582, when he was recalled from his post by Queen Elizabeth following widespread complaints of his brutality. But book 5 also confronts us, more directly than any other part of the poem, with the personality of Edmund Spenser, colonial bureaucrat and Irish plantation owner. In the years he wrote *The Faerie Queene*, from 1580 through 1596, Spenser made his living as a functionary in the Anglo-Irish colonial administration, serving as secretary to a succession of highly placed officials, beginning with Grey himself, as clerk of faculties in the Irish Court of Chancery, as deputy clerk in the council of Munster, as sheriff-designate of Cork. In 1589, his stake in the colonial project became material, when he was granted possession of an estate carved from the confiscated lands of the rebellious Earl of Desmond.[11]

In book 5, where Artegall serves as an obvious surrogate for Lord Grey and the hapless Irena as a fantasy of Ireland without the Irish, such biographical realities exert an unmistakable pressure on the poet's imagination and sympathies. As William Butler Yeats puts it, "When Spenser wrote of Ireland, he wrote as an official, and out of thoughts and emotions that had been organised by the State"; "he saw nothing but work for the Iron man."[12] C. S. Lewis offers a blunter assessment, saying, "Spenser was the instrument of a detestable policy in Ireland, and in his fifth book the wickedness he had shared begins to corrupt his imagination." Like Warren before him, Lewis takes issue not only with Spenser's moral conception of justice but with the overt topicality of the fiction by which it is conveyed: the historical references in which book 5 abounds are, in his view, "of interest to the critic chiefly in so far as they explain how some bad passages came to be bad," but "[s]ince this does not make them good—since to explain by causes is not to justify by reasons—we shall not lose very much by ignoring the matter." Book 5, he concludes, "is not, and ought not to be, a favourite."[13]

Few critics today would assent to Lewis's efficient demarcation of policy from poetry. "The distinction is a comforting one," as Ciaran Brady observes, "but it is hardly satisfactory": the "rising fear of imminent catastrophe," compounded of political anxiety and professional disappointment, that beset Spenser in the years he wrote both the *View* and the second half of *The Faerie Queene* imbue prose and poem alike with "an acute sense of crisis."[14] Nor can the Legend of Justice be cordoned off from the rest of *The Faerie Queene*: the sense of crisis may be most urgently felt in book 5, but as Stephen Greenblatt argued in his landmark reading of the destruction of the Bower of Bliss at the end of book 2, "Ireland is not only in book 5 of *The Faerie Queene*; it pervades the poem."[15] Even so, the sense persists that in book 5 both poet and reader are uniquely and unhappily constrained. "The basic problem," Judith Anderson argues, "is evident enough": "If the very subject of justice leads to the dream of a Golden Age, it leads also to the presence of topical, or historical, allegory in Book Five, a painful reminder of Elizabethan shortcomings. The logical structure of Book Five has a vicious, circular validity, and the figure of Artegall is enmeshed in it."[16] So too are Spenser's readers, for to look for more rarified or exalted meanings within book 5 can feel a lot like ignoring the actual bodies interred in its allegorical landscape. Unable to escape history, criticism is reduced to an obvious and unsatisfying accounting of correspondences between fiction and fact—a grim sort of double-entry bookkeeping that records without redeeming the poet's defects of imagination and feeling. For critics accustomed to identifying the study of literature in general and of *The Faerie Queene* in particular with the improvement of intellect and the expansion of moral sympathy, the experience of reading book 5 is chastening, not to say demoralizing: Spenser's allegory in book 5 is "painfully obvious," A. C. Hamilton writes; "Spenser's vision at this point becomes disturbingly narrow," observes Michael O'Connell; "the failure of the fiction to negotiate the demands of Elizabethan realpolitik," as Elizabeth Jane Bellamy notes, "not only sabotages attempts to reconcile justice with *The Faerie Queene*'s overall epic purpose, but also impedes literary interpretation itself."[17]

There are those who insist that this gets it backward: that the problem with book 5 is that readers have failed to negotiate the demands of Spenser's fiction. Responding to critics who "lament . . . Book Five's collapse of allegory into referent," Richard Rambuss argues, "Spenser is not the state instrument he seems to be," and the allegory of book 5 is "anything but transparent."[18] "The received view" of the Legend of Justice—its "narrowness of vision" and "loss of moral complexity"—"is just too simple," concurs Tobias Gregory. Book 5, he argues, is not an unthinking brief for totalitarianism but "a shifting, ambivalent discourse on the ill effects of half-measures in the public sphere."[19] The burden for discerning its subtleties falls on the critic: Spenser's "analysis of justice and law," writes Andrew Hadfield, "may appear upon investigation more astute than is habitually thought, which in turn ought to encourage a second look at even the darkest sections of his work."[20] Sounding "a note of caution" against the "new orthodoxy" of historicism, Willy Maley detects "an element of glibness taking root" in scholarship on book 5, in which "[a]esthetic concerns have arguably been overshadowed" by the desire to make criticism itself historically responsive and politically engaged.[21] But in Maley's view, the "critical commodification and fetishizing of Ireland" and the "reduction and oversimplification" of Spenser's perspective on it are, at bottom, a refusal to do the hard and necessary work of interpretation: "*The Faerie Queene* is, on one level, a poem about reading," he declares, "and while reading 'Ireland,' in all its complexity, in Spenser's life and texts may be a fruitful exercise, it can never exhaust the range of meanings in the poem."[22] This conviction has the happy effect of making readers' efforts to see past the apparent defects of the Legend of Justice the very act of judgment that fulfills the promise of its title: Artegall's shortcomings elicit our compensatory efforts, by which the book's seemingly absent virtue is restored and perfected. "It is no wonder that Artegall cannot cope with the tasks he has been set," Hadfield argues. "He does not know how to read the icons of justice properly."[23] We do, and it is up to us to do better.

For all their flattering implications about the redemptive power of literary criticism, these revisionary accounts of book 5 involve Spenser's readers in a contract whose terms we may wish to resist. It isn't only that, as Bellamy notes, critiques of earlier accounts of book 5 as reductive or simplistic have an uncomfortable tendency to shift responsibility onto Spenser's critics, making it "the reader's burden" to supply the apparent defects of the poem.[24] Although Hadfield and Maley both accuse C. S. Lewis of "circular logic" for insisting that, to the extent book 5 of *The Faerie Queene* was political, it was therefore not a poem, there is something similarly circular in Hadfield's insistence that "complicated texts require careful decoding" or Maley's that "the best way to approach 'Spenser' and 'Ireland' is to assume, first of all, the complexity of both."[25] Either assertion rests on a tacit faith, not so different from Lewis's own, in the virtue of complexity itself. Such faith, Heather Love has argued, is endemic to modern humanistic study, in which "richness is an undisputed—if largely uninterrogated—good," and it frequently licenses a slippage between textual difficulty, readerly sophistication, critical authority, and ethical virtue. Although there is no "necessary connection between the capacity to interpret such texts and the ability to respond justly and empathetically to the ethical dilemmas represented in them," the distinction between the two tends to vanish when the work of close reading—of attending to textual ambiguities—is identified with a capacity for moral judgment, for reckoning with ethical complexity.[26] Love and other dissenters from the "hermeneutic of suspicion"—advocates for the protocols of what Stephen Best and Sharon Marcus christened "surface reading"—have been accused of quietism, or of beating a pessimistic retreat from the political imperatives of Marxist and postmodern critique; and a desire to avoid certain exhausted or simply exhausting strains of contention is clearly at play among critics of book 5 of *The Faerie Queene*.[27] But arguments over how to read the Legend of Justice also stand at a usefully oblique angle to the debate over surface reading, for those who advocate reading the text more deeply, subtly, and suspiciously are hoping to mitigate, if not altogether avoid, the pressure of politics in and on the poem. For the problem with book 5 is that even the least suspicious reader cannot help recognizing the ideological ills to which its symptoms point; its politics and its prejudices are hardly latent enough.

Love's brief for what she calls "'thin' description"—criticism that strives for attentiveness rather than dazzlingly unexpected insight—ends with an expression of doubt that the regime of complexity will ever be toppled: "For who among us is willing to exchange the fat and the living for the thin and the dead" (388)? It is a question that ought to give Spenserians particular pause, recalling as it does both the emaciated figure of Marinell on his deathbed and—more pointedly—his real-life counterparts in Spenser's Ireland, the victims of the famine that ensued in the district of Munster as a result of Lord Grey's scorched-earth tactics. In a now notorious passage in *A View of the Present State of Ireland*, Irenius recalls the suffering of those victims not with regret but with a wish that it might be extended across Ireland, subduing (or simply eradicating) its rebellious inhabitants once and for all. "By . . . hard restraint," he says, "they would quickly consume themselves, and devour one another":

> The proofe whereof, I saw sufficiently exampled in these late warres of *Mounster*, for notwithstanding that the same was a most rich and plentifull countrey, full of corne and cattle, that you would have thought they should have beene able to stand long, yet ere one yeare and a halfe they were brought to such wretchednesse, as that any stony heart would have rued the same. Out of every corner of the woods and glynnes they came creeping forth upon their hands, for their legges could not beare them, they looked like anatomies of death, they spake like Ghosts crying out of their graves, they did eate the dead Carrions, happy were they could finde them, yea, and one another soone after, insomuch as the very carcasses they spared not to scrape out of their graves, and if they found a plot of water-cresses or Shamrocks; there they flocked as to a feast for the time, yet not able long to continue therewithall, that in short space there were none almost left, and a most populous and plentifull countrey suddainely left voyde of man and beast. (72)

The impulse to find in book 5 of *The Faerie Queene* the qualities this passage so painfully lacks—an ambivalence about suffering, a capacity for sympathetic identification, or an edge of ironic detachment—is understandable, but to imbue these bodies with allegorical depth, figurative density, or a wider range of reference is to efface their material reality: the bare facts of hunger, suffering, and death.

Spenser himself surely shared this faith in the recuperative power of reading. Indeed, the culture of Christian humanism depended on the belief that inventive readers—especially inventive allegorical readers—could salvage meaning and value from the corrupt and fragmentary texts of classical antiquity, whose wisdom had to be carefully sifted from, and was perhaps even encoded in, their errors and superstitions. St. Augustine provides the key image and justification for such interpretive effort in *De doctrina Christiana*, when he likens the reading of pagan literature to the vessels of Egyptian gold, which the Hebrews "going out of Egypt appropriated to themselves, designing them for a better use."[28] Spenser explicitly recalls Augustine's metaphor and adopts his method—which humanists termed *euhemerism*—at the start of canto 7 in book 5, on the threshold of the Temple of Isis, when he praises the Egyptian myth of Osiris as a repository of both moral insight and historical knowledge, "[w]ith fayned colours shading a true case" (5.7.2.7).[29] The Legend of Justice as a whole presents something of the same euhemeristic challenge, and the same temptation, to critics: to discover in its ideological falsehoods and self-serving half-truths a range of meanings more worthy of the poem and its readers. It is no coincidence that one of the boldest and most effective rereadings of book 5 in the twentieth century, Angus Fletcher's *The Prophetic Moment*, explicitly calls upon Britomart's prophetic vision at the Temple as an antidote to the ceaseless violence of Talus, "the grim reaper of Time's harvest," who is barred from entering with her. The Temple is a resting place and sanctuary, Fletcher notes, but it is also the house of the prophet, whose "visionary interpretation" of history infuses errant time with the mythic urgency and messianic appeal of crisis. Along the way, it rescues the poem from mere politics: "Spenser's myth here is strong," Fletcher writes, "whatever may have been his personal motives."[30] The impulse to salvage something from the rubble persists. But Cymoent's refusal of the redemptive promise of interpretation might spur the reader of book 5 to a different conclusion, not that the Legend of Justice is unreadable, or that it requires better, deeper, subtler reading to counter its apparent crudities, but that it is "no time to scan": a straitened extremity of the poem in which reading itself is both accelerated and attenuated, exposed as less profound and less transformative an enterprise than we often wish to believe.

Required Speed

The pressures to which reading is subjected in book 5 are not only historical but narrative: the Legend of Justice is the only book of *The Faerie Queene* whose action unfolds on (or, more often, behind) a fixed schedule—the only book, too, in which speed proves as seductive a temptation as delay. The hero of book 5, Artegall, is introduced to readers in book 4, where he falls in love with and promises to marry the female knight, Britomart. But as Artegall explains to his betrothed, the marriage cannot take place until he has fulfilled his promise to Gloriana, to free the maiden Irena from the tyranny of the wicked Grantorto. He vows, however, to return "speedily": "No lenger space thereto he did desire, / But till the horned moone three courses did expire" (4.6.43.8–9). As readers of book 5 discover, he fails to keep that appointment when he allows himself to be captured by the Amazon Radigund. Artegall's failure to arrive by "the vtmoste date / Assigned to his return" (5.6.3.6–7) creates an anomalous slackness in Britomart's experience, as the bold and forthright maid is forced to keep idle for a now indeterminate stretch of time. In this unsettling meantime, she occupies herself with what Spenser terms an "errour":

> She fayn'd to count the time againe anew,
> As if before she had not counted trew.
> For houres but dayes; for weekes, that passed were,

> She told but moneths, to make them seeme more few:
> Yet when she reckned them, still drawing neare,
> Each hour did seeme a moneth, and euery moneth a yeare. (5.6.5.4–9)

As J. K. Barret notes, Britomart's "bald-faced bid for temporal control" is a failure: the more she dwells on the passage of time, the more slowly it seems to pass.[31] In this sense, even as the passage teases her for treating time as something that might be "count[ed] . . . anew," it confirms that error as an experiential fact: for the individuals who exist within it, time does flow at variable rates.

Barret names the peculiar slackness of time Britomart experiences in the first half of book 5 "vacant time" (5), an interval in which there is, literally, nothing to be done; crisis, marked by the perception that something—anything—must be done, is its essential opposite. Artegall's time in book 5 is oddly split between vacancy and crisis: when he is not chatting with dwarves, officiating at weddings, giving advice to spatting siblings, or learning to spin while wearing a dress in Radigund's basement, he is hurtling through the poem toward appointments he seems destined to miss. Indeed, his most important appointment of all is one we learn of only after he has failed to keep it. In canto 11, Artegall encounters "good Sir *Sergis*" (5.11.38.2), Irena's faithful knight, who upbraids him for his lack of faith:

> For she presuming on th'appointed tyde,
> In which ye promist, as ye were a Knight,
> To meete her at the salvage Ilands syde,
> And then and there for triall of her right
> With her unrighteous enemy to fight,
> Did thither come, where she afrayd of nought,
> By guilefull treason and by subtill slight
> Surprized was, and to Grantorto brought,
> Who her imprisond hath, and her life often sought. (5.11.39)

This is the first we hear of "th'appointed tyde" fixed for Artegall's combat with Grantorto, and it casts the previous ten cantos—almost the whole of book 5—in a newly dubious light: what we thought was a quest for justice was a catastrophic deferral of it. Or, a near-catastrophic deferral: inexplicably—but luckily for Artegall—Grantorto does not kill Irena outright, allowing "ten daies . . . of grace" for her rescuer to arrive. He makes it, but only just; "The terme approching fast, required speed" (5.11.65.9).

That single line epitomizes the temporal logic of book 5, which consists in the paradoxical interdependence of aimlessness and urgency. If, as Barret argues, delay is weirdly destigmatized in the Legend of Justice, that is partly because Artegall's dilatory progress engenders and legitimates the demand for speed. The answer to that demand is embodied in Artegall's robotic associate, Talus, who enters the poem in canto 1, just as Astraea, the goddess of justice, abruptly leaves it:

> But when she parted hence, she left her groome
> An yron man, which on her did attend
> Alwayes, to execute her stedfast doome,
> And willed him with *Artegall* to wend,
> And doe whatever thing he did intend.
> His name was *Talus*, made of yron mould,
> Immouable, resistlesse, without end.
> Who in his hand an yron flale did hould,
> With which he thresht out falshood, and did truth unfould. (5.1.12)

Begotten of the crisis of Astraea's untimely departure, Talus himself is, as Lynsey McCulloch observes, what Spenser clearly hoped book 5 itself would be: "a timely intervention" into a project on the brink of disaster.[32] He is nonetheless oddly abstracted from the sense of history and futurity crisis entails: "Attend[ing] / Alwayes," "without end," Talus is pure presence, possessed of neither hope nor fear for what is to come, endowed only with the capacity to make it so.

As James Nohrnberg points out, Talus's relation to Artegall is complicated by the fact that he has not one but two classical namesakes: the metal guardsman who patrols the shores of Crete according to the (pseudo-)Platonic *Minos* and Apollonius of Rhodes's *Argonautica*, circling the island three times a day and hurling rocks at intruders, and the nephew of Ovid's master craftsman Dedalus, an apprentice who surpasses his teacher by inventing both the saw and the compass, at which point Dedalus kills him in fit of envy, hurling him from a precipice much as Spenser's Talus hurls the Egalitarian Giant.[33] Embedded in the character and conduct of *The Faerie Queene*'s iron man is thus the long history of human ambivalence toward tools and their makers, a deep-seated anxiety that the objects we expect to serve us might one day surpass us, that things are a potential threat to the primacy of human nature. To whom, after all, does the pronoun in line 5 ("And doe whatever thing *he* did intend") refer—to Artegall or to Talus? Spenser makes a point of the incongruity of Talus's own tool, his iron flail, calling it "his strange weapon, neuer wont in warre" (5.4.44.2), but this underrates the aptness of the implement as an emblem of how Talus processes the poem itself—how he reduces its rich and variable imagery to a single, objective truth: whatever thing he did intend.

To read like Talus, then, is to read instrumentally and for the present, having an immediate end in mind and rejecting anything that detracts or distracts from it. For despite what the poem says, Talus's flail is never used to winnow truth from falsehood (that task falls to Artegall); instead, it serves to distinguish relevant from irrelevant inputs, signal from noise. We see this discriminating intelligence at work in the very first description we get of Artegall's page in action, as the pair approach a bitterly weeping "Squire in squallid weed" (5.1.13.7). Talus's perspective on the scene is knit to the knight's own by plural pronouns, right up to the point that Artegall's feelings are engaged, by the revelation of the cause of the squire's grief, the decapitated corpse of a lady:

> To whom as *they* approched, *they* espide
> A sorie sight, as euer seene with eye;
> An headlesse Ladie lying him beside,
> In her owne blood all wallow'd wofully,
> That her gay clothes did in discolour die.
> Much was *he* moued at that ruefull sight.... (5.14.1–6; emphasis added)

Talus's eye, it would seem, is not included in the universal claim of line 2; an unwritten adjective—human? living?—silently modifies the noun "eye." This unfeeling, unblinking, indistractible eye makes Talus a uniquely effective navigator of the landscape of book 5, as the rest of the encounter with the weeping squire makes clear. Filled with righteous indignation and impatient zeal, Artegall interrogates the squire about the identity of the lady's murderer:

> Aread (sayd he) which way then did he make?
> And by what markes may he be knowne againe?
> To hope (quothe he) him soone to overtake,
> That hence so long departed is but vaine:
> But yet he pricked ouer yonder plaine,
> And as I marked, bore vpon his shield,
> By which its easie him to know againe,
> A broaken sword within a bloodie field;
> Expressing well his nature, which the same did yield. (5.1.19)

This fleeting description of a knight pricking across a plain inevitably recalls the image with which *The Faerie Queene* began, of the Redcrosse Knight, "pricking on the plaine," his shield bearing "the cruell markes of many a bloodie field" (1.1.1.4). But the resemblance serves to indicate a more pervasive and consequential distinction between reading in book 1 of the poem and reading in book 5. The difficulty in book 1 is that the marks on the Redcrosse Knight's shield don't, at least to begin with, express his nature well: the impossibility of knowing any knight by his armor, or truth by outward sign, is the central challenge of the Legend of Holinesse, to which even Una succumbs. But in book 5, interpretation is evidently no longer an issue: "its easie him to know againe," the squire insists, if only you could find him. Now time and distance—figured by the vast and increasingly unknowable expanse of the poem itself—stand as obstacles to readerly success: there is too much for any human reader, however interpretively gifted, to master.

This is a challenge to which Talus is fantastically well suited, as Artegall is the first to realize:

> No sooner sayd, but streight he after sent
> His yron page, who him pursew'd so light,
> As that it seem'd aboue the ground he went:
> For he was swift as swallow in his flight,
> And strong as Lyon in his lordly might.
> It was not long before he ouertooke
> Sir *Sanglier*; (so cleeped was that Knight)
> Whom at the first he ghessed by his looke,
> And by the other markes, which of his shield he tooke. (5.1.20)

Again, it is worth noting the difference from book 1: in the Legend of Holiness, first guesses are inevitably suspect, reliant as they are on mere outward form. In the Legend of Justice, by contrast, immediacy is a necessity or even a virtue—deliberation may be an essential element of judicial practice, but it is a luxury the time-bound nature of Artegall's quest cannot always afford and does not always reward. There is a further revelation here, too: speed is not only useful in book 5; it is beautiful, as the description of Talus skimming across the surface of the poem, "so light," "swift as swallow in its flight," unexpectedly emphasizes.[34] Although it is Talus's brutality we tend to remember, the poem identifies him here with an enviable virtuosity, an effortless and instantaneous comprehension of reality that distills reading from process to revelatory point, from criticism to crisis.

Coming to terms with the straitening of readerly experience in book 5 therefore means coming to terms with Talus, who has long borne the brunt of the critical animus against book 5, and with the temporal exigencies that shape our own readerly judgment, whether we acknowledge them or not. "[A]ll the most unpleasant results and the useless slaughters which follow from [Artegall's] judgments or actions are taken in hand by Talus, the Iron Man," declares Warren in her 1898 preface (xvi). Indeed, Warren comes close to interpreting Talus as a figure for the ineluctable pressure of history itself, which in book 5 transforms Spenser, against his will, into a lesser poet and a lesser human being:

> Talus, as the groom of Artegall, is usually supposed to stand for the executive power which carries out the decrees of justice, and as such he has some rightful place in the story; but that an Iron Man, incapable of human

> feeling, should be the sole attendant upon Justice is a woeful limitation to impose upon our conception of the virtue which Aristotle thought the most perfect of all. Spenser having limited himself to a picture of Justice as he saw it during a short period of his own century, and in a few places, had then of necessity to limit his conception of the virtue itself. (xvi–xvii)

The phrase "of necessity" says openly what Warren's evasively passive syntax only hints: if Talus is unfeeling by nature, Spenser is unfeeling by accident—made so, that is, by the literal accidents of time and place to which his allegory of justice is unhappily tethered.

Talus's thingness is essential to the revulsion he inspires: Jane Aptekar, the first critic to devote an entire monograph to the Legend of Justice, describes him as a monstrous hybrid of animal and machine, "a bloodhound and a police helicopter"; A. C. Hamilton refers to him as Spenser's "robo-cop"; and Elizabeth Jane Bellamy refuses him a place even in the poem's figurative ecology, deeming him "neither an organic being nor, for that matter, a figure of allegory, but rather a war-machine utterly lacking the humanity that, by definition, underwrites humanism itself."[35]

The resistance to Talus is as much methodological as it is moral: the problem isn't simply his objecthood but his objective—and relentlessly immediate—perspective on the poem itself. The speed and scale at which the iron man conducts his assaults exceed the capacity of human understanding; the rigor of his discernment excludes the richness and texture of human experience; and the opacity (or, perhaps, the absence) of his motives and the obduracy of his being defy human sympathy. Thanks to Talus, Heather James argues, the Legend of Justice becomes an "experiment in *how* poetry fails"—and how reading, unaided by a larger aesthetic, philosophical, or moral sense of purpose, fails with it:

> In the delimited space of Book V, Spenser gives up the charisma and aura of fiction based on antique legends. He presses hard on the *difference* between history and poetry. And he enlists readers in the unexpected project of reading locally but not objectively: it would be comforting to think that local or historical reading in Book V might lead to mastery over the book's questions of moral and political philosophy, but Spenser characterizes the "local" view as a fall into passion, bias, and misinterpretation. To give up a focus on philosophical and transhistorical concerns and read for the moment, in Book V, is to read with "envy, and suspition."[36]

Our task, then, is to refuse the temptation of reading "for the moment"—with an eye fixed only on the immediate substance of history—and, in so doing, to release book 5 from Talus's "iron paw." "Let me lay my cards on the table," James declares: "I blame Talus." The iron man's name, as she points out, literally means "joint"—the *talus* is a knucklebone—and it gestures to the family of Latin words (*talis*, *tale*, and *talia*) that introduce rhetorical comparisons. For James, this cluster of associations makes Talus a cautionary figure for the lure of analogy and the efficiencies of ideological interpretation, with its tendentious drive to efface differences and collapse distinctions between the abstract and the particular, the transcendent and the ordinary, the philosophical and the merely historical. To read book 5 like Talus is to proceed with "a will, a plan, and a destination" already in mind, "absorb[ing] the violence and bad faith of history and carr[ying] it forward to future times."

But before the twentieth century—and, in fact, for several decades into it—such reading constituted almost the entirety of the reception history of book 5, which appealed to readers precisely for the qualities more recent critics have tended to deplore. As I show in the following section, there have always been those for whom the unbending rigor and blatant self-interest of Spenser's Legend of Justice were points in its favor—and, indeed, attributes to be emulated, by readers who enlist the poem and its characters in contemporary disputes. Their responses to book 5 are "local" in precisely the sense James deplores: unabashedly partisan and willfully presentist, they subject the poem and its author alike to reductive misreading, regularly lapsing, as James suggests they must, into passion, bias, and misrepresentation. Allowing such readings to influence our own approach to the Legend of Justice is risky, to be sure: they do not deepen, enrich, or complicate our understanding of the poem so much as call into question the values of depth, richness, and complexity. Reading against time is reading that disavows textual and situational nuance, makes virtues of obviousness and generality, and insists, as Spenser does in the *View*, that its insights and conclusions are not "of will, but of verie urgent necessitie." Even as we flinch from such reductive and coercive methods, however, it is worth asking what they illuminate in book 5 that we, in all our subtlety, have missed or preferred to disregard.

For the bias toward complexity entails economies of its own, as Elaine Freedgood and Cannon Schmitt observe:

> One of the odd lessons of literary criticism of the modern novel might turn out to be that it teaches us how to leave parts of texts alone; it prescribes a rigid division of reading labor. Only certain matter needs our attention. Other words, phrases, even entire plotlines might be read more lucidly by nautical, medical, botanical, ontological, or spiritualist readers, for example. Denotative, literal, and technical language has heretofore given us space to breathe, allowing us to look through or around it rather than at it. To refuse that space, to confront the opacity of such language, would be tantamount to transforming it into a *thing*.[37]

The lessons Freedgood and Schmitt here identify with criticism of the novel are, as previous chapters of this book have shown, essential to the pedagogy of *The Faerie Queene*, a poem in which knowing how to read very often means knowing how—or what—not to read. From this angle, book 5 looks less like a revolt against the poem's faith in interpretation than an intensification of the shortcuts and half-measures such faith has always, in practice, entailed. The difficulty is that in book 5, the literal and denotative overwhelm the allegorical; the part consumes the whole; the inescapable salience of historical reality leaves no room for any other sort of interpretation; the poem becomes a thing and its reader an automaton. Insisting either on the complexity and ambiguity of history itself or on the complexity and ambiguity of Spenser's relation to it is one way to restore "breathing room" to the poem, space for interpretation to reassert its value and necessity. The alternative, Freedgood and Schmitt suggest, is not to refuse to read, but to look unblinkingly at what remains, accepting both the iron-clad limits and the unseemly expediencies of reading for the moment.

Speaking of expediency: I suspect that it is Talus's speed, as much or more than his brutality, that has made him seem antithetical to the aims of literary criticism. For whatever our methods, whether historicist or formalist, symptomatic or surface-oriented, suspicious or reparative, what critical readers have in common is our insistence on taking our time: "We are 'critical' in that we are slow readers," Freedgood and Emily Apter have argued, "able to muse and Google and cross-reference at length, unencumbered by other fulltime employment."[38] That definition relies, however, on fairly dubious and increasingly untenable assumptions about the nature of academic employment and the lives of scholars; better, perhaps, to say that what we call criticism—the "reading" we produce in writing for perusal by other critics—strives to maintain an illusion of unhurried encounter with a text, an encounter purified of the evasive maneuvers ("browsing and abridging, skimming and snoozing") to which Apter and Freedgood themselves confess (140). But even as a disciplinary ideal, this ethos of slow reading is at odds with what we all know from experience, that the transformation from lay reader to scholarly interpreter is almost entirely regulated—motivated, shaped, directed, constrained, and often cut short—by the passage of time: by deadlines and due dates, day-care hours, academic calendars, teaching schedules, grant terms, employment contracts, and tenure clocks. If we are prone to celebrate the virtues of slow reading, as a scholarly protocol, an aesthetic pleasure, and even an ethical obligation, we do so in denial or disavowal of criticism's essential economies, of the inborn skills and learned techniques of inattention on which professional success so often depends.

Book 5 of *The Faerie Queene*—the book in which Spenser most closely confronts the exigencies and accommodations of his own professional career—offers us an opportunity to reflect more openly, and less defensively, on the instrumental, expedient, and urgently motivated character of criticism, both now and in the past. For as Spenser reminds us at the very end of book 4, deadlines can be liberating, even revelatory; the prospect of imminent catastrophe licenses the renegotiation—or breaching—of all kinds of contracts, including the contract between reader and text. And as various earlier readers of book 5 have discovered, the same holds true in the world outside the poem, where the rhetoric of crisis offers a powerful justification for effacing the claims of textual precision, historical difference, and authorial intent. Those readers—Talus-like in their fixity of purpose and their willful inattentiveness to what conflicts with their foregone conclusions—fall far outside the norms and values of modern criticism, but they make meaning from book 5 in a way that more recent critics have struggled to do, expanding the reach of its historical allegory by fashioning opportunistic analogies between then and now. Indeed, exploring the pre-twentieth-century reception history of book 5 reveals a paradoxical truth: although the Legend of Justice contains the most local and time-bound of Spenser's allegorical narratives, it is the part of the poem readers have most often invoked in answer to the requirements of their immediate circumstances. In part, this reflects the historical character of historicism itself: early readers of *The Faerie Queene* did not necessarily share our conviction that it, or any text, had to be read as a product of a particular historical and cultural moment. But even after the mid-eighteenth-century rise of literary historicism, book 5 retained its appeal as a commentary on the present—not because readers failed to recognize its relation to the late sixteenth-century political landscape, but because that context itself seemed to anticipate, explain, or even allegorize more recent events. For such readers, the impetus to attend to book 5 came not from a desire to understand the past but from the need to make sense of the present, as Talus does, by recognizing—or re-knowing—it as an instance of what has already occurred.

Poem of the Ironsides

The first reader to interpret the Legend of Justice as a pointed address to his own political circumstances had good reason for doing so: he was the son and heir of the Scots queen whose 1587 trial and execution for treason by Elizabeth were rendered—cautiously but unmistakably—in the trial and execution of Duessa in book 5, canto 9. As the English ambassador to Scotland, Robert Bowes, reported to the queen's treasurer, Lord Burghley, in November 1596, just after the six-book second edition of *The Faerie Queene* appeared in print, James VI interpreted the episode as a targeted attack on his royal legitimacy:

The K[ing] hath conceaved great offense against Edward [sic] Spencer publishing in prynt in the second p[ar]t of the Fairy Queene and ixth chapter some dishonorable effects (as the k. demeth therof) against himself and his mother deceassed. He alledged that this book was passed with priviledge of her ma[jes]t[y]s Commision[er]s for the viewe and allowance of all wrytinges to be receaued into Printe. But therin I haue (I thinke) satisfyed him that it is not giuen out with such p[ri]viledge: yet he still desyreth that Edward Spencer for his faulte, may be dewly tryed & punished.[39]

As the parenthetical asides suggest, Bowes was careful to separate himself from James's understanding of the poem and, especially, from his angry assumption that Elizabeth had approved or even solicited its depiction of his mother. But as Jonathan Goldberg argues, and Bowes surely realized, the king's resentment at the contents of book 5, canto 9 had less to do with the historical conflict it represented between Protestant Elizabeth and Catholic Mary than with the ongoing struggle between Elizabeth and James himself over the line of English succession, "James continually wanting assurances that his mother's treason did not bar his way to the English throne [and] Elizabeth recalcitrantly withholding her wishes for a successor."[40] For all his protestations about honoring his mother's memory, Richard McCabe concurs, the king's real anger over the publication of the 1596 *Faerie Queene* (and the motive for his ban on the poem's circulation in Scotland) "was largely for himself": "he appears to have regarded Book V as a personal insult" and "a calculated contribution to the debate over succession." Indeed, absent that pressing concern for his own political future, James appears to have had no quarrel with Spenser's poem: "once firmly established on the throne," McCabe points out, "he made no effort to prohibit the publication of the 1609 folio."[41]

The instinct to interpret the historical allegory of book 5 in light of more immediate anxieties was, in James's case, likely justified; certainly, he was not the only contemporary reader to interpret the poem as an allegory of the succession crisis. A year after he issued his ban on the 1596 *Faerie Queene*, an English reader named John Dixon—described by his modern editor, Graham Hough, as "literate but not particularly literary," and in no way sharing James's aspirations for England—annotated his copy of the 1590 *Faerie Queene* with a partially encrypted key identifying various characters in books 1, 2, and 3 with rivals for Elizabeth's favor at court.[42] Dixon's preoccupation with court politics, and his determination to enlist Spenser on his side in every instance, strikes Hough as perverse: "What to more modern readers has seemed the secondary meaning of the poem was to him the primary one."[43] But he confessed that in his myopia, Dixon saw things that those modern readers missed. For instance, even lacking the assistance of the historical allegory of book 5, Dixon was confident that

Duessa was meant to be Mary, Queen of Scots—or, as he refers to her in his alphabetical cipher, "dhrrar bs fpbggrf"—and he interprets the delivery of her letter at the end of book 1 as "[a] fiction of a challenge by Q[ueen] of S[cots]: that the religion maintained by hir maintained to be the truth," a reading Hough calls "surely right," although until the twentieth century, no other commentator advanced it.[44] "[I]ndifferent to the courtly and romantic aspects of *The Faerie Queene*" and with "very little interest in the narrative line ... which indeed he often misunderstands," Dixon nonetheless produced what even his disapproving editor recognized as a compelling version of the poem in his own image: "strongly Protestant and patriotic, [and] devoted to the Queen as the protagonist of the true faith in England."[45]

Reading *The Faerie Queene* in the immediate wake of its publication, James VI and John Dixon had sharply different reactions to its politics, but they agreed on what those politics were. In the decades and centuries after Spenser's death, however, even the most overtly politicized elements of the poem, many of them concentrated in the Legend of Justice, took on a curious malleability, susceptible to enlistment on either side of any current conflict or debate. Stranger still, it was Talus who served as the rhetorical hinge—the joint—on which such readings frequently depended, his blank efficiency making him a suitable agent for any cause. The iron page makes his first appearances outside *The Faerie Queene* in the late 1640s, at the height of the English Civil War, just as the word "crisis" itself entered general circulation. He appears not as a character from Spenser's allegory of colonial justice but as a portable figure of political urgency, a kind of shorthand for the radical action crisis demands. He first assumes this function in 1648, just after negotiations between Parliament and King Charles I finally collapsed, when an anonymous royalist republished book 5, canto 2 of *The Faerie Queene* under the title *The Faerie Leveller*, claiming it, in the words of the title page, as "A lively representation of our times."[46] "[C]ulled out by it selfe, and set forth for present use," the episode of Talus's encounter with the Egalitarian Giant was legible in a new way, as a prophetic allegory of the ongoing conflict between royalists and republicans: now "Talus ... with his iron flayle" stood for those loyal to the king's cause, while the Giant was Oliver Cromwell, news of whose defeat in Scotland the author eagerly anticipated, and his followers "the movers of Sedition ... lately risen up and now reigning amongst us." In the preface to his explanatory key, the anonymous author describes the extract from Spenser's poem as "now revised," but the text itself is unaltered; revising here has the literal sense of seeing anew or again—in the author's word, "applying all to these times" (3–4).

But a year later, in an exasperated aside in *Eikonoklastes*, a response to the king's elegiac *Eikon Basilika* and a defense of his execution by Parliament, John Milton enlists Talus in the republican cause, declaring, "If there were a man of iron, such as *Talus*, by our Poet *Spencer*, is fain'd to be, the page of Justice, who with his iron flaile could doe all this, and expeditiously, without theose deceitfull formes and circumstances of law, worse then ceremonies in religion; I say God send it don, whether by one *Talus*, or by a thousand." With his very next breath, Milton suggests that this apocalyptic vision has already come to pass: "It was not the Kings grace or princely goodness, but this iron flaile, the People, that drove the Bishops out of thir Baronies, out of thir Cathedrals, out of the Lords House, out of thir Copes and Surplices, and all those Papistical innovations, threw down the High Commission and Star-Chamber, gave us a triennial Parlement, and what we most desired."[47] That the republican Milton could call upon *The Faerie Queene*'s instrument of royal justice as a figure for the triumph of a populist revolt against the Crown is only partly explicable by the similarities between the Irish troubles of the 1580s and the 1640s, which Cromwell, like Grey before him, brutally repressed.[48] The larger point is that the extremity of political need to which Talus answers in *The Faerie Queene* licensed a comparable extremity in readers, whose polemical appropriations of Spenser's meaning were surely intended, in some measure, to startle.

As these early examples suggest, the contemporaneity and particularity of the historical allegory in book 5 was no obstacle to its redeployment on subsequent occasions of need; on the contrary, the topicality of the Legend of Justice seems to have served as an invitation for readers to seek in it a commentary on the present. Indeed, far from limiting the pool of readers to whom Spenser appeared as an ideological ally, the pointedly political character of book 5 made it susceptible to citation by opposite parties in a debate—each blaming the other for wanton misreading. The most mischievous instance of this occurred in 1713, at the height of the controversy over the Hanoverian succession, when a Whig churchman named Samuel Croxall, writing under the pen name "Nestor Ironsides," published what he claimed to be *An Original Canto of Spencer*, described as a lost fragment of *The Faerie Queene*'s fifth book.[49] The imposture wasn't meant to fool anyone: the supposedly original canto offered a naked satire of the current Tory administration, with Queen Anne appearing as a haplessly enthralled Britomart and her chief minister, Robert Harley, as the villainous Archimago. But Croxall didn't simply borrow Spenser's characters; he also claimed descent from one of their originals. In a joky preface "Nestor" said he found the manuscript in the papers of his great-grandfather, "Sir Caleb Ironside," "Schoolfellow and intimate Acquaintance of Mr Spencer's," whom the poet affectionately dubbed "Talus" (3). Croxall's own Talus retains the flavor of this imagined friendship: he appears at the end of the *Original Canto* as "trusty Talus," tasked not with the destruction of Archimago but with rousing Artegall to action, "Wishing him strait, ere Tyde might be too late / To hie with him, and snatch her from the Jaws of Fate" (29–30). The canto ends on a note of suspense, with

Artegall, "prict inly" by Talus's words and trusting to his guidance, racing to avert the impending catastrophe (30).

Croxall's Talus is not an executioner but a gadfly, his real-world counterpart not the military commander but the political pamphleteer—and Croxall hints that this is the proper function of poetry, as well. The preface to the *Original Canto* ends with the teasing promise of a forthcoming verse miscellany, to be titled "Poems of the Ironsides." "For you must know," Nestor assures us,

> all the Ironsides have had some smattering of Poetry more or less; or at least have pretended to it. There the Reader shall be entertain'd with the fashionable Flourishes of every Age, from the Ballad of Sidrophel Ironside, in the Reign of Henry the Fourth, to the Satyr of Nestor Ironside, Esq; in the Time of Charles the Second. (6)

It was this bit of humor, as much as the contents of the canto itself, that rankled the author of an anonymous rebuke to Croxall in the Tory *Examiner*. The piece in the *Examiner* has relatively little to say about the succession crisis; instead, it is aimed against the idea that Nestor Ironsides and his ilk might have any place in the history of English poetry. "[T]he itch of Politicks is ... on him," the author rails, "certainly an intollerable corruption of poetry." "Criticism, a very useful art," he adds, "is perfectly excluded by it." The figure most injured by the *Original Canto* is therefore not Robert Harley but "the deceased Immortal Spenser," who must suffer "Treason and Sedition utter'd in his Name and Language"—that is, in the name of poet and the language of poetry.[50] In his reply to the *Examiner* (followed, shortly thereafter, by the publication of *Another Original Canto*), Croxall retorted that what the anonymous writer dismissively termed "State-Poetry" was not a bastardization of the art but integral to it: "good Poets you see have been Prophets, and will, I hope, always be so."[51] The response was hardly necessary, for his antagonist had already made the point for him, with Spenser's help. The diatribe in the *Examiner* ends with a pointed quotation from book 5, canto 8: the chilling description of the poet with his tongue nailed to a post outside Mercilla's gate, tortured for his slanderous verses against the queen. "It must not be forgotten," the anonymous author observes, "that these ... Stanza's are to be found in the Description of the Palace of MERCY." However menacing in intent, that reminder backfires in the context of an essay against political poetry, underscoring the fact that *The Faerie Queene* itself violates the mandate to "render us Humane, Courteous, Benevolent, and mutual Promoters of each others Ease and Satisfaction."[52] It was always already a Poem of the Ironsides.

Diverse though their politics may be, those who appeal to book 5 as a reference point in the seventeenth and eighteenth centuries share a sense of urgency about the present: they make critical interventions not by taking their time with Spenser's poem but by insisting there is no time to lose. Such overtly instrumental readings of *The Faerie Queene* fell out of fashion in the later eighteenth century, however, as the myth of "gentle Spenser," poet of fancy, took hold. In the notes to his 1758 edition of *The Faerie Queene*, John Upton makes a strikingly defensive case for at least attending to the historical context of book 5, arguing that although history affords a "lesser view" of the poet's intentions, "[t]he historical allusions in this [fifth] book are so very apparent, that the most superficial reader of Spenser could never mistake them." Even so, he anticipates resistance from readers who will think "my arguments too flimsy, and extended beyond their due limits," and asks skeptics only "to consider what latitude of interpretation all typical and symbolical writings admit": for Upton, it seems, the danger of historical allegory is not that its insights will be too obvious or narrow, but that they will appear entirely far-fetched.[53]

Not until 1882 did Upton's defense of historical allegory find an echo, in an essay by Edward Dowden, first Professor of English Literature at Trinity College, Dublin, titled "Spenser, The Poet and Teacher" and prefaced to the London Spenser Society's edition of the *Complete Works*, edited by Alexander Grosart.[54] Eager to rescue Spenser from the sticky-sweet clutches of Romantic critics like William Hazlitt and James Russell Lowell, Dowden proposed to revive the standing of the "sage and serious Poet" hailed by Milton in *Areopagitica* as "a better teacher than Scotus or Aquinas."[55] But his own reading of *The Faerie Queene* owes more to the Milton of *Eikonoklastes*, in its attachment to the militancy of book 5: "The sternness of Spenser in this fifth Book is remarkable," Dowden observes, and belies any conception of the poet as "forgetful of England, forgetful of earth, lulled and lying in some bower of fantasy." Indeed, he admits, "it may be a difficulty with some readers to bring into harmony with their conception of Spenser his emphatic approval of the terrible policy of Lord Grey, the hero of this book, towards the Irish people." Like Milton, however, Dowden accounts for the brutality of book 5 by appealing to a more recent crisis, explaining, "towards the Irish people Spenser felt as an old Anglo-Indian might feel towards Sepoys in time of mutiny" (335). The reference is to the Indian Mutiny of 1857, which began when sepoys—native troops serving under the command of the British East India Company—rebelled against Company rule, motivated in part by rumors that the cartridges of their Enfield rifles had been greased with beef tallow. The mutiny was suppressed, but it prompted the dissolution of the East India Company, the reorganization of the entire colonial administration, and the establishment of the British Raj: for Dowden, book 5 of *The Faerie Queene* offers a transhistorical and global perspective on the crises of English empire—latitude of interpretation, indeed.

What is merely an aside in Dowden's essay becomes a full-fledged thesis in the essay that launched *The Faerie Queene* into the age of Anglo-American global politics, Edwin Greenlaw's 1912 article on "Spenser and British Imperialism." "In *The Faerie Queene*," Greenlaw writes, "is found abundant evidence that Spenser ... made use of current politics for the purposes of his allegory."[56] Far from decrying this fact, Greenlaw argues that it produced in book 5 "the zenith" of Spenser's poetic achievement, "a revelation of the mature thought of the poet" and "one of the most remarkable productions of its kind" (351). What Kate M. Warren saw as the "woeful limitation" of allegory in the Legend of Justice, Greenlaw embraces as a dazzling refinement. In it, he writes, Spenser's "mastery of allegory is complete ... , everything being subordinated to the treatment of problems of government" (351). "[H]ow admirable is Spenser's method and how complete his interpretation of contemporary history," he marvels:

> The most important events in the history of Elizabeth's development of a powerful government are treated, not baldly and incoherently as in the chronicles, but in an allegory that unifies and interprets. ... Each minor adventure leads toward the climax in the triumph of authority, showing how lawlessness, bribery, selfish quarrelling and jealousy among the leaders, the danger from womanish theories of mildness, all contribute to thwart the purposes of the ministers of the sovereign. ... Here in truth is a turning of the barren precepts of philosophy into pregnant images of life, a life not merely of men and measures, but also breathing the spirit of the new imperial England. (355–57)

Reading such effusions, it is hard to avoid the suspicion that Greenlaw's appreciation for book 5 is colored, like so many earlier readings, by more immediate interests—certainly his description of "the spirit of the new imperial England" reflects the triumphalism of the early twentieth century better than the ambivalence of the Elizabethan age. And in fact, seven years later, after the outbreak of a world war that cemented the Anglo-American alliance and stretched the British empire to its greatest extent, Greenlaw included excerpts from *The Faerie Queene* under the heading "Training for Empire" in *The Great Tradition*, an anthology of English and American literature coedited by James Holly Hanford, "illustrating the national ideals of freedom, faith, and conduct."[57] Meant to nurture the "idealism, sleeping but not dead, that swept America like a divine fire in the months following April of 1917," Greenlaw's anthology opened with a summons to politically engaged literary criticism: "Other crises remain to be met, for the warfare never ends. It is the task of the school and college to guard the flame" (xxii).

A year earlier, in 1918, as World War One raged and anticolonial unrest roiled Ireland, the Clarendon Press in Oxford released its new edition of book 5, with a frankly jingoistic preface by Alfred B. Gough. Gough recommends the

Legend of Justice as "the most suitable book to introduce the young student to the study of Spenser":

> Particularly at the present crisis, when Britain has once more appeared as a champion of oppressed nations, and especially of "the Lady Belge," yet again the innocent victim of a monstrous tyrant, who has moreover, like Grantorto, fanned the smouldering embers of Irish sedition into a flame, and has threatened our shores with a mightier Armada than Philip's, a new and singular interest attaches to the book in which the Elizabethan poet broadly interprets the similar struggle of his day as an elemental conflict between justice and injustice.[58]

Gough here makes explicit the way that crisis, supposedly the phenomenon of an instant, perpetuates itself across time, becoming an endlessly reusable justification for violent response. In this view, the specific political crisis from which book 5 of *The Faerie Queene* emerged—the "struggle of [Spenser's] day"—is not a limitation on its meaning but the renewable source of its significance in the present, as "a true reflection of the ardent patriotism, the adventurous temper, the steadfast energy, and the religious and moral zeal" of "English warriors and statesmen" (xlix). So long as crises continue to present themselves—and when do they not?—the poem retains its power; allegories of conquest expand with the empires that beget them, and warfare, like Talus, never ends.

This perception of book 5, as the record of a past that isn't really past, need not, however, be taken to legitimate the business of empire as usual, as an essay by the Irish priest and scholar Matthew Kelly in the December 1844 issue of the *Dublin Review* illustrates with astonishing power. Kelly had been recently appointed professor of belles lettres at Maynooth College, and his essay is ostensibly a work of literary criticism, occasioned by the publication of a new Routledge edition of *The Works of Edmund Spenser*, but it begins with a stark disclaimer:

> It is not our intention to discuss the poetical merits of Spenser.... Ours is a more humble and more ungracious task—to speak of plain facts which have been overlooked by his admirers—to consider him, not as a poet establishing all the virtues in his Faery Realm, but as a politician applying his philosophy to an earthly kingdom; not as polishing the language and exalting the poetry of England, but as expressing her prejudices and swaying her councils in the government of a land which must bitterly regret that he ever set foot on her shores.[59]

That land, of course, is Ireland—but despite its name, the *Dublin Review* was a London publication, founded in 1836 by journalist Michael Joseph Quin, Cardinal Nicholas Wiseman, and politician Daniel O'Connell, to champion Irish

Catholic interests and opinions to a potentially sympathetic English readership.[60] And at the end of 1844, that mission was on the verge of failure: O'Connell, known as the Liberator for his role in the passage of the 1829 Catholic Emancipation Act, was arrested the previous year for leading a massive campaign to repeal the 1801 Act of Union incorporating Ireland into Great Britain. Tried and convicted of sedition by British authorities, he spent much of 1844 in prison, and although the conviction was overturned in the fall, new troubles threatened. The failure of the repeal campaign had lent legitimacy to more radical members of the independence movement, who favored violent uprising, and rumors had begun to spread of a devastating agricultural blight, deadly to the potato plants on which the Irish diet—thanks in part to ruinous tariffs on grain—almost entirely depended.

Kelly invokes those pressing concerns as the necessary frame for reading both Spenser's 1596 prose treatise, *A View of the Present State of Ireland*, and book 5 of *The Faerie Queene*, the twin texts to which the bulk of his essay is dedicated. What links them to each other, he asserts, is also what makes them essential reading in the present, their shared foundation in the catastrophe from which modern Ireland was born:

> It is certain, that the reign of Elizabeth was the great crisis of modern Ireland. It is certain that succeeding reigns, with a few brief intervals, adopted, with greater or less severity, the maxims of Elizabeth's policy; and it is equally certain, we fear, that whatever was irritating or oppressive in that policy, was, if not originated, at least recommended by the gentle Spenser. (415–16)

The epithet is evidently ironic, but only partly so: Kelly recognizes, more, perhaps, than most modern critics, the aesthetic appeal of book 5, its lush descriptions of the Irish landscape and its vivid touches of local color. "Spenser is a tempter, depicting the glowing charms of helpless beauty," he observes, and it is precisely the grandeur and purity of his ideals that makes his embodiment of them in Artegall so offensive, "an outrage unparalleled in the annals of literary curiosities" (435, 419). Talus, by contrast, appears as a worthy addition to the Legend of Justice, being "the true emblem of British justice in Ireland" (421): what countless critics have rejected as a crude and dehumanizing portrait of justice strikes Kelly as the only honest element in it.

Kelly's account of *The Faerie Queene* is remarkable not only for its insistent focus on book 5 as the epitome of Spenser's dubious poetic gifts but for its continual, self-reflexive defense of its own methodology: when it comes to Spenser, Kelly—trained as an antiquarian—claims presentism as the only responsible version of historicism. Although he frequently indulges in casual analogies between the 1580s and the 1840s ("To form some idea of the government of Ireland by the Lord Grey of Queen Elizabeth, we have only to call to mind the government of the Lord Grey of Queen Victoria" [418]; Spenser's complaints of corrupt colonial soldiers "look like a description of the Shinrone police" [431]), he also insists that Spenser was a product of his time: "He spoke the feelings of his day" (423). That comment follows immediately upon Kelly's citation of the description of the starving people of Munster in Spenser's *View*—but it is not meant as mitigation. Rather, Kelly insists, it is precisely the representative character of Spenser's inhumanity that makes *The Faerie Queene*—and, especially, its fifth book—far more dangerous than any mere artifact of history. Spenser's imperial day is one on which the sun hasn't begun to set. "The errors of Spenser and his compeers, like all great national lies, will last as long as the system from which they sprang," Kelly explains, and that system endures into the present: "it must not be forgotten that Spenser's calumnies and policy are still the maxims of British governors and, unfortunately, the public opinion of a large class of Englishmen toward Ireland" (424, 444).

It is that large class of Englishmen to whom Kelly addresses his argument: by the end what is at stake is not so much the reputation of a particular poet but the habits and attitudes of a reading public whose proprietary stake in English literary tradition—and in *The Faerie Queene* as part of that tradition—depends on their propensity to treat poetry and politics, past and present, as fully alienable categories. "Thousands know Spenser's poetry who never heard of his politics," he observes, and toward those readers he adopts a pose of calculated humility: "we feel some apology is due, for raking up these heavy charges on his memory." But the apology is immediately retracted, since for an Irish reader, the memory of colonial oppression doesn't need raking up: "Spenser's spirit survives in Irish misgovernment. His work is the fruit and food of prejudices injurious to some of our fellow-subjects and disgraceful to all." The essay concludes with a fatalistic pronouncement: "Such is the fate of the errors of genius, especially when they are the errors of an age" (444). The "especially" gives the argument an unexpected final twist: genius is not what transcends history but what is amplified and transmitted by it. The enduring power of *The Faerie Queene* is not a mark of timelessness but proof that its age—the age of empire—is not yet ended.

A reader like Kelly hardly needed Edward Dowden to remind him that "Spenser was no dreamer" (338)—the evidence of the poet's real-world influence lay all about him—but his perspective on the poem was not welcomed by mainstream Spenserians. In a lengthy appendix to his 1882 edition of Spenser's *Works*, in which Dowden's essay appears, Alexander B. Grosart singles out Kelly's *Dublin Review* essay as an egregious instance of the "Vials of wrath—filled to the brim" that "have been poured out from generation to generation by (so-called) patriotic Irish Historians and Biographers and Essayists and Reviewers [on] the head of *Spenser*" (449). Calling it "a pitiably partizan and perpetually blundering paper," Grosart rejects the essay's reading of book 5 through the lens of current Irish politics as a "mere assertion of ignorance, not knowledge . . . throughout characterized by the most illiberal and provocative spirit" (450). What Grosart really objects to, however, is not the forging of historical analogies per se, but the unflattering portrait this particular analogy between Ireland in the 1580s and Ireland in the 1840s paints of Spenser and of English empire. He counters it with an analogy of his own: the poet's "scheme of 'starving out'" the inhabitants of Munster was, he says, "identical with Germany before Paris in our own time," when Otto von Bismarck—Kaiser Wilhelm's "Iron Chancellor"—first shelled and then starved the people of the city into submission. "[W]ere rebellion to arise to-day in Ireland in such lines as were laid in Elizabeth's time," Grosart darkly concludes, "the truest mercy were as absolute a use of force as England's resources could command" (499).

Kelly's reading of Spenser in the 1844 *Dublin Review* is indeed extraordinary, both in its insistence on the fundamentally (and destructively) political character of the poet's legacy and its determination to evaluate that legacy from the perspective of its anonymous casualties. But in its embrace of what we might call the hermeneutic of crisis, it is exemplary of a critical mainstream to which Grosart himself clearly belongs, a tradition of presentist reading that allowed Spenser's historical allegory of the 1580s to be repurposed as Royalist prophecy and Republican polemic, Whig satire and Tory propaganda, record of colonial injustice and summons to imperial aggression. To a modern critical eye, the results of such reading are not especially edifying. Especially in the jingoistic accounts of Grosart, Greenlaw, and Gough, the poetry of *The Faerie Queene* is not simply instrumentalized but weaponized—as Edward Dowden writes, "that which appears pliant as the blades of summer grass may prove at our need to be a sword of steel" (339). The martial metaphor isn't simply distasteful; it gets at what we are likely to find least appealing in early readings of book 5: the willing sacrifice of ambiguity to obviousness, the pliancy of poetry to the steeliness of propaganda. But the legitimacy Dowden confers on readerly necessity, as a force that can transform texts, activating them for uses beyond the bounds of authorial intention or original context, is not restricted to those who see in Spenser the flattering image of their own imperial ambitions and ideological prejudices. Talus's victims can learn from his methods—as Kelly's unrelenting assault on Spenser's policies and poetry shows.

Near the beginning of Kelly's essay, just after he describes the unyielding character of Talus, he points *A View of the Present State of Ireland* as a clarifying and galvanizing image of Talus out of "his poetic dress." Talus, Kelly observes, "is forbidding enough," but in the poet's description of his emaciated neighbors, we see "the naked horrors" of the justice he served (422–23). At the end of the essay, however, Kelly returns to *A View*, countering the earlier citation with a second extract, which, he says, would "cover a multitude of [Spenser's] sins" if it, too, were read through the lens of present necessity. The latter passage, containing Irenius's appeal to English lawmakers to counter the abuses of Irish tenant farmers by wealthy landowners, is a rare expression of what seems like a real concern for justice on Spenser's part, not only for himself but for his Irish neighbors—but this is not why Kelly cites it. "[I]t is clear," he says, that "Spenser's motive was not humanity, but policy": many wealthy Irish landlords were members of the "Old English" elite antagonistic to Lord Grey's reforms. But Spenser's sensibilities are not the point: if Irenius's proposed reforms were finally adopted, Kelly argues, the most pressing cause of poverty and food insecurity in nineteenth-century Ireland would be removed. Then, and only then, would Spenser's "moral delinquency" be redeemed, for "how few the victims, how slight the rapid havoc of war, compared to the millions of hearts broken by the tyranny of landlords" (445).

Less than a year after Kelly's essay appeared in the *Dublin Review*, the Irish potato crop failed. Over the next five years, as Irish tenant farmers continued to export large quantities of food and cash to English landowners, more than a million people died of starvation and famine-related diseases; millions of others were forced to emigrate, hurried on their way by mass evictions. Faced with the tyranny of landlords, as an eyewitness account suggests, sympathy counted for nothing, could even become an excuse for inaction:

> The wailing of women—the screams, the terror, the consternation of children—the speechless agony of honest industrious men—wrung tears of grief from all who saw them. I saw officers and men of a large police force, who were obliged to attend on the occasion, cry like children at beholding the cruel sufferings of the very people whom they would be obliged to butcher had they offered the least resistance. The landed proprietors in a circle all around—and for many miles in every direction—warned their tenantry, with threats of their direct vengeance, against the humanity of extending to any of them the hospitality of a single night's shelter ... and in little more than three years, nearly a fourth of them lay quietly in their graves.[61]

The slip from the screams of the terrified children to the childlike tears of their oppressors shows how easy it is to expand the range of sympathetic identification right over the distinction between victim and victimizer, to equate the helplessness of those forced from their homes at gunpoint with those "obliged" to hold the guns. Among its many merits, the essay in the *Dublin Review* refuses to credit Spenser for the ambivalence—the pliancy of feeling and imagination—that leads him to depict Artegall and Britomart quailing at the spectacle of Talus's "rapid havoc." The legal violence for which they righteously stand is the poem's real and abiding horror, and if Spenser is to be redeemed, it is law that must redeem him. Sympathy and self-doubt are poetical merits that not all readers can afford; in a crisis, one seizes what is at hand, even if that hand is the unfeeling hand of the law.

The Faerie Queene Express

The reception history of the Legend of Justice does much to confirm the wariness with which modern critics have approached book 5 of Spenser's poem; those to whom it has appealed tend to be precisely the kinds of readers Spenserians would like to disavow—warmongers, ideologues, and apologists for empire—and their once timely commentaries on it pass rapidly into obsolescence, seeming at best quaint and at worst bigoted. But the variety of seemingly incommensurate uses to which politically minded readers have put book 5 suggests the potential of crisis as a hermeneutic strategy, its capacity to extend the range of allegorical reference across time and space. Talus, in particular, serves to trigger that response: even Northrop Frye, quintessential formalist of the mid-twentieth century, pauses in his superbly refined analysis of "The Structure of Imagery in *The Faerie Queene*," to note that Spenser's iron man, "who must surely be one of the earliest 'science fiction' or technological symbols in poetry, and who kills without discrimination for the sake of discrimination," puts him in mind of nothing so much as "a South African policeman."[62] More recently, in an interview conducted in October 2003, seven months after the start of the US- and Britain-led invasion of Iraq, Irish poet Seamus Heaney observed that "it would be an instructive, self-educational thing at this minute to read Edmund Spenser in relation to Iraq.... You wouldn't have to accuse Spenser of writing bad poetry, but you'd have to understand him historically, in the full and present realization that civilized people can do bad things."[63] The pressing immediacy of crisis—reading Spenser "at this minute," with a "full and present realization" of his significance—need not be opposed to historical understanding, Heaney suggests; on the contrary, it is constitutive of it in the fullest sense, by insisting on the multiplicity of moments at which a poem might mean something new.

Such reading necessarily entails risks scholarly critics are trained to avoid, exposing interpretive claims to charges of ignorance, bias, anachronism, and opportunism. But in the final section of this chapter, I want to run those risks, and to count the cost of avoiding them, by offering a speculative reading of book 5 shaped by an imminent sense of disciplinary crisis, in which the phrase "no time to scan" has taken on meanings no sixteenth-century writer would have anticipated. For Talus offers readers in the economically straitened, politically volatile, and digitally sped twenty-first century something that scholars within the discipline of literary criticism have been calling for with increasing frequency: what Johanna Drucker calls "a humanistically informed theory of ... technology," reflecting the interdependence of the human and the non- or post-human in the work of textual interpretation.[64] By the same token, the tools and theories of the digital humanities offer readers of book 5 a perspective on Spenser's iron man that is neither overly defensive nor sentimentalized, one from which Talus can be seen as embodying the fraught instrumentality of all reading, whether done on-screen or by means of that no less transformative technology, the book.

Indeed, as the responses to Talus in the previous section reveal, Spenser's iron man offers readers of *The Faerie Queene* an opportunity to think through what Tara MacPherson has identified as the central problem of media studies, its seeming effacement or evasion of the embodied histories of race and empire. Talus reminds us that the questions MacPherson asks of digital computation—"Might we ask whether there is not something *particular to the very forms* of electronic culture that seems to encourage just such a movement, a movement that partitions race off from the specificity of media forms? Put differently, might we argue that the very structures of digital computation develop at least in part to cordon off race and to contain it?"[65]—have antecedents in questions Spenser scholars have asked of the technologies of manuscript and print, essential to the poet's professional career. As Christopher Burlinson and Andrew Zurcher note, Spenser's role as "copyist, certifier, sealer, and dispatcher" of letters made him a key channel between Ireland and London, "a husbander of secrets, but also a medium of communication" in an environment in which news was a vital and often scarce commodity, but the very official trappings of those documents has helped distance their contents from the substance of his verse.[66] Talus may be the figure in *The Faerie Queene* most conspicuously alien to the allegorical poet, but he is an obvious surrogate for the colonial functionary, impersonal instrument of colonial domination.

Unbound by time and immune to distraction, Talus's perspective on the poem he inhabits is inhumanly wide *and* deep, swift *and* patient, concentrated *and* diffuse. Sent after Sir Sanglier in canto 1, he skims across the surface of the allegorical landscape like a "swallow in her flight" (5.1.20.4), identifying his quarry at first glance; keen to sniff out Munera in canto 2, by contrast, he becomes like "a limehound" or bloodhound, who "all things secrete wisely could bewray," searching "at length" until he finds her hiding place beneath a heap of gold and draws her out (5.2.25.3–5). Throughout book 5 he is repeatedly deployed by Artegall to wield his flail against crowds so massive they lose—in his and our eyes—any semblance of humanity, appearing instead like "a swarme of flyes" (5.2.53.6, 5.11.58.1–2), "a flush of duckes" (5.2.54.2) or "squirrels" (5.11.59.3), massed in "heapes ... of slaughtred carkasses" (5.7.36.4–5), "flock[ed] together in confusde array" (5.11.43.8), and "scattred all over the land, / As thicke as ... seed" (5.12.7.8–9). Such scenes require Talus's intervention both because they exceed Artegall's capacity for judgment and because they fall short of it: it's the sort of "big data" processing or "macroanalysis"—scanning in the modern sense—we now delegate to algorithmic codes and computer search engines, the automated sidekicks on which we rely to navigate the ever expanding and notoriously unreliable landscape of digitized information.

But we needn't look so far ahead as the EEBO-TCP N-gram browser or Google to discover analogues—or antidotes—to Talus's "iron paw." In the summer of 1820, while marking his copy of *The Faerie Queene* for Fanny Brawne, John Keats added a stanza to the close of book 5, canto 2, where Artegall and Talus defeat the Egalitarian Giant. "To Spenser," Herbert Cory notes, "the giant's radical notions were naturally revolting and the henchmen of Justice kicked him off a cliff," but Keats, "his eyes dilated by the French Revolution and by many new political visions," imagines a sequel to the episode.[67] In this version, technology turns on Artegall and Talus, reanimating the giant's radical politics with the power of mass media and the popular press:

> In after-time, a sage of mickle lore
> Yclep'd Typographus, the Giant took,
> And did refit his limbs as heretofore,
> And made him read in many a learned book,
> And into many a lively legend look;
> Thereby in goodly themes so training him,
> That all his brutishness he quite forsook,
> When, meeting Artegall and Talus grim,
> The one he struck stone-blind, the other's eyes wox dim.[68]

For Keats, print itself contained the germ of resistance to Spenser's autocratic vision; the solution to the injustices of book 5 lay not in a rejection of Talus's mechanized efficiency but in the supersession of it by newer and more powerful means of producing and disseminating texts. (Fittingly enough, the stanza itself was published posthumously by Keats's friend Charles Brown in a newspaper, the *Plymouth and Davenport Weekly Journal*.)

Or we might go back further still, to 1609, when the publishers of the first folio edition of *The Faerie Queene* made the seemingly slight but massively consequential decision to number the stanzas within each canto of the poem. Numbered stanzas are so basic to our experience of the poem today—indeed, it would be impossible to teach, write articles, or give conference presentations about *The Faerie Queene* without them—that it is surprising to realize that readers ever encountered the poem without them; in fact, however, they appear in neither of the editions printed in Spenser's lifetime. The numbering of

Spenser's stanzas in the 1609 folio constitutes a crisis in *The Faerie Queene* in the sense that numbered stanzas are the precondition of criticism about *The Faerie Queene*. Without a simple, standardized mechanism for referring to particular places within the poem's more than four thousand stanzas, it would be impossible to do anything with the poem other than recite it verbatim or summarize its contents: critical reading of the poem—reading that weds close attention to particular textual effects with a more capacious interest in large-scale phenomena of allegorical structure, imagistic patterning, narrative sequence, or thematic development—absolutely depends on the ability to move easily between textual instances and to rapidly adjust the scale of our attention, zooming in to or out from the text as the work of interpretation demands. For these purposes, numbered stanzas are indispensible: they allow a reader to reconstruct the poem as an argument, a motivated reading in which particular passages are excerpted for special attention, returned to on multiple occasions, coupled with passages remote from them in the poem itself, and offered as examples of something other than or in addition to their immediate function in the unfolding of Spenser's verse.

In his efficient processing of Artegall's commands, his ability to reduce the complexities of judgment to mere sequencing and pattern recognition, Talus can thus be read as anticipating the unforeseen and unforeseeable effects of print on the reception of *The Faerie Queene*—the ways that new formats like the numbered stanza or new genres like the newspaper enabled new readings. By the same token, for twenty-first-century readers, Talus helps to illuminate the increasing sway of what Stephen Ramsay and Geoffrey Rockwell call "the most problematic—and, perhaps, the most ubiquitous—category of digital tools," tools that "don't explain or argue but simply facilitate."[69] Facilitation is Talus's raison d'être: left to his own devices, the iron man iterates the inputs of judgment without end, ceaselessly and pointlessly, which is why both Artegall and Britomart are repeatedly forced to call him off. But Talus also exposes the inadequacy of a phrase like "simply facilitate," for his perspective, however detached, reshapes the poem in its own image, effacing difference and ambiguity. So, too, of course, do the rubrics that converted printed documents into machine readable texts: "We accept the compromises inherent in such transformations," Ramsay writes elsewhere, "in order to reap the benefits of speed, automation, and scale that computational representations afford."[70] Talus's participation in Artegall's quest entails similar compromises and reaps similar benefits; it is a media shift that inflects the ends of justice, for better and for worse, much as numbering *The Faerie Queene*'s stanzas transformed the purposes for which the poem could be read, much as our technologically enhanced methods of scanning—in the anachronistic modern sense of the word—are shaped by the prostheses on which we rely.[71]

Granting Talus a more intimate and familiar place in our readings of book 5 means reckoning with the instrumentalized, networked, inhuman nature of those readings. But it is also an occasion for reflecting on the occasionally supernatural acuity of the inhuman, the specters of meaning that things alone can conjure. The promise of the digital humanities is that algorithms, databases, and search engines can deliver us from crisis by fortifying humanist inquiry with the methodological prestige and epistemological confidence of the sciences, opening new sources of funding and institutional support and liberating individual researchers from the constraints of time, of which none of us have as much as we need. The most extreme version of this promise, however, the hope that machine learning will progress to true artificial intelligence, to algorithms capable of setting their own agendas and arriving at insights no human reader could, presents an inescapable conundrum: If machine reading did generate an independent and otherwise inaccessible result, how would we—how could we—verify and interpret that finding? What if our attempts to do so failed?

Since digital tools do not share human readers' assumptions about what counts as a meaningful or legitimate resemblance, or our habits of chronological and narrative sequencing, they are especially prone to forging connections that are, on closer inspection, merely adventitious. This is their weakness—the kind of error machine learning works to overcome—but also their strength, for in it inheres their capacity to tell us things we do not know, would not have guessed, and might not even recognize as true. The problem is what to do with such insights. As James E. Dobson writes,

> the important difference between human and machine classification ... is what draws us to categorize data into categories and our doubt about this categorization. The algorithm assumes all data will "fit." Within machine learning there are concepts to label the degree to which data fits into categories: we call any potential uncertainty within classification confusion or simply "error." The outlier, that peculiar object not belonging to the domain of one law or another, might present some difficulty to categorize for the algorithm, but it is of high interest to the human interpreter because it represents a problem.[72]

Let me turn, then, to an outlier, a peculiar object brought to my attention when, faced with a looming deadline for a conference paper, I delegated the task of making sense of Talus to my own laptop computer by searching for the phrase "Faerie Queene machine" on Google. Mostly I got links back to digital texts of the poem itself, but the very first result directed me to a Wikipedia entry titled "Fairy Queen (locomotive)." This was almost certainly not what I needed for my conference paper, but I clicked the link anyway, and then clicked several more links, eventually arriving at a website for the Indian Railways Fan Club (http://irfca.org), where I found a photograph of a brightly painted steam engine, ornamented with gold stars and a nameplate reading "Fairy Queen Express."

As certified by the 1998 *Guinness Book of World Records*, the Fairy Queen Express, also known as Engine 22 of the East Indian Railway Company (EIR 22), was—until 2016, when it was finally retired—the world's longest-running steam-powered locomotive. It was built in a factory in Leeds in 1855 and shipped to Calcutta, where it was put into use as a mail train. Two years later, when the Sepoy Mutiny sparked a widespread anticolonial uprising, EIR 22 was pressed into emergency service in the East India Company military, hauling ammunition, weaponry, and British troops across the colonial territories.[73] Further research revealed that railways were crucial to the survival of British rule in India: when the city of Delhi fell to native insurgents, the last-minute arrival of a siege-train carrying heavy battery allowed British troops to finally destroy the city's defenses. Records kept by members of the Royal Corps of Engineers reveal that military operations were often focused on preventing anticolonial forces from seizing or destroying essential railroad routes and engines.[74] Thanks in part to their control of the country's railways, the combined forces of the East India Company and the British government put an end to the rebellion in 1858—although the East India Company itself was dissolved not long after, replaced by the British Raj. EIR 22 returned to its ordinary function, lapsing into disuse in the early twentieth century before it was restored as a tourist attraction. Today the Fairy Queen Express is a government-certified national treasure, transporting day-trippers and train enthusiasts from Delhi to the picturesque town of Alwar and back.

In the instant of discovery, the Fairy Queen Express seemed to me an uncanny expression of Talus's reach beyond the poem, across the history and geography of British empire. Here, again, was the iron machine, racing across a colonial landscape in the service of a profoundly inequitable vision of justice. And the afterlife of the Fairy Queen Express, its transformation from instrument of oppression to historical and cultural icon, seemed to echo the fortunes of *The Faerie Queene*, book 5, foregrounding the ethical ambiguities that make that part of Spenser's poem such uneasy reading. There was just one problem: further research utterly failed to bear these intuitions out. EIR 22 wasn't christened the "Fairy Queen Express" until the end of the nineteenth century, and there is no evidence I can find that the name has anything to do with Spenser's poem (more likely, perhaps, is a reference to Shakespeare's Titania). As an avatar of Talus, the Fairy Queen Express is not a relic of literary history but an artifact of the haphazard course of Internet research—a casualty of reading in the digital present.

As the reception history of book 5 repeatedly shows, reading against time—in the sense of reading in haste and under pressure—begets readings against time, readings that resist the logic of cause and effect, before and after, in favor of a hasty poetics of analogy. The norms of scholarly research suggested I ought to let it go, but the Fairy Queen Express has proved stubbornly hard to dislodge from my thinking about book 5 of *The Faerie Queene*, as obdurate in its way as Talus himself. The stereotype of digital humanistic research is that it can reveal patterns too vast, diffuse, and elusive for any human reader to perceive, but digital research can also forge connections that would not otherwise have occurred at all: What then? I have been urging an analogy between Talus and the various tools upon which readers, past and present, rely to organize their responses to Spenser's poem. But Talus is also an "outlier," impossible either to assimilate or to ignore; begotten of Spenser's tragic misjudgments in colonial Ireland, he persists as an atavistic residue of aggression, the ghost in *The Faerie Queene* machine.

"Voluminous databases contain hidden knowledge," Kenneth Cory observes, and empires forge strange bonds, too, linking places, peoples, and events in what Lisa Lowe terms "the intimacies of four continents."[75] (In 1845, for instance, the first major relief effort for victims of the Great Hunger arrived in the form of a £14,000 donation from Irish soldiers enlisted in the service of the East India Company in Calcutta.) Empires and databases can also, of course, produce illusions of knowledge, control, and meaningful connection where there is really only coincidence and contingency. For all the associations between the digital and the objectively verifiable, computer-enabled searches frequently generate uncanny excesses of signification. As scholars, we are trained to ignore these hints if they cannot be confirmed by textual evidence and traditional methods of inquiry and, if they can be confirmed, to furnish them with more legitimate stories of origin—we cite the scholarly text or archival document that gives heft to the unexpected association or random result, not the Google query that sent us down the research rabbit hole in the first place. And yet, as Elaine Freedgood argues, such moments of "algorithmic divination" remind us that "[r]eading literature is always in this sense divinatory" (224)—always interpretive, always creative, and (less happily) always vulnerable to misjudgment.

We can lament this fact, or we can accept it as the ground of humanistic study: a "scientific criticism," Stephen Ramsay declares, "would cease to be criticism," and "in pouring the 'well of English undefiled' through the thin opening of Von Neumann's bottleneck"—a reference to the built-in processing limits of personal computers—"we discover strange tensions, exceptions and potential" (*Reading Machines*, 15, 34). The phrase "well of English vndefyled" is, oddly enough, from *The Faerie Queene*—it's Spenser's praise in book 4, canto 2 of "Dan Chaucer," "On Fames eternall beadroll worthie to be fyled" (4.2.32.8–9).

Ramsay doesn't footnote it, and perhaps it serves him only as a suitably orotund invocation of literary tradition, but it fits his context uncannily well, since the way Spenser chooses to honor Chaucer in book 4 is by rewriting his narrative: updating his file, lest "cursed Eld, the cankerworme of writes" causes it to be "deuoured, and brought to nought by little bits" (4.2.33.6, 9). The transformations wrought by the bits and bytes of digital data are, in this sense, merely the extension of a very long history of poetic remediation, fueled by the very human impulse to, as Ramsay says, "fill in gaps, make connections backward and forward, explain inconsistencies, resolve contradictions, and, above all, generate additional narratives" (*Reading Machines*, 62).

Nowhere in *The Faerie Queene* is that impulse more openly resisted than at the end of book 4, when Cymoent declines to make sense of the prophecy on which her son's life seemingly depends, and nowhere is it more openly courted than in canto 6 of book 5, when Talus is temporarily loosed from the control of his human minders, "not belonging," as Dobson describes the algorithmic error, "to the domain of one law or another." The crisis is triggered back in canto 5, when Artegall willingly surrenders to the Amazon Radigund, who dresses him in female garb and makes him her slave. Unable to countermand his master's decree by freeing him and unwilling to stand by while the course of justice is perverted, Talus sets off in pursuit of someone who can relieve his dilemma, overriding the contradictory imperatives to which he is bound. At the start of canto 6, we see him racing headlong toward the castle where Britomart waits, impatiently counting the time again anew. Seeing the iron man approach, she races out to meet him, "to know his tidings somme" (5.6.8.9), at which point Talus suffers an extraordinary, if momentary, collapse:

> Euen in the dore him meeting, she begun;
> And where is he thy Lord, and how far hence?
> Declare at once; and hath he lost or wun?
> The yron man, albe he wanted sence
> And sorrowes feeling, yet with conscience
> Of his ill newes, did inly chill and quake,
> And stood still mute, as one in great suspence,
> As if that by his silence he would make
> Her rather reade his meaning, then him selfe it spake. (5.6.9)

A number of recent critics have been struck by Talus's strange onset of interiority at this moment, the rush of what Abraham Stoll calls "Hamlet-like conscientiousness" into Spenser's iron man at the very moment when he is literally, uncharacteristically inanimate, standing "still mute." Stoll attributes this inflection of Talus's character to his proximity to Britomart: the iron man catches his "inner life of feeling" from Spenser's most fully felt fictional creation. "The crisis within Talus," he writes, "becomes a crisis within the poetics of *The Faerie Queene* for Talus's suddenly rich inner life defeats our expectations of psychomachia": What do we do when an allegorical instrument takes on a life of its own, a life uncannily like our own? [76] But that reading takes on faith the equivalences implied by "as" and "as if"—words that reveal the narrator's complicity in making sense of, by humanizing, a moment of machine failure. And the possibilities the narrator imagines aren't wholly benign; he interprets Talus's muteness not simply as an expression of emotional turmoil (if it is that) but a rhetorical strategy: "As if that by his silence he would make / Her rather reade his meaning, then him selfe it spake." Given the ethical unease reading the Legend of Justice itself induces, this is an explanation worth taking seriously. Interpretation abhors a vacuum—and in the rush to fill one with meaning, it assumes the burden of that meaning. This explanation suggests that Talus has begun to master not empathy but the logic of blame-shifting, which would make Britomart the agent of her own disappointment. To speak "ill news" is to be responsible for its transmission, but to stand silent and have one's meaning read redistributes that responsibility to the reader.

Initially Britomart resists the bait. Uninterested in the meaning of Talus's silence or his hypothetical feelings, she forces him to speak his piece, giving her news of Artegall "what euer it be, good or bad" (5.6.10.2). Talus replies that "a Tyranesse . . . him captiued hath in hapless woe" (5.6.11.2–3). At that, like Cymoent before her, Britomart assumes a figurative meaning—and a thinly veiled one at that: "Cease thou bad newes-man," she rebukes him, "badly doest thou hide thy maisters shame, in harlots bondage tide. / The rest myself too readily can spell" (5.6.11.4–6). Only after several stanzas of weeping and lamenting is Talus able to reassert himself, and what he speaks then to Britomart is the entirety of the poem we have been reading: "[t]he whole discourse . . . In sort as ye haue heard the same as late" (5.6.17.1–2) (It's *The Faerie Queene* express.) Britomart's response to this compressed recital is instructive: "when she with hard enduraunce had / Heard to the end," she "streight her selfe did dight and armor don," riding forth "vppon her readie way" (5.6.17.4–8, 5.6.18.1). But "[s]adly she rode and never word did say" (5.6.18.2). In the stanzas that follow, Britomart is drained of the lively, expressive warmth with which she is singularly endowed by Spenser, both armored and reduced to a state of being much closer to Talus's own. The transformation doesn't last: before long, she arrives at the Temple of Isis, where Talus cannot join her, and is given a vision that redeems her knowledge both mythically and prophetically, making it scannable once more. In the dull interval, however, she and her iron companion model a "hard enduraunce" that *The Faerie Queene*'s readers might try to emulate: a refusal to look aside from those parts of the poem whose cruelty cannot be ignored, whose defects cannot be salvaged, and whose persistence across time is, and isn't, ours to justify.

6

Blatant Beasts

ENCOUNTERS WITH OTHER READERS

JOHN UPTON's advance copy of his 1758 edition of *The Faerie Queene* contains handwritten sketches of many of the scholarly notes that would accompany the groundbreaking volume in print, including philological commentary, historical references, and allusions to classical and contemporary authors, as well as a running elucidation of the poem's allegory and plot. But one unusually long note is more personal in tone, registering Upton's bemusement at an apparent contradiction, trivial but annoying, in the narrative of book 1, canto 9. Enlisted by Una to aid the vanquished Redcrosse Knight, Arthur has just defeated Orgoglio, rescued Redcrosse from his dungeon, and banished the stripped Duessa to the wilderness; after an interval of rest, the two knights prepare to take their leave and continue on their separate ways. "But ere they parted," writes the narrator, "Vna faire besought / That straunger knight his name and nation tell; / Least so great good, as he for her had wrought, / Should die vnknown, and buried be in thankles thought" (1.9.2.6). Arthur demurs:

> Faire virgin (said the Prince) yee me require
> A thing without the compas of my witt:
> For both the lignage and the certein Sire,
> From which I sprong, from mee are hidden yitt. (1.9.3.1–4)

As he goes on to explain, Arthur is a changeling, stolen from his mother's breast by a faerie knight and delivered to the care of Merlin:

> Him oft and oft I askt in priuity,
> Of what loines and what lignage I did spring.
> Whose answer bad me still assured bee,
> That I was sonne and heire vnto a king,
> As time in her iust term the truth to light should bring. (1.9.5.5–9)

In the very next stanza, however, Una asks a further question, revealing that she, at least, has no doubt as to Arthur's identity: "But what aduenture, or what high intent / Hath brought you hether into Fary land, / Aread Prince Arthure, crowne of martiall band?" (1.9.6.3–5). Why ask Arthur his name if she knew it all along?

As is always the case in an allegorical text, there are ways of making the discrepancy meaningful: Una, after all, is Truth; perhaps what we are reading is the very moment in which the truth of his identity is brought to light for Arthur (as it will later be for the Redcrosse Knight on Contemplation's Mount). But Upton can't seem to get past the strangeness of the exchange in human terms. In the margins of his book, alongside stanzas 2 and 3, the learned editor gropes his way toward a more satisfying explanation:

> Una knew the name this stranger knight was called by in Faery Land in plain see st[anza] VI below—But Faery Knights were called by various names, & they often concealed their real names. Una therefore does not know whether the name he went by *Prince Arthur* were his real or assumed name.—Good manners therefore led her to inquire ... In the first book *George* is the real name of the Redcrosse Knight.—Arthegall goes by the name of the Salvage Knight.—Britomart passes for a man.[1]

As explanations go, this confuses rather more than it clarifies. Upton seems to be suggesting that Una's real question is whether Arthur, whom she knows as Arthur, goes by "Arthur" in Faerie Land, or whether he—like her own Redcrosse Knight, but also like Artegall and Britomart, two characters neither Una nor the reader have yet encountered—has adopted a special, pseudonymous disguise for his adventures in Spenser's poem. Rather as a teacher might ask students on the first day of class whether they prefer nicknames or particular pronouns, it is simply etiquette for a lady to ask a strange knight whether he has *nom de faerie*: "Good manners therefore led her to inquire."

At a local level, this raises questions of its own—surely, if disguises and secret identities are a common and often deliberately cultivated feature of Faerie life, good manners would dictate that one not press a new acquaintance on this point too directly—but as a hermeneutic approach to *The Faerie Queene*, the explanation from etiquette opens up a tantalizing array of possibilities. What would it mean to approach Spenser's poem sociologically, as a document of the manners and mores of a people very much, but not entirely, like ourselves? What other of the poem's baffling features might be explained as accommodations to an alien culture, with its own elaborate and often unspoken rituals, prohibitions, and understandings? Such rituals, prohibitions, and understandings also inform the fraught interactions between *The Faerie Queene* and its readers, who must often exert themselves, like John Upton, to smooth over what seem like violations of the poem's own logic and laws. What counts as good manners when it comes to reading, and what are such manners good for?

Ironically, or perhaps fittingly, Upton's appeal to "good manners" occurs in a genre of writing, the marginal annotation—manuscript forerunner of the footnote or endnote—that entails its own complex etiquette. His 1758 edition of *The Faerie Queene* is justly lauded for its notes, which labor heroically to assuage the complaints of those who longed—in the words of Upton's dedicatory epistle—"to get some kind of intimacy with those, whom from their writings we cannot but esteem," but who found that the difficulty of Spenser's poem kept them at an uncomfortable arm's length. Bringing such readers closer to *The Faerie Queene* without infringing on their pride or the poem's own dignity, balancing intimacy and esteem, took deft maneuvering on Upton's part. As Jonathan Kramnick writes, "Upton's edition is the first to treat Spenser as a classic, and of all the period's Spenser editions, the most elaborate in its annotation and glossary."[2] Commercially speaking, that elaborate editorial apparatus was as much a selling point for the edition as the text of the poem itself. A *Proposal for printing by subscription a new edition of Spenser's "Fairy Queen," with notes by John Upton, prebendary of Rochester*, issued in advance of the publication, consists of three pages, the first outlining the terms of subscription, the second showing a page proof of the first four stanzas of book 1, canto 1, and the third giving readers a glimpse of Upton's copious notes on those stanzas, which occupy every bit as much space as the verse itself.[3] And Upton prepared readers of his edition to receive his notes as friendly counsel: this, at least, seems to be the purpose of the *Letter concerning a new edition of Spenser's "Faerie Queene." To Gilbert West, Esq.*, which Upton published seven years earlier, in 1751.[4] The *Letter* runs to forty typeset pages, includes extracts from Greek, Latin, and Italian sources, indulges in lengthy disquisitions on orthography and prosody, and is accompanied by an alphabetical index; in its final paragraph Upton confesses to West that the handwritten document is far too bulky to be sent by mail—if, indeed, that was ever his intention. But the device of the familiar letter helps to frame its learned contents, and the forthcoming edition, as a conversation between equals, joined in their admiration of and affection for Spenser's poem.

Both editing and annotating require tact, as Upton clearly realized, and a tactless editor or annotator—as Upton deemed his "unscholarlike" predecessor, John Hughes, whose 1715 edition of Spenser's *Works* dared to improve the poet's end rhymes—risks not only the corruption of his source but the outrage of fellow readers. Indeed, although the scorn Upton heaps on poor Hughes over the question of Spenser's spelling augurs in a particular way the emergence of orthography as a test of scholarly rigor (as I argue in chapter 1), it also serves as an instance of the territorial hostility that frequently threatens to erupt between custodians of a common text. Of course, Upton disguises his aggression as a form of courtesy, citing Hughes's unmannerly neglect of Spenser's prior editors as his own rationale for ignoring Hughes. "Methinks every reader would require that the last editor should consult every former edition, and that he should faithfully and fairly exhibit all the various readings of even the least authority," he complains at the start of the *Letter* to Gilbert West. Having failed to do so to Upton's satisfaction, Hughes can therefore justly be dismissed in turn: "But enough already concerning editors and editions, critics and critical science," Upton declares; "Let us return to our intended specimen" (sig. B[1]r–v). And yet he can't help himself; Upton turns back to Hughes time and again in the *Letter*, inevitably finding fault with his judgment or mocking his taste, needing him, it would seem, as the coarse and blundering foil to his own more elegant interventions. "You may be certain, if there is a worse reading, to meet with it in *Hughes*," reads a snide parenthesis in a section on Virgilian allusions (22): shared admiration and affection might be the utopian grounds on which readers meet in Upton's *Letter*, but rivalry and resentment are often the actual themes of the encounter.

All of which brings us back to Una and Arthur. The narrator explains that Una asks his name out of anxiety that his brave deeds will go unnoted by posterity: "Least so great good, as he for her had wrought, / Should die vnknown, and buried be in thankles thought" (1.9.2.8–9). Arthur answers by assuring her, as Merlin assured him, that "time in her iust term the truth to light should bring" (1.9.5.9). The scholarly and critical work of salvaging a neglected history of readerly engagement—of putting now forgotten or forever anonymous readers back in conversation with a poem and its present audience—can feel like an act of restorative justice, or at least of a gesture of what Upton calls "good manners." But discovering the presence of other readers, whether in the archive, the critical tradition, the pages of a manuscript, or the margins of a printed text, can also feel like a violation of the seemingly exclusive bond between reader and text. The realization that someone has already had the response one has to a particular poem or passage can bring a pleasing sense of community, a glow of mutual understanding—or it can inspire panic, forcing a confrontation with the banal and predictable character of one's inmost thoughts. By the same token, the discovery that someone else has read a poem or passage in an utterly different sense than oneself can yield exhilaration, amusement, delight, and fascination—or it can provoke incomprehension, irritation, insecurity, or shame.

Above all, the awareness that one is not alone with what one reads transforms the scene of reading into a space requiring careful displays of deference or sudden and self-preserving acts of aggression—a space, in short, much like the sixth and final book of the 1596 *Faerie Queene*. Shame and irritation are far more pervasive in the Legend of Courtesy than understanding or delight, and they must be managed or modulated rather than dispelled. The virtuous knights and ladies of book 6 enjoy intervals of success, satisfaction, and recreation, but those intervals are never lasting, and they require conspicuous effort to sustain. Depending on one's tastes, book 6 supplies either a pleasingly low-key or an unnervingly downbeat finish to a poem about heroic self-fashioning; set in what C. S. Lewis describes as "the gracious valley of Humiliation," the adventures of its champion, Sir Calidore, are modest and provisional in comparison to those of his allegorical fellows.[5] This is perhaps because the aims of courtesy are necessarily ameliorative and compensatory: in contrast to the transcendent virtues of holiness, temperance, chastity, friendship, and justice—ideals that, however unattainable in this life, retain an unsullied perfection in the imagination—courtesy assumes human frailty as its reason for being, and Spenser's Legend of Courtesy offers both characters and readers an ideal so hedged by contingency that it verges on improvisation. But that very improvisatory quality makes courtesy an eminently useful frame for thinking about reading. Dispensing both with the ideal of singular perfection and with many of its earlier anxieties about aimlessness and indirection, the final book of the 1596 *Faerie Queene* stages reading as an ongoing intersubjective encounter between readers, texts, and other readers: a conversation in the continual making.

Entering the Conversation, Exiting the Poem

Few metaphors of scholarly discourse are more pervasive, and none more seemingly benign, than conversation. To "enter the conversation," as we repeatedly urge students to do in their writing, is, first of all, to acknowledge that a conversation already exists—that one is not the only person to read, puzzle over, question, challenge, or otherwise engage with a particular text, topic, or problem. Implicitly, too, it is to recognize that joining that conversation means making a contribution to the collective understanding: it is not enough simply to repeat what has already been said or, contrarily, to say something that has no bearing on what has already been said. In writing *The Faerie Queene*, Spenser himself was keenly conscious of entering a conversation—in his case, a poetic conversation spanning multiple cultures and language traditions over two thousand years. With its conspicuous nods to Virgil and Ariosto, the first stanza of the proem to book 1 of *The Faerie Queene* establishes the poem as an expression of Spenser's determination, in Gabriel Harvey's words, to "overgo"—which is to say, both to retrace and to exceed—the courses plotted by his classical and continental precursors.[6] Entering the conversation thus requires self-promotion and self-effacement: the delicate balance of ambition and reticence that Spenser terms courtesy. "As a practice that allows one to cross social boundaries without threatening them, to enter a closed circle without puncturing it," writes

Michael Schoenfeldt, "courtesy is transgression under the guise of accommodation."[7] As Schoenfeldt observes, Spenser's own social and professional trajectory—from "pore scholar" at the Merchant Tailors School and "sizar," or scholarship student, at Cambridge to aristocratic secretary, colonial gentleman, and (by self-appointment) the queen's own poet—required the continual sublimation of ambition into deference and of deference itself into a seemingly unforced and spontaneous grace. The career of Sir Calidore, hero of book 6, turns on his mastery of the same double sleight of hand: for Calidore, master of the art of entering the conversation, successful self-transformation always comes by way of an apparent submission to things as they are.

Oddly, however, when we arrive at the proem to book 6, Spenser's desire—and his need—to engage with other voices seems to have vanished from the poem. Instead, we find the poet-narrator alone and at large, simultaneously wearied and refreshed by his traversal of "this delightfull land of Faery," whose "waies . . . / Are so exceeding spacious and wyde, / And sprinckled with such sweet variety" that the effort of invention is forgotten in the pleasures of discovery and exploration (6.proem.1.2–4). Indeed, the pathways through this final book of the poem seem to be not simply uncharted but uninhabited: "strange waies, where neuer foote did vse," as the narrator boasts, "Ne none can find, but who was taught them by the Muse" (6.proem.2.8–9). Calidore himself gives this description a more melancholy cast in the opening stanzas of canto 1, greeting Artegall on his return to court from Ireland:

> But where ye ended haue, now I begin
> To tread an endless trace, withouten guyde,
> Or good direction, how to enter in,
> Or how to issue forth in waies vntryed,
> In perils strange, in labours long and wide,
> In which although good Fortune me befall,
> Yet shall it not by none be testified. (6.1.6.1–7)

Together with the proem, these odd lines, half-proud and half-pessimistic, forecast book 6's preoccupations with secrecy and hiddenness, with the threat of exposure and the pleasure (and anxiety) of estrangement, with social and pedagogical rites of indoctrination and exclusion, and with the kind of passing—entering in and issuing forth—that Schoenfeldt describes as "transgression under the guise of accommodation."[8] They also hint at its fondness for digression—either, in Stanley Stewart's view, as a fit expression of the "occasional . . . nature of courtesy" or, as Corey McEleney argues, at the direct expense of allegorical coherence.[9] Finally, and perhaps most importantly, they gesture at a conviction that the quest for courtesy is an obscure one, its victories greatest when least noted. In this respect, the Legend of Courtesy remains oddly resistant to the very idylls of sociability it works so hard to imagine. "[U]nlike the other important knights in Spenser's poem," as George Rowe notes, Calidore "has no companion," and when a willing and suitable companion presents himself in canto 2 in the form of the well-born and well-mannered Tristram, Calidore politely declines his services.[10] And this "belief in his own sufficiency" has strange effects on his quest, Jane Grogan observes, as a "strong instinct for self-preservation replaces the drastic corrective action we might expect of a Spenserian knight"; indeed, Calidore's detachment can verge on disengagement, most conspicuously when he abandons the poem altogether in cantos 4–8.[11]

But if Calidore insists upon isolation—and this, too, is a dimension of courtesy, James Nohrnberg reminds us, as a mode of "respect accorded to another person's determination upon inward possession"[12]—that isolation proves difficult to secure, for the thoroughfares and byways of book 6 are in fact crowded with fellow travelers. Far from wandering in an unmarked wasteland, Spenser's Knight of Courtesy can hardly take a step in his own quest without tripping over the bodies, belongings, and business of others. Courtesy would seem ideally suited to soothe such embarrassments: as Rowe writes, adherence to the decorums of courtesy "testifies to the importance of an essential privacy beneath the garment of social discourse; it reflects an awareness that certain boundaries must not be crossed, that speaking and interpreting must not be too insistent, and that the desire to know can be a form of violence."[13] In fact, however, Calidore's courtesies frequently succeed only in involving him in further unsought entanglements—and in an increasingly dubious set of ethical compromises, ranging from the telling of a polite lie to the despoliation of an enemy corpse. Disengagement would be a dereliction of knightly duty, but the results of engagement are rarely satisfying or heroic.

Even the grace-filled Arthur is stymied by the overcrowded terrain of book 6, repeatedly confusing friend with foe. He appears in canto 5 on the verge of a catastrophic error—mistaking the unfortunate Serena's protector for an aggressor, he is narrowly prevented from killing the kindly salvage man—and follows that misadventure with a series of equally abortive efforts at restoration: he tries and fails to secure a permanent remedy for the shameful injuries suffered by his squire, Timias; is won to an uneasy and temporary peace with Turpine by the guileful Blandina; and is prevented from dealing a deathblow to the villainous Disdain by the intervention of Mirabella, a maid condemned for her pride to suffer the scorn of others. Checked by her plea, Arthur accedes to Mirabella's request that she be left to endure her penance unaided and departs from the poem on this anticlimactic note: grace itself is reduced by courtesy to the minimal self-discipline of tact.

Behind the awkward contortions and uneasy compromises of book 6 lurk the vicious and voluble threat of the Blatant Beast, the many-tongued monster whom it is Calidore's quest to subdue. The Blatant Beast enters the poem at the end of the Legend of Justice as the pet of Envie and Detraction, who appear in book 5's final stanzas to jeer at the homeward-bound Artegall. Envie is a familiar menace, the same self-murdering evil that parades with Lucifera in book 1 and partially afflicts Britomart at the end of the 1590 version of book 3. But Detraction is something new—and worse, as the narrator tells us, a perverter of the economy of praise and mutual interest on which both knightly honor and poetic patronage depend:

> For what soeuer good by any sayd,
> Or doen she heard, she would streightwayes inuent,
> How to depraue, or slaunderously vpbrayd,
> Or to misconstrue of a mans intent,
> And turne to ill the thing, that well was ment.
> Therefore she vsed often to resort,
> To common haunts, and companies frequent,
> To hearke what any one did good report,
> To blot the same with blame, or wrest in wicked sort.
>
> And if that any ill she heard of any,
> She would it eeke, and make much worse by telling,
> And take great ioy to publish it to many,
> That euery matter worse was for her melling,
> Her name was hight *Detraction*, and her dwelling
> Was neare to *Enuie*, euen her neighbour next;
> A wicked hag, and *Enuy* selfe excelling
> In mischiefe: for her selfe she onely vext;
> But this same both her selfe, and others eke perplext.
>   (5.12.34–35)

"[C]ombynd in one, / And linckt together gainst Sir Artegall," Envie and Detraction fail to unsettle the imperturbable Knight of Justice, "who seem'd of them to take no keep" (5.12.42.9), but their vicious tongues leave a scar nonetheless, "Bit[ing] him behind, that long the marke was to be read" (5.12.39.9). And, once unleashed, there is no recalling their hideous pet, who

>   by them set on
> At him began aloud to barke and bay,
> With bitter rage and fell contention,
> That all the woods and rockes nigh to that way,
> Began to quake and tremble with dismay;
> And all the aire rebellowed againe.
> So dreadfully his hundred tongues did bray.

It is this beast, a nightmare embodiment of conversation itself, that Calidore is tasked with capturing and subduing in the Legend of Courtesy. And in response, both Spenser's knight and his poem retreat to a self-protective crouch: if you can't say anything nice, best to say nothing at all.

Part of what makes the Blatant Beast so horrifying, as readers of book 6 discover, is that the Beast himself may not mean any harm. In canto 3, when the innocent Serena wanders forth to enjoy the mild weather and gather flowers, she goes "[w]ithout suspect of ill or daungers hidden dread" (6.3.23.9), obviously a perilous state for an unaccompanied maiden in the woods of romance, or for the unsuspicious reader of an allegorical poem. It's no surprise then (to us, at least) when Serena is set upon "all sodainely" in the next line of the poem by the ravening Blatant Beast, who finds her "loosely wandring here and there"—"loosely" of course allowing for the usual double entendre, setting in motion the assault on her reputation—"And in his wide great mouth away her bare" (6.3.24.3–4). But what is surprising (indeed, almost inexplicable) is that the encounter also seems to come as a shock to the Beast himself, whom the narrator describes as "forth rushing *vnaware*" (6.3.24.1; emphasis added). Is "vnaware" simply a transferred epithet, fleetingly reassigning Serena's state of mind to her attacker? Even if so, how strange is the effect of that transfer, which displaces Serena's blithe innocence onto the Beast and leaves the moral responsibility for her injury nowhere at all.

The same peculiar absence of intentionality recurs in canto 5, where we learn how Arthur's squire, Timias, now the devoted servant of Belphoebe, falls prey to the Beast. This time, the attack does have an agent—three of them, Timias's determined enemies Despetto, Decetto, and Defetto—who, when their repeated attempts on the squire's life and honor fail, send "that Blatant Beast to be a baite, / To draw him from his deare beloved dame, / Vnwares into the daunger of defame" (6.5.15.3–5). Once again, Timias's own lack of awareness seems to be shared by the Beast, whose status as "baite" implies that he, as much as the squire, is the target of others' malevolent designs. And, indeed, in the following stanza, it is Timias who assaults the Beast, not vice versa:

> The hardy boy, as they deuised had,
> Seeing the vgly Monster passing by,
> Vpon him set, of perill naught ydrad,
> Ne skilfull of the vncouth ieopardy;
> And charged him so fierce and furiously,
> That his great force vnable to endure,
> He forced was to turne from him and fly:
> Yet ere he fled, he with his tooth impure
> Him he heedlesse bit, the whiles he was thereof secure. (6.5.16)

As is often the case in scenes of Spenserian combat, pronoun confusion makes it difficult to tell who is inflicting damage on whom, but in this instance, the grammar seems most straightforwardly to suggest that it is the Beast who is set upon by Timias, the Beast who is unable to endure the force of the attack, the Beast who must turn and flee, and the Beast who, in fleeing Timias's relentless assault, "[h]im . . . heedlesse bit." As with "vnaware" in the stanza describing Serena's injury, "heedlesse" floats between "[h]im" and "he," victim and assailant, neither of whom seem to have an inkling of their mutual peril; if anything, the monster's role in the encounter is the more purely reactive. It is as if the Blatant Beast roams the landscape of book 6 openmouthed and empty-headed, continually surprised by humans who insist on impaling themselves on his teeth. He isn't aggressive so much as in the way.

He may also be indispensible. At the end of book 6, near the close of canto 12, Calidore succeeds in capturing the Blatant Beast, but the remedy is temporary; rather than slaying the Beast, Calidore only muzzles and leashes him. And in the final stanzas of book 6 (which are also the final stanzas of the 1596 edition of the poem), the Beast escapes to roam the world once more. Incapable now of any restraint, he turns his poisoned tongues and terrible teeth on the poem that begot him:

> Ne may this homely verse, of many meanest,
> Hope to escape his venemous despite,
> More then my former writs, all were they clearest
> From blamefull blot, and free from all that wite,
> With which some wicked tongues did it backebite,
> And bring into a mighty Peres displeasure,
> That neuer so deserved to endite.
> Therefore do you my rimes keep better measure,
> And seeke to please, that now is counted wisemans threasure. (6.12.41)

The lurking implication of the weirdly passive attacks on Serena and Timias—it was all their fault, anyway—is here strenuously resisted, but it makes no difference to the outcome. The once potent and enabling art of courtesy amounts, in the end, to a grim regimen of self-policing, while the avoidance of ill occasion requires a radical sequestration of poetry itself. In his final act of courtesy to those he may have offended, the narrator of *The Faerie Queene* assumes the burden of showing himself the door.

Whether one finds the tenor of book 6 depressing or refreshingly modest, an unmistakable lapse in confidence besets the 1596 *Faerie Queene*, from the ambition of the poem's opening stanza, in which the poet is chosen by "the sacred Muse . . . / To blazon broade emongst her learned throng" the neglected praises "of Knights and Ladies gentle deedes" (1.proem.1.5–8) to the bitter self-recrimination of its final lines. That lapse admits of many explanations, from the biographical (by 1596, Spenser had witnessed the disappointment of many of his own hopes for advancement at court, resigning himself to bureaucratic exile in Ireland) to the allegorical (the path from holiness to courtesy traces a circle of increasing inwardness and self-limitation). Or perhaps the frustration was global, even existential: as one critic argues, "the failure of courtesy ... dramatizes Spenser's implicit avowal that the potential ideal which his epic was designed to embody has been defeated by a world hopelessly antagonistic to its realization."[14] But the most immediate cause for pessimism at the end of book 6 seems to be a shift from the anxiety of influence to the anxiety of reception—or, to put it another way, from the problem of other poets to the problem of one's own readers. In the proem to book 1, Spenser finds it easy enough to incorporate the voices of Virgil and Ariosto into harmony with his ambitions; the loud mouths, wicked tongues, and venomous fangs of his own real and imagined readers—past, present, and future—are another matter altogether.

As I argue in chapter 4, a similar shift marks the close of the final book of the 1590 edition of the poem, although there the combined efforts of chastity and a very different sort of courtesy supply Spenser with an unexpectedly generous way of imagining, enabling, and even inviting the participation of others. The close of book 6 offers no such consoling vision: no text, however artful or capacious, Spenser now insists, can fully anticipate or defend against the responses of its readers, and no reader, however well-intentioned, can avoid inflicting some harm. The oddly hapless Blatant Beast, with his literally innumerable tongues—a "hundred" (5.12.41.7) when he first appears at the end of book 5; "a thousand" (6.12.27.1) by the final canto of book 6—is the incarnation of this truth, a monstrous realization not of the poem's failure to find an audience but of its success. One last instance of pronoun near-confusion drives the point home, as the "you" of line 8 temporarily wavers between the poet's rhymes and the person or persons to whose keeping they are now entrusted. If "keep better measure" is the 1596 *Faerie Queene*'s last stern injunction to itself, it also resonates as a plea to the poem's readers, whose numerousness might threaten its integrity even as their multiplication guarantees its survival.

Marginal Skirmishes: Reading as Rivalry

If it is to remain anything other than a linguistic fossil—which is something *The Faerie Queene* sometimes seems on the verge of becoming—a poem cannot do without readers, which means that readers of *The Faerie Queene* also cannot do without one another. Yet even the most well-intentioned readers of the poem can find themselves getting in one another's way; when it comes to courtesy, as book 6 reminds us, good intentions are no guard against injury. Like the Blatant Beast, Calidore doesn't mean to trouble those on whose private idylls he repeatedly intrudes, from Calepine and Serena in canto 3 to Colin Clout and the dancing graces on Mount Acidale in canto 10, but trouble them he does. Indeed, the most lasting and painful harm Calidore inflicts in book 6 is suffered by someone to whom he bears nothing but goodwill, the bumbling shepherd Coridon, whose long-cherished desire for the shepherdess Pastorella Calidore spoils simply by showing up at the start of canto 9. The poem works hard to keep us from taking Coridon's humiliation too much to heart: we are assured from the start that Pastorella herself has no interest in Coridon, and in that sense, there is no preexisting relationship for Calidore to disrupt. And the competition between shepherd and knight is ludicrously one-sided: Calidore excels Coridon at every shared pursuit, from courtship to wrestling to milking the ewes, and he hardly seems to regard Coridon as a rival at all. On the contrary, Calidore takes every opportunity to place Coridon in a more favorable light, offering him in his own place at the head of the country dance and crowning him with the garlands he wins at the shepherds' games—all of which, of course, works only to make Calidore himself seem more wonderful in the eyes of Pastorella.

Such aggression is impossible to resist, as the narrator observes, for it masquerades as cooperation: "[E]ven they, the which his riuals were, / Could not malign him, but commend him needs: / For courtesie amongst the rudest breeds / Good will and fauour" (6.9.45.3–6). This summary itself repeats the trick: what is initially visible as a privation of will and power—"Could not malign him, but commend him needs"—is transfigured in the lines that follow into a generous and unforced bequest. By the end of canto 11, Coridon has been exposed as a wholly unworthy lover for Pastorella, fleeing "through cowherd feare" when brigands capture her, steal her flock, and kill her parents (6.10.35.3). As the pun on "coward" and "cowherd" makes clear, we are meant to understand Coridon's unworthiness as the twin function of character and class, both of which disqualify him from true rivalry with the bold and well-bred knight. The coup de grâce comes after Calidore kills the brigands and rescues Pastorella, when he bestows all of the stolen sheep on Coridon, an act of unmerited largesse that acts as his ultimate triumph over the clownish shepherd, who rests indebted to the knight for his livelihood and his life. The final line of canto 11— "So droue them all away, and his loue with him bore" (6.11.51.9)—includes Coridon among those driven away by Calidore's relentless and irresistible grace.

Coridon's predicament is not the frustration of Colin Clout on Mount Acidale—not, that is, the predicament of the poet-piper who must submit his perfect creation to the gaze of potentially unworthy onlookers. Rather, his predicament is closer to that of the reader whose untroubled attachment to a poem—and Pastorella's name clearly identifies her as a kind of poem—depends on the conviction that it is as much his as anyone else's. Coridon might never have won Pastorella's hand, but until Calidore came along, he could content himself with the fact that no one had or would (as the narrator puts it, "Yet neither she for him, nor other none / Did care a whit, nor any liking lend" [6.9.10.7–8]). But the affection Pastorella displays toward the stranger knight upsets the face-saving fiction that she has no interest in love, and when that illusion vanishes, Coridon reacts with none of the equanimity the narrator leads us to expect: he sulks and grumbles, "scoule[s] and pout[s]," "loure[s] / And byte[s] his lip," challenging Calidore to ill-advised contests of strength and complaining about Pastorella to the other shepherds (6.9.38.7, 6.9.39.2–3). Coridon can tolerate Pastorella's chill unresponsiveness to his attentions; what he can't bear is the thought that she might be more forthcoming with others.

Spenser's readers may likewise be chafed by the realization that other readers have gotten to his poem first and left their marks on it. And as the pages of certain well-used copies of *The Faerie Queene* can attest, that irritation is heightened when readers share not only a common text but a single copy of that text, struggling to claim space for themselves and their views in an already crowded volume. In the margins of copies of *The Faerie Queene* annotated by multiple hands—they are easy to find on the shelves of any university library or used bookstore—the injunction to keep better measure frequently manifests as a charge leveled from one reader at another, across decades and even centuries, in tones of increasing desperation. The margins of such books not only shed light on the interpretive histories of the works they contain; they can also illuminate the less reputable environs of the readerly psyche.

Take, for instance, the book now known as Cambridge University Library SSS.22.27, a 1590 edition of *The Faerie Queene* that passed through the hands of various members and acquaintances of a family of Yorkshire gentry over the course of the seventeenth century. Littered with handwritten marks, the book nonetheless contains few traces of engagement with Spenser's poem. Instead, the vast majority of the marginal annotations in SSS.22.27 consist in readers' competing and increasingly contentious claims to be the book's rightful owner. The opening salvo is fired on page 2, where the name "John Lyndley" is written twice alongside the proem to book 1. On the opposite page, however, are two additional signatures, "Jane Lind[ley]" and "Henry." On page 19, at the start of canto 2, "Jane" signs her name again, alongside "Alice F," who then re-signs herself as "Alice Fawsett." Over the course of the next six hundred-some pages, John Lindley writes his name thirteen more times, Jane writes hers twelve more times (including eight times on the back flyleaf), and they are joined not only by "Henry" (who reappears on page 364, and may be the "Henry Lassel" who signs his name twice on page 300) and "Alice Fawcett" (who appears once more, on page 246) but by nine additional readers: "FF" (once, on the title page), "John

Bryan" (twice, on pages 265 and 267), "Richard Simbon" (page 290), "Simon" (page 364), "Adam Spenser" (page 387), "Daniell Lindley" (page 471), "Tomis: Lindley" (page 482), and "John Ritchman" and "Mare Lindley" (both on the back flyleaf). All in all, there are forty-six signatures in SSS.22.27, representing at least thirteen different individuals.

As Heather Wolfe has shown, paper was not an unaffordable luxury in most early modern English households: although some of the marks left in SSS.22.27 may be pen trials, it is extremely unlikely that the book's signatories had nowhere else to write.[15] On the contrary, the accumulation of signatures strongly suggests that they signed the pages of *this* book precisely because others had done so before. That likelihood is amplified to a near-certainty by the fact that most of the individuals who left their marks in the margins of SSS.22.27 didn't simply sign their names but also staked seemingly defensive claims of ownership: "John Lindley is the true possessor of this booke 1620 I:R:," reads the note on page 130. "Alise Fawsett est himself [herself?] booke," counters a note on page 246. "Henry Lassels Booke also," reads a note on page 300, and reiterates, just below, "Henry Lassels Booke." Then, on page 354, we find: "Jane Lindley owe[s] this boke / god geiue hir grace on it to looke." John reasserts himself on page 364—"John Lindley Booke"—though that claim is followed immediately by the signatures of "Simon" and "Henry." "Daniel Lindley Booke," declares a note on page 471, and on page 482 we read, "Tomis: Lindley habet usum his Libris." Page 526 contains both a signature from Jane and an apparently defiant and slightly incoherent response: "I am ye son John John John Booke." On the back flyleaf Jane both signs her name multiple times and makes what seems like a bequest: "to the right nobel ualorous knight John Lindley of Yorke / fines Jane Lindley the mother," which is followed by an obscure and only partly legible valediction from John: "Be it known unto all men ... that, John Lindley of York; gentleman / euer known and respected: my time / fines John Lindley."

In whatever rudimentary sense, the inscriptions in SSS.22.27 thus form a conversation—indeed, a heated one, though its import to the participants is hard to discern. It doesn't seem to have much to do with the content of Spenser's poem, to which only one hand, John Lindley's, makes reference; ownership, and not interpretation, is the readerly relation that matters here. Whose was this particular copy of *The Faerie Queene*, and why do its rival claimants find that such a difficult question to adjudicate? Absent an authenticated family tree and much more careful paleographic analysis of the various signatures and hands, it is hard to reconstruct the circumstances behind the contested provenance of SSS.22.27, although an amateur genealogical website maintained by a modern descendent of the Lindleys of Yorkshire (http://lindleyancestry .com//) contains some hints in a transcription of the 1613/1614 will of John Lindley, brother of Henry and Francis (married to Jane), father to Thomas,

William, and Margaret, and grandfather to John Lindley the younger, on whom the family estate was settled. Here, at least, are many of the names that appear in the margins of SSS.22.27, and they suggest that what seems like a struggle for simultaneous possession may instead be a record of serial possession, as the book traveled across a multigenerational network of family and friends. But that possibility makes the insistent, often angry tone of the annotations even more striking. Familiarity, friendship, and inheritance are appealing and readily available metaphors for the bonds forged across time among readers of a common text, and in this case they were also literally true, but they aren't the affective relations evoked by the inscriptions left in the margins of SSS.22.27. On the contrary, the evidence of this peculiar book suggests that reading in company is an occasion for mutual resentment and thinly masked aggression—a struggle to leave one's mark in an increasingly crowded field.

A similar and still more pointed lesson emerges from the pages of Osborn Z76 O75, a 1609 folio edition of *The Faerie Queene* now held in the collection of the Beinecke Library at Yale University but, for much of the nineteenth century, in heavy circulation among the members of a college society known as the "Brothers in Unity" (whose name is stamped in gold on the book's leather cover and binding). The book's undergraduate users not only read its pages and annotated its contents but autographed its flyleaves, doodled in its margins, colored its printer's ornaments, added rude speech bubbles to its illustrations, and penned witticisms and in-jokes in any available blank space. A handwritten note on page 1 of the poem reflects glowingly on this legacy of fraternal use: "Honorable book, you have come down to us from former generations!!" But the encounters between readers within the pages of Osborn Z76 O75 are rarely so elevated (or genial) in tone. To be sure, shared reading material can extend the intimacies of real life: in the margins of book 1, canto 9, one reader seems to have recognized the hand of another and leaves a teasing answer to his rueful comment on a description of love's inescapable folly. "True every word, I know it by experience," laments the first reader, to which the second reader responds, "You don't say so, Mr. Fisher" (39).[16] More typical, however, are the barbed exchanges between a different pair of hands, readers of the poem whose relationship to one another inheres only in the accidental sharing of this particular text.

As Eve Houghton has established, the first of these readers was Phineas Bacon Wilcox, Yale College class of 1821, who left a lightly penciled running commentary on the poem at the bottom of numerous pages; the second was Edward Baldwin, Yale college class of 1846, whose experience of *The Faerie Queene* two decades later seems to have been entirely warped by the obtrusive presence of Wilcox's notes. Both the comedy and the fascination of the exchanges between Wilcox and Baldwin inhere in the fact that only one of them—Baldwin—knows it is a conversation at all. Wilcox, the earlier reader, clearly wrote with an audience in mind; he made his annotations in a library book, after all, and they are far too studied and self-conscious to pass as mere notes to himself. Indeed, he even—like William Henry Ireland's Shakespeare— goes so far as to sign and date them for posterity: "P. B. Wilcox, April 6, 1820," reads a flourishing inscription in the margin of book 5, canto 4 (260). But the audience he seems to have imagined for his annotations is quietly receptive, impressed by his acumen and grateful for his insights—nothing like the choleric, quick-witted, and irreverent Baldwin, whose attitude toward the wisdom of "former generations" is summed up by a note he scrawls in the margins of book 2: "Spenser had better learn to spell" (106). Driven first to distraction and finally to profane exasperation by Wilcox's pretentious chatter, Baldwin retaliates by making his predecessor's remarks the foil for his savage mockery.

P. B. Wilcox was in training for a law career—after graduation from Yale, he moved to Ohio, where he passed the bar and made his living as a litigator—and his commentary on *The Faerie Queene* is, to put it kindly, lawyerly: judicious, skeptical, evenhanded, and often unbearably smug.[17] Unmoved by the poem's moral content and immune to its narrative fascination, he is enthralled by technicalities and ever eager to display his own erudition. Of the description of a battle, in which the "cruell steele ... so greedily doth bite / In tender flesh" (1.5.9.3–4), he pompously observes, "Bite: I believe this word was first applied in this way by Chaucer" adding, "Dryden uses it thus—it is highly poetical" (21). Although his tastes are not noticeably more refined than those of the average undergraduate, he adopts the pose of a connoisseur, registering either his benign approbation of Spenser's artistic achievement or his regret at the poem's deficiencies. "This is on the whole one of the most agreeable stories in the book," he writes of the Squire of Dames (159), and of the buffoonish Braggadochio, "This character is always a relish to the reader of the Fairy Queen" (69). But the marriage of the Thames and the Medway in book 4 fills him with dismay: "This is quite a blemish, or rather mistake in Master Spenser, [and] tedious to the modern reader" (237, 241). As an aspiring magistrate, he takes particular umbrage at book 5, whose depiction of justice, in his view, "deserves but little praise" (281). And his pedantry shades into peevishness when it comes to the poem's female characters, whose adventures, unless they are mostly naked, instantly sour his mood. "There is indeed nothing admirable in the character of Britomart," he declares at the start of book 3, canto 3. "She is certainly unfit for love and her sex condemns her heroisms" (140).

As a reader of *The Faerie Queene*, P. B. Wilcox is, in short, insufferable: at once jejune and pretentious, high-minded and heavy-handed. But on the last page of Osborn Z76 O75, he gets his comeuppance. There, beneath the final printer's ornament, where Wilcox signs his name again, in ink—"P. B. Wilcox 1820"—a second hand adds, in pencil, "is an ass." The hand in question is Edward Baldwin's, who signs his own name above the argument to book 1, canto 6. Baldwin's clear, cursive notes are scattered throughout the rest of the poem as well—although, unlike Wilcox, he doesn't exactly seem to be reading it. Instead, his responses are targeted almost exclusively at Wilcox's annotations, or at Wilcox himself. Only once does he engage with the substance of his predecessor's analysis: in answer to Wilcox's repeated complaints about Artegall's lax treatment of the bad knight Sangliere, Baldwin demands, "Doth not this loggerheaded critic perceive that it was a greater punishment for Sangliere to bear the dead body of his mangled lady continually before him than to be slaid forthwith?" (252). For the most part, he contents himself with taking sly jabs at Wilcox's self-regard and ruthless advantage of his obtuseness. On the rare occasion that Wilcox admits to some minor confusion—"Where did the Redcross Knight come from?" he puzzles over the sudden reappearance of that name in 3.1.63.2—Baldwin snaps, "Turn back one leaf and see. The Redcrosse Knight appears to be the one whom Britomart found engaged with the six" (129). And when Wilcox notes of Spenser's treatment of the Lear story in book 2, canto 10, that "Shakespeare gives a different account of this affair," Baldwin rolls his eyes at the obviousness of the observation: "Does he? Aye?" (105). Wilcox's attempts at sophistication please him no better: "Of all the cants that are canted in this canting world," he complains after one especially fulsome annotation, "though the cant of hypocrisy may be the worst, the cant of criticism is the most disgusting strain" (251)—and again, later on, "From the cant of criticism good Lord deliver us" (277). Above all Baldwin objects to his predecessor's high-handed judgments of Spenser's art: Wilcox's distaste for Britomart spurs Baldwin to a rhyming rebuke—"Ne let a man, if e'er he can / This work dare criticise" (141)—but even his observation that a phrase in book 6, canto 10 is "a most happy idea and most happily expressed" infuriates with its condescension: "[A]gain, how dare you" (340).

That last outraged expostulation might be read as a gesture of courtesy, a defense of the poem and its author against an obviously unworthy reader. But it is hard not to suspect that Baldwin's animus against Wilcox was personal, too. For Wilcox is a perfectly blatant beast: he may not mean any harm—may, indeed, regard himself as providing a polite service to his fellow students—but one can hardly get through a canto of Osborn Z76 O75 without getting snagged on one of his cringe-inducing observations. The cringe is induced by the idiocy but also by the aspiration to critical sophistication, which Baldwin—editor of the *Yale Literary Magazine*—obviously shared. How mortifying for a smart and worldly undergraduate, a self-identified literary type, to open a poem like *The*

Faerie Queene and discover its pages blotted in advance by a caricature of his own intellectual and cultural ambitions. Indeed, it would be hard for anyone susceptible to academic striving (and perhaps anyone who has been an English major) not to identify wincingly with Wilcox's clumsy performance of readerly savoir faire. What Baldwin sees in his predecessor's annotations—what, I suspect, he cannot forgive—is the funhouse image of his own desire to be adequate to his text.

That, at least, is one hypothesis for his ruthless and efficient skewering of Wilcox. Another—and they are not mutually exclusive—is that Baldwin is engaged in an artful performance of his own, this one also for the benefit of undergraduate readers yet to come, readers whom Baldwin assumes will share his low opinion of Wilcox and delight in his handy takedown of him. Such marginal posturing appears to be a frequent feature of the books that fill university library shelves: after spending time with Osborn Z76 O75 in the Beinecke archives, I began noticing versions of it wherever I went, books in which generations of student readers had used one another's annotations as whetstones of wit and foils for rude humor. On the basis of my far-from-rigorous survey of such materials, it seems that stupidity and sloppiness are less offensive than self-regard. Excessive underlining or overobvious asides may be annoying, but they don't often attract comment, whereas annotations that too conspicuously perform the intelligence, sophistication, or seriousness of their author inspire eye-rolling rebuke.[18] The fact that the original author will almost certainly never register that rebuke hardly seems to matter: the joke—and the lesson—is for the benefit of future readers. Sharing a text thus becomes an indoctrination into a transhistorical society of readers—not necessarily brothers in unity but a community nonetheless, with subtle hierarchies and strictly enforced decorums of self-presentation. If we approach Osborn Z76 O75 in that light, not simply as the relic of a historically specific local community of readers—nineteenth-century Yale boys with a casual interest in Spenser—but as a microcosm of the much broader collective of readers of any shared text, P. B. Wilcox's indispensable role in securing that community becomes much more evident. Wilcox is a *useful* idiot, his earnest attempts at critical sophistication the necessary foil to Baldwin's genuinely sophisticated sense of irony and wit—which may explain why, on page 252, when Baldwin accidentally rubs out part of Wilcox's whining objection to Arthur's treatment of Sangliere in the process of subscribing his answer to "this loggerheaded critic" beneath it, he carefully repencils in the effaced letters in his own clear hand. Or perhaps, although Baldwin is eager to dismantle Wilcox's pose of critical erudition, there are laws of courtesy, or rules of readerly engagement, even he won't breach. It is one thing to insult a fellow reader; it is another, impermissible thing to erase him.

Courtesy, Critique, and the Minimal Ethics of Readerly Engagement

Of course, we need not look to the distant past or the margins of library books for reminders that contact between readers can spark conflict; scholarly journals and lecture halls supply ample scope for our own rivalries and resentments. Above all, there is the genre of the academic book review, a form designed to subject one reader's encounter with a text to the potentially hostile scrutiny of another. In 1968 Paul Alpers gave Spenserians a master class in such interreaderly hostility, in a blistering review of a new study of book 6 of *The Faerie Queene*. The review appeared in *Essays in Criticism* under a misleadingly bland and encouraging title—"How to Read *The Faerie Queene*"—which perhaps partly accounts for the fact that it was subsequently (and continues to be) reprinted in collections of essays intended for the use of student readers.[19] But the review might better be titled "How Not to Read *The Faerie Queene*," for (unlike Alpers's 1967 *The Poetry of "The Faerie Queene*," which is packed with supremely useful counsel to novice and expert readers alike), its tenor is relentlessly, even brutally, negative.

To be fair to Alpers—who could not have anticipated the contexts in which his review would later appear—the late 1960s were a charged moment in the field of Spenser criticism: the dismissive attitudes of the New Critics toward *The Faerie Queene* had succeeded in marginalizing the poem within the discipline of literary studies; scholarship on the poem—and those who produced it—had a reputation for being dry, dull, stodgy, and old-fashioned. Alpers begins his review of Donald Cheney's *Spenser's Image of Nature: Shepherd and Wild Man in "The Faerie Queene"* (1967) not by challenging this widespread impression but lamenting its accuracy: "Despite the recent flood of books on Spenser, the common reader can still find little to help him read *The Faerie Queene* with pleasure, understand how, in its alien mode, it has the complexity and human importance we expect of great poetry." Cheney's book, which "should provide such help," in Alpers's view emphatically does not, although he is willing to concede that the author's intentions were probably good. Indeed, early on, he finds grounds for sympathy between Cheney's conception of *The Faerie Queene* and his own, particularly with respect to the poem's complexity, internal contradictions, and shifting perspectives. But sympathy rapidly shades into severity: "[F]or all its real and potential virtues," he writes, "*Spenser's Image of Nature* has most of the faults of most books on *The Faerie Queene*—most importantly, rigid interpretations and the distortion of details in the interest of a previously determined point of view or argument" (749). In the end, Alpers deems Cheney's book "an exceptionally striking, and therefore instructive, instance of the gaps that can exist between intelligent general statements and particular critical analyses and demonstrations" (750).

For its part, Alpers's review is an exceptionally striking, and therefore instructive, instance of the proximity between criticism and cruelty. Licensed by concern for "the common reader"—and motivated, no doubt, by the disregard in which *The Faerie Queene* was held by the dominant critics of the previous three decades—he is free to indulge in an unusually naked form of scholarly aggression: book reviewing as blood sport. The effort would seem less savage if it were not so ostentatiously fair-minded; again and again Alpers catches Cheney in violation of his own avowed critical precepts, above all his desire not "to reduce [Spenser's] world to any neat conceptual pattern, or to exclude any discordant impulse,"[20] and mourns "his inability to put his general theories into critical practice." The tone oscillates between disappointment and cutting disparagement, mild regret and sudden ferocity. After quoting with approval Cheney's warning against "the reductive reading" of such subtle allegorical landscapes as the "wandering wood," for example, Alpers continues: "And now, alas, let us see what Cheney actually says about this passage" (751). Cheney's plodding anatomy of the wood into its component moral features is then reproduced at tedious length, only to be summarily discounted by Alpers: "Almost every one of these statements seems to me totally without foundation in the poem" (752). What praise is offered is modest or hedged, while the criticisms are absolute. Cheney's arguments "are always based on close analysis of individual stanzas," Alpers acknowledges, but the terms of that analysis "are as unreal as they are untraditional" (752, 753); "he has plausible and interesting ideas," but "their irrelevance reveals his inability to put his general theories into critical practice" (752); his readings of particular episodes contain "many felicitous and useful observations," but he "consistently reduces moral issues to judgments of character," "going ... against the nature of allegory as Spenser inherited it and the nature of *The Faerie Queene* itself" (750, 753). Moreover, his "attitude towards moral discourse is totally foreign to Spenser," his sense of irony not "the true Spenserian irony" but a "presumed sophistication," and his "actual readings and interpretations" inevitably "disappointing" (753, 754). Incapable of following Alpers's cardinal rule for reading *The Faerie Queene*—"Trust the verse" (757)—Cheney emerges from the review a pathetic, almost tragic, figure: "One can readily imagine that Cheney, seeing what was involved in single stanzas, did not trust the verse, or perhaps did not trust himself, enough to see the poem through to the end on its own terms"; for all his good intentions, "he cannot reveal the poem he knows is there" (757, 752).

In the end, it is up to Alpers to reveal the poem to us, and in the final section of the essay he does so brilliantly, tracking the "unfolding" of four different stanzas with characteristic precision, sensitivity, and wit. *That* is how to read *The*

Faerie Queene. And that, presumably, is why A. C. Hamilton chose to include "How to Read *The Faerie Queene*" in his 1972 collection of *Essential Articles for the Study of Edmund Spenser*, an installment in a new series of edited collections that promised to winnow the "[i]mmense resources ... now available for literary study in England and America" to those essays and articles that "consistently reappear on graduate seminar shelves and on undergraduate program reading lists." The chosen pieces were meant to be doubly exemplary: they "make up a body of knowledge that cannot fail to be valuable, and they act as models of the kind of contributions to learning which we are training our students to make themselves."[21] Is "How to Read *The Faerie Queene*" such a model? An oddly abashed prefatory note hints that Hamilton himself had qualms on this point: "Late in the planning of this edition, the rising costs of permission to reprint required that excerpts from books be omitted," it reads. "In particular, I regret the omission of an extract from Donald Cheney's *Spenser's Image of Nature: Wild Man and Shepherd in 'The Faerie Queene,'* which was designed to introduce Paul J. Alpers' review and allow his answer to it."[22] As it was, the review stood alone.

No such apologetic note appears in the 1993 (or the 2014) Norton Critical Edition of *Edmund Spenser's Poetry*, where "How to Read *The Faerie Queene*" appears again—and where I first encountered it, while drawing up the syllabus for an introductory poetry seminar that included a unit on Spenser. Drawn by the title, I was startled by the contents; ultimately, I decided not to assign it, for fear that students would be terrorized by its ferocity—or, worse, inspired to mimic it in class. But the discomfort I felt, and still feel, at reading "How to Read *The Faerie Queene*" also has to do with what Alpers might call the striking and instructive gap between my own pedagogical ideals and critical practice. When I teach *The Faerie Queene* to students, undergraduate or graduate, much of my energy is expended in the service of what might be called courtesy: fostering an environment of mutual respect and generosity in which students are free to take interpretive risks without fearing they will meet with impatience or ridicule—even, perhaps especially, when they get the poem wrong. This, to put it mildly, is not the ethos of Alpers's review; in contrast to the warm and well-mannered decorum of the classroom, his gladiatorial approach comes as a shock. But the shock is partly one of recognition: I find the experience of reading "How to Read *The Faerie Queene*" oddly mortifying, not only because it is so easy to identify with the target of Alpers's scathing wit, but also because it is so easy to identify with its agent, the nakedness of whose aggression threatens to expose my own least flattering readerly instincts.

The review is a minor critical genre, but it can be a singularly revealing one: for the subject of the review, but also for the author, and for the collective readership for whom he or she claims to speak. "How to Read *The Faerie Queene*" transmits the urgency of a moment at which Spenser's poem very nearly was a lost cause for criticism, when dissenting too mildly from moribund ways of interpreting it might have condemned it to obsolescence; Alpers may be blatantly beastly to Cheney, but unlike Spenser's beast, he had his reasons. Even now, when the urgency of that particular moment has passed, "How to Read *The Faerie Queene*" retains its rude vigor. Indeed, its very rudeness challenges some of the chief pieties of contemporary literary scholarship: that studying the humanities makes us more humane; that reading develops our capacity for empathy; that debate is the hallmark of civil society; and that participating in professional academic discourse means entering a conversation, not suiting up for combat. It even tests the more basic assumption that academic debate, however heated, is and ought to be impersonal—that a bad review is a reflection on the quality of an argument, not a referendum on the character of its author. Above all, Alpers's reading of Cheney reading *The Faerie Queene* exposes academic discourse's competitive stakes, transforming what Alpers himself idealistically describes as "an open-ended poem" into a limited and frankly contested domain. For however firmly we may believe and profess that the readers of a shared text are colleagues, not competitors for a finite store of understanding or enjoyment (or professional prestige), such amiable convictions falter in the face of a colleague like Alpers: "How to Read *The Faerie Queene*" makes reading into rivalry, like it or not.

This is where the very minimalism of Spenserian courtesy may come in useful. For as John Upton reminds us, encounters between the inhabitants of Spenser's Faerie Land are shaped by ritual, precept, and convention: codes that work not to eliminate confusion, uncertainty, mistrust, and distaste but to make a contained space for them. In the poem's final book, these codes allow an unsettling proportion of the enemies of courtesy to go more or less free—not only the Blatant Beast itself but also lesser villains like Briana and Crudor, Sangliere, Blandina, Turpine, and the tormenters of Mirabella. Such escapes can feel frustratingly anticlimactic—hence P. B. Wilcox's annoyance at Calidore's treatment of Sangliere—but they are also ways of ensuring that courtesy does not succumb to the totalitarian and genocidal tendencies of Spenserian justice. Sometimes perpetuating conflict is more vital than ending it: in *The Faerie Queene*, courtesy keeps arguments and antagonists alive, if not unbloodied. Literary scholarship has evolved techniques of its own for sustaining debate while keeping it within bounds: the allusion and the citation, the block quote and the paraphrase, the footnote or endnote, the list of works cited and the bibliography. The gradations of acknowledgment entailed in these gestures are no less subtle than the rules of a joust, and equally charged with the potential either to prevent or to inflict harm. The "review article" itself might be regarded as such a technique writ large, a hybrid genre designed to accommodate both a reviewer's obligation to speak to her text and her wish to have her own say.

In that respect, Alpers's essay has the form of Spenserian courtesy, however abrasive its content. And there is one place in "How to Read *The Faerie Queene*" when Alpers appears conscious of having transgressed the norms of his genre. Toward the end of the review essay, seeking a suitably stultifying passage to sum up his disdain for Cheney's book, he resorts to citing its promotional copy, claiming that it "summarizes an aspect of Cheney's thought more clearly than anything in the book." In any case, he adds, "[w]ith a book so elliptically written that the wild man and the shepherd of the subtitle are not mentioned until p. 174, one may be excused for quoting the dust-jacket" (757). Maybe, but that defensiveness seems the mark of a guilty conscience: it is one thing for a reviewer to hold an author responsible for his own bad prose, but another to lampoon him for someone else's. Much in Alpers's review of Cheney's book is ungenerous, but only here is he unmannerly—and he knows it.

The minimal ethic of courtesy as Spenser depicts it thus offers itself as both an antidote to the more poisonous tendencies of critical culture and a safeguard against misguided sentimentality. Such an offering seems particularly valuable at present, when a growing number of literary scholars have expressed dissatisfaction with the relentless skepticism and predictable negativity of what Paul Ricoeur dubbed the "school of suspicion" and Bruno Latour calls "critique."[23] Prompted both by the self-questioning of scholars like Latour and Eve Sedgwick and by a widespread (perhaps largely economic and structural) sense of disciplinary malaise, such critics have made efforts to negotiate a truce, not only among readers but between readers and their texts, proposing such alternatives as "postcritical" reading, "the hermeneutics of susceptibility," "just reading," "surface reading."[24] As the names suggest, the proponents of these methods tend to embrace the rhetoric of minimalism: first, do no harm. But the ethical claims they make on behalf of their methods are often quite grand, even utopian. Most influential of all, in this respect, is Sedgwick's 2003 essay on paranoid and reparative reading, which calls for a new discipline of readerly vulnerability, grounded in a willingness to be caught off guard by texts, interpretations, and history itself. Paranoia—which results when suspicion metastasizes from "a possibility among possibilities" to "a mandatory injunction"—mandates "a distinctively rigid relation to temporality, at once anticipatory and retroactive, averse above all to surprise," Sedgwick writes. Resisting that mandate allows us "to glimpse the lineaments of other possibilities": "to read from a reparative position is to surrender the knowing, anxious paranoid determination that no horror, however apparently unthinkable, shall ever come to the reader as new; to a reparatively positioned reader, it can seem realistic and necessary to experience surprise."[25]

This is more or less exactly how Paul Alpers believes one ought to read *The Faerie Queene* ("Trust the verse!"), but Alpers's way of communicating that lesson, by publicly excoriating a fellow reader, reminds us of why many readers may yet resist Sedgwick's injunction: it is difficult to come away from "How to Read *The Faerie Queene*" without feeling slightly more paranoid about the enterprise of literary criticism. That is another reason that Alpers's review essay strikes me as a fitting place to conclude this book, for both the pleasure and the embarrassment of being caught off guard have been an enormous part of the experience of researching and writing it. From the discovery that my studied respect for Spenser's spellings might be an artifact of scholarly self-mythologization to the realization that earlier readers were oblivious to or dismissive of historical and political contexts I have learned to regard as both indispensible and inescapable, encountering readers of *The Faerie Queene* from other eras has often shaken my confidence in what I thought I knew, about the poem and about reading itself. Some surprises were delightful or revelatory, others harder to assimilate. And not every outworn or neglected instance of reading proved worth the trouble of its excavation, though I have enjoyed the license to include some such instances anyway, resisting the basic expectation that readings must be relevant in order to qualify as such. But delving into reception history has also filled me with fresh appreciation for the work that readerly antagonism does in making relevance happen: for the surge of annoyance that prompts one reader to respond sharply to another, the aggression that makes one insist on one's own reading, the savage delight in demolishing someone else's.

As Heather Love points out, Sedgwick herself shared that appreciation; indeed, even in the celebrated essay on reparative reading, it can be hard to square her stated commitment to "multiplicity, surprise, rich divergence, consolation, creativity, and love" with the scouring, hypervigilant eye she brings to the foibles of critics with whom she disagrees.[26] "[D]espite the methodological gains and affective appeal of the turn away from critique," Love writes, "I just don't think it's possible to read Sedgwick's essay ... *only* as a call for reparative reading" (238). Nor, she continues, would it be desirable to do so: the point of Love's essay isn't "to catch Sedgwick" in her own paranoid aggression (though Love is careful not to disavow that motive altogether) but "to acknowledge the negativity and aggression at the heart of psychic life and to recognize that thinking is impossible without [them]" (238). "[J]ust as allowing for good surprises means risking bad surprises, practicing reparative reading means leaving the door open to paranoid reading," she concludes, for "there is risk in love, including the risk of antagonism, aggression, irritation, contempt, anger—love means trying to destroy the object as well as trying to repair it" (240). Calidore's insistence on giving Pastorella's flocks as a parting gift to Coridon, at the end of book 6, canto 11, just before he takes away Pastorella herself for good, is just such an instance of aggressive reparation, or reparative aggression. And I am tempted to claim the moment when Edward Baldwin carefully retraces the letters of P. B. Wilcox's annotation, the better to mock him, as another. In such ambivalent gestures, suspended between courteous acknowledgment and the instinct to annihilate, we can recognize the divided impulses that make us want to take apart a text we love and obsess over a text we can't stand, to bask in the fellow feeling of reading in community and snarl at the approach of a rival interpreter, to resist any intrusion on the solipsistic scene of reading and keep, at all costs, the conversation going. Book 6 of *The Faerie Queene*, the Legend of Courtesy, supplies a genuinely minimal protocol for managing those competing impulses, an ethic of readerly engagement that assumes no mutual goodwill, that makes no claims for the inherently civilizing instincts of human beings or humanistic studies, and that restrains—but does not silence—the tongues of even the most obnoxious fellow readers.

CODA

Reading to the End

The Faery Queen, it is said, has never been read to the end.
—VIRGINIA WOOLF, THE MOMENT AND OTHER ESSAYS, 1947

Without being insensible to the defects of the Fairy Queen, I am never weary of reading it.
—ROBERT SOUTHEY, LETTER TO WALTER SAVAGE LANDOR, 1811

IT ISN'T really the case, but Virginia Woolf insisted that the opening line of her essay on *The Faerie Queene* conveyed a certain psychological truth: "Such remarks however exaggerated probably give pleasure, like a child's laugh at a ceremony," she reflects, "because they express something we secretly feel and yet try to hide."[1] Even Robert Southey seems to have felt the occasional twinge of impatience at the poem he loved so much—how else to explain the running list he kept in his commonplace book of wittily disparaging things people said or wrote about *The Faerie Queene*?[2] Because it is dense, difficult, didactic, and strange; because it is an allegory; because its language is pseudoarchaic and its spelling weird; because it meanders and digresses, shedding characters and entire plotlines as it goes; above all, because it is so extraordinarily long, Spenser's poem tests our readerly loyalties and often defeats our instinct to see a story through. If the reception history of *The Faerie Queene* appeared in the guise of one of the poem's own allegorical pageants, Delight and Discipline would lead the way, but Drowsiness, Distraction, Bewilderment, Boredom, and Fatigue would dog their heels.

But the opening line of Woolf's essay could also be taken straight: *The Faerie Queene* never *has* been read to the end, for the simple reason that no one can quite say where, or if, it ends at all. This peculiar fact—the joint product of biographical accident, editorial intervention, and what might or might not be poetic ingenuity—has consequences for the poem as a whole. To begin with, it makes it unusually difficult to speak of the poem *as* a whole. As Barbara Herrnstein Smith has written, poetic closure "is an effect that depends primarily upon the reader's experience of the structure of the entire poem."[3] But for the first two decades *The Faerie Queene* was in print, that experience kept changing: to begin with, there was the three-book poem of 1590, whose last stanzas depict the ecstatic union of Amoret and Scudamore, with Britomart standing off to the side; six years later came the six-book poem of 1596, in which Britomart finds Artegall, Scudamore loses Amoret, and the Blatant Beast rampages out of the closing lines; finally—though "finally" is in some ways just the wrong word here—there was the folio edition of 1609, in which the last page of book 6 sits directly opposite what looks like a continuation of the poem, or perhaps a new beginning: "Two Cantos of Mutabilitie: Which, both for Forme and Matter, appear to be parcell of some following Booke of the Faerie Queene, Vnder the Legend of *Constancie*. Neuer before imprinted."[4]

The source of that descriptive heading is unknown: it can't have been Spenser himself, since the poet had died ten years before, and the hesitancy of the language suggests that it wasn't a close friend or literary executor, either. In all likelihood, the heading was the work of the folio's printer, Matthew Lownes, who acquired the rights to *The Faerie Queene* after the death of their original publisher, William Ponsonby, in 1604. But whoever composed them, those few tentative lines remain our sole source of information as to the nature and purpose of what follows: 116 additional stanzas, telling the story of the rebellious rise and fated downfall of the titaness Mutabilitie. In keeping with the design of *The Faerie Queene*'s first six books, those stanzas are distributed into cantos, numbered 6 and 7, each preceded by a four-line verse "Argument"; there is also the two-stanza beginning of an eighth canto, "vnperfite" (363). Beyond these formal features, the relation between the so-called *Cantos of Mutabilitie* and the hypothetical Legend of Constancie from which they may derive, as well as the relation between that Legend and the rest of *The Faerie Queene*, is unclear: there is no knightly protagonist in view, nor any hint of a larger narrative in process, only Mutabilitie and her quest for dominance.

The addition of the *Mutabilitie Cantos* to *The Faerie Queene* did more than fractionally increase the length of an already long poem; it violated the twofold expectation—of continuity and closure, in that order—by which reading "to the end" is typically governed and sustained. "The perception of poetic structure is a dynamic process," writes Herrnstein Smith:

> Structural principles create a state of expectation continuously modified by successive events. Expectation itself, however, is continuously maintained, and in general we expect the principles to continue operating as they have operated. Now it is clear that a poem cannot continue indefinitely; at some

point the state of expectation must be modified so that we are prepared not for continuation but for cessation. Closure, then, may be regarded as a modification of structure that makes *stasis*, or the absence of further continuation, the most probable succeeding event. Closure allows the reader to be satisfied by the failure of continuation, or, put another way, it creates in the reader the expectation of nothing. (33–34)

But the early manuscript and print history of *The Faerie Queene* had already put this structure of expectation under considerable stress: Spenser appears to have written the poem out of narrative sequence and over the course of at least a decade and a half; he allowed portions of it to circulate among friends and acquaintances; he published it in installments, making significant revisions to the plot between editions; and he wrote repeatedly of his intentions to continue adding to it, perhaps until it attained the full twelve-book form projected in the 1590 "Letter of the Authors." Indeed, the title pages of the two editions of *The Faerie Queene* produced in his lifetime both describe it proleptically as "Disposed into twelue books." For all these reasons, as Gordon Teskey notes, and because at his death in 1599, "he was still young enough to believe he would do it," "there was no reason not to expect materials from the promised second half of *The Faerie Queene* eventually to come to light."[5] The addition of the *Two Cantos of Mutabilitie* to the poem in 1609 was, if not "the most probable succeeding event," an event for which Spenser's readers had been amply prepared—not only by *The Faerie Queene*'s publication history but by its plot. If the italicized and capitalized *FINIS* beneath the *Cantos*'s closing stanzas was legible as yet another intermission in an unusually ruptured and protracted publication history, the prayer for rest and fulfillment those stanzas contain could be interpreted as both a prophetic summons to the absent rest of the poem and an echo of the narrative "not yet" with which so many of its protagonists must learn to be content. In the world of *The Faerie Queene*, the point at which expectation yields to satisfaction can always be postponed.

Spenser's early readers appear to have learned this lesson well, for the extension of the 1609 *Faerie Queene* to a point of terminal uncertainty does not seem to have troubled them—or, indeed, to have attracted much notice. No one appears to have questioned Lownes's judgment in publishing the *Mutabilitie Cantos* or in placing them as he did, although that decision did prompt readers to wonder how much more of *The Faerie Queene* Spenser had completed and whether any of it survived in manuscript.[6] Sir James Ware's 1633 preface to *A View of the Present State of Ireland* helped to launch the rumor of an additional six books—the entire promised second half of the poem—completed by Spenser and "unfortunately lost by the disorder and abuse" of a servant entrusted with transporting them from Ireland to England.[7] That claim, which

Ware later retracted, continued to circulate for centuries after, keeping the hope of further manuscript discoveries alive. Indeed, of the hundred or so seventeenth- and early eighteenth-century references to Spenser collected by R. M. Cummings, the only one to mention the *Two Cantos of Mutabilitie* in particular is a 1660 letter from John Worthington to Samuel Hartlib fantasizing about the lost works of Spenser's that might yet "lie hid in some libraries or closets."[8] Maybe this poem *would* continue indefinitely.

But as decades, and then centuries, passed with no further discoveries or additions, Lownes's *FINIS* came to seem like the real thing, and *The Faerie Queene* settled firmly into the guise it assumed in 1609: six book-length Legends of Holiness, Temperance, Chastity, Friendship, Justice, and Courtesy, and the *Two Cantos of Mutabilitie*, extracted perhaps from some lost Legend of Constancy. The relative ease of that posthumous transformation has a great deal to do with the obscure and chaotic circumstances of Spenser's own end—of disease, hunger, or perhaps heartbreak in the streets of London, following the ransacking of his Irish estate by rebels—which served as an ample excuse for the obscure and chaotic ending of his poem. But it also owes something to the *Cantos* themselves, and to the uncanny aptness with which they seem to anticipate and justify their effect on *The Faerie Queene*. As the title given to them by Lownes indicates, change is the force that dominates the *Mutabilitie Cantos*: Mutabilitie's quest to rule in the heavens as she does on earth forms a miniature epic of the near-triumph of impermanence and flux over constancy, time over eternity. In their melancholic embrace of Mutabilitie's power, till that apocalypse when "all shall changed bee" (7.7.59.4–9), the *Cantos* function almost as a gloss on the strange unraveling of the work to which they belong: as John Upton wrote in the notes to his 1758 edition of *The Faerie Queene*, "Proud Change or Mutabilitie, that insulting Titanesse, who has plaid her cruel pranks to many a man's decay and ruin, has made her depredations likewise on our poet's poem."[9] Now legible only as a ruined remnant or partial prefiguration of itself, *The Faerie Queene* joins the ranks of Mutabilitie's hapless subjects, awaiting an apocalyptic redemption.

That melancholy yet hopeful posture of expectation has seemed to many readers like an ideal conclusion: indeed, the very neatness with which the final, fragmentary cantos of the 1609 *Faerie Queene* comment on the poem's narrative and bibliographic unraveling can make their appearance in it feel perfectly crafted, even fated. Not simply thematically but formally, as James Nohrnberg has pointed out, the relation of the two full cantos to their pair of trailing stanzas mirrors the relation of the two major installments of the 1590 and 1596 *Faerie Queene* to the brief appendage of 1609. So richly suggestive are the parallels between part and whole that it is hard to not see the hand of some poetic providence at work in Lownes's belated discovery, bringing order out of disorder and redemption out of disappointment. Beginning with John Hughes's 1715 edition of *The Faerie Queene*, the *Mutabilitie Cantos* have tended to be read in just this light: as both "a noble Fragment" and "the most sublime and the best invented Allegory in the whole Work."[10] Generations of critics have found them "equal, if not superior, to any of the rest,"[11] "rising to a sublime strain of invention,"[12] containing "stronger testimony of mature thought"[13] and "more powerful poetry" than anything else Spenser wrote.[14] "More than a coda," writes A. C. Hamilton, the *Mutabilitie Cantos* "are central to the poem, a final and clarifying vision of all that has gone before."[15]

It is thus easy to forget that this almost certainly wasn't *Spenser's* vision of *The Faerie Queene*.[16] On the contrary, it is a vision predicated on the poet's absence from the poem, and on the likely frustration or abandonment of his plans for it. Although it is "conceivable," as Spenser's biographer Andrew Hadfield puts it, that the manuscript for the *Mutabilitie Cantos* was given to Matthew Lownes while Spenser was still alive, perhaps even by the poet himself, the textual evidence points strongly in the other direction; both the lapse in time before they appeared in print and the tentative terms in which they are described make it "most likely that Lownes inherited them from [William] Ponsonby's papers."[17] Indeed, Andrew Zurcher's bibliographic analysis of the 1609 folio leads him to conclude that the placement of the *Cantos* at the end of the book was a last-minute decision, not a premeditated design. And even if Spenser did intend the *Mutabilitie Cantos* as a postscript to the six-book *Faerie Queene*, he could not have anticipated the significance that would accrue to them in light of his untimely passing. "[F]or us," as Gordon Teskey observes, "the poet's death has become part of the meaning of this poem, . . . confirm[ing] what the broken structure of the *Mutabilitie Cantos* bears witness to mutely: the incompleteness of all our projects in this world" (336). Far from weakening the *Cantos*'s relation to *The Faerie Queene*, however, this haunting symmetry of life and work has only enhanced their appeal and strengthened their authority in the eyes of readers: however inexplicable or even unauthorized their arrival in the poem, the addition of the *Two Cantos of Mutabilitie* has had the paradoxical effect of making the rest seem more intelligible, more perfect, and more wholly Spenser's own. By whatever obscure and haphazard means the *Two Cantos of Mutabilitie* came into *The Faerie Queene*, almost no one has wished for it to do without them.

Almost no one: in the June 1880 issue of *Macmillan's Magazine*, a dissenting voice was briefly and consequentially raised. The eye-catching headline of Sebastian Evans's article, "A Lost Poem by Edmund Spenser," trumpets a new discovery—perhaps one of the works carelessly mislaid by that apocryphal servant. In fact, however, the poem Evans claims to have discovered was none other than the *Two Cantos of Mutabilitie*, which he grandly characterized as "practically lost to the world for more than two centuries and a half."[18] What Evans meant wasn't that no one had read the *Mutabilitie Cantos*—after all, they were included in every print edition of *The Faerie Queene* from 1609 on—but that no one had read them properly: "as a complete and highly finished poem, with a distinct beginning, middle and end of its own, and though similar in form to the *Faerie Queene*, utterly different from it in matter and in aim" (147). Not so much lost as hiding in plain sight, this last great work of Spenser's career had been buried in the massy bulk of the poem to which it was assumed to belong. "[I]t is high time," Evans declared, "that these *Two Cantos of Mutabilitie* should at last be recognised not as a wholly incongruous and only half-intelligible appendage to the *Faerie Queene*, but as one of the noblest independent poems of the noblest age of English poetry" (151).

In truth, though, what impressed him about the *Mutabilitie Cantos* was how little they seemed like a product of their age. Evans read the *Cantos* as unexpectedly, preternaturally forward-looking, bearing traces of Spenser's up-to-the-minute engagement with Copernican astronomy and hinting at his anticipation of some of the most recent and radical developments in nineteenth-century physics. As proof of the poet's prophetic genius, he cites Nature's verdict against Mutabilitie at the close of canto 7, in which the great goddess explains that

> [A]ll things stedfastnes doe hate
> And changed bee, yet being rightly wayd
> They are not changed from their first estate,
> But by their change their being do dilate:
> And turning to themselves at length again,
> They worke their owne perfection so by fate:
> Then over them Change doth not rule and raigne;
> But they raigne ouer change, and doe their states maintaine.
>
> (*MUTABILITIE CANTOS* 7.58.2–9)

"It is startling," Evans writes, "to find thus fantastically tricked out in the garb of poetic Elizabethan allegory one of the latest doctrines of logical Victorian science"—namely, Julius Robert Mayer's 1842 law of the conservation of energy, which provided a corollary to Antoine Lavoisier's 1785 law of the conservation of mass. "It is perhaps too much to credit Spenser with enunciating the theory that while every particle of matter is moved in every particle of time, the sum of all matter and all motion remains immutable," but Evans insists that "a strict analysis of this poem will show that its conclusions cannot be translated into the terminology of modern physics by any less extensive proposition." Indeed, he judges Spenser's formulation of constancy-in-mutability "clearly preferable" to the existing laws of conservation of mass and energy "as at once co-ordinating [each] doctrine with its complementary one"—though he was content to leave the final verdict on that matter "for others to determine" (151). (In the event, it would be another two and half decades before science caught up to Spenser, with Albert Einstein's synthesis of the two laws of conservation into the special theory of relativity and the equation $e = mc^2$.)

Despite his essay's title, the mystique of the lost work was part of the nostalgic mind-set Evans wanted Spenser's readers to forswear: the missing six books of *The Faerie Queene*, he argued, were only missing in the sense that people had insisted on missing them. What Evans discovered in the *Two Cantos of Mutabilitie*, by contrast, was not a lost poem but a new and forward-looking incarnation of Spenser himself—indeed, a version of the poet to whom novelty mattered much more than antiquity. This Spenser, he insisted, would never have consented to the posthumous prolongation of *The Faerie Queene*: "the whole of the poem printed in the poet's lifetime" was, in fact, the whole of the poem (145). Dismissing the description of a twelve-book *Faerie Queene* as merely "a sketch of [Spenser's] general plan" and not "a definite promise as to what he will write in future," Evans argues that the six-book version of 1596

> is committed to the world as ended if not consummated, and a careful survey of the internal evidence discloses no promise of any contemplated completion.... And, in fact, Spenser must have felt that the world wanted no more *Faerie Queene*. In 1579 the conception of the poem was an inspiration. In 1596 its continuation would have been an anachronism. (145–46)

An anachronism, of course, is precisely what most critics *had* made of *The Faerie Queene*, regarding it as both a purposeful exercise in poetic archaism and the crumbling relic of a bygone age: in the well-known metaphor of John Hughes's 1715 edition, the poem survives like the ruins of some great work of "Gothick Architecture." Evans counters that image with an architectural analogy of his own, between the six-book *Faerie Queene* and Alexander Hausmann's recent (and controversial) redesign of the crooked byways of medieval Paris into a regular and spacious urban grid:

> This *Faerie Queene* is not a cathedral of Beauvais, where the colossal choir among its disproportionate surroundings records the fate of over-sanguine ambitions: it is rather one of Hausmann's Boulevards, which comes to an end at a street corner, not because it could not be continued in exactly the same style for any number of leagues further, but simply because it is not wanted. (146)

No superannuated ruin, haunted by the ghost of its own incompletion, this vision of *The Faerie Queene* was distinctly and bracingly *modern*: modular, functional, and meticulously well planned, with nothing redundant or out of place. What isn't there, wasn't—and isn't—wanted.

This, however, is where Evans's own foresight failed him. For as it turned out, what wasn't in the 1596 *Faerie Queene*—not only the *Two Cantos of Mutabilitie* but the vision of poetic fulfillment for which they stood—was wanted, quite badly, by some readers. The backlash to Evans's essay was swift and severe: shortly after its publication, Alexander B. Grosart devoted an entire appendix in his 1882–84 edition of Spenser's *Complete Works* to dismantling what he disparagingly calls "this noticeable essay": "as a simple matter-of-fact," he declares, "every single statement [in it] is historically and critically inaccurate."[19] Grosart mocked Evans's pretensions to scientific expertise, dismissed his critical insights as "unhistoric and ... frivolous," and scoffed at his supposed knowledge of Spenser's private intentions for *The Faerie Queene*. Most damningly, he amassed an impressive array of instances in which the poet declared his determination to continue the 1596 poem. The conclusions reached by Evans's "noticeable essay" were thus doubly dismissed, as both "'not proven' and disproved" (1:508). The vehemence of Grosart's reaction suggests that Evans's essay had gotten under his skin, and the account he provides of *The Faerie Queene*'s lost or unwritten second half in his own "Life" of Spenser suggests why. For Grosart, the *Mutabilitie Cantos* were more than a precious remnant of those missing books; they were proof of Spenser's fidelity to his readers, proof that he never wholly abandoned his intention to complete his poem, even as "the announced purpose must have become a remorseful memory" (215). Spenser, he writes, "was a strong-souled Englishman," and even the destruction of his home by Irish rebels could not have dampened his ambition; the fragment of a seventh book recovered by Lownes "go[es to] show that" he had "given himself afresh to the mighty task" (221). To sever the *Mutabilitie Cantos* from *The Faerie Queene* was thus to deprive readers of an essential confidence in the poet, the poem, and the worthiness of their own efforts to understand it in full: to grasp to the best of their knowledge and ability the entirety of what Spenser wished to communicate.

In a purely practical sense, Grosart prevailed: in the decades that followed, as the field of literary studies took root within the university and the corpus of scholarship on *The Faerie Queene* burgeoned, Evans's essay was almost completely stricken from the record. A footnote to Herbert Ellsworth Cory's 1917 study of Spenser for the newly launched University of California series in Modern Philology invokes it only to bury it, declaring, "It is hardly worthwhile to pause here to lay to rest the ghost of a rumor that these cantos do not belong to the *Faerie Queene*."[20] It appears again in a bibliography in the 1938 *Variorum*

Edition: "The Faerie Queene" Books Six and Seven, but as the title of the volume indicates, the *Variorum* editors wholly disregarded the substance of Evans's argument.[21] Indeed, no modern editor of *The Faerie Queene* ever adopted his radically separatist position on the *Two Cantos of Mutabilitie*, which continued to appear at the end of *The Faerie Queene* under the same heading as in 1609. Even those who shared Evans's suspicions about the *Cantos* balked at his solution: "Neither in thought nor treatment do they evince any similarity to the seventy-two cantos to which they are appended," Thomas J. Wise confessed in the preface to his 1895–97 edition. "Nevertheless, to the end that the present edition of Spenser's masterpiece may be rendered as complete as possible, it has been decided to append them."[22] Critics took much the same approach, treating the *Cantos* as functionally, if not designedly, integral to the work with which they had so long been associated—indeed, as the only perspective from which one could see *The Faerie Queene* whole. As Frye (who otherwise shared Evans's taste for a six-book *Faerie Queene*) put it, "The poem brings us to the poet's 'Sabbath's sight' after his six great efforts of creation, and there is nothing which at any point can be properly described as 'unperfite.'"[23]

The *Mutabilitie Cantos* were wanted, and so they stayed. But—wanted or not—Evans's "ghost of a theory" stayed, too. For when it came to Spenser's intentions, even Alexander Grosart had to admit that Evans had a point: we have no certain knowledge of what the *Cantos* were meant to be. In a grudging postscript to his rebuttal, Grosart concedes, "I do not mean by this that it is not still open for argument whether the 'Two Cantoes of Mutabilitie' and the two stanzas were or were not intended by Spenser to be incorporated in the *Faery Queen*" (510). That "still" rather understates the matter: for nearly three hundred years, the question of whether or not the *Mutabilitie Cantos* belonged to *The Faerie Queene* never *was* raised, but in the century and a half since Evans posed it, it has proved—as Grosart seems irritably to anticipate—impossible either to answer or to evade. In a plot twist that would gladden Mutabilitie's own rebellious heart, by striving to fix the bounds of *The Faerie Queene* more narrowly and securely, Evans's essay opened the poem to an onslaught of dissension and doubt. As Jane Grogan writes in the introduction to a collection of essays on the *Mutabilitie Cantos* published on the four hundredth anniversary of their appearance in print, those who study the final 116 stanzas of *The Faerie Queene* must reckon with an intimidating array of unknowns:

> Notoriously little of the relevant circumstantial details are known to us: what is it exactly? Why was it written? When did the printer get hold of it, and how? Where should it be situated with respect to *The Faerie Queene*, and indeed within early modern literary culture?[24]

Behind such questions lurk other doubts, both practical and existential: What were Spenser's plans for *The Faerie Queene*, and how fully did he execute them? Are any of the versions of the poem we have complete, or is each the fraction of a larger whole? If so, what shape might that larger whole have assumed? And what difference, if any, should all this make to how we interpret the poem (or, as Evans would have it, poems) we possess? Is any reading of *The Faerie Queene*, however careful and comprehensive, doomed to failure in the end?

Now notorious, as Grogan says, such anxieties appear to have been entirely unfelt by readers of *The Faerie Queene* before 1880. The impact of Sebastian Evans's argument—to put it in terms Evans himself might appreciate—has been less like Einstein's 1905 theory of special relativity, which fixed the speed of light in a vacuum as a universal constant, than like Heisenberg's 1927 uncertainty principle, which pried knowledge of a subatomic particle's velocity loose from any sure conception of where it might be found. The analogy is less fanciful than it might seem, for as Evans pointed out, the judgment that had secured the *Mutabilitie Cantos*'s position in relation to the rest of *The Faerie Queene* was founded on an explicit and unfounded guess as to what they were—and vice versa. In an impressive feat of circular reasoning, the questions "What is it exactly?" and "Where should it be situated?" had both been answered by appeal to the same unsourced and frankly speculative assertion: Two Cantos Of Mutabilitie: *Which, both for Forme and Matter, appear to be parcell of some following Booke of the* Faerie Qveene, Under The Legend Of *Constancie*. Offered as a description of the stanzas that follow, the 1609 heading had, as Evans argued, taken on a prescriptive power:

> The editor, if indeed the volume had any other editor than Matthew Lownes the printer, prints the poem accordingly as if it were the sixth and seventh cantos of some lost book of the *Faerie Queene*, with a fragment of an eighth. Now supposing the editor to have been simply an honest blunderer, the palpable influence from this heading is that in some way or another he had become possessed of this poem, and finding it written in the same metre and style as the *Faerie Queene*, had come to the conclusion that it probably formed part of that poem; and thereupon, arbitrarily, if not allegorically, placed his sixes and sevens at the head of the cantos. The very phrase, "*appear* to be," is absolutely conclusive against his having any authoritative information on the subject. If, however, it is justifiable to hint a doubt as to whether Matthew Lownes, or whoever the real culprit may have been, being quite so scrupulously conscientious as all of Spenser's later editors, it may be surmised that if he were fortunate enough by any means to "acquire" a poem undoubtedly by Spenser, which it might be possible to palm off as a part of the *Faerie Queene* supposed to be irrecoverably lost, he would hardly scruple to suppress

any tell-tale introductory verse or verses it might have possessed in MS., with a view to rendering his new book more irresistibly tempting to the British public. (146)

Evans's reasoning here is hardly airtight: as Alexander Grosart would want us to note, he has gone from the confident assertion that in 1596 Spenser himself knew that "the world wanted no more *Faerie Queene*" to the equally confident and contradictory assertion that in 1609 the prospect of more *Faerie Queene* would have been "irresistibly tempting." And although he derides the fantasy of the parts of the poem "supposed to be irrecoverably lost," he does not hesitate, in the next breath, to invent a no less suppositious lost fragment—the "telltale introductory verse or verses [the *Cantos*] might have possessed in manuscript"—in support of his own pet theory.

But this, perhaps, is the point: the very fantastical and contradictory nature of Evans's argument about the end of *The Faerie Queene* forced its scholarly custodians to confront the wishful thinking that undergirded their own approach to the poem. And the ire with which Grosart reacted suggests that Evans's scorn for the generations of editors who had accepted the 1609 account of the *Mutabilitie Cantos* without "ever vouchsaf[ing] the slightest hint as to their real character and significance" painfully hit home. Even if it did not change Grosart's mind, or his editorial practice, it needled him into a revealingly defensive response. Grosart's edition of the *Complete Works*, it is worth recalling, was aimed at an audience of specialists and connoisseurs, published by subscription only and advertised as including a new biography of the poet and an array of explanatory essays "BASED ON ORIGINAL RESEARCHES" by a team of scholars whose academic qualifications and affiliations were listed prominently on the title page of volume 1.[25] In his preface to the edition, Grosart promised to remove Spenser's life and works from the hands of unthinking traditionalists: "[I]n dealing with hereditary mistakes and mendacities, I have not shunned to call a spade a spade," he avowed. "No criticism or difference is advanced without a statement of its ground" (1[v]). The grudging postscript to his appendix on Sebastian Evans suggests that he was as good as his word: when it came to the nature and purpose of the *Mutabilitie Cantos*, there was almost no ground on which to stand.

For the most part, that continues to be the case. Barring some extraordinary archival find, even the most rigorously fact-based arguments about the end of *The Faerie Queene* incorporate a significant measure of fantasy and guesswork. As Andrew Zurcher admits in an article that attempts to reconstruct the features of the lost manuscript source from which the printed text of the *Cantos* was set, "facts are scarce, the inquiry speculative, and the conclusions hypotheses merely."[26] "[T]he evidence does not amount to proof," concurs J. B.

Lethbridge at the start of his effort to date the composition of the *Cantos* through biographical clues and stylistic features. "[O]bviously I give it partly because I find it compelling," Lethbridge writes, "but of course the strength of my personal conviction and the strength of my argument are not the same thing."[27] But the two can be surprisingly difficult to disentangle: Zurcher's long catalogs of bibliographic features are meticulously objective, but his judgments as to which features are authentically "Spenserian" and which editorial depend on a far more intuitive sense of the poet's aims, while Lethbridge's survey of stylistic minutiae is anchored in a speculative account of the tumultuous final weeks of Spenser's life. Perhaps as a result, the versions of the *Mutabilitie Cantos* that emerge from their analyses are wholly incompatible: Zurcher argues that the *Cantos* came to Lownes's hands through an unreliable source, that they were probably never meant for incorporation into *The Faerie Queene*, and that the numbers assigned to them are a dubious editorial supposition; Lethbridge, by contrast, claims that Spenser wrote (or at least "compiled") the *Cantos* just before death, left them deliberately unfinished, and may have numbered them "to suggest precisely the incomplete nature of *The Faerie Queene*, his life's work" (329). According to one body of evidence, the *Mutabilitie Cantos* are a purely accidental, if fortuitous, part of *The Faerie Queene*; according to another, they reflect Spenser's most deeply felt longings for his poem. In each case—and Lethbridge and Zurcher are admirably frank on this point—the divergent conclusions reached are rooted in divergent preferences, not only about how to read the *Two Cantos of Mutabilitie* but about how to read, period. Biography or bibliography, formal analysis or the charting of page signatures and running titles: much as Sebastian Evans suggested, where we place the end of *The Faerie Queene* is a function of what we want, from Spenser's poem and for the discipline of literary criticism.

Evans published his essay just as that discipline was coming into its own, at a moment when its relationship to more established fields of research, especially in the natural and social sciences, was notably precarious. As Herbert Cory writes in the introduction to the study that reduced Evans to a footnote,

> If literary criticism is to exonerate itself from parasitism, from triviality and pedantry in the community of new sciences of man, . . . [it] must examine constantly its scientific fellows, general biological evolution, paleontology, ethnology, heredity, general psychology, comparative psychology, parapsychology, economics, history, the empirical study of ethical values, and the empirical study of aesthetic values in the other arts, for hints of method, for facts, and for relevant interpretations.[28]

It is possible Evans believed himself to be doing just that, anchoring poetry in science by claiming a place for Spenser in the lineage of modern physics; if so, the attempt backfired badly. Instead, his accusation that *The Faerie Queene*'s editors and critics had been foolishly credulous in accepting Lownes's account of the *Two Cantos of Mutabilitie* struck an exposed nerve among the poem's scholarly readers, who revenged themselves by ridiculing and then effacing him. (Ironically, a number of Evans's seemingly far-fetched claims about Spenser's scientific interests, such as his familiarity with the writings of Lucretius and Giordano Bruno, later entered the critical mainstream, but they were purged of association with his essay.[29]) But he remains among the most influential of Spenser's critics—not because he succeeded in persuading others that the *Mutabilitie Cantos* had, as he put it, "no real connection" with *The Faerie Queene*, but because he showed where that connection was necessarily to be found, in the minds of Spenser's readers. Indeed, as Gordon Teskey acknowledges, in the sense of doubt it articulates and the doubts it has engendered, the poem's elusive ending reveals "the inseparability of Spenser's work as a writer ... from our work as readers" (336). In the face of such terminal uncertainty, what we accept as evidence is a function of what we want—and of what we cannot bear to lose.

For there is one possibility about the end of the 1609 *Faerie Queene* that Evans himself doesn't entertain: namely, that it isn't by the author of *The Faerie Queene* at all. In his imagined account of the *Mutabilitie Cantos*'s arrival in Lownes's print shop, Evans describes the manuscript as "undoubtedly by Spenser"—although, since the manuscript has vanished, that attribution must rest on the same potentially spurious resemblance of "metre and style" that Evans derided as a basis for including it in *The Faerie Queene* (146). What is to prevent us, then, from elaborating his skeptical fantasy to include someone besides the doltish or duplicitous Lownes, a devoted admirer or archimitator of *The Faerie Queene* for whom the six existing books of Spenser's poem served as the template for an astonishing feat of impersonation: the Earl of Oxford, perhaps, or Francis Bacon, or—why not—William Shakespeare? In fact, one reader did imagine something almost like this: in 1914, Edward George Harman produced a six-hundred-page-long treatise arguing for Bacon's authorship of Spenser's entire poetic oeuvre, as well as the complete works of Shakespeare. Oddly, however, although he is willing to relinquish almost every other supposed certainty about *The Faerie Queene*, Harman's views of the *Mutabilitie Cantos* are restrained, even conservative. Although he scoffs at the "pretence" of their posthumous appearance in Lownes's print shop "with no explanation as to their origin"—Bacon, still alive in 1609, has a clear advantage over Spenser in this regard—he accepts without question their relation to *The Faerie Queene*: "They are obviously the work of the author of the previous six books." Indeed, because he has no need to wonder how the manuscript made its way into Lownes's hands ten years after the death of its author, Harman can dispense with the sort of worries that plague other critics of the *Cantos*: although they appear fragmentary, they were, he insists, "evidently added to give a close to the poem."[30] Dispensing with the assumption that either the *Mutabilitie Cantos* or *The Faerie Queene* itself is by Spenser thus allows Harman to secure the relationship between the two. Once Bacon is recognized as the true author, everything else about the *Cantos* becomes "obviously" and "evidently" clear: their continuity with the first six books of *The Faerie Queene*, their status as the poem's intended ending, even their Irish setting and their seemingly belated appearance in 1609 (the same year, Harman points out, in which Bacon wrote a memorandum to King James urging the "replantation" of the Irish colonial settlements).

With the exception of Harman, Spenser's authorship of the *Cantos* has been treated as axiomatic, the ground on which all further speculations necessarily rest: as Jane Grogan puts it, "Only the 'who' is reasonably clear: that this is the work of Edmund Spenser."[31] And yet the evidence for that assertion is less conclusive than one might suppose. It is true that the *Cantos* have all the stylistic hallmarks of *The Faerie Queene*, from its intricately rhymed nine-line stanza and its antiquated diction to its narrator's penchant for parenthetical asides. And with their Irish setting and their nods to the poet's earlier writings, they pointedly advertise their connection to Spenser's life and career, soliciting fond recognition from readers. As the narrator demands in one of those characteristic asides, "Who knows not Colin Clout?" No one, it would seem, for even those who doubt that the *Mutabilitie Cantos* belong to *The Faerie Queene* agree that they belong to the author of *The Faerie Queene*. But if one wished to make a case against that claim—and that is not my real purpose here—it would be relatively easy to do, beginning with the unavoidable fact that the *Cantos* surfaced a decade after Spenser's death and were never mentioned in his lifetime, not even among the unpublished and possibly lost works listed by Gabriel Harvey in 1580 and William Ponsonby in 1595. The wording of the heading given to them in the 1609 folio implies that Lownes himself had little notion of where they came from and only a shaky intuition of what they were for, an implication that Andrew Zurcher's account of the folio's confused compilation confirms. And the rationale Lownes offers for including them in *The Faerie Queene*—the conspicuous resemblances of "Forme and Matter"—might just as well be counted against them, since stylistic hallmarks can be imitated; indeed, the more conspicuous a feature, the easier to forge—and any forger worth his or her salt surely would take care to advertise his text's ties to its supposed original. If we look past the *Cantos*'s more obviously "Spenserian" features to the subtle stylistic markers on which ascriptions of authorship more reliably rest, the evidence is still more mixed: for all their apparent kinship to Spenser's verse, the *Mutabilitie Cantos* are also, as numerous critics have noted, unlike anything else he wrote. "The themes, the intellectual framework, the physical setting, the tone, and the temporal orientation are all somewhat different from *The Faerie Queene*," as Teskey notes, and their formal composition, F. M. Padelford observed, is "marked by certain peculiarities."[32] Grogan describes them as "delivered in . . . a startling new vein," and stylometric analysis bears her out: studies of specific words, phrases, and tropes have produced no consensus about when or why the *Mutabilitie Cantos* were written except to affirm that they stand apart from every other book in *The Faerie Queene*, containing "fewer digressions [and] fewer ornaments," lacking many of the poem's most frequently used words and phrases, and featuring "nothing remotely like" its formulaic repetitions.[33] Indeed, J. B. Lethbridge concludes, "the *Cantos* are written almost as it were by a different person to the rest of *The Faerie Queene*" (316).

Almost as it were by a different person—and yet no one, not Evans, not even Harman, has ever suggested that they were. Given how many possible ends readers of *The Faerie Queene* have imagined since the late nineteenth century, why has this one possibility been silently ruled out of court? The likelihood is vanishingly small, but it would explain much that has seemed inexplicable: why Spenser's last work took so long to appear in print, and why we know so little about how it did; why the poetry of the *Mutabilitie Cantos* is at once so conspicuously like and so noticeably unlike the rest of Spenser's verse; how the contents of the narrative can reflect so aptly the fragmentary and belated form of its publication. Of course, that is how conspiracy theories work: the acceptance of one vast unlikelihood—that Spenser anticipated and encoded the key discoveries of modern physics, or that Francis Bacon secretly and single-handedly wrote the bulk of the early modern English literary canon—is urged because it is seen to remedy a host of lesser confusions and unlikelihoods. My point is simply that in the case of the *Mutabilitie Cantos*, this oddly inelastic economy of doubt applies as much to the orthodox scholarly theories as to their far-fetched alternatives. When it comes to the end of *The Faerie Queene*—when *we* come to the end of *The Faerie Queene*—there is, it seems, only so much uncertainty we can handle.

In his history of the Shakespeare authorship controversy, James Shapiro traces its origins to William Henry Ireland's highly public confrontation with Edmund Malone, whose use of orthography as a means of literary authentication helped secure the privileged status of "Spenser's spelling."[34] It may also have helped secure the status of the *Two Cantos of Mutabilitie*: once the old-spelling *Faerie Queene* became the only acceptable version of Spenser's poem, the text—with all its conspicuous gaps and ragged edges—acquired an impression of uniformity that must have seemed impossible to fake. But the real explanation may be simpler: for the vast majority of Spenser's readers, it has been difficult to conceive of *The Faerie Queene* as finished—or of finishing *The Faerie Queene*—without this fortuitous and graceful addition; in its absence, the burden of our effort seems too great and its reward too little. Even those who question the *Cantos'* relation to *The Faerie Queene* treasure it as the summation of a poetic career; even the one person who doubted it was by Spenser was sure it belonged to the man who wrote *The Faerie Queene*. The judgment rendered by Nature against Mutabilitie at the close of canto 7, that all things "turning to themselves at length againe, / Do worke their own perfection" (*Mutabilitie Cantos*, 7.58.6–7), may not be the scientific breakthrough Evans claimed, but it is an insight on which the field of Spenser criticism has depended, a proposition that reconciles Spenser's ambition to his achievement, his immeasurable energy to the insupportable mass of his verse. "From the high ground of Arlo Hill," as William Blissett writes, "perhaps more of Spenser's total work can be held in conspectus than from any other vantage point."[35]

Yes—and more of our work, too. For all its unwieldy vastness, the six-book *Faerie Queene* can feel not nearly long enough: there is too much irresolution and too little satisfaction, too scanty a return on our efforts to comprehend it. Neither a narrative conclusion nor an allegorical summation, the *Mutabilitie Cantos* are not a fulfillment of Spenser's plans for *The Faerie Queene* so much as a benediction on the labor of his readers. The fragmentary addition supplies what Frank Kermode termed "the sense of an ending"—a fullness of meaning and aesthetic pleasure that comes only through instability, contradiction, and strife. The fable of Mutability's rise and the prophecy of her downfall is a consoling fiction of human existence, as Kermode argues, reconciling "those great complementary opposites: the earthly and heavenly cities, unity and multiplicity, light and dark, equity and justice, continuity . . . and ends."[36] As a story about endurance amid loss and change, it is also a consoling fiction of Spenser's career, reconciling poetic intention to human error and historical accident, and sublime inspiration to the undignified hazards of embodiment. Finally, and perhaps most crucially, it is a consoling fiction of what it is like to read *The Faerie Queene*. Following on thousands of stanzas whose intricate rhyme scheme is a continual interplay of constancy and change, the final 116 stanzas of the poem provide what Blissett simply and beautifully calls "a stopping place."[37] Over time they have become, in Nohrnberg's nicely paradoxical phrase, "an indispensible supplement," bound to the poem, and to Spenser, by the force of our affection and need.[38]

The inexhaustible quality that makes reading *The Faerie Queene* so daunting—the sense that there are always more questions to answer and further challenges to surmount—can also make it an obsessive, even addictive, pleasure. "Spenser . . . I could have read forever," Walter Scott confessed, recalling his boyhood infatuation with *The Faerie Queene*.[39] For Scott's contemporary

Southey, that passion never waned, although he was aware that not everyone shared it: "Do you love Spenser? I have him in my heart of hearts," he wrote to a friend in 1816. As a young man, Southey cherished a plan to write *The Faerie Queene*'s unfinished second half, "collect[ing] every hint and indication of what Spenser meant to introduce in the progress of his poem, and . . . plann[ing] the remaining legends," and even in middle age, he contemplated his failure to do so with regret: "What I have done as a poet falls far short of what I had hoped to do." His first action in the afterlife, he confided, would be to seek out Spenser's soul and ask "to hear the lost books of the Faery Queen."[40] Such insatiability is as much a hallmark of *The Faerie Queene*'s reception history as the irritability and impatience to which Virginia Woolf gives voice. Indeed, for some of Spenser's readers, Woolf's opening line gets it exactly wrong: it isn't finishing *The Faerie Queene* that's hard; it's accepting that the poem is over, that there are no further "parcells" to be discovered, no lost fragments still in circulation, no way to bind up all of the loose ends and frayed edges. "[A] poem cannot continue indefinitely," as Herrnstein Smith sensibly maintains, but *The Faerie Queene* teased readers with the possibility that it might—and inspired at least a few with the determination to see that it would.

"Certainly, Timoclea, you have a passion for the marvellous beyond all power of gratification," begins a letter sent in October 1719 from Sir Thomas Fitzosborne to a bookish lady friend:

> There is not an adventurer throughout the whole regions of chevalry, with whom you are unacquainted; and have wandered thro more folios than would furnish out a decent library. Mine, at least, you have totally exhausted, and have so cleared my shelves of knights-errant, that I have not a single hero remaining that ever was regaled in bower or hall. But tho you have drained me of my whole stock of romance, I am not totally unprovided for your entertainment.

Fitzosborne explains that his library has recently been enlarged by the addition of a strange and seemingly singular manuscript, given to him by a nameless friend:

> He discovered it, he tells me, among some old manuscripts, which have been long, it seems, in the possession of his family: and, if you will rely upon his judgment, it is . . . by Spenser's own hand. There was a short dedication affixed to it, inscribed "To the most vertuous and beautiful lady, the Lady Carew." But this, my correspondent tells me, is entirely devoured by the rats.

All that remains is a date, "September 1591," a signature—"the initial letters E. S. subscribed at the bottom [and] perfectly legible"—and a poem, or the fragment of one, a transcript of which is appended to the letter.

At first glance, or to an uncritical eye, it looks very much like a missing piece of *The Faerie Queene*: nineteen nine-line stanzas, rhyming ababbcbcc and ending with an alexandrine, written in a faintly archaic species of poetic diction, and recounting a supposedly ancient fable, the pseudo-Ovidian tale of Lycon and Euphormius, "[w]hich for ensample drad my muse shall here unfold." The plot of the fable bears a distant resemblance to the tale of Faunus and Molanna in the *Mutabilitie Cantos*: "Unaw'd by conscience, of no gods afraid," proud Lycon seeks to thwart the courtship of his daughter by the son of the wise old shepherd Euphormius, making "[f]ull many a mean devise ... / The hoped day of spousal to with-hold." When he discovers the lovers have wed in secret, he casts his daughter out, "[f]orelore, the houseless child of misery, / Expos'd to killing cold, and pinching penury." The girl is rescued by Euphormius, and Jove himself descends from heaven to mete out justice. "Transmew'd to blatant beast," Lycon becomes "[a] wolf in form as erst a wolf in soul," while Euphormius is invited to "join the throng / Of glitt'rand lights that gild the glowing sky." Fitzosborne offers it to Timoclea with his compliments, though he makes no guarantee of its authenticity, leaving that "to be settled between my friend and the criticks."[41]

It was, of course, a complete fabrication—and so, for that matter, was Sir Thomas Fitzosborne. Both poem and gentleman were the inventions of William Melmoth, chancery court official, translator of Cicero and Pliny, and pseudonymous author of the popular epistolary compendium known as *Fitzosbornes Letters*, first published in 1742 and reprinted at least fourteen times in the subsequent fifty years. (Letter LXXII, "To Timoclea," first appeared in the expanded second edition of 1748.) Melmoth's authorship of *Fitzosbornes Letters* was an open secret—a witty game for those in the know—and it sparked both admiration and impatience in his peers. According to William Shenstone, the *Letters* were "written with Judgment, Elegance, and Fancy; but rather too much with an Eye to the Press."[42] "From the author of 'Fitzosborne's Letters,' I cannot think myself in much danger," Samuel Johnson told Boswell; "I met him only once, about thirty years ago, and in some small dispute reduced him to whistle." "For my part," professed Thomas De Quincey, "I have never looked into the 'Fitzosborne's Letters' since my boyhood, but the impression I then derived from them was, that Melmoth was a fribble in literature, and one of the 'sons of the feeble.'"[43]

But his impersonation of Spenser was not an element of Melmoth's notoriety; indeed, hardly anyone seems to have taken it seriously. This is likely as Melmoth intended: "The Transformation of Lycon and Euphormius," as it is titled, reads less like a wholehearted attempt at literary forgery, such as William Henry Ireland's annotation of "Shakespeare's *Faerie Queene*," than as a burlesque of Spenserian types and tropes. The joke, such as it was, was supposed to be on

Spenser—of whom, as the following letter, "To Clytander," makes clear, Melmoth was no great admirer. In that letter, Melmoth disparages "our English bard" for his clunky reanimations of classical deities and the literal-mindedness of his allegorical personations. Pronouncing such conceits tolerable in small doses, "when such shadowy beings are . . . just shewn to the imagination, and immediately withdrawn again," he declares them ridiculous in a poem like *The Faerie Queene*: "I can relish them no farther than as figures only: when they are extended in any serious composition beyond the limits of metaphor, and exhibited under all the various actions of real persons; I cannot but consider them as so many absurdities" (2:120). Far from expecting readers to greet "The Transformation of Lycon and Euphormius" as a genuine addition to the Spenserian corpus, then, Melmoth seems to have intended it as a spoof on a poem that was, in his view, too long already.

Readers, however, are unpredictable creatures, and the pseudonymous Timoclea, that insatiable and inexhaustible consumer of romance, had an unlikely real-life counterpart in the learned Scottish antiquary John Callander. Callander read the second edition of *Fitzosbornes Letters* in 1749, as he was in the midst of compiling notes for what he seems to have hoped would become a new annotated edition of *The Faerie Queene*, the first since John Hughes's 1715 edition. And for all his erudition, he greeted the supposed discovery of "The Transformation of Lycon and Euphormius" with unfeigned enthusiasm, copying the contents of the letter to Timoclea into his 1611/1612 edition of the *Works of Edmund Spenser* and noting with excitement that the newly discovered work was "wrote in the same stanza as the Fairy Queen, and its language . . . for the most part even more obsolete." Himself a scholar of both early modern English poetry (his annotated *Paradise Lost* appeared in print the following year) and classical Greek verse, Callander should have known better—indeed, he may have done so. "If it be an imitation of our authors manner," he adds in a hesitant disclaimer, "it is very well executed."[44] But as Eve Houghton observes, "Callander seems to want to have it both ways: he expresses skepticism about the poem's authenticity even as he indulges in the fantasy that a poem by a major English poet has been discovered in an Elizabethan manuscript, picturesquely gnawed by rats."[45] In the end, readerly desire trumped scholarly caution: the learned antiquarian transcribed the pseudo-Spenserian poem's opening stanza into the pages of his rare and valuable book, calling it "very beautifull."

Callander's annotated edition of Spenser never made it into print, so we cannot know whether he would have seriously attempted to secure Melmoth's forgery a place in the poet's published *Works*, but "The Transformation of Lycon and Euphormius" was a supplement that his own version of *The Faerie Queene*, at least, could not do without. It would be easy to mock Callander for this credulity; how "unscholarlike," as his contemporary and fellow Spenser editor

John Upton would say. But the reception history of *The Faerie Queene* suggests that many of us want it both ways, too—Upton, with his pseudoscholarly defense of the charms of old spelling, emphatically included. Like Callander, we crave fact and fantasy, accuracy and enchantment, and we are not always good at telling the two apart. Indeed, Callander's ambivalent attachment to what he knew was likely a mere imitation betrays a double consciousness that will resonate with anyone for whom reading is both discipline and delight, labor and its reward. Such powerfully mixed feelings do not pertain only to the reading of very long poems—poems that defy our capacity to finish them—but they may be intensified by it. Wallace Stevens thought so: "Anyone who has read a long poem day after day as, for example, *The Faerie Queene*, knows how the poem comes to possess the reader and how it naturalizes him in his own imagination and liberates him there."[46] Possessed and liberated by his reading of Spenser's poem, John Callander was *The Faerie Queene*'s reader, which made *The Faerie Queene* his poem, to do with as he wished. But I am fond of Callander for another reason, too: together with the audacious and irreverent Melmoth, he supplies a cheerful antidote to the atmosphere of melancholy that tends to accrue at the close of any study of *The Faerie Queene*, thanks in part to the wistful final stanzas of the *Mutabilitie Cantos*, with their evocative, impassioned, and still unanswered prayer for rest. The single stanza from "The Transformation of Lycon and Euphormius" that Callander penciled into his copy of Spenser's *Works* is hardly equal to those extraordinary lines; it is not great poetry, or even—pace Callander—a convincing simulacrum of it. But Melmoth's forgery nonetheless afforded Callander a slyly inverted glimpse of *The Faerie Queene*'s "Sabbath's sight": the vision of a poem that never does end, so long as there is someone, somewhere, who wishes it to continue.

ACKNOWLEDGMENTS

I'm grateful to all of the friends, family members, colleagues, neighbors, and passing acquaintances who have encouraged, entered into, or cheerfully endured my six-year-long preoccupation with *The Faerie Queene*. Writing a book about a poem very few people read ought to be a fairly solitary endeavor, but writing this one has been a joyously sociable experience throughout.

Thanks first of all to J. K. Barret, Briallen Hopper, Ruth Kaplan, Jill Richards, Sunny Xiang, Leslie Harkema, and Anna Zayaruznaya for their friendship and support—I am fortunate to have such brilliant, kind, tough, principled, passionate, and deeply caring companions in this work.

Thanks secondly to my students: our shared delight, bewilderment, hilarity, mystification, and fascination with this poem is what made me want to write about it in the first place, and what has sustained and buoyed me along the way. I am so very lucky to learn with and from you. Special thanks to Eve Houghton for a spectacular summer's worth of research assistantship and to Ben Card for getting me to the finish line on time.

I'm grateful, too, to David Kastan, Larry Manley, and John Rogers for their continued mentorship and their willingness to read multiple iterations of almost every page I write. Kathryn James introduced me to William Henry Ireland's copy of *The Faerie Queene* and converted me to the pleasures of archival research. Lanny Hammer was an enthusiastic champion of this project from the start and made sure that it got a receptive reading when it counted most. Gary Tomlinson invited me to join the vibrant community of the Whitney Humanities Center, whose Hilles Publication Fund made it possible to include a slightly profligate number of illustrations in this book.

I'm grateful for the chance to have shared pieces of the manuscript with members of the early modern communities at Columbia, Stanford, and Yale. Special thanks to Gabe Bloomfield, Michael West, Julie Crawford, Jean Howard, Luke Barnhart, Ivan Lupic, and Hannah Smith-Drelich for their incisive feedback and warm hospitality. Thanks as well to the editors of *Modern Language Quarterly*, *English Literary History*, and the *Spenser Review* for publishing earlier versions of or extracts from chapters one, two, and four, and for allowing me to reuse that material here.

My first scholarly publication was in *Spenser Studies*, and Anne Prescott's editorial note to me about it remains one of the most lavishly generous and gratuitously kind responses my work has ever received—a model of how to make a fledgling scholar feel like she belonged. In general, the community of Spenser scholars is astonishingly hospitable to newcomers, and I am immensely glad to have found my way into it. I'm particularly grateful to Joe Moshenska, Ayesha Ramachandran, Joe Loewenstein, Andrew Hadfield, Maureen Quilligan, and David Miller for their advice, encouragement, and wise counsel.

I cite Jeff Dolven with exceptional frequency in the pages of this book, but that frequency doesn't come close to reckoning what his scholarship, mentoring, and encouragement have meant to me in the course of writing it. No one makes *The Faerie Queene*—or the profession of literary criticism—more inviting.

Margreta de Grazia doesn't particularly care for *The Faerie Queene*, but she does an incredible job of caring for her students, even those who have long since ceased to be her professional responsibility. I will always be grateful for her patient, perceptive, terrifyingly acute scrutiny of my writing, and for her boundless confidence in my ability to improve it.

Anne Savarese at Princeton University Press has taken excellent care of this book throughout the publishing process, not least by securing for it two remarkably careful, detailed, imaginative, and capacious reader's reports. My thanks to the readers for their diligence and insight, and to Anne for her usefully stern attitude toward deadlines.

Thanks to my parents, my brothers, and the extended Nicholson-Levenson clan for their loving support. None of them read *The Faerie Queene*, but they are gratifyingly proud of me for doing so.

This book is dedicated to the four people who have lived most intimately, affectionately, and patiently with it—and me—over the past six years and more: to Marc Levenson, who helps me make a life with space for reading and writing and so much more, and who lets me sleep in every weekend; to Miriam Levenson, who was small enough to review children's adaptations of *The Faerie Queene* for me when this project began and old enough to spot errors in the page proofs by the time it was done, and whose line-edits are amazingly apt; to Ruthie Levenson, who made me narrate the entire plot of the poem, including the *Mutabilitie Cantos*, over several weeks' worth of bedtimes, dressed up as a lady-knight for Halloween, and wrote a version of Book One in which *another dragon* is waiting at the end; and to Eli Levenson, who came along just in time for the final edits and is the happy ending we've all been waiting for.

NOTES

Introduction

1. Edmund Spenser, *The Faerie Queene*, ed. A. C. Hamilton (New York: Longman, 2007). Unless otherwise specified, all subsequent citations from the poem refer to this edition and are given parenthetically by book, canto, stanza, and line.

2. Anthony Grafton, "The Humanist as Reader," in *A History of Reading in the West*, ed. Guglielmo Cavallo and Roger Chartier, trans. Lydia G. Cochrane (Amherst: University of Massachusetts Press, 1999), 183. Along with Jean-François Gilmont's chapter on "Protestant Reformations and Reading" in the same volume, Grafton's chapter offers a useful account of the ways that reading was both regularized and refracted by the intellectual, political, economic, and religious transformations of the fifteenth and sixteenth centuries. As both scholars emphasize, the rise of humanism, the invention of print, and the Reformation produced certain broad shifts in the culture and practice of reading—away from reverence for the *auctoritates* of the medieval university, for instance, and toward a culture of independent scholarship, or away from the presumption of universal Latinity and toward a culture of vernacularization—but such general trends are complicated by innumerable regressions and countermovements.

3. Judith Anderson, "What I Really Teach When I'm Teaching Spenser," *Pedagogy* 3.2 (Spring 2003): 178.

4. Isabel MacCaffrey, *Spenser's Allegory: The Anatomy of Imagination* (Princeton, NJ: Princeton University Press, 1976), 59.

5. Spenser, "Letter," in *The Faerie Queene*, 716.

6. Persuasive versions of this argument—which is often made with much more subtlety than in my summary here—can be found in Richard Foster Jones, *The Triumph of the English Language* (Oxford: Oxford University Press, 1953); Richard Helgerson, *Forms of Nationhood: The Elizabethan Writing of England* (Chicago: University of Chicago Press, 1992); Paula Blank, *Broken English: Dialects and the Politics of Language in Renaissance Writings* (New York: Routledge, 1996); Claire McEachern, *The Poetics of English Nationhood, 1590–1612* (Cambridge: Cambridge University Press, 1996); David J. Baker, *Between Nations: Spenser, Shakespeare, Marvell, and the Question of Britain* (Stanford, CA: Stanford University Press, 1997); and Andrew Hadfield, *Shakespeare, Spenser and the Matter of Britain* (New York: Palgrave Macmillan, 2004).

7. Anderson, "What I Really Teach When I'm Teaching Spenser," 178.

8. Ibid., 179.

9. See especially Sheila T. Cavanaugh, "'Clowdily Enwrapped in Allegorical Deuices': The Joys and Perils of Teaching Spenser's Epic," *Pedagogy* 3.2 (2003): 171–76, which describes the highly

polarized responses *The Faerie Queene* tends to elicit in the classroom, based on the results of a survey of instructors at a range of institutions.

10. I have written elsewhere about Mulcaster's pioneering role in establishing English in the grammar school curriculum; see Catherine Nicholson, *Uncommon Tongues: Eloquence and Eccentricity in the English Renaissance* (Philadelphia: University of Pennsylvania Press, 2014), 40–44.

11. Richard C. Frushell, *Spenser in the Early Eighteenth Century: Education, Imitation, and the Making of a Literary Model* (Pittsburgh: Duquesne University Press, 1999), 3.

12. Gerald Graff, *Professing Literature: An Institutional History*, 20th anniversary ed. (Chicago: University of Chicago Press, 1987, 2007), 4.

13. Jeff Dolven, *Scenes of Instruction in Renaissance Romance* (Chicago: University of Chicago Press, 2007), esp. 136–71, on the making of examples out of bad students.

14. "M.R.," letter to the *Spectator*, July 3, 1712; reprinted in Joseph Addison and Richard Steele, *The Spectator*, vol. 4, ed. Donald F. Bond (Oxford: Clarendon Press, 1965), 432, and quoted in R. M. Cummings, ed., *Spenser: The Critical Heritage* (London: Routledge & Kegan Paul, 1971), 239.

15. Ibid.

16. Thomas Babington MacCauley, "Southey's *Edition of the Pilgrim's Progress*," *Edinburgh Review* 65 (1831): 452. As various critics have noted, the jest seems to reveal that MacCauley himself did not finish the poem, since the Blatant Beast is alive and well at the end of book 6.

17. C. S. Lewis, *English Literature in the Sixteenth Century* (Oxford: Clarendon Press, 1954), 393.

18. Spenser, "A Letter of the Authors," in *The Faerie Queene*, ed. Hamilton, 714.

19. James Nohrnberg, *The Analogy of "The Faerie Queene"* (Princeton, NJ: Princeton University Press, 1976), 39; the 1590 and 1596 title pages are reproduced in *The Faerie Queene*, ed. Hamilton, 26–27.

20. Anthony Trollope, *The Eustace Diamonds*, ed. Helen Small (Oxford: Oxford University Press, 2012), 165.

21. Charles and Mary Cowden Clarke, *Recollections of Writers*, 2nd ed. (London: Sampson Low, Marston, Searle & Rivington, 1878), 126.

22. Henry A. Beers, *A History of English Romanticism in the Nineteenth Century* (New York: H. Holt, 1899), 120.

23. The Larkin note is quoted in Kingsley Amis, "Oxford and After," in *Larkin at Sixty*, ed. Anthony Thwaite (London: Faber, 1982), 25, and cited in Andrew Hadfield, *Edmund Spenser: A Life* (Oxford: Oxford University Press, 2012), 503n109.

24. See Alexander Gill, *Logonomia Anglica* (London: John Beale, 1619); and John Milton, *Areopagitica* (London: 1644), 12–13. On the place of Spenser in Gill's pedagogy, see Frushell, *Spenser in the Early Eighteenth Century*, 25–26. I discuss Gill's handling of Spenser in the *Logonomia* at greater length in chapter 1 and Milton's fraught relationship to the poet in chapter 5. On Milton's misremembering of the Cave of Mammon episode, in which he wrongly places Guyon's Palmer, see also Patterson, Quilligan, and George F. Butler, "Milton's 'sage and serious Poet Spencer': Error and Imitation in *The Faerie Queene* and *Areopagitica*," *Texas Studies in Literature and Language* 49.2 (Summer 2007): 101–24. It is worth pointing out that the error may be unintended—there is, after all, so much poem to remember, and the Palmer does accompany Guyon everywhere else in book 2.

25. See Frushell, *Spenser in the Early Eighteenth Century*, 26–44.

26. Folger MS W.A. 126; quoted in Frushell, *Spenser in the Early Eighteenth Century*, 38.

27. William Hazlitt, *Lectures on the English Poets* (London: Taylor and Hessey, 1818), 74.

28. David Hume, *The History of England Under the House of Tudor*, 2 vols. (London: A. Millar, 1759), 2:738–39.

29. Virginia Woolf, *The Moment and Other Essays* (London: Hogarth Press, 1947), 25. The essay was published posthumously; it was likely written a decade earlier.

30. Virginia Woolf, *A Writer's Diary*, ed. Leonard Woolf (London: Harcourt, 1981), 230.

31. Woolf, *The Moment*, 25.

32. Ibid., 29.

33. Woolf, *A Writer's Diary*, 231.

34. Horace Walpole, *Letters* (London: R. Bentley, 1840), 3:25; Robert Southey copied the slur into his commonplace book, *Southey's Commonplace-Book* (London: Longman, Brown, Green, and Longmans, 1851), 4:312.

35. Walter Scott, 1805 letter to Anna Seward, quoted in John Gibson Lockhart, *Memoirs of the Life of Sir Walter Scott* (Cambridge, MA: Riverside Press, 1902), 1:436–37.

36. Robert Southey, letter to Walter Savage Landor, January 11, 1811, quoted in Charles Cuthbert Southey, *The Life and Correspondence of Robert Southey* (New York: Harper and Brothers, 1851), 3:295.

37. Walter Savage Landor, letter to Robert Southey, 1810, quoted in John Forster, *Walter Savage Landor: A Biography*, 2 vols. (London: Chapman and Hall, 1879), 1:259.

38. Samuel Richardson, letter to Susannah Highmore, June 22, 1750, in *The Correspondence of Samuel Richardson*, ed. Anna Laetitia Barbauld (London: R. Phillips, 1804), 2:245.

39. The letter was printed in June 1580 in a pamphlet titled *Three proper, and wittie, familiar letters: lately passed betvveene tvvo vniuersitie men: touching the earthquake in Aprill last, and our English refourmed versifying With the preface of a wellwiller to them both* (London: H. Bynneman, 1580), 7. I have chosen to cite original print editions and manuscripts wherever possible in this book, so that others can consult them if they wish, but this and many other early references to Spenser and *The Faerie Queene* can also be found in two indispensible resources: R. M. Cummings's *Spenser: The Critical Heritage* (London: Routledge & Kegan Paul, 1971), which covers the period 1579–1715, and the website *Spenser and the Tradition: English Poetry 1579–1830*, compiled by David Hill Radcliffe and found at http://spenserians.cath.vt.edu/.

40. Harvey and Spenser, *The Proper, and wittie, familiar letters*, 41, 50 (these are sequential pages; the pagination in the pamphlet is oddly erratic).

41. Thomas Nashe, *Pierce Peniless his Supplication to the Divell* (London: John Busbie, 1592), [41], sig. [L4]v.

42. Ben Jonson, *Timber; or Discoveries*, in *Workes* (London: Richard Bishop, 1640), 2.116–17.

43. John Harington, *Orlando Furioso* (London: Richard Field, 1591), 373; "Of Monsters. To my Lady Rogers," *The most elegant and witty epigrams of Sir Iohn Harrington, Knight digested into foure bookes: three vvhereof neuer before published* (London: John Budge, 1618), sig. [G8]v.

44. Samuel Daniel, "Sonnet 51," *Delia and Rosamond augmented. Cleopatra* (London: Simon Waterson, 1594), sig. E2r.

45. Michael Drayton, *Idea, the shepheards garland. Fashioned in nine eglogs* (London: Thomas Woodcock, 1593), 13; *Poly-Olbion* (London: Matthew Lownes, 1612), 71, 84.

46. John Hughes, ed., *The Works of Mr. Edmund Spenser* (London: Jacob Tonson, 1715), lxix–lxx; Thomas Warton, *Observations on the Faerie Queene of Spenser*, 2 vols. (London: R. and J. Dodsley, 1762), 1:8.

47. James Russell Lowell, *Literary Essays* (Boston: Houghton Mifflin, 1871), 326.

48. Alexander B. Grosart, ed., *The Complete Works in Verse and Prose of Edmund Spenser* (printed for private circulation, 1882–84), 1:294, 1:298.

49. The foundational and still immensely valuable study of this disciplinary history is Graff, *Professing Literature*; on the particular role played by the novel—or, at least, newly branded—technique of close reading, see John Guillory, "Close Reading: Prologue and Epilogue," *ADE Bulletin* 149 (2010): 8–14, and Joseph North, *Literary Criticism: A Concise Political History* (Cambridge, MA: Harvard University Press, 2017), 24.

50. Chris Baldick, *Criticism and Literary Theory 1890 to the Present* (London: Longman, 1996), 20.

51. David Hill Radcliffe, *Edmund Spenser: A Reception History* (Columbia, SC: Camden House, 1996), 157. Radcliffe's entire book is a trove of information and insight, but his account of the fruitful interdependence of Spenser studies and what he calls "the massed forces of professional philology" has been especially valuable to me here (166).

52. See Graff, *Professing Literature*, 6–8, on the rise of historical specialization and the displacement of departments of rhetoric and literature tradition by the "field coverage" model of the modern English department.

53. Radcliffe, *Edmund Spenser*, 157.

54. Edwin Greenlaw, *The Province of Literary History* (Baltimore: Johns Hopkins University Press, 1931), 59–60; see also 68–74. James Holly Hanford, "Edwin Greenlaw and the Study of Literature," *Studies in Philology* 29.2 (April 1932): 141–48, also notes Greenlaw's reverence for Warton.

55. Graff, *Professiong Literature*, 5, 140; see also Radcliffe, *Edmund Spenser*, 163–67.

56. Quoted in Graff, *Professing Literature*, 140, who does not attribute the phrase. Hazard Adams attributes it to Brents Stirling, a Renaissance scholar who studied under Greenlaw's collaborator Frederick M. Padelford, and who warned Adams as a young scholar, "Don't buck the Greenlaw trust" (Hazard Adams, *Academic Child: A Memoir* [Jefferson, NC: McFarland, 2008], 82, 188). Adams interpreted Stirling's caution as both a general commentary on the perils of academic politics and a measure of Greenlaw's peculiarly outsized influence on the field in Stirling's own youthful days. On the latter, see also James Holly Hanford, "Edwin Greenlaw and the Study of Literature," *Studies in Philology* 29.2 (April 1932): 141–48.

57. Edwin Greenlaw and James Holly Hanford, eds., *The Great Tradition: A Book of Selections from English and American Prose and Poetry; Illustrating the National Ideals of Freedom, Faith, and Conduct* (New York: Scott, Foresman, 1919), xiv. The production of such a popular anthology is less contrary to Greenlaw's scholarly self-image than it might seem: "Despite its rationalizing tendencies," as Radcliffe notes, his writing about literary study "everywhere emphasizes romance and romanticism" (164).

58. Jewel Wurtsbaugh, *Two Centuries of Spenserian Scholarship* (Baltimore: Johns Hopkins University Press, 1936), 160.

59. T. S. Eliot, "Charles Whibley" (1931), in *Selected Essays, 1917–1932* (New York: Harcourt, Brace, 1932), 405.

60. W. L. Renwick, "Review of the Hopkins *Works of Edmund Spenser*," *Modern Language Review* 28 (1933): 508; quoted in Radcliffe, *Edmund Spenser*, 166.

61. William Empson, *Seven Types of Ambiguity*, rev. 2nd ed. (London: Chatto and Windus, 1947), 33–34.

62. Quoted in David Gervais's contribution to the F. R. Leavis special issue of the *Cambridge Quarterly* 25.4 (1996): 312.

63. On Richards, see F. R. Leavis, "Dr. Richards, Bentham, and Coleridge (Review of *Coleridge on Imagination*)," *Scrutiny* 3 (1935): 382; on Tillyard, see F. R. Leavis, *The Common Pursuit* (London: Chatto and Windus, 1952), 40; on Eliot, see F. R. Leavis, "T. S. Eliot's Stature as Critic: A Revaluation," *Commentary* 26 (November 1, 1958): 404. The judgment to which Leavis objects appears in T. S. Eliot, "What is Minor Poetry?," *Sewanee Review* 54.1 (1946): 5.

64. Eliot, "What is Minor Poetry?," 8; and J. B. Bamborough, "The Influence of F. R. Leavis," *Spectator*, October 25, 1963, 24.

65. Derek A. Traversi, "Revaluation: *The Vision of Piers Plowman*," *Scrutiny* 5 (1936); reprinted in *A Selection from "Scrutiny*,*"* vol. 2, ed. F. R. Leavis (Cambridge: Cambridge University Press, 1968), 234, 240.

66. On Leavis's influence in particular, see Arthur Mizener, "The Scrutiny Group," *Kenyon Review* 10.2 (1948): 355–60; Gabriel Gersh, "The Moral Imperatives of F. R. Leavis," *Antioch Review* 28.4 (1968): 520–28; and Morris Freedman, "The Oracular F. R. Leavis," *American Scholar* 70.2 (2001): 93–99.

67. John Crowe Ransom, "Criticism, Inc.," *Virginia Quarterly Review* 13.4 (1937): 593.

68. The recollection appears in Lowell's 1974 obituary for Ransom and is quoted in Richard Danson Brown, "MacNiece in Fairy Land," in *Edmund Spenser: New and Renewed Directions*, ed. J. B. Lethbridge (Madison, NJ: Fairleigh Dickinson University Press, 2006), 353n5; and in Robert Lowell, *Collected Prose*, ed. Robert Giroux (New York: Farrar, Straus and Giroux, 1987), 23.

69. Allen Tate, *Reactionary Essays on Poetry and Criticism* (New York: Charles Scribner's Sons, 1936), 82, 91.

70. See Harry Berger Jr., "Backlooping: Life in a Revisionary Enclave," *A Touch More Rare: Harry Berger, Jr., and the Arts of Interpretation*, ed. Nina Levine and David Lee Miller (New York: Fordham University Press, 2009), 274. To be fair, these are the recollections of one of *The Faerie Queene*'s most passionate twentieth-century defenders, Harry Berger Jr., but they correspond well enough with Brooks's published comments on the poem.

71. Brooks, *Modern Poetry and the Tradition* (Chapel Hill: University of North Carolina Press, 1939), 181.

72. I am indebted for this anecdote to my colleague, Leslie Brisman, who was *The Faerie Queene*'s valiant would-be defender.

73. Cleanth Brooks, *The Well-Wrought Urn: Studies in the Structure of Poetry* (New York: Reynal and Hitchcock, 1947), 58; Yvor Winters, *Forms of Discovery: Critical and Historical Essays on the Forms of the Short Poem in English* (Chicago: Swallow Press, 1967), 28.

74. Mark van Doren, *The Noble Voice: A Study of Ten Great Poems* (New York: H. Holt, 1946), 231, 242.

75. Merritt Y. Hughes, "Spenser, 1552–1952," *Transactions of the Wisconsin Academy of Sciences, Arts, and Letters* 42 (1953): 5.

76. Hayden Carruth, "Spenser and His Modern Critics," *Hudson Review* 22.1 (1969): 139.

77. Northrop Frye, *The Anatomy of Criticism: Four Essays* (Princeton, NJ: Princeton University Press, 1957), xiii.

78. Harry Berger Jr., *The Allegorical Temper: Vision and Reality in Book Two of Spenser's "Faerie Queene"* (New Haven, CT: Yale University Press, 1957).

79. Angus Fletcher, *Allegory: The Theory of a Symbolic Mode* (Ithaca: Cornell University Press, 1964); and Rosemond Tuve, *Allegorical Imagery: Some Medieval Books and Their Posterity* (Princeton, NJ: Princeton University Press, 1966).

80. Paul Alpers, *The Poetry of "The Faerie Queene"* (Princeton, NJ: Princeton University Press, 1967), 4–5.

81. James Nohrnberg, *The Analogy of "The Faerie Queene"* (Princeton, NJ: Princeton University Press, 1976), ix.

82. Jonathan Goldberg, *Endlesse Worke: Spenser and the Structures of Discourse* (Baltimore: Johns Hopkins University Press, 1981), xi.

83. Quilligan and Montrose have written at length and over many years on these subjects, but their first major treatments of it both appeared in 1983: see Maureen Quilligan, *Milton's Spenser: The Politics of Reading* (Ithaca: Cornell University Press, 1983); and Louis Montrose, "Shaping Fantasies: Figurations of Gender and Power in Elizabethan Culture," *Representations* 2 (Spring 1983): 61–94.

84. Stephen Greenblatt, *Renaissance Self-Fashioning from More to Shakespeare* (Chicago: University of Chicago Press, 1980), 175.

85. Harry Berger Jr., in Harry Berger Jr., Irene Reti, and Cameron Vanderscoff, "The Critical World of Harry Berger, Jr.: An Oral History," ed. Reti and Vanderscoff (UC Santa Cruz Regional History Project, 2015), https://escholarship.org/uc/item/4rg173mr.

86. Michael Warner, "Uncritical Reading," in *Polemic: Critical or Uncritical*, ed. Jane Gallop (New York: Routledge, 2004), 13.

87. Ibid., 15.

88. Christina Lupton, *Reading and the Making of Time* (Baltimore: Johns Hopkins University Press, 2018), 2.

89. Ann Blair, *Too Much to Know: Managing Scholarly Information before the Modern Age* (New Haven, CT: Yale University Press, 2010).

90. Stanley Fish, *Is There a Text in This Class? The Authority of Interpretive Communities* (Cambridge, MA: Harvard University Press, 1980), 326. The impulse is not restricted to scholars: popular writers, too, have been eager to champion attention as an antidote to the ills of contemporary culture, politics, and daily life. Three recent offerings in the burgeoning corpus of self-help literature on this subject are Cal Newport's *Digital Minimalism: Choosing a Focused Life in a Noisy World* (New York: Portfolio, 2019), a follow-up to his best-selling *Deep Work: Rules for Focused Success in a Distracted World* (New York: Grand Central, 2016); Jenny Odell's *How to Do Nothing: Resisting the Attention Economy* (New York: Melville House, 2019); and Brigid Schulte's *Overwhelmed: How to Work, Love, and Play When No One Has the Time* (New York: Sarah Crichton Books, 2014). Kenneth Rogers offers an incisive analysis of the phenomenon in which these books participate in *The Attention Complex: Media, Archaeology, Method* (New York: Palgrave Macmillan, 2014), while Natalie Phillips's *Distraction: Problems of Attention in Eighteenth-Century Literature* (Baltimore: Johns Hopkins University Press, 2016) helpfully traces the instinct to fetishize attention back well before the rise of digital media or the advent of neoliberalism or global capitalism.

91. Sharon Best and Stephen Marcus list "Attention to surface as a practice of critical description" as the primary shared impulse of the practices they christened "surface reading" ("Surface Reading: An Introduction," *Representations* 108.1 [2009]: 11); "To read [the] expressiveness [of objects] presents a challenge not so much of excavation as of attentiveness," writes Anne Anlin Cheng in "The Wayward Life of Objects," *Forum: What Can Reading Do?, Novel* 45.1 (Spring 2012): 4. On attention's distinctive and even constitutive relation to literary experience, see also David Marno, *Death Be Not Proud: The Art of Holy Attention* (Chicago: Chicago University Press, 2016); and Margaret Koehler, *Poetry of Attention in the Eighteenth Century* (New York: Palgrave Macmillan, 2012). For a critique of the tendency among such critics to fetishize attentiveness as, precisely, inattentive to other aspects of reading in theory and practice, see Ellen Rooney, "Live Free or Describe: The Reading Effect and the Persistence of Form," *differences: A Journal of Feminist Cultural Studies* 21.3 (2010): 112–39.

92. Martin Amis, *Lionel Asbo: State of England* (London: Jonathan Cape, 2012), 6–7.

93. Theo Tait, "*Lionel Asbo* by Martin Amis—Review," *Guardian*, online edition, June 8, 2012.

Chapter 1: "The Falsest Twoo": Forging the Scholarly Reader

1. William Henry Ireland, *The Confessions of William Henry Ireland* (London: Thomas Goddard, 1805), 196.

2. William Henry Ireland, manuscript annotations in *The Faerie Queene* (1794–95) (Beinecke Rare Books Library 2014 160), 2, 59, 134.

3. James Boaden, *A Letter to George Steevens, Esq. Containing a Critical Examination of the Papers of Shakspeare; Published by Mr. Samuel Ireland* (London: Martin and Bain, 1796), 14.

4. Quoted in Arthur Sherbo, "The Earliest[?] Critic of the Ireland Shakespeare Forgeries," *Notes and Queries* 35/233.4 (1988): 499.

5. Quoted in Peter Martin, *Edmond Malone, Shakespearean Scholar: A Literary Biography* (Cambridge: Cambridge University Press, 1995), 196.

6. [Anonymous], "Cento Verborum Ex Shakespeareâ HIBERNIAE," *Gentleman's Magazine* 66 (February 1796): 93.

7. Edmund Malone, *An Inquiry Into the Authenticity of Certain Miscellaneous Papers and Legal Instruments, published Dec. 24, 1795. And attributed to Shakspeare* (London: H. Baldwin, 1796), 62.

8. Thomas P. Roche and C. Patrick O'Donnell, "A Note on the Text," in *The Faerie Queene*, ed. Roche and O'Donnell (New York: Penguin Classics, 1979; repr. 1987), 7.

9. Andrew Hadfield and Anne Lake Prescott, "Introduction," in *Edmund Spenser's Poetry*, ed. Hadfield and Prescott, 4th ed. (New York: W. W. Norton, 2013), xi; Hiroshi Yamashita and Toshiyuki Suzuki, "Textual Introduction," in *The Faerie Queene*, ed. A. C. Hamilton, rev. ed. (London: Pearson/Longman, 2007), 21.

10. Joseph Loewenstein gave an account of this editorial debate in a presentation at the Dublin 2015 International Spenser Society Conference titled "What EEBO-TCP Should Mean to Editors (of Spenser and Others)."

11. Robert Kellogg and Oliver Steele, "Introduction," in *Books 1 and 2 of "The Faerie Queene": "The Mutabilitie Cantos," and Selections from the Minor Poetry*, ed. Kellogg and Steele (New York: Odyssey Press, 1965), vii.

12. Emma Field Pope, "Renaissance Criticism and the Diction of *The Faerie Queene*," *PMLA* 41.3 (1926): 606–7.

13. Bruce McElderry, "Archaism and Innovation in Spenser's Poetic Diction," *PMLA* 47.1 (1932): 146. Paula Blank offers a persuasive modification of Pope's and McElderry's arguments in *Broken English: Dialects and the Politics of Language in Renaissance Writings* (New York: Routledge, 2002), 112–17, although she suggests that contemporary objections to Spenser's diction had more to do with class and region—with "rusticity"—than with archaism.

14. See https://earlyprint.wustl.edu/. The *Early English Books Online* corpus "contains digital facsimile page images of virtually every work printed in England, Ireland, Scotland, Wales and British North America and works in English printed elsewhere from 1473–1700"—more than 125,000 texts (see http://eebo.chadwyck.com/home). EEBO-TCP is a joint production of EEBO and the Text Creation Partnership, with the aim of converting the roughly 70,000 unique first editions in EEBO into "fully searchable" XML/SGML electronic texts (that work is still in progress: as of 2014, at least 25,000 texts had been converted and made publicly available; by 2020, the entire 70,000 may be publicly available; see http://www.textcreationpartnership.org/tcp-eebo/).

15. Anupam Basu and Joseph Loewenstein, "Spenser's Spell: Archaism and Historical Stylometrics," *Spenser Studies* 33 (2019): 1, 29.

16. Martha Craig, "The Secret Wit of Spenser's Language," in *Elizabethan Poetry: Modern Essays in Criticism*, ed. Paul Alpers (New York: Oxford University Press, 1967), 447–72. The spelling of "geaunt" is one of Craig's central examples that are drawn almost exclusively from the text of book 1; it is worth wondering whether such etymological punning is particular to the Legend of Holiness or whether it extends evenly across all six books of the poem.

17. On this turn and its sequelae, see John Guillory, "Close Reading: Prologue and Epilogue," *ADE Bulletin* 149 (2010): 8–14; Jane Gallop, "Close Reading in 2009," *ADE Bulletin* 149 (2010): 15–19; and N. Katherine Hayles, "How We Read: Close, Hyper, Machine," *ADE Bulletin* 150 (2010): 62–79. On the conflict over *The Faerie Queene* between the New Critics and their successors, see my introduction above. For a compelling account of how book 1 of *The Faerie Queene* works as an introduction to the method and ethic of close reading, see Judith H. Anderson, "What I Really Teach When I'm Teaching Spenser," *Pedagogy* 3.2 (2003): 177–83. Anderson's insistence on the necessity of readerly disorientation as a precursor to readerly skill goes some way, I think, to explaining why Spenser critics—who, these days, are almost always also Spenser teachers—have been so reluctant to abandon the poem's old spellings.

18. Paul Alpers, *The Poetry of "The Faerie Queene"* (Princeton, NJ: Princeton University Press, 1967), 14.

19. David Lee Miller, *The Poem's Two Bodies: The Poetics of the 1590 "Faerie Queene"* (Princeton, NJ: Princeton University Press, 1988), 84; A. Leigh DeNeef, *Spenser and the Motives of Metaphor* (Durham, NC: Duke University Press, 1982), 143; Jonathan Goldberg, *Endlesse Worke: Spenser and the Structures of Discourse* (Baltimore: Johns Hopkins University Press, 1981), 3; Andrew Hadfield, "The 'sacred hunger of ambitious minds': Spenser's Savage Religion," in *Religion, Literature, and Politics in Post-Reformation England, 1540–1688*, ed. Donne B. Hamilton and Richard Strier (Cambridge: Cambridge University Press, 1995), 30, quoted in Willy Maley, *Salvaging Spenser: Colonialism, Culture and Identity* (New York: St. Martin's Press, 1997), 6.

20. Alpers, *The Poetry of "The Faerie Queene,"* 102, 100.

21. Angus Fletcher, *The Prophetic Moment: An Essay on Spenser* (Chicago: University of Chicago Press, 1971), 99–101.

22. Catherine Bates, "The Point of Puns," *Modern Philology* 96.4 (1999): 423–24.

23. Margaret Ferguson, "Fatal Cleopatras and Golden Apples: Economies of Wordplay in Some Shakespearean 'Numbers,'" in *The Oxford Handbook of Shakespeare's Poetry*, ed. Jonathan Post (Oxford: Oxford University Press, 2013), 78–81. Ferguson's essay draws on Jacques Derrida's discussion of puns and other forms of verbal wit in "Proverb: 'He that would pun . . .,'" in *Glassary*, ed. John P. Leavey Jr. (Lincoln: University of Nebraska Press, 1986); and Gregory Ullmer, "The Puncept in Grammatology," in *On Puns: The Foundation of Letters*, ed. Jonathan Culler (New York: Basil Blackwell, 1988), 164–89, both of which emphasize the fundamental arbitrariness of linguistic representation that puns expose.

24. Edmund Spenser, *The Faerie Queene* (London: Printed [by John Wolfe] for William Ponsonby, 1590), 13 [1.1.37–38].

25. Alexander Hume, *Of the Orthographie and Congruitie of the Britan Tongue* (1620), ed. Henry B. Wheatley (London: Early English Text Society, 1865), 1.

26. Franco Moretti, *Distant Reading* (New York: Verso, 2013), 48–49.

27. "What EEBO-TCP Should Mean," 1.

28. Basu and Loewenstein, "Spenser's Spell," 35.

29. Daniel Shore, "WWJD? The Genealogy of a Syntactic Form," *Critical Inquiry* 37.1 (2010): 24.

30. Randall McLeod, "Spellbound: Typography and the Concept of Old-Spelling Editions," *Renaissance and Reformation* n.s. 3 (1979): 50–65. For reasons I discuss at greater length below, Shakespeare scholars—and scholars of early modern drama more generally—have long parted company with Spenserians over the value and validity of old-spelling editions.

31. Ben Jonson, *Timber or Discoveries, Made Upon Men and Matter* (London: 1641), 116; on Jonson's spelling, see Joseph Loewenstein, *Ben Jonson and Possessive Authorship* (Cambridge: Cambridge University Press, 2002), 154–55; and Kevin J. Donovan, "Jonson's Texts in the First Folio," in *Ben Jonson's 1616 Folio*, ed. Jennifer Brady and Wyman H. Herendeen (Newark: University of Delaware Press, 1991), 23–37.

32. Edmund Spenser, *"The Faerie Queen": "The Shepheards Calender": Together With the Other Works of England's Arch-Poët, Edm. Spencer* (London: H[umphrey] L[ownes] for Matthew Lownes, 1617), 5.

33. A. C. Hamilton, "On Annotating Spenser's *Faerie Queene*: A New Approach to the Poem," in *Contemporary Thought on Edmund Spenser*, ed. Richard C. Frushell and Bernard J. Vondersmith (Carbondale: Southern Illinois University Press, 1975), 41.

34. See F. R. Johnson, *A Critical Bibliography of the Works of Edmund Spenser Printed before 1700* (Baltimore: Johns Hopkins University Press, 1933); David Lee Miller, *The Poem's Two Bodies: The Poetics of the 1590 "Faerie Queene"* (Princeton, NJ: Princeton University Press, 1988); Joseph Loewenstein, "Spenser's Retrography: Two Episodes in Post-Petrarchan Bibliography," in *Spenser's Life and the Subject of Biography*, ed. Judith H. Anderson, Donald Cheney, and David A. Richardson (Amherst: University of Massachusetts Press, 1996), 99–130; Carol A. Stillman, "Politics, Precedence, and the Order of the Dedicatory Sonnets in *The Faerie Queene*," *Spenser Studies* 5 (1985): 143–48; Jean R. Brink, "Materialist History of the Publication of *The Faerie Queene*," *Review of English Studies* 54 (2003): 1–26; and Wayne Erickson, ed., *The 1590 "Faerie*

Queene": *Paratexts and Publishing*, special issue of *Studies in the Literary Imagination* 38.2 (Fall 2005).

35. Andrew Zurcher, "Printing *The Faerie Queene* in 1590," *Studies in Bibliography* 57 (2005/2006): 115–50.

36. The pioneering account of *The Faerie Queene*'s spelling as a function of compositorial labor is in Hiroshi Yamashita, Haruo Sato, Toshiyuki Suzuki, and Akira Takano, *A Textual Companion to "The Faerie Queene," 1590* (Tokyo: Kenyusha, 1993), 407–8.

37. Here a word of further caution is in order, for, as Jeffrey Masten has recently pointed out, the whole field of compositorial analysis depends in an assumption that sixteenth-century spelling is, if not regular per se, at least particular to an individual, a kind of compositorial or writerly fingerprint, and that assumption may also be anachronistic (see *Queer Philologies: Sex, Language, and Affect in Shakespeare's Time* [Philadelphia: University of Pennsylvania Press, 2016], 39–66). But Masten's overarching point—that in the early modern period "the autobiographical subject practices no fully auto-orthographical consistency" (44)—is crucial to my own argument here.

38. Edwin Greenlaw, Charles Grosvenor Osgood, and Frederick Morgan Padelford, "Textual Appendix," in *The Works of Edmund Spenser: A Variorum Edition*, vol. 1 (Baltimore: Johns Hopkins University Press, 1932; reissued 2001), 521.

39. [Edmund Spenser and Gabriel Harvey], *Three proper, and wittie, familiar letters* (London: H. Bynneman, 1580), 7.

40. E.K.'s preface and gloss to *The Shepheardes Calender* undoubtedly influenced Spenser's reputation for linguistic archaism and eccentricity—as they were intended to do (see Emma Field Pope on this point). But apart from "eglogues," I can find no trace of a connection between E.K. and the later perception or treatment of Spenser's spelling, and the orthography of *The Shepheardes Calender* was standardized along with that of the rest of Spenser's poems in the seventeenth century.

41. Alexander Gill, *Logonomia Anglica* (London: John Beale, 1619), 91.

42. [Ralph Knevett], *A Supplement of the "Faery Queene"* (1635), Cambridge University Library MS. Ee.3.53; [Anonymous], *The Faerie Leveller: or, King Charles his leveller descried and deciphered in Queene Elizabeths dayes. By her poet laureat Edmond Spenser, in his unparaleld poeme, entituled, "The faerie queene." A lively representation of our times* ([London]: 1648), title page; [Edward Howard], *Spencer redivivus containing the first book of the "Fairy queen" his essential design preserv'd, but his obsolete language and manner of verse totally laid aside deliver'd in heroick numbers, by a person of quality* (London: Thomas Chapman, 1687), [A2r], A4r.

43. John Hughes, ed., *The Works of Mr. Edmund Spenser* (London: Jacob Tonson, 1715), 1:iii–iv.

44. William Duncombe, "Preface," in *Poems on several occasions. With some select essays in prose. By John Hughes* (London: J. Tonson and J. Watts, 1735), viii; Samuel Johnson, "Hughes," in *Prefaces, Biographical and critical, to the Works of the English Poets*, vol. 4 (London: J. Nichols, 1779), 9.

45. Thomas Warton, *Observations on the Faerie Queen of Spenser*, expanded 2nd ed., 2 vols. (London: R. and J. Dodsley, 1762), 1:15.

46. Thomas Birch, ed., *The Faerie Queene. By Edmund Spenser. With an exact collation of the two* ORIGINAL EDITIONS, *Published by Himself at London in Quarto*, 2 vols. (London: J. Brindley, 1751), 1:xxxvii.

47. John Upton, *A letter concerning a new edition of Spenser's "Faerie Queene." To Gilbert West, Esq.* (London: G. Hawkins, 1751), 34, 32.

48. John Upton, ed., *Spenser's "Faerie Queene." A new edition with a glossary, and notes explanatory and critical*, 2 vols. (London: J. and R. Tonson, 1758), 1:xli.

49. Ralph Church, ed., *The Faerie Queene, by Edmund Spenser. A new edition, with notes critical and explanatory*, 4 vols. (London: William Faden, 1758), 1:iii.

50. Jonathan Kramnick, *Making the English Canon: Print Capitalism and the Cultural Past, 1700–1770* (Cambridge: Cambridge University Press, 1998), 137.

51. John Bell, ed., *The Poetical Works of Edmund Spenser*, 8 vols. (Edinburgh: Apollo Press, 1778), 1:[lxxxviii].

52. Henry John Todd, ed., *The Works of Edmund Spenser* (London: F. C. and J. Rivington, 1805), 1:A3r–A4r.

53. John Guillory, "Literary Study and the Modern System of the Disciplines," in *Disciplinarity at the Fin de Siècle*, ed. Amanda Anderson and Joseph Valente (Princeton, NJ: Princeton University Press, 2002), 26.

54. E.K., "To the moste excellente and learned both Orator and Poete, Mayster Gabriell Haruey," in *The Shepheardes Calender* (London: Hugh Singleton, 1579), sig. ¶iir.

55. Thomas Tyrwhitt, ed., *The Canterbury Tales of Chaucer*, 5 vols. (London: T. Payne, 1775), 1:ii, xx. The continuing questions about how to edit Chaucer's spelling—or, rather, the orthographies of the various manuscripts in which Chaucer's poetry survives—are too complex to summarize here, but overlap with the question of how to edit Spenser's spelling, including digital analysis to adjudicate among variants. See Simon Horobin, "Chaucer's Spelling and the Manuscripts of *The Canterbury Tales*," in *Placing Middle English in Context* (Berlin: Mouton de Gruyter, 2000), 199–207, and *The Language of the Chaucer Tradition* (Cambridge: D. S. Brewer, 2003); Larry Benson, "Chaucer's Spelling Reconsidered," *English Manuscript Studies, 1100–1500* 3 (1992): 1–22; and Geoff Barnbrook, "Computer Analysis of Spelling Variants in Chaucer's Canterbury Tales," in *New Directions in English Language Corpora: Methodology, Results, Software Developments*, ed. Gerhard Leitner (Berlin: Mouton de Gruyter, 1992), 277–87.

56. Edmund Malone, ed., *The Plays and Poems of William Shakspeare* (London: H. Baldwin, 1790), 1:xliv.

57. The question of whether to restore old spelling—or, as Randall McLeod argues it might better be termed, "old typesetting"—to Shakespeare's plays wholesale has occasionally been revived but has never gained much traction, in part because the discrepancies among various printed sources are so vast; see McLeod, "Spellbound." But the mystique of orthographic intentionality may still govern the way scholars have approached compositorial analyses of Shakespeare's playtexts, as Masten argues in *Queer Philologies*.

58. On this point, see Jeffrey Kahan, "Shakespeare and the Forging of Belief," *Critical Quarterly* 43.2 (2001): 19–33.

59. Anthony Grafton, *Forgers and Critics: Creativity and Duplicity in Western Scholarship* (Princeton, NJ: Princeton University Press, 1990). See also Margreta de Grazia's observation that "the appearance of forgeries, written and painted, coincided historically with the very criterion of authenticity they attempted to replicate" (*Shakespeare Verbatim: The Reproduction of Authenticity and the 1790 Apparatus* [Oxford: Oxford University Press, 1991], 110–11).

60. Thomas Warton, *An Enquiry into the Authenticity of the Poems Attributed to Thomas Rowley* (London: J. Dodsley, 1782), 3, 27, 92.

61. Marjorie Garber, *Academic Instincts* (Princeton, NJ: Princeton University Press, 2000), 42–47.

62. John Russell Brown, "The Rationale of Old-Spelling Editions of the Plays of Shakespeare and His Contemporaries," *Studies in Bibliography* 13 (1960): 60.

63. Thomas Raynesford Lounsbury, *Studies in Chaucer: His Life and Writings* (New York: Harper, 1892), 3:268.

64. "Textual Appendix," in *The Faerie Qveene: Book One*, ed. Greenlaw, Osgood, and Padelford, 522. Spelling is something of a problem for the *Variorum* editors, since it casts doubt on their conviction that the 1596 edition, which they use as a copy-text for books 1 through 3, was produced "very probably under the author's supervision." The 1596 text they claim, "shows sufficient alteration for the better to justify the opinion that Spenser was responsible for an incidental revision," but add, "It is not our belief that 1596 represents Spenser's correction of 1590 line by line; the number of spelling variants and their inconsistency would make such a view untenable" (516).

65. Roland M. Smith, "Spenser's Scholarly Script and 'Right Writing,'" *Studies in Honor of T. W. Baldwin*, ed. Don Cameron Allen (Urbana: University of Illinois Press, 1958), 97.

66. Margreta de Grazia and Peter Stallybrass, "The Materiality of the Shakespearean Text," *Shakespeare Quarterly* 44.3 (Autumn 1993): 255–83; see especially 262–67.

67. Basu and Loewenstein, "Spenser's Spell," 34–35.

Chapter 2: Una's Line: Child Readers and the Afterlife of Fiction

1. C. S. Lewis, *The Allegory of Love* (Oxford: Clarendon, 1936), 299.

2. Edmund Spenser, "A Letter of the Authors" (1590), in *The Faerie Queene*, ed. A. C. Hamilton (New York: Longman, 2007), 714.

3. Samuel Taylor Coleridge, *Coleridge's Miscellaneous Criticism*, ed. Thomas Middleton Raysor (Cambridge, MA: Harvard University Press, 1936), 36.

4. Isabel MacCaffrey, *Spenser's Allegory: The Anatomy of Imagination* (Princeton, NJ: Princeton University Press, 1976), 51.

5. Judith H. Anderson, "What I Really Teach When I'm Teaching Spenser," *Pedagogy* 3.2 (2003): 178. Not all recent critics are so emphatic about the folly or futility of seeking "characterological realism" or psychological insight in book 1—see especially Jeff Dolven's bravura analysis of the psychology of Redcrosse's bolt from the false Una in "Panic's Castle," *Representations* 120.1 (Fall 2012): 1–16; and Joseph Campana's sensitive reading of the sexual and corporeal anxieties expressed in figures like Fradubio and Duessa in *The Pain of Reformation: Spenser, Vulnerability, and the Ethics of Masculinity* (New York: Fordham University Press, 2012)—but such readings tend to concentrate on the experiences and emotions of the Redcrosse Knight and the various characters he encounters in his wayward career apart from Una. Una is handled with due allegorical reverence or not at all.

6. C. S. Lewis, "Edmund Spenser," in *Fifteen Poets* (Oxford: Oxford University Press, 1941), 40.

7. C. S. Lewis, *The Voyage of the Dawn Treader* (New York: Collier Books, 1970), 215–16.

8. Kevin Pask, *The Fairy Way of Writing: Shakespeare to Tolkien* (Baltimore: Johns Hopkins University Press, 2013), 126.

9. Oscar Wilde, "The Decorative Arts" (1882), quoted in Douglas Mao, *Fateful Beauty: Aesthetic Environments, Juvenile Development, and Literature, 1860–1960* (Princeton, NJ: Princeton University Press, 2008), 5.

10. Mao, *Fateful Beauty*, 4.

11. Carolyn Steedman, *Strange Dislocations: Childhood and the Idea of Human Interiority* (Cambridge, MA: Harvard University Press, 1995), 18–20.

12. Samuel F. Pickering, *Moral Instruction and Fiction for Children, 1749–1820* (Athens: University of Georgia Press, 1993), viii, 2–3.

13. Karen Sánchez-Eppler, *Dependent States: The Child's Part in Nineteenth-Century American Culture* (Chicago: University of Chicago Press, 2005), 18.

14. Michael McKeon, *The Origins of the English Novel, 1600–1740* (Baltimore: Johns Hopkins University Press, 1987), 295–314. The example with which McKeon begins, Thomas Burt's recollection of reading *Pilgrim's Progress* as a boy as if it were "a solid literal history" (297) has striking affinities with the memories of childish misreadings of Spenser I catalog in this chapter, and *Pilgrim's Progress* acts as a kind of shadow text for *The Faerie Queene* throughout: it was written about by critics in very similar ways, was widely available in illustrated children's editions, and was adapted for young readers in the same fashion as *The Faerie Queene*. That said, the particular quasi-erotic attachment former child readers often felt for Una, and for *The Faerie Queene*, is not, I suspect, as common among Bunyan's readers.

15. Felicity A. Hughes, "Children's Literature: Theory and Practice," *ELH* 45.3 (Autumn 1978): 542–61.

16. On the emergence of the lineaments of what we now term children's literature out of sixteenth-century texts like courtesy manuals, John Foxe's *Actes and Monuments*, ballad- and jest-books, and Aesop's *Fables*, see Warren W. Wooden's *Children's Literature of the English Renaissance* (Lexington: University of Kentucky Press, 1986).

17. Katie Trumpener, "On Living in Time," in *On Periodization and Its Discontents*, ed. Virginia Jackson (Cambridge, MA: English Institute in collaboration with the American Council of Learned Societies, 2010), para. 196; see also Trumpener, "The Making of Child Readers," in *The Cambridge History of English Romantic Literature*, ed. James Chandler (Cambridge: Cambridge University Press, 2009), 553–78.

18. Abraham Cowley, "Of Myself," in *The Works of Mr. Abraham Cowley* (London: Henry Herringman, 1668), 144.

19. Thomas Sprat, "Account of the Life and Writings of Mr. Abraham Cowley," in *The Works of Mr. Abraham Cowley* (1668), sig. A2.

20. Gordon Teskey, "The Thinking of History in Spenserian Romance," in *Romance and History: Imagining Time from the Medieval to the Early Modern Period*, ed. Jon Whitman (Cambridge: Cambridge University Press, 2015), 217.

21. Elizabeth Palmer Peabody, *Record of a School: Exemplifying the General Principles of Spiritual Culture* (Boston: James Munroe, 1835), 14; emphasis in the original. Elizabeth Palmer Peabody is a fascinating figure in her own right—a reformer and social activist caricatured by Henry James as Miss Birdseye in *The Bostonians* and credited with popularizing the idea of kindergarten education. For more on her fraught relationship to Alcott, whom she both idolized and mistrusted, see Josephine E. Roberts, "Elizabeth Peabody and the Temple School," *New England Quarterly* 15.3 (1942): 497–508; Bruce A. Ronda, *Elizabeth Palmer Peabody: A Reformer on Her Own Terms*

(Cambridge, MA: Harvard University Press, 1999), 112–42; Megan Marshall, *The Peabody Sisters: Three Women Who Ignited American Romanticism* (Boston: Houghton Mifflin, 2005), 312–26; and Derek Pacheco, *Moral Enterprise: Literature and Education in Antebellum America* (Columbus: Ohio State University Press, 2013), 83–90.

22. Sánchez-Eppler, *Dependent States*, xxvi.

23. Patricia Parker, *Inescapable Romance: Studies in the Poetics of a Mode* (Princeton, NJ: Princeton University Press, 1979), 65.

24. "Tension between the characteristic values of idyllic pastoral and those of theological discourse becomes especially intense at this moment," Gless observes (*Interpretation and Theology in Spenser* [Cambridge: Cambridge University Press, 1994], 108). See also William Oram, "Human Limitation and Spenserian Laughter," *Spenser Studies* 30 (2015). For a reading of the fauns and satyrs more resolutely committed to their status as theological emblems, see Kathryn Walls, *God's Only Daughter: Spenser's Una as the Invisible Church* (Manchester: Manchester University Press, 2013), 103–22.

25. Alistair Fowler, *Renaissance Realism: Narrative Images in Literature and Art* (Oxford: Oxford University Press, 2003), 99.

26. Rosemund Tuve, *Allegorical Imagery* (Princeton, NJ: Princeton University Press, 1966), 337.

27. James Kearney, *The Incarnate Text: Imagining the Book in Reformation England* (Philadelphia: University of Pennsylvania Press, 2009), 113.

28. Susanne Lindgren Wofford, *The Choice of Achilles: The Ideology of Figure in the Epic* (Stanford, CA: Stanford University Press, 1992), 220.

29. Paul Alpers, "Narration in *The Faerie Queene*," *ELH* 44.1 (1977): 27–28.

30. John Calvin, *Institutes of the Christian Religion*, ed. John T. McNeill, trans. Ford Lewis Battles (Louisville, KY: Westminster John Knox Press, 1960), 251.

31. Geneva Bible (1560), Genesis 3:14–16. It is possible to use the typological association between Eve and the Church to make a kind of consistent moral allegory out of the middle cantos of book 1 (see, for instance, Walls, *God's Only Daughter*), but the comic, almost slapstick tenor of these cantos resists that effort, in my view.

32. As David Lee Miller points out, the *Variorum* Spenser reveals that nineteenth- and early twentieth-century critics were especially fond of this stanza—a sign of the "neo-chivalric sexual politics" that drew them to Spenser's heroines generally and to Una in particular ("*The Faerie Queene*, 1590," in *A Critical Companion to Spenser Studies*, ed. Bart van Es [New York: Palgrave Macmillan, 2006], 152–55).

33. Joe Moshenska, "The Forgotten Youth of Allegory: Figures of Old Age in *The Faerie Queene*," *Modern Philology* 110.3 (2013): 389–414.

34. Oram, "Human Limitation and Spenserian Laughter," 42.

35. See *Oxford English Dictionary*, s.v. "care."

36. On eighteenth- and nineteenth-century Spenserians as "revisionary" readers, see Michelle O'Callaghan, "Spenser's Literary Influence," in *The Oxford Handbook of Edmund Spenser*, ed. Richard A. McCabe (Oxford: Oxford University Press, 2010), 672–73; and Greg Kucich, *Keats, Shelley, and Romantic Spenserianism* (Philadelphia: University of Pennsylvania Press, 2010). For indictments of the blindness or obtuseness of romantic Spenserians and their nineteenth-century heirs, see Paul Alpers, ed., *Edmund Spenser: A Critical Anthology* (Harmondsworth: Penguin

Books, 1969), 68–69; A. C. Hamilton, *The Structure of Allegory in "The Faerie Queene"* (Oxford: Clarendon Press, 1961), 4; Maureen Quilligan, *Milton's Spenser* (Ithaca: Cornell University Press, 1983), 20; and Benjamin Lockerd, *The Sacred Marriage: Psychic Integration in "The Faerie Queene"* (Lewisburg, PA: Bucknell University Press, 1987), 17.

37. Alexander Pope, letter to John Hughes, October 7, 1715; quoted in Howard Erskine-Hill, "Pope, Alexander," in *The Spenser Encyclopedia*, gen. ed. A. C. Hamilton (Toronto: University of Toronto Press, 1990), 555; Samuel Taylor Coleridge, *Biographia Literaria*, ed. Walter Jackson Bate and James Engell (London: Routledge and Kegan Paul, 1983), 1:36.

38. John Hughes, ed., *The Works of Mr. Edmund Spenser* (London: Jacob Tonson, 1715), lxix–lxx.

39. Henry More, "To his dear father," in *Philosophical Poems* (Cambridge: Roger Daniel, 1647), sig. A2v.

40. David Sandner, *Critical Discourses of the Fantastic, 1712–1831* (Surrey: Ashgate, 2011), 9.

41. Thomas Rymer, "The Preface of the Translator," in René Rapin, *Reflections on Aristotle's Treatise of Poesie* (London: H. Herringman, 1674), sigs. [A6v]–[A7r].

42. Joseph Addison, "An Account of the Greatest English Poets," in *The Annual Miscellany: for the Year 1694, Being the Fourth Part of Miscellany Poems* (London: Jacob Tonson, 1694), 318–19.

43. Evidently, *The Faerie Queene* was a suitable text for readers in their second childhood as well: Pope's recollection was inspired, in Spense's account, by his recently having read part of the poem aloud to "an old lady between seventy and eighty years of age," likely his mother. "There is something in Spenser that pleases one as strongly in one's old age as it did in one's youth," Pope remarks (Joseph Spense, *Anecdotes, Observations, and Characters of Books and Men* [ca. 1740], ed. Samuel Weller Singer [London: W. H. Carpenter, 1820], 296).

44. John Gibson Lockhart, ed., *Memoirs of the Life of Sir Walter Scott* (Edinburgh: Robert Cadell, 1837), 1:35–36.

45. Letter to John May, January 19, 1823, in *The Life and Correspondence of Robert Southey*, ed. Charles Cuthbert Southey (London: Longman, Brown, Green, and Longmans, 1849), 1:85.

46. John Dryden, "To the Right Honourable John, Lord Houghton," in *The Spanish Fryar, or The Double Discovery* (London: Richard and Jacob Tonson, 1681), sig. A3r.

47. Letter to Walter Savage Landor, January 11, 1811, in *The Life and Correspondence of Robert Southey*, 3:295.

48. From Scott's anonymous review of John Henry Todd's *Variorum* edition of Spenser, which he read hoping that it would "recal the sensations of our earlier studies" and found disappointing, burdened as it was by the "learned lumber" of critical comment (*Edinburgh Review* 7 [October 1805]): 203–4, 217.

49. William Hazlitt, *Lectures on the English Poets* (London: Taylor and Hessey, 1818), 68.

50. Leigh Hunt, *Lord Byron and some of his Contemporaries; with Recollections of the Author's Life, and of his Visit to Italy* (London: H. Colburn, 1828), 373.

51. Leigh Hunt, *Imagination and Fancy, or Selections from the English Poets* (1860) (London: Smith, Elder, 1891), 55.

52. James Russell Lowell, *Literary Essays* (Boston: Houghton Mifflin, 1871), 313.

53. David Mannings, *Sir Joshua Reynolds: A Complete Catalog of His Paintings* (New Haven, CT: Yale University Press, 2000), 143.

54. John Chilton Scammell, *The Library of Entertainment: A Thousand Hours of Enjoyment with the World's Great Writers; Handbook* (Chicago: George L. Shuman, 1915), ix–x.

55. Ibid., vol. 11 (1918), 270–78.

56. Eliza Weaver Bradburn, *Legends from Spenser's "Faerie Queene," for the Children* (London: John Mason, 1829), 3.

57. Julie Pfeiffer, "'Dream Not of Other Worlds': *Paradise Lost* and the Child Reader," *Children's Literature* 27 (1999): 3.

58. Jonathan Sircy, "Educating Milton: *Paradise Lost*, Accommodation, and *The Story of 'Paradise Lost' for Children*," *Milton Quarterly* 45.3 (2011): 173, 184.

59. These adaptations have received little attention from scholars, but there is a useful overview in the entry on "*The Faerie Queene*, children's versions" by Brenda M. Hosington and Anne Shaver in *The Spenser Encyclopedia*, ed. A. C. Hamilton (Toronto: University of Toronto Press, 1990), 289–91.

60. John S. Hart, *An Essay on the Life and Writings of Edmund Spenser, with a Special Exposition of the "Fairy Queen"* (New York: Wiley and Putnam, 1847), 210.

61. Sophia L. MacLehose, *Tales from Spenser; Chosen from "The Faerie Queene"* (Glasgow: James MacLehose and Sons, 1892), 1.

62. Both MacLehose's *Tales from Spenser* and Jeanie Lang's *Stories from "The Faerie Queene": Eight Tales for Children* (London and Edinburgh: E. P. Dutton, 1906) make Una the heroine of their opening tales; Naomi Gwladys Royde-Smith's *Una and the Redcrosse Knight, and Other Tales from Spenser's "Faery Queene"* (New York: E. P. Dutton, 1905) even gives her top billing in the title.

63. M. H. Towry, *Spenser for Children* (London: Chatto and Windus, 1885), vi.

64. Elizabeth Palmer Peabody, *Holiness, or, The Legend of St. George: A Tale from Spencer's Faerie Queene, by a Mother* (Boston: E. R. Broaders, 1836), iv.

65. It's worth noting that Eliza Peabody's own marriage, to Nathaniel Peabody, was not an easy one; Nathaniel had a terrible temper and struggled to keep the family out of poverty. The publication of *Holiness* was at least partly intended to alleviate the couple's financial difficulties (see Marshall, *The Peabody Sisters*, 82–84).

66. Sophia's journal entries during her marriage to Nathaniel can be found in Patricia Dunlavy Valenti, "Sophia Peabody Hawthorne's *American Notebooks*," *Studies in the American Renaissance* (1996): 115–85; this quote, from an entry made on April 7, 1844, is on p. 147.

67. Letter to Sophia Peabody Hawthorne, May 27, 1844, in *The Centenary Edition of the Works of Nathaniel Hawthorne*, vol. 16, ed. Thomas L. Woodson, L. Neal Smith, and Norman Holmes Pearson (Columbus: Ohio State University Press, 1985), 37; hereafter cited as *CE*. A good deal has been written about the Hawthornes' Transcendentalist-inflected visions of marriage, family life, childhood, and their eldest daughter, and although most of these accounts mention Spenser only in passing, they give a vivid sense of how simultaneously romantic and allegorical those visions tended to be; in addition to Patricia Dunlavy Valenti's introduction to "Sophia Peabody Hawthorne's *American Notebooks*," see her *Sophia Peabody Hawthorne: A Life*, 2 vols. (Columbia: University of Missouri Press, 2004, 2015); Sánchez-Eppler, *Dependent States*, 52–60; and T. Walter Herbert, *Dearest Beloved: The Hawthornes and the Making of the Middle-Class Family* (Berkeley: University of California Press, 1995).

68. Hillard's letter is quoted in its entirety in Julian Hawthorne's biography of his parents, *Nathaniel Hawthorne and His Wife* (Boston: Houghton Mifflin, 1893), 276.

69. George S. Hillard, "Preface," in *The Poetical Works of Edmund Spenser* (Boston: Little, Brown, 1839), liii. According to Gary Scharnhorst, Hawthorne is the likely author of an approving review of this edition published anonymously in the *Boston Post* in November 1839 ("Hawthorne and *The Poetical Works of Spenser*: A Lost Review," *American Literature* 61.4 [1989]: 668–73).

70. The letter, written in 1850–51, is recorded in Rose Hawthorne Lathrop's *Memories of Hawthorne* (Boston: Houghton Mifflin, 1897), 122.

71. As such, Matthiessen regarded her "worth dissecting," but also "worth murdering, most modern readers of fiction would hold, since the tedious reiteration of what she stands for betrays Hawthorne at his most barren" (*American Renaissance: Art and Expression in the Age of Emerson and Whitman* [Oxford: Oxford University Press, 1941], 278). The tendency to lament Spenser's influence is pervasive in twentieth-century criticism of Hawthorne's fiction.

72. Nathaniel Hawthorne, *The Scarlet Letter*, ed. Seymour Gross, Sculley Bradley, Richard Croom Beatty, and E. Hudson Long (New York: W. W. Norton, 1988), 140, 76.

73. Sacvan Bercovitch, *The Office of the Scarlet Letter* (Baltimore: Johns Hopkins University Press, 1991), 144.

74. Nathaniel Hawthorne, *Twice-Told Tales* (Boston: John B. Russell, 1837), 172.

Chapter 3: Load Every Rift: Avid Readers in the Legend of Temperance

1. John Keats, "To PERCY BYSSHE SHELLEY, Wednesday 16 Aug. 1820," in *The Letters of John Keats*, ed. Maurice Buxton Forman, rev. 3rd ed. (Cambridge: Chadwyck-Healey, 1999).

2. Marjorie Garber, *Academic Instincts* (Princeton, NJ: Princeton University Press, 2000), 4; William A. Read, *Keats and Spenser* (Heidelberg: E. Geisendörfer, 1897), 30.

3. Miriam Allott, "John Keats," in *The Spenser Encyclopedia*, gen. ed. A. C. Hamilton (Toronto: University of Toronto Press, 1990), 416.

4. Charles and Mary Cowden Clarke, *Recollections of Writers*, 2nd ed. (London: Sampson Low, Marston, Searle & Rivington, 1878), 126.

5. Quoted in David Masson, *Wordsworth, Shelley, Keats, and Other Essays* (London: Macmillan, 1874), 147. "Sea-shouldering whales" is another image from book 2; it appears in 2.12.23.6, as Guyon and the Palmer make their voyage to the Bower of Bliss.

6. Matthew Arnold, "Homer, Spenser, and Keats," in *Passages From the Prose Writings of Matthew Arnold* (London: Smith, Elder, 1880), 22. On Keats's borrowings from Spenser, see William A. Read, *Keats and Spenser*, and William T. Arnold, "Introduction," in *The Poetical Works of John Keats*, ed. W. T. Arnold (London: Kegan Paul, Trench, 1884), xxiv–xxv.

7. M. Allott, "John Keats," 416.

8. Desiderius Erasmus, *De duplici copia verborum ac rerum comentarii duo* (*De Copia*) (1512; rev. and expanded 1514, 1526, 1534), trans. Betty I. Knott, in *The Complete Works of Erasmus*, ed. Craig R. Thompson, vol. 24 (Toronto: University of Toronto Press, 1978), 295; hereafter *CWE*.

9. Abraham Fraunce, *The Arcadian Rhetorike* (London: Thomas Orwin, 1588), sig. A2v.

10. George Puttenham, *The Arte of English Poesie* (London: Richard Field, 1589), 114.

11. Michel de Certeau, *The Practice of Everyday Life*, trans. Steven Rendell (Berkeley: University of California Press, 1984), 174.

12. Hazel Wilkinson, *Edmund Spenser and the Eighteenth-Century Book* (Cambridge: Cambridge University Press, 2017), 64.

13. Certeau, *The Practice of Everyday Life*, 176.

14. Ibid.

15. Jeff Dolven, *Scenes of Instruction in Renaissance Romance* (Chicago: University of Chicago Press, 2007), 170.

16. Jonathan Brody Kramnick, *Making the English Canon: Print-Capitalism and the Cultural Past, 1700–1770* (Cambridge: Cambridge University Press, 1999), 138.

17. Thomas Warton, *Observations on the Faerie Queene of Spenser*, 2 vols. (London: R. and J. Dodsley, 1762), 1:8.

18. Kramnick, *Making the English Canon*, 146.

19. The first three descriptions are from John Spiers's introductory "Survey of Medieval Verse," in *The Pelican Guide to English Literature, Vol. 1: The Age of Chaucer*, ed. Boris Ford (Harmondsworth, UK: Penguin Books, 1954), 65; the last is from Derek Traversi's essay in the same volume on "Spenser's *Faerie Queene*," 227.

20. Traversi, "Spenser's *Faerie Queene*," 212, 213, 217, 224.

21. Harry Berger Jr., *The Allegorical Temper: Vision and Reality in Book II of Spenser's "Faerie Queene"* (New Haven, CT: Yale University Press, 1957), 121.

22. Berger coins the phrase "conspicuous irrelevance" in explicit homage to Thorsten Veblen's theory of "conspicuous consumption," the ostentatious expenditure of wealth or acquisition of luxury goods as a public display of social status, whether actual or imagined. Reading, for Berger, is thus already framed as an economic transaction, where interest is the currency and understanding assumed to be the desirable commodity.

23. Dolven, *Scenes of Instruction*, 170.

24. Adam Smyth, *"Profit and Delight": Printed Miscellanies in England, 1640–1682* (Detroit: Wayne State University Press, 2004), xv.

25. Erasmus, *De Copia*, in *CWE*, 24:636.

26. Erasmus, "To Pieter Gillis," in *Parabolae sive similia* (1514, rev. and expanded 1515, 1516, 1522), trans. R.A.B. Mynors, in *CWE*, 23:130.

27. Richard Tottel, "To the reder," in *Songes and Sonettes, written by the right honorable Lorde Henry Haward late Earle of Surrey, and other* (London: Richard Tottel, 1557), fol. 1v.

28. Fraunce, *Arcadian Rhetorike*, sig. [D7]r.

29. Ibid., sig. E4r.

30. On these volumes and other miscellanies from the period, see Elizabeth W. Pomeroy, *The Elizabethan Miscellanies: Their Development and Conventions* (Berkeley: University of California Press, 1973).

31. Dora Anna Scribner, "The History of Spenser's Literary Reputation" (unpublished MA thesis from the University of Chicago, 1906), 7. D.E.L. Crane observes that Allott had just completed the compilation of *Wits Theater of the Little World* for Ling and John Bodenham in 1599: "Both Ling and Allott, having recently worked with Bodenham, would have known of his immediate plans, and *Englands Parnassus* bears many signs of having been hastily assembled to compete with two Bodenham books also published in the same year," *Bel-vedére* and *Englands Helicon* ("Note," to *Englands Parnassus* [Menston: Scolar Press, 1970], unnumbered]). If this is the case, recourse to *The Faerie Queene*, with an emphasis on descriptive passages, seems to have

been part of the competitive strategy: *Bel-vedére* concentrates on proverbs, similitudes, and examples, largely drawn from classical authors, and *Englands Helicon* on pastoral verse.

32. As Pomeroy observes of *Englands Parnassus*, "Aphorism is clearly valued less than poetic invention in this apparent handbook for imitation" (*The Elizabethan Miscellanies*, 25).

33. I have formatted these lines as Allott does, without a break between the end of stanza 12 (line 9) and the start of stanza 13 (line 10).

34. T.W., *The Tears of Fancie. Or, Loue Disdained* (London: William Barley, 1593), sig. D3v.

35. James A. Riddell and Stanley Stewart, *Jonson's Spenser: Evidence and Historical Criticism* (Pittsburgh: Duquesne University Press, 1995), 32–33.

36. All of the following citations of Jonson's annotations are taken from Riddell and Stewart's transcriptions in *Jonson's Spenser*, 161–86.

37. A. J. Fletcher, "Honour, Reputation, and Local Officeholding in Elizabethan and Stuart England," in *Order and Disorder in Early Modern England*, ed. Anthony Fletcher and John Stevenson (Cambridge: Cambridge University Press, 2009), 100; "James Ryther of Harewood and His Letters to William Cecil, Lord Burghley," *Yorkshire Archaeological Journal* 56 (1984): 117n9.

38. The online *Catalogue of English Literary Manuscripts, 1450–1700* lists Hoby's Spenser (SpE 90) as "untraced," but it is entered in the Bodleian collection as F.2.62.Linc. All annotations cited here have been transcribed from the Bodleian copy; I have given folio page numbers for the pages on which they occur.

39. James Nohrnberg, *The Analogy of "The Faerie Queene"* (Princeton, NJ: Princeton University Press, 1976), 285.

40. Ibid., 356–57.

41. Ibid., 291–92.

42. The shelf mark is British Library, G.11537; the marks mentioned can be found in volume 2, pages 25 and 517. Altogether, I have counted fifty-four marked similes; the reader also marks two dozen sententiae in volume 2. This and several other annotated *Faerie Queenes* are discussed in Alastair Fowler, "Oxford and London Marginalia to 'The Faerie Queene,'" *N&Q* 206 (November 1961): 416–18.

43. Bodleian Library, Malone 7; the attribution of the marginalia to Thomas and Joseph Warton was first made by Edmund Malone, who writes on the flyleaf, "This book formerly belonged to Thomas [or Thomes], and afterwards to Joseph Wharton." Parenthetical citations of the annotations give both the book, canto, and stanza in which the marking appears (where relevant) and the page number in Malone 7.

44. See Kramnick, *Making the English Canon*, 139–46.

45. Warton, *Observations*, 1:122, 114.

46. Edwin Greenlaw, Charles Grosvenor Osgood, and Frederick Morgan Padelford, eds., *The Works of Edmund Spenser: A Variorum Edition*, vol. 2, *The Faerie Queene, Book Two* (Baltimore: Johns Hopkins University Press, 1966), 472.

47. The details of Digby's 1628–29 voyage can be found in Joe Moshenska, *A Stain in the Blood: The Remarkable Voyage of Sir Kenelm Digby* (London: William Heinemann, 2016), which also offers an engaging account of Digby's early life.

48. Joe Moshenska, "'Spencerus Isthic Conditur': Kenelm Digby's Transcription of William Alabaster," *Spenser Studies* 27 (2012): 316.

49. Kenelm Digby, *Observations on the 22. stanza in the 9th. canto of the 2d. book of Spencers Faery Queen* (London: Daniel Frere, 1643), 25.

50. Quoted in Riddell and Stewart, *Jonson's Spenser*, 176–77. The page on which Jonson writes his note, however, has been trimmed, lopping off some of the writing, and letters in triangular brackets have been supplied by Riddell and Stewart, including, significantly, the second half of the word "actuator," on which much of their case against Digby depends; see ibid., 102–3.

51. These are: Bodleian MS Perrott 7 (early seventeenth century; a folio volume of state tracts, in various hands); Bodleian MS Tanner 82 (pre-1640; a folio volume of letters and state papers); BL Add MS 44848 (possibly pre-1640; a folio composite volume of state letters and papers); BL Egerton MS 2725 (ca. 1640; a quarto miscellany of verse and some prose); BL Harley MS 4761 (early seventeenth century; a folio composite volume of state letters); BL Sloane MS 20 (seventeenth century; manuscript copy of the *Observations* with an ownership inscription to Tho: Austin); BL Harley MS 7375 (ca. 1630; "Sʳ Kenelm Digbys remarks on Spencers Fairy Queen," on thirteen quarto leaves, bound with Harley MS 4153); Bradford Archives, 32D86/44 (mid-seventeenth century; a quarto volume of state letters); Cambridge University Library, MS Dd. 3. 85, item 12 (a composite volume of twenty tracts); Cornwall Record Office, EL/655/8 (ca. 1629–32; copy, in a professional secretary hand, subscribed "Kenelme Digby" and dated January 13, 1628[/9]; in a folio composite volume of state tracts and letters); Lord Egremont, Petworth House, HMC MS 61 (ca. 1637; folio volume of state letters); Folger, MS V.a.239 (ca. 1630; copy headed "Sr: Kenelme Digbies Letter to Sr: Edward Stradlinge . . . abord his shipp," in a quarto volume of state letters); Folger, MS V.b.234 (ca. 1630s, copy, headed "Sr Kenolme Digby to Sr Ed: Stradling . . ." [etc.], subscribed "Kellam Digbie," in a folio volume of state letters and papers); Huntington, HM 36836 (ca. 1630s, a folio volume of transcripts of state letters); Pierpont Morgan Library, MA 1162 (mid-seventeenth century; a small quarto volume of state letters and papers, in a single secretary hand).

52. A. P. Riemer, "An Annotated Copy of *The Faerie Queene*," *Sydney Studies in English* 9 (1983–84): 107–8; includes a full transcription of the annotations.

53. The transcription is in ibid., 107–8.

54. See Riddell and Stewart, *Jonson's Spenser*, 110–15.

55. William Austin, *Haec Homo, Wherein the Excellencie of the Creation of Woman is Described, By way of an Essay* (London: R. Mabb, 1637), sigs. E3v–E4r.

56. BL Sloane MS 20, mentioned above.

57. Bodleian Malone MS 16 (p. 39), and British Museum Addit. MSS. 21433 (fol. 165v) and 25303 (fol. 187). Bibliographic details and transcription from Malone MS 16 can be found in Helen E. Sandison, "Three Spenser Allusions," *Modern Language Notes* 44.3 (March 1929): 161–62.

58. John Keats, autograph letter to Fanny Brawne (Kentish Town, July 4[?], 1820); MS Keats 1.82.

59. Greg Kucich, "'A Lamentable Lay': Keats and the Making of Charles Brown's Spenser Volumes," *Keats-Shelley Review* 3 (1988): 2.

60. MS letter from Fanny Brawne to Fanny Keats, reproduced in *The Letters of Fanny Brawne to Fanny Keats*, ed. Fred Edgcumbe (Oxford: Oxford University Press, 1937), 88.

61. Gordon Teskey, "Notes on Reading in *The Faerie Queene*: From Moment to Moment," in *Spenser in the Moment*, ed. Paul J. Hecht and J. B. Lethbridge (Madison, NJ: Fairleigh Dickinson University Press, 2015), 219.

Chapter 4: Half-Envying: The Interested Reader and the Partial Marriage Plot

1. Andrew Hadfield and Anne Lake Prescott, "Preface to the Fourth Edition," in *Edmund Spenser's Poetry*, 4th ed., ed. Hadfield and Prescott (New York: W. W. Norton, 2014), ix.

2. Judith Anderson, "What I Really Teach When I'm Teaching Spenser," *Pedagogy* 3.2 (Spring 2003): 178–79.

3. Walter J. Ong, *Interfaces of the Word: Studies in the Evolution of Consciousness and Culture* (Ithaca: Cornell University Press, 1982; 1st ed. 1977), 53.

4. Ibid., 70.

5. Ibid., 73. Returning to the point several years later, Ong put it more strongly still: "The ways in which readers are fictionalized is the underside of literary history, of which the topside is the history of genres and the handling of character and plot" (*Orality and Literacy: The Technologizing of the Word* [London: Routledge, 2002; 1st ed. 1982], 101).

6. Edmund Spenser, *The Faerie Queene* (London: William Ponsonby, 1590), sig. [A1]v.

7. Louis Montrose, "Shaping Fantasies: Figurations of Gender and Power in Elizabethan Culture," *Representations* 2 (Spring 1983): 61–94. Montrose has dilated this argument in dazzling series of articles and monographs; see especially, "The Elizabethan Subject and the Spenserian Text," in *Literary Theory/Renaissance Texts*, ed. Patricia Parker and David Quint (Baltimore: Johns Hopkins University Press, 1986), 303–40; "Spenser and the Elizabethan Political Imaginary," *ELH* 69.4 (Winter 2002): 907–46; and *The Subject of Elizabeth: Authority, Gender, and Representation* (Chicago: University of Chicago Press, 2006).

8. Maureen Quilligan, *Milton's Spenser: The Politics of Reading* (Ithaca: Cornell University Press, 1983), 177, 179–80.

9. David Lee Miller, "The Chastity of Allegory," *Spenser Studies* 29 (2014): 3. Miller's essay shares this chapter's interest in the distorting effect of Elizabeth's imagined gaze on the poem as Spenser writes it (and its debt to Quilligan), but it locates the effects of that anxiety in more familiar places—in the violence wrought by allegorical and poetic representation, and in the Petrarchan discourse of unsatisfied male desire—and finds its remedy, as is also usual, in the emergent ideal of companionate marriage.

10. "Allegory's primary work is to force meaning on beings who are reduced for that purpose to substance," writes Gordon Teskey (*Allegory and Violence* [Ithaca: Cornell University Press, 1996], 25). See also Angus Fletcher's well-known account of allegorical "daemonism" (*Allegory: Theory of a Symbolic Mode* [Ithaca: Cornell University Press, 1967], 25–69). For an account of allegory "disarmed" by narrative in the Garden of Adonis, see Joseph Campana, *The Pain of Reformation: Spenser, Vulnerability, and the Ethics of Masculinity* (New York: Fordham University Press, 2012), 204–23.

11. Edmund Spenser, *Colin Clouts Come Home Againe* (1595), ll. 358–67, in *The Yale Edition of the Shorter Poems of Edmund Spenser*, ed. William A. Oram (New Haven, CT: Yale University Press, 1989), 539.

12. *Amoretti* 33, ll. 1–14, in *The Yale Edition of the Shorter Poems of Edmund Spenser*, 620.

13. Jeff Dolven, "Inescapable Romance," *Spenser Review* 44.1.4 (Spring–Summer 2014).

14. Lewis's annotated copy of the poem is held in the Rare Book Collection at the University of North Carolina-Chapel Hill (call number RBC PR2358.A3 S6 1897 c.1); I am grateful to Jerrod Nathan Rosenbaum for consulting and transcribing the annotations for me.

15. Colin Burrow, "C. S. Lewis and *The Allegory of Love*," *Essays in Criticism* 53.3 (2003): 293.

16. C. S. Lewis, *The Allegory of Love: A Study in Medieval Tradition* (Oxford: Oxford University Press, 1958), 315–16, 331, 332.

17. Bracketed dates distinguish between the endings of the 1590 and 1596 book 3.

18. Donald Cheney, "Spenser's Hermaphrodite and the 1590 *Faerie Queene*," *PMLA* 87.2 (March 1972): 192–200.

19. Ibid., 196. For a similar view, see David Lee Miller, who writes that "if [Britomart's] response is half-envious it is also full of yearning and remains thoroughly mimetic": only the "incompleteness" of her desire sets her apart from the married lovers, for "the object of her unsatisfied desire is still '*like* happinesse'" (*The Poem's Two Bodies: The Poetics of the 1590 "Faerie Queene"* [Princeton, NJ: Princeton University Press, 1988], 285.) As I will argue below, it is precisely the notion of "like happinesse"—happiness that is similar but not identical to the happiness of others—that the 1596 version of the poem refuses to entertain, instead treating all happiness as singular and exclusive.

20. A. Bartlett Giamatti, *Play of Double Senses: Spenser's "Faerie Queene"* (New York: Norton, 1975), 133. For more recent, skeptical takes on Spenserian eros, see Melissa Sanchez, "'Modesty or Comeliness': The Predicament of Reform Theology in Spenser's *Amoretti and Epithalamion*," *Renascence: Essays on Values in Literature* 65.1 (2012) and *Erotic Subjects: The Sexuality of Politics in Early Modern English Literature* (Oxford: Oxford University Press, 2011), 58–86; Campana, *The Pain of Reformation*, 163–203; Jonathan Goldberg, *The Seeds of Things: Theorizing Sexuality and Materiality in Renaissance Representations* (New York: Fordham University Press, 2009), 63–122; and William Junker, "Spenser's Unarmed Cupid and the Experience of the 1590 *Faerie Queene*," *ELH* 79.1 (2012): 59–83.

21. Susanne Lindgren Wofford, "Gendering Allegory: Spenser's Bold Reader and the Emergence of Character in *The Faerie Queene* III," *Criticism* 30 (1988): 15.

22. Williams is referring specifically to the image of the Hermaphrodite at the end of the 1590 book 3, which she calls "a symbol of marriage, but of marriage as itself a symbol" ("Venus and Diana: Some Uses of Myth in *The Faerie Queene*," *ELH* 28 [1961]: 115). This emblematic understanding of Spenserian marriage is exceedingly widespread, though there are variations in the precise species of unity for which marriage is taken to stand. To cite just a few instances: C. S. Lewis understands Spenserian marriage as a sign of "the triumphant union of romantic passion with Christian monogamy" (*The Allegory of Love: A Study in Medieval Tradition* [Oxford: Clarendon Press, 1936], 345); Thomas P. Roche as a figure of the discordia concors that is the highest aim of all Spenser's poetry (*The Kindly Flame: A Study of the Third and Fourth Books of Spenser's "Faerie Queene"* [Princeton, NJ: Princeton University Press, 1964], 208–9); Giamatti as an embodiment of the promise that "all duality will cease and wholeness, that human kind of holiness, will be ours" (*Play of Double Senses*, 133); and Miller in *The Poem's Two Bodies* as "a fantasy of . . . healing of the breach between culture and nature that defines the 'human' condition" (278).

23. David Quint, "Archimago and Amoret: The Poem and Its Doubles," in *Worldmaking Spenser: Explorations in the Early Modern Age*, ed. Patrick Cheney and Lauren Silberman (Lexington: University Press of Kentucky, 2000), 37–38. For more on the Scudamore family and its relationship to Spenser's poem, see "Scudamore" in *The Spenser Encyclopedia*. An account of the Scudamore-Shelton affair and Elizabeth's violent reaction is given in Violet A. Wilson, *Queen Elizabeth's Maids of Honour and Ladies of the Privy Chamber* (London: John Lane, 1922), 83, 106–7;

Wilson's source is a letter written by Eleanor Bridges, another of Elizabeth's ladies-in-waiting, to the Earl of Rutland.

24. Singleton was arrested and narrowly escaped punishment—the amputation of his right hand—for his part in helping to publish John Stubbs's *A Gaping Gulph* (1579), written in opposition to the proposed match with the Duke of Anjou. Philip Sidney, the poem's dedicatee, risked his precarious favor at court by writing a letter to the queen against the match; he left court not long afterward, though it isn't clear that the letter was the cause (see Alan Stewart's account of the affair in *Philip Sidney: A Double Life* [London: Chatto and Windus, 2000], 218–22). The queen later retaliated by expressing her own displeasure at his engagement to Francis Walsingham, although she declared herself willing to "pass over the offense" (quoted in ibid., 250). Stewart depicts the court in 1579–80 as a hotbed of secret marriages, each an outrage to the queen's sense of propriety (213–15).

25. On Spenser's relationship to Raleigh and the Raleigh-Throckmorton affair, see Kathrine Koller, "Spenser and Ralegh," *ELH* 1.1 (1934): 37–60; and Jeffrey B. Morris, "To (Re)fashion a Gentleman: Ralegh's Disgrace in Spenser's Legend of Courtesy," *Studies in Philology* 94.1 (1997): 38–58.

26. Jürgen Habermas, *The Structural Transformation of the Public Sphere: An Inquiry into a Category of Bourgeois Society* (1962), trans. Thomas Burger and Frederick Lawrence (Cambridge, MA: MIT Press, 1989), 28, 46. See also Michael McKeon, *The Secret History of Domesticity: Public, Private, and the Division of Knowledge* (Baltimore: Johns Hopkins University Press, 2005), 110–61. For examples of how Habermasian notions of private and public domain are given a Spenserian provenance, see Louis Montrose, "Spenser's Domestic Domain: Poetry, Property, and the Early Modern Subject," in *Subject and Object in Renaissance Culture*, ed. Margreta de Grazia et al. (Cambridge: Cambridge University Press, 1996); Christopher Warley, "'So Plenty Makes Me Poore': Ireland, Capitalism, and Class in Spenser's Amoretti and Epithalamion," *ELH* 69.3 (Fall 2002): 567–98; and George E. Rowe, "Privacy, Vision, and Gender in Spenser's Legend of Courtesy," *MLQ* 50.4 (1989): 309–36. Book 6 is certainly the place where Spenser comes closest to a modern sense of privacy as personal entitlement.

27. Paul Alpers, *The Poetry of "The Faerie Queene"* (Princeton, NJ: Princeton University Press, 1967), 8–9.

28. "Argument" to "Aprill," in *The Shepheardes Calender* (1579), in *The Yale Edition of the Shorter Poems of Edmund Spenser*, ed. William A. Oram, Einar Bjorvand, Ronald Bond, Thomas H. Cain, Alexander Dunlop, and Richard Schell (New Haven, CT: Yale University Press, 1989), 70. All subsequent citations of Spenser's poems, except for *The Faerie Queene*, refer to this edition. Line numbers will be given in the text. On Colin's ode as a "national epithalamion" celebrating "the mystical marriage of Virgin Queen and England," see Cain's introduction to the eclogue, 69.

29. The subtitle identifies the poem as "A Spousal Verse made by Edm. Spenser in honovr of the dovble marriage of the two Honorable & virtuous Ladies, the Ladie Elizabeth and the Ladie Katherine Somerset, Daughters to the Right Honourable the Earle of Worcester" (*Shorter Poems*, 754). I'm reading the poem against the critical grain: for most critics the challenge has been to explain how the symbolic power of marriage overcomes and redeems the speaker's alienation; marriage is never, so far as I can tell, read as an exacerbation of his alienation, though that is literally how it functions in the poem. See Einar Bjorvand's introduction to the *Prothalamion* in *The Yale Edition of the Shorter Poems of Edmund Spenser*, 756–57; Harry Berger, "Spenser's

Prothalamion: An Interpretation," *Essays in Criticism* 15.4 (October 1965): 363–80; Lawrence Manley, "Spenser and the City: The Minor Poems," *Modern Language Quarterly* 43 (1982): 203–27; and Andrew Hadfield's discussion of the poem in *Edmund Spenser: A Life* (Oxford: Oxford University Press, 2012), 358–59: "What cannot be disputed," Hadfield claims, "is the poem's celebration of marriage." For a more muted account of how the poem's putative marital ideal modulates its speaker's despair, see David Lee Miller, *Fowre Hymns and Prothalamion*, in *The Oxford Handbook of Edmund Spenser*, ed. Richard A. McCabe (Oxford: Oxford University Press, 2011), 293–313.

30. The first quotation is from Theresa Krier, *Gazing on Secret Sights: Spenser, Classical Imitation, and the Decorums of Vision* (Ithaca: Cornell University Press, 1990), 13. Krier's argument about the significance of marital privacy as a figure for Spenser's desire for imaginative freedom has much in common with Richard Helgerson's: "Whatever the laureate's obligation to the public world, it is in this private realm [of love and marriage] that he finds the source of his inspiration" (*Self-Crowned Laureates* [Berkeley: University of California Press, 1987], 97). The second is from Joseph Loewenstein, "Spenser's Retrography: Two Episodes in Post-Petrarchan Bibliography," in *Spenser's Life and the Subject of Biography*, ed. Judith H. Anderson, Donald Cheney, and David A. Richardson (Amherst: University of Massachusetts Press), 120. Paul Alpers uses the term "poetic domain" to describe "the qualified but nonetheless genuine independence" Spenser achieves through the pastoral fiction of *The Shepheardes Calender*, his "freedom to poeticize and possess his own space" ("Pastoral and the Domain of Lyric in Spenser's *Shepheardes Calender*," *Representations* 12 [1985]: 95). Montrose argues that it is in the marital and familial contexts of *Amoretti and Epithalamion* that that freedom is most fully realized, thanks in part to an emergent Protestant ethos of patriarchal authority and a nascent capitalist ideology of private possession ("Spenser's Domestic Domain").

31. Frances E. Dolan, *Marriage and Violence: The Early Modern Legacy* (Philadelphia: University of Pennsylvania Press, 2009), 3–4.

32. "But if they cannot absteine let them mary, for it is better to mary then to burne": 1 Corinthians 7:9, in *The Newe Testament of Ovr Lorde Iesus Christ*, trans. Theodore Beza and L.T. (London: Christopher Barker, 1578), 182v; Richard Mallette, *Spenser and the Discourses of Reformation England* (Lincoln: University of Nebraska Press, 1997), 84–142; and Melissa Sanchez, "'Modesty or Comeliness': The Predicament of Reform Theology in Spenser's *Amoretti and Epithalamion*," *Renascence: Essays on Values in Literature* 65.1 (2012): 5–24. On the complexity and diversity of Reformation-era attitudes toward marriage, see also Heather Dubrow, *A Happier Eden: The Politics of Marriage in the Stuart Epithalamion* (Ithaca: Cornall University Press, 1990), 12–27.

33. "An Homyly of the State of Matrimonie," in *The Second Tome of Homilies* (London: Richard Jugge, 1563), 253r.

34. Thomas Cranmer, *Certaine Sermons appointed by the Quenes Maiesty, to be declared and read* (London: Richard Jugge, 1563), sig. D2r

35. Martin Luther, "A Sermon on the Estate of Marriage" (1519), in *Martin Luther's Basic Theological Writings*, ed. Timothy F. Lull (Minneapolis: Fortress Press, 1989), 637.

36. Augustine of Hippo, "Of Marriage and Concupiscence," book 1, ch. 7, in *St. Augustine: Anti-Pelagian Writings*, trans. Peter Holmes, Robert Ernest Wallace, and Benjamin B. Warfield, in *Select Library of Nicene and Post-Nicene Fathers*, ser. 1, vol. 5 (New York: Christian Literature

Company, 1893), 180. See also *The City of God against the Pagans*, book 14, ch. 17, ed. and trans. R. W. Dyson (Cambridge: Cambridge University Press, 1998), 615–16.

37. Augustine, "Of Marriage and Concupiscence," 1:36.

38. Augustine, *City of God*, book 14, ch. 18, 617.

39. Luther, "A Sermon on the Estate of Marriage," 633–34.

40. *The boke of common praier and administracion of the sacramentes* (London: Richard Grafton, 1552), fol. 113r–v.

41. See Patricia Parker, *Inescapable Romance: Studies in the Poetics of a Mode* (Princeton, NJ: Princeton University Press, 1979); and, more recently, Corey McEleny, "Spenser's Unhappy Ends: The Legend of Courtesy and the Pleasure of the Text," *ELH* 79.4 (2012): 797–822.

42. Spenser, "A Letter of the Authors," 716.

43. Gordon Teskey, "Notes on Reading in *The Faerie Queene*: From Moment to Moment," in *Spenser in the Moment*, ed. Paul J. Hecht and J. B. Lethbridge (Madison, NJ: Fairleigh Dickinson University Press, 2015), 226–27.

44. The canonical accounts of the early modern origins of privacy are Lawrence Stone, *The Family, Sex and Marriage in England, 1500–1800* (New York: Harper and Row, 1977); Norbert Elias, *The Civilizing Process*, trans. Edmund Jephcott (New York: Pantheon Books, 1978–82); and Roger Chartier, Philippe Ariès, and Georges Duby, eds., *A History of Private Life: Passions of the Renaissance*, vol. 3, trans. Arthur Goldhammer (Cambridge, MA: Belknap Press, 1993). For perspectives emphasizing the relative lack of public/private distinctions in early modern England, see Jonathan Gil Harris, "This Is Not a Pipe: Water Supply, Incontinent Sources, and the Leaky Body Politic," in *Enclosure Acts: Sexuality, Property, and Culture in Early Modern England* (Ithaca: Cornell University Press, 1994), 203–28; and Lena Cowen Orlin, *Locating Privacy in Tudor London* (Oxford: Oxford University Press, 2007), which highlights the "controversial privacies" registered within legal and municipal records not as entitlements but as "disruptions of community and interruptions of social knowledge" (3).

45. Patricia Fumerton, *Cultural Aesthetics: Renaissance Literature and the Practice of Social Ornament* (Chicago: University of Chicago Press, 1991), 62–77, and *Unsettled: The Culture of Mobility and the Working Poor in Early Modern England* (Chicago: University of Chicago Press, 2006), 1–32.

46. Orlin, *Locating Privacy*, 10.

47. Richard Mulcaster, *Positions concerning the training up of children* (London: Thomas Vautrollier, 1581), 185–86.

48. Nohrnberg, *The Analogy of "The Faerie Queene"* (Princeton, NJ: Princeton University Press, 1976), 770.

49. Harry Berger Jr., "The Discarding of Malbecco," in *Revisionary Play: Studies in the Spenserian Dynamics* (Berkeley: University of California Press, 1988), 170.

50. See Berger, "The Spenserian Dynamics," in *Revisionary Play*, 23–28; Jeff Dolven, "Panic's Castle," *Representations* 120.1 (Fall 2012): 1–16; on Malbecco see p. 3.

51. Roche, *The Kindly Flame*, 200–211; see also Kathleen Williams's claim that "the Legends of Chastity and Friendship . . . examine the same subject of love with slightly different emphasis; love is a kind of friendship, friendship a kind of love" ("Venus and Diana," 106); Lauren Silberman, *Transforming Desire: Erotic Knowledge in Books III and IV of "The Faerie Queene"* (Berkeley: University of California Press, 1995), 9–10, 76–79.

52. Orlin, *Locating Privacy*, 138–39.

53. Once again, it is striking how strictly Spenser enforces this law: immediately before Merlin reveals to Britomart that she will have a son, he informs her that Artegall will die (3.3.28, 29)—in *The Faerie Queene*, marital intimacy can't even make room for the children it produces.

54. John R. Gillis, *For Better, For Worse: British Marriages, 1600 to the Present* (Oxford: Oxford University Press, 1985), 11. See also Ariès et al., *A History of Private Life*, vol. 3, on the French custom of charivari, rowdy public commotions that preceded a wedding and aired any communal grievances against it (531–69).

55. Orlin, *Locating Privacy*, 141.

56. Nohrnberg, *The Analogy of "The Faerie Queene,"* 662; see also Rowe, "Privacy, Vision, and Gender." Michael Schoenfeldt, "The Poetry of Conduct: Accommodation and Transgression in *The Faerie Queene*, Book 6," in *Enclosure Acts: Sexuality, Property, and Culture in Early Modern England*, ed. Richard Burt and John Michael Archer (Ithaca: Cornell University Press, 1994), 152.

57. Richard Neuse, "The Triumph over Hasty Accidents: A Note on the Symbolic Mode of the *Epithalamion*," *Modern Language Review* 61 (1966): 164.

58. Thomas Greene, "Spenser and the Epithalamic Convention," *Comparative Literature* 9 (1957): 226–27.

59. George Puttenham, *The Arte of English Poesie* (London: Richard Field, 1589), 40.

60. Lodowick Bryskett, *A discourse of ciuill life containing the ethike part of morall philosophie. Fit for the instructing of a gentleman in the course of a vertuous life* (London: Edward Blount, 1606), 5.

Chapter 5: Reading against Time: Crisis in *The Faerie Queene*

1. J. Hillis Miller, *On Literature: Thinking in Action* (New York: Routledge, 2002), 122

2. See *Oxford English Dictionary Online*, s.v. "scan (v.)."

3. Jonathan Goldberg, *Endlesse Worke: Spenser and the Structures of Discourse* (Baltimore: Johns Hopkins University Press, 1981), 10–11.

4. C. S. Lewis, *The Allegory of Love: A Study in Medieval Tradition* (Oxford: Clarendon Press, 1936), 321.

5. Joannes de Vigo, *The most excellent workes of chirurgerye*, trans. Bartholomew Traheron ([London]: Edwarde Whytchurch, 1543), sig. §§.iiv. See also *Oxford English Dictionary*, s.v. "crisis," 1.

6. *Oxford English Dictionary*, s.v. "crisis," 3.

7. Ciaran Brady, "Spenser's Irish Crisis: Humanism and Experience in the 1590s," *Past and Present* 111 (May 1986): 29. Brady's essay is, in part, a response to Nicholas Canny, "Edmund Spenser and the Formation of an Anglo-Irish Identity," *Yearbook of English Studies* 13 (1983): 1–19, which argues that Spenser's view of Ireland was typical of his class and generation. The debate between Canny and Brady continues in *Past and Present* 120 (August 1988): 201–15.

8. At least one surviving manuscript of the *View* is dated 1596. The treatise was entered into the Stationers' Register by Matthew Lownes in 1598 but no edition followed; what I cite here is the first print edition, in James Ware's *Two Histories of Ireland* (Dublin, 1633), 76.

9. Paula Blank, "The Proverbial 'Lesbian': Queering Etymology in Contemporary Critical Practice," *Modern Philology* 109.1 (August 2007): 118. For a thoroughgoing account of

etymology's appeal to and influence on English Renaissance writers, including Spenser, see Hannah Crawforth, *Etymology and the Invention of English in Early Modern Literature* (Cambridge: Cambridge University Press, 2013). Crawforth's chapter on Ben Jonson focuses on how "etymological moment[s]" warp time, both by "look[ing] to the increasingly distant past" and by creating "a particular sense of the present" (65–66).

10. Kate M. Warren, "Preface," in Edmund Spenser, *The Faerie Queene, Book V* (Westminster: Archibald Constable, 1898), vii.

11. On Spenser's career in Grey's employ and his persistent defense of Grey's conduct and policies, see Andrew Hadfield, *Edmund Spenser: A Life* (Oxford: Oxford University Press, 2012), 153–95; on the legally complex (and contested) acquisition of his estate at Kilcolman from the confiscated lands of the Earl of Desmond, see Hadfield, *Edmund Spenser*, 197–207.

12. W. B. Yeats, "Introduction," in *Poems of Spenser* (Edinburgh: T. C. and E. C. Jack, 1906), xxxii, xx.

13. Lewis, *Allegory of Love*, 349.

14. Brady, "Spenser's Irish Crisis," 49.

15. Stephen Greenblatt, *Renaissance Self-Fashioning: From More to Shakespeare* (Chicago: University of Chicago Press, 1980), 186. Spenserians (and other Renaissance scholars) have been exceedingly responsive to this claim: in addition to the works referenced directly in this chapter, major studies of the Irish context of *The Faerie Queene* include the essays collected in Patricia Coughlan, ed., *Spenser and Ireland: An Interdisciplinary Perspective* (Cork: Cork University Press, 1989); Claire McEachern, *The Poetics of English Nationhood, 1590–1612* (Cambridge: Cambridge University Press, 1996); Andrew Hadfield, *Edmund Spenser's Irish Experience: Wilde Fruit and Salvage Soyl* (Oxford: Clarendon Press, 1997); Christopher Highley, *Shakespeare, Spenser, and the Crisis in Ireland* (Cambridge: Cambridge University Press, 1997); David Baker, *Between Nations: Shakespeare, Spenser, Marvell and the Question of Britain* (Stanford, CA: Stanford University Press, 1997); Willy Maley, *Salvaging Spenser: Colonialism, Culture, and Identity* (London: Macmillan, 1997); Andrew Murphy, *But the Irish Sea Betwixt Us: Ireland, Colonialism, and Renaissance Literature* (Lexington: University of Kentucky Press, 1999); and Richard A. McCabe, *Spenser's Monstrous Regiment: Elizabethan Ireland and the Poetics of Difference* (Oxford: Oxford University Press, 2002). See also Lisa Jardine, "Encountering Ireland: Gabriel Harvey, Edmund Spenser, and English Colonial Ventures," in *Representing Ireland: Literature and the Origins of Conflict, 1534–1660*, ed. Brendan Bradshaw, Andrew Hadfield, and Willy Maley (Cambridge: Cambridge University Press, 1993), 60–75; and Julia Reinhard Lupton, "Mapping Mutability: or, Spenser's Irish Plot," in *Representing Ireland*, 93–115.

16. Judith H. Anderson, "'Nor Man It Is': The Knight of Justice in Book Five of Spenser's *Faerie Queene*," *PMLA* 85.1 (January 1970): 65.

17. A. C. Hamilton, "General Introduction," in *The Faerie Queene* (Harlow, UK: Longman, 2007), 13; Michael O'Connell, *Mirror and Veil: The Historical Dimension of Spenser's "Faerie Queene"* (Chapel Hill: University of North Carolina Press, 1977), 13; Elizabeth Jane Bellamy, "*The Faerie Queene* (1596)," in *The Oxford Handbook of Edmund Spenser*, ed. Richard McCabe (Oxford: Oxford University Press, 2008), 279.

18. Richard Rambuss, *Spenser's Secret Career* (Cambridge: Cambridge University Press, 1993), 113–14.

19. Tobias Gregory, "Shadowing Intervention: On the Politics of *The Faerie Queene* Book Five, Cantos 10–12," *ELH* 67.2 (2000): 365–66,

20. Andrew Hadfield, "The Death of the Knight with Scales and the Question of Justice in *The Faerie Queene*," *Essays in Criticism* 65.1 (2015): 13.

21. Willy Maley, "'To Weet to Work *Irenaes* Franchisement': Ireland in *The Faerie Queene*," *Irish University Review* 26.2 (1996): 303–4.

22. Willy Maley in Andrew Hadfield and Willy Maley, "The Present State of Spenser Studies: Dialogue-Wise," in *Edmund Spenser: Essays on Culture and Allegory*, ed. Jennifer Klein Morrison and Matthew Greenfield (Burlington, VT: Ashgate, 2000), 194–95.

23. Hadfield, "The Death of the Knight with Scales," 27.

24. Bellamy, "*The Faerie Queene* (1596)," 282.

25. On the circularity of Lewis's argument—which I do not dispute—see Hadfield, "The Course of Justice: Spenser, Ireland, and Political Discourse," *Studia Neophilologica* 65.2 (1993): 187; and Maley, "'To Weet to Worke *Irenaes* Franchisement,'" 306; Hadfield's pronouncement on the complexity of book 5 appears in "The Death of the Knight with Scales," 14; Maley's on the complexity of Spenser and Ireland is in "The Present State of Spenser Studies," 195.

26. Heather Love, "Close but Not Deep: Literary Ethics and the Descriptive Turn," *New Literary History* 41.2 (2010): 371.

27. See, for instance, Crystal Bartolovich, "Humanities of Scale: Marxism, Surface Reading—and Milton," *PMLA* 127.1 (2012): 115–21; Kristina Straub, "The Suspicious Reader Surprised, or, What I Learned from Surface Reading," *Eighteenth Century* 54.1 (Spring 2013): 139–43; Ariana Reilly, "Always Sympathize! Surface Reading, Affect, and George Eliot's *Romola*," *Victorian Studies* 55.4 (2013): 629–46; and Sara S. Poor, "Why Surface Reading Is Not Enough: Morolf, the Skin of the Jew and German Medieval Studies," *Exemplaria* 26.2–3 (2014): 148–62. The phrase "hermeneutic of suspicion" originates with Paul Ricoeur, who uses it to describe the shared impulse to decode or disillusion that animates the writings of Marx, Freud, and Nietzche (*Freud and Philosophy: An Essay on Interpretation* [New Haven, CT: Yale University Press, 1970]); on the influence of Ricoeur on literary studies, see Rita Felski, "Critique and the Hermeneutic of Suspicion," *M/C Journal* 15.1 (2012). The term "surface reading" first appears in Stephen Best and Sharon Marcus, "Surface Reading: An Introduction," *Representations* 108 (2009), where it is most pointedly opposed to Frederic Jameson's "symptomatic reading" of literary texts in *The Political Unconscious: Narrative as a Socially Symbolic Act* (Ithaca: Cornell University Press, 1981).

28. Augustine, *De Doctrina Christiana: A Classic of Western Culture*, trans. Duane W. H. Arnold (Notre Dame, IN: University of Notre Dame Press, 1995), 15.

29. On the place of euhemerism in Renaissance histories more generally, and in books 2 and 5 of *The Faerie Queene* in particular, see Bart van Es, *Spenser's Forms of History* (Oxford: Oxford University Press, 2002), 112–38. Van Es notes the potential uses of euhemeristic interpretation to modern readers of book 5, writing that "An active engagement with that system allows the reader of Book V to transform what is sometimes considered a rather flat narrative into a text that is three- or even four-dimensional" (124).

30. Angus Fletcher, *The Prophetic Moment: An Essay on Spenser* (Chicago: University of Chicago Press, 1971), 37, 278, 286–87.

31. J. K. Barret, "Vacant Time in *The Faerie Queene*," *ELH* 81.1 (2014): 1.

32. Lynsey McCulloch, "Antique Myth, Early Modern Mechanism: The Secret History of Spenser's Iron Man," in *The Automaton in English Renaissance Literature*, ed. Wendy Beth Hyman (Burlington, VT: Ashgate, 2011), 76. McColluch's essay, one of several recent attempts to add nuance to the critical portrait of Talus, influences my own reading of Talus throughout this chapter. McCulloch emphasizes two aspects of Talus that earlier critics have tended to miss: his affiliation with ancient and early modern discourses of wonder and his function as a mediator between Artegall and Britomart. See also Jonathan Sawday on Talus and other Renaissance automata as both "figure[s] of horror" and "thing[s] of beauty and admiration" ("'Forms Such as Never Were in Nature': The Renaissance Cyborg," in *At the Borders of the Human: Beasts, Bodies, and Natural Philosophy in the Early Modern Period*, ed. Erica Fudge, Ruth Gilbert, and Susan Wiseman [New York: Palgrave, 2002], 190–91).

33. James Nohrnberg, *The Analogy of "The Faerie Queene"* (Princeton, NJ: Princeton University Press, 1976), 409–25. See also McCulloch, "Antique Myth, Early Modern Mechanism," in *The Automaton*, ed. Hyman, 75–76.

34. McCulloch draws attention to this passage, arguing that it "warn[s] against the reading of a singular Talus, one inevitably cast in cruelty and indomitability" ("Antique Myth, Early Modern Mechanism," in *The Automaton*, ed. Hyman, 67). I might say, rather, that it warns against the assumption that such qualities are at odds with aesthetic appeal.

35. Jane Aptekar, *Icons of Justice: Iconography and Thematic Imagery in Book V of "The Faerie Queene"* (New York: Columbia University Press, 1969), 42; A. C. Hamilton, ed., *The Faerie Queene*, 512n; Bellamy, "*The Faerie Queene* (1596)," 280.

36. Heather James, "The Problem of Poetry in *The Faerie Queene*, Book V," *Spenser Review* 45.1.1 (Spring–Summer 2015); http://www.english.cam.ac.uk/spenseronline/review/item/45.1.1.

37. Elaine Freedgood and Cannon Schmitt, "Denotatively, Technically, Literally," *Representations* 125 (2014): 3–4.

38. Elaine Freedgood and Emily Apter, "Afterword," special issue on "The Way We Read Now," *Representations* 108 (2009): 141.

39. Quoted in Jonathan Goldberg, *James I and the Politics of Literature* (Baltimore: Johns Hopkins University Press, 1983), 1. The letter also appears in Frederic Ives Carpenter, *A Reference Guide to Edmund Spenser* (Chicago: University of Chicago Press, 1923), 41–42.

40. Ibid., 2.

41. Richard A. McCabe, "The Masks of Duessa: Spenser, Mary Queen of Scots, and James VI," *English Literary Renaissance* 17.2 (Spring 1987): 224.

42. Graham Hough, *The First Commentary on "The Faerie Queene"* (Chichester: Moore and Tillyer, 1964), 18.

43. Ibid., 19.

44. Ibid., 10; the annotations appear at 1.12.26 and 2.1.21. Dixon's code, which he uses at irregular intervals for what he may have regarded as especially sensitive topical commentary, is a simple alphabetical substitution, decoded by counting fourteen letters ahead.

45. Ibid., 1, 18.

46. [Anonymous], THE FAERIE LEVELLER: OR, King CHARLES his Leveller descried and deciphered in Queene ELIZABETHS dayes (London: 1648).

47. John Milton, *Eikonoklastes in answer to a book intitl'd Eikon basilike* (London: Matthew Simmons, 1649), 34.

48. On the incongruity of Spenser's politics and Milton's, see Maureen Quilligan, *Milton's Spenser: The Politics of Reading* (Ithaca: Cornell University Press, 1983), 12; on the potential similarities in their perspectives on Ireland, see McCulloch, "Antique Myth, Early Modern Mechanism," in *The Automaton*, ed. Hyman, 63–64.

49. [Samuel Croxall], *An original canto of Spencer: Design'd as part of his Fairy queen, but never printed. Now made publick, by Nestor Ironside, Esq.* (London: A. Baldwin, [1713] [title page reads 1714]).

50. *Examiner* 5:6 (London: John Morphew, December 18, 1713).

51. [Samuel Croxall], *The Examiner Examin'd. In a letter to the Englishman. Occasion'd by the Examiner of Friday Dec. 18. 1713. Upon the Canto of Spencer* (London: J. Roberts, 1713), 6–7. *Another Original Canto of Spencer* (in which Talus reappears in still more flattering guise, as Britomart's valiant companion) was published by James Roberts in 1714.

52. *Examiner* 5:6.

53. John Upton, ed., *Spenser's "Faerie Queene"* (London: J. and R. Tonson, 1758), 633–35.

54. On the circumstances that led to Dowden's writing the essay, see David Gardiner, "'To Go There as a Poet Merely': Spenser, Dowden, and Yeats," *New Hibernia Review* 1.2 (1997): 113.

55. Edward Dowden, "Spenser, the Poet and Teacher," in *The Complete Works in verse and Prose of Edmund Spenser*, ed. Alexander B. Grosart ([Manchester]: Spenser Society, 1882–84), 305. The reference is to John Milton, *Areopagitica; a speech of Mr. John Milton for the liberty of vnlicens'd printing, to the Parlament of England* (London: 1664), 13.

56. Edwin A. Greenlaw, "Spenser and British Imperialism," *Modern Philology* 9 (1912): 347.

57. Edwin A. Greenlaw and James Holly Hanford, *The Great Tradition: A Book of Selections from English and American Prose and Poetry, Illustrating the National Ideals of Freedom, Faith, and Conduct* (New York: Scott, Foresman, 1919).

58. Alfred B. Gough, "Preface," in *The Faerie Queene, Book V* (Oxford: Clarendon Press, 1918), [iii].

59. [Matthew Kelly], "Art. VI—*The Works of Edmund Spenser*. London: Routledge. 1844," *Dublin Review* 17 (December 1844): 415. The identification of the essay's author is made in Walter E. Houghton, ed., *The Wellesley Guide to Victorian Periodicals, 1824–1900* (Toronto: University of Toronto Press, 2006), 2:44. A reverential account of Kelly's life is given by Rev. D. McCarthy in a "Memoir" prefixed to Kelly's posthumously published *Dissertations, Chiefly on Irish Church History* (Dublin: James Duffy, 1864), i–xiii.

60. On the founding and early history of the *Dublin Review*, see L. C. Casartelli, "Our Diamond Jubilee," *Dublin Review* 119 (1986): 245–72; see also Houghton, *The Wellesley Guide to Victorian Periodicals*, 2:9–20.

61. Quoted in John T. Walters, *Ireland's Wrongs and How to Mend Them* (London: Hodder and Stoughton, 1881), a pamphlet addressed to the "middle-class ... electors" of England, urging them to support the passage of the 1881 Land Act.

62. Northrop Frye, "The Structure of Imagery in *The Faerie Queene*," *University of Toronto Quarterly* 30.2 (January 1961): 124.

63. In Dennis O'Driscoll, *Stepping Stones: Interviews with Seamus Heaney* (New York: Farrar, Straus and Giroux, 2008), 455. In his introduction O'Driscoll notes that the text of this particular interview, "'An ear to the line': Writing and Reading," was generated on two occasions in October 2003 (viii).

64. Johanna Drucker, "Humanistic Theory and Digital Scholarship," in *Debates in the Digital Humanities*, ed. Matthew K. Gold (Minneapolis: University of Minnesota Press, 2012), 87.

65. Tara McPherson, "Why Are the Digital Humanities So White? or Thinking the Histories of Race and Computation," in *Debates in the Digital Humanities*, 143.

66. Christopher Burlinson and Andrew Zurcher, "Spenser's Secretarial Career," in *The Oxford Handbook of Edmund Spenser*, 76; see also Rambuss, *Spenser's Secret Career*.

67. Herbert E. Cory, "Spenser, Thomson, and Romanticism," *PMLA* 26 (1911): 73n2.

68. Quoted in ibid., 73. Fittingly enough, the stanza was published in a newspaper after Keats's death by his friend Charles Brown, where it was advertised as his final poetic production (see the *Plymouth and Davenport Weekly Journal* [July 4, 1839]); the annotated volume itself, believed lost for many decades, was rediscovered by Greg Kucich in 1988: see "'A Lamentable Lay': Keats and the Making of Charles Brown's Spenser Volumes," *Keats-Shelley Review* 3 (1988): 1–22.

69. Stephen Ramsay and Geoffrey Rockwell, "Developing Things: Notes toward an Epistemology of Building in the Digital Humanities," in *Debates in the Digital Humanities*, 78.

70. Stephen Ramsay, *Reading Machines: Toward an Algorithmic Criticism* (Chicago: University of Illinois Press, 2011), 8.

71. For media theorists, old and new, this is not a radical insight: although there are still those who insist that computer-based text analysis is only a tool, a way of accelerating and expanding the techniques and objects of traditional literary historical study, scholars are increasingly conscious of how digital methods reify interpretive judgments, "creat[ing] at least the illusion (or delusion) of fixity" (Drucker, "Humanistic Theory and Digital Scholarship," 88). Nonetheless, however often we remind ourselves that, as Geoffrey C. Bowker writes, "'raw data' . . . is an oxymoron," the charts and graphs and scatterplots that result from our digital queries entice us to forget it (*Memory Practices in the Sciences* [Cambridge, MA: MIT Press, 2005], 183–84). For a long historical perspective on this problem, surveying print as well as digital information technologies, see the essays collected in Lisa Gitelman, ed., *"Raw Data" Is an Oxymoron* (Cambridge, MA: MIT Press, 2013).

72. James E. Dobson, "Can an Algorithm Be Disturbed? Machine Learning, Intrinsic Criticism, and the Digital Humanities," *College Literature* 42.4 (2015): 559. Dobson draws on Sigurd Burkhardt's earlier account of the value of the "stumbling block," the disturbance or discrepancy within a reader's experience of a poem that propels the work of interpretation ("Notes on the Theory of Intrinsic Interpretation," in *Shakespearean Meanings* [Princeton, NJ: Princeton University Press, 1968], 289).

73. "The Fairy Queen (locomotive)," Wikipedia, https://en.wikipedia.org/wiki/Fairy_Queen _(locomotive).

74. See Whitworth Porter and Charles Moore Watson, *History of the Corps of Royal Engineers* (London: Longmans, Green, 1889).

75. Kenneth Cory, "Discovering Hidden Analogies in an Online Humanities Database," *Library Trends* 40.1 (1999): 60; Lisa Lowe, *Intimacies of Four Continents* (Durham, NC: Duke University Press, 2015).

76. Abraham Stoll, "Spenser's Allegorical Conscience," *Modern Philology* 111.2 (2013): 182, 201–2. See also the discussions of this scene in McCulloch ("Antique Myth, Early Modern Mechanism," in *The Automaton*, ed. Hyman); and Tiffany Jo Werth, "'Degendered': Spenser's 'Yron Man' in a 'Stonie' Age," *Spenser Studies: A Renaissance Poetry Annual* 30 (2015).

Chapter 6: Blatant Beasts: Encounters with Other Readers

1. Beinecke Osborn pc76, 106.

2. Jonathan Brody Kramnick, *Making the English Canon: Print-Capitalism and the Cultural Past, 1700–1770* (Cambridge: Cambridge University Press, 1999), 165.

3. *Proposal for printing by subscription a new edition of Spenser's "Fairy Queen," with notes by John Upton, prebendary of Rochester* ([London]: [1758?]).

4. John Upton, *A Letter concerning a new edition of Spenser's "Faerie Queene." To Gilbert West, Esq.* (London: G. Hawkins, 1751).

5. C. S. Lewis, *The Allegory of Love*, 350. Critical perspectives on book 6 are divided between those who find its slackness disappointing and those for whom it comes as a blessed release from the rigors of the Legend of Justice. "The Legend of Courtesy ends with no picture of triumph," observes Kate M. Warren in the introduction to her 1900 edition of book 6, adding: "This is out of Spenser's own experience. In the years in which he was engaged upon the *Faerie Queene* he was learning, little by little, one of the hardest truths that the lover of the ideal has to learn in this life—the enormous strength of evil in the world, of cruelty, hypocrisy, injustice, falsehood, jealousy, malice, and all the rest; and how infinitely small is the headway that any single man or woman can make against it" ("Introduction," in *The Faerie Queene: Book VI*, ed. Warren [Westminster: Archibold Constable, 1900], xi). Richard Neuse offers a similar account in "Book VI as Conclusion to *The Faerie Queene*," *ELH* 35 (1968): 329–53, noting that "the dominant sense of Book VI is one of disillusionment" (331). By contrast, Northrop Frye regarded book 6 as an ideal ending, "a summing up and conclusion for the entire poem and for Spenser's poetic career" ("The Structure of Imagery in *The Faerie Queene*," *University of Toronto Quarterly* 30.2 [1961]: 135). A. C. Hamilton strives to reconcile these perspectives, describing the Legend of Courtesy as both "a decline" and "a higher awakening" ("General Introduction," in *The Faerie Queene*, ed. Hamilton [Harlow: Pearson Longman, 2007], 14).

6. Lines 1–4 of the opening stanza to the proem of book 1 echo the pseudo-Virgilian Latin verses prefixed to most sixteenth-century editions of the *Aeneid*, in which the poet narrates his progress from pastoral through georgic to epic—what came to be known as the Virgilian *rota*. Lines 5 and 9 rework (and, as Thomas Cain and John Watkins point out, also challenge and critique) Ariosto's own imitation of Virgil in the opening of the *Orlando Furioso* (Cain, *Praise in "The Faerie Queene"* [Lincoln: University of Nebraska Press, 1978], 39–40; and Watkins, *The Specter of Dido: Spenser and Virgilian Epic* [New Haven, CT: Yale University Press, 1995], 61). The claim that Spenser meant to "overgo" Ariosto's epic romance in *The Faerie Queene* appears in Harvey's letter to the poet printed as one of *Three Proper and Wittie Familiar Letters* in 1580. A. C. Hamilton claims in the notes to his edition that the device of the "proem" is itself one for which Spenser "lacked any precedent in classical or Italian epic."

7. Michael Schoenfeldt, "The Poetry of Conduct: Accommodation and Transgression in *The Faerie Queene*, Book 6," in *Enclosure Acts: Sexuality, Property, and Culture in Early Modern England*, ed. Richard Burt and John Michael Archer (Ithaca: Cornell University Press, 1994), 152. Norbert Elias provides a large-scale account of this process—what he calls "the courtization of warriors"—within early modern culture, politics, and society in *The Civilizing Process*, trans. Edmund Jephcott, 2 vols. (New York: Pantheon Books, 1978–82), esp. 2:235–36.

8. Schoenfeldt, "The Poetry of Conduct," 152.

9. Stanley Stewart, "Sir Calidore and 'Closure,'" *Studies in English Literature, 1500–1900* 24.1 (Winter 1984): 73; Corey McEleney, "Spenser's Unhappy Ends: The Legend of Courtesy and the Pleasure of the Text," *ELH* 79.4 (Winter 2012): 797–822.

10. Rowe, "Privacy, Vision, and Gender," 312.

11. Jane Grogan, *Exemplary Spenser: Visual and Poetic Pedagogy in "The Faerie Queene"* (Farnham, Surrey: Ashgate, 2009), 150.

12. Nohrnberg, *The Analogy of "The Faerie Queene,"* 662.

13. Rowe, "Privacy, Vision, and Gender," 313.

14. Richard Neuse, "Book VI as Conclusion to *The Faerie Queene*," 331.

15. See Wolfe's blog post, "Was Early Modern Writing Paper Expensive?," *Collation*, February 13, 2018, https://collation.folger.edu/2018/02/writing-paper-expensive/.

16. The response suggests that the initial annotation may be the work of the "James C. Fisher, Class of 1826," who signed the bottom of page 262.

17. I am indebted to Houghton for these biographical details and for drawing my attention to Osborn Z76 O75. See her detailed and lively description of the book and its annotators for the Beinecke Library website: "'Honorable book, you have come down to us from former generations!': *The Faerie Queene* annotated by Yale Undergraduates, 1820–1841," *On the Margins* blog, April 15, 2015, https://beineckemargins.wordpress.com/2015/04/15/honorable-book-you-have-come-down-to-us-from-former-generations-the-faerie-queene-annotated-by-yale-undergraduates-1820-1841/.

18. Two volumes stand out especially in my memory, both copies of Jonathan Goldberg's *Endlesse Worke*. One, in the Lincoln College Library at Oxford, was annotated by a reader using an elaborate and inscrutable system of symbols: there was the usual assortment of straight lines and squiggles, crosses and asterisks, but also an arcane selection of interlocking circles, various-sized pyramids of dots, and what looked vaguely like zodiacal signs. Beneath a particularly dense concentration of such doodles, another reader wrote: "I quite agree, and would like to add: [picture of a potted plant]." The other is in the Bass Undergraduate Library at Yale; it was annotated by a reader who repeatedly wonders why Goldberg cites deconstructionist critics instead of invoking Plato; the third time this query appears, another hand writes: "SHUT UP ABOUT PLATO."

19. Paul Alpers, "How to Read *The Faerie Queene*," in *Edmund Spenser's Poetry*, ed. Anne Lake Prescott and Andrew Hadfield, 4th ed. (New York: W. W. Norton, 2014), 749–58. Originally published in *Essays in Criticism* 18 (1968): 429–42.

20. Donald Cheney, *Spenser's Image of Nature* (New Haven, CT: Yale University Press, 1967), 22; quoted in Alpers, "How to Read *The Faerie Queene*," 751.

21. Bernard N. Schilling, "Foreword," in *Essential Articles for the Study of Edmund Spenser*, ed. A. C. Hamilton (Hamden, CT: Archon Press, 1972), ix.

22. Hamilton, "Preface," in *Essential Articles*, xi.

23. Paul Ricoeur, *Freud and Philosophy: An Essay on Interpretation* (1970), trans. Denis Savage (New Haven, CT: Yale University Press, 2008), 32; Bruno Latour, "Why Has Critique Run Out of Steam? From Matters of Fact to Matters of Concern," *Critical Inquiry* 30 (2004): 225–48. On the relation between suspicion and critique, see Rita Felski, "Critique and the Hermeneutics of Suspicion," *M/C Journal* 15.1 (November 2011); available at http://journal.media-culture.org.au/index.php/mcjournal/article/view/431.

24. On "postcritical" reading practices, see Rita Felski, *Uses of Literature* (New York: Wiley-Blackwell, 2008) and *The Limits of Critique* (Chicago: University of Chicago Press, 2015); on the "hermeneutics of susceptibility" and "surface reading," see the special issue of *Representations* on "The Way We Read Now," coedited by Stephen Best and Sharon Marcus in 2009, especially Best and Marcus, "Surface Reading: An Introduction," *Representations* 108.1 (Fall 2009): 1–21; and Anne Anlin Cheng, "Skins, Tattoos, and Susceptibility," *Representations* 108.1 (Fall 2009): 98–119; "just reading" is a term Marcus coins in *Between Women: Friendship, Desire, and Marriage in Victorian England* (Princeton, NJ: Princeton University Press, 2005).

25. Eve Kosofsky Sedgwick, *Touching Feeling: Affect, Pedagogy, Performativity* (Durham, NC: Duke University Press, 2003), 125, 146.

26. Heather Love, "Truth and Consequences: On Paranoid Reading and Reparative Reading," *Criticism* 52.2 (Spring 2010): 237.

Coda: Reading to the End

1. The first epigraph above is from Virginia Woolf, *The Moment and Other Essays* (London: Hogarth Press, 1947), 25, and appears on the same page as the quote given here. The second epigraph is from Robert Southey, letter to Walter Savage Landor, January 11, 1811, quoted in Charles Cuthbert Southey, *The Life and Correspondence of Robert Southey*, 6 vols. (New York: Harper and Brothers, 1851), 3:295.

2. Robert Southey, *Southey's Commonplace-Book* (London: Longman, Brown, Green, and Longmans, 1851), 4:311–12. Southey's list was my original source for a number of the complaining comments I cite in the introduction to this book.

3. Barbara Herrnstein Smith, *Poetic Closure: How Poems End* (Chicago: University of Chicago Press, 1968), viii.

4. Edmund Spenser, *The Faerie Queene* (London: Matthew Lownes, 1609), 353.

5. Gordon Teskey, *Two Cantos of Mutabilitie*, in *The Oxford Handbook of Edmund Spenser*, ed. Richard A. McCabe (Oxford: Oxford University Press, 2010), 334.

6. Some assumed the poem was unfinished at Spenser's death; others that pieces of it were lost or destroyed. For instance, a 1607 epigram by Sir John Stradling laments the loss of "some manuscript copies" of Spenser's in a fire (*Epigrammatum Libri Quator*, quoted and translated in *A Reference Guide to Edmund Spenser*, ed. Frederic Ives Carpenter [Chicago: University of Chicago Press, 1923; repr. New York: Peter Smith, 1950], 128), while a 1616 poem by William Browne describes the poet as "rapt" to heaven "ere he ended his melodious song" (*Britannia's Pastorals: The Seconde Booke*, quoted in *Spenser: The Critical Heritage*, ed. R. M. Cummings [London: Routledge and Kegan Paul, 1971], 133–34). Both are quoted and discussed in J. B. Lethbridge, "Spenser's Last Days: Ireland, Career, Mutability, Allegory," in *Edmund Spenser: New and Renewed Directions*, ed. J. B. Lethbridge (Madison, NJ: Fairleigh Dickinson University Press, 2006), 307–8.

7. See Edmund Spenser, *A View of the Present State of Ireland (1596; 1633)*, ed. Andrew Hadfield and Willy Maley (Oxford: Blackwell, 1997), 5. See also Lethbridge, "Spenser's Last Days," in *Edmund Spenser*, 307–8.

8. In Cummings, *Spenser: The Critical Heritage*, 197.

9. John Upton, "Notes on Two Cantos of Mutabilitie," in *Spenser's "Faerie Queene"* (London: J. and R. Tonson, 1758), 659.

10. John Hughes, "Remarks on the 'Faerie Queene,'" in *The Works of Mr. Edmund Spenser*, ed. Hughes (London: Jacob Tonson, 1715), xc–xci; quoted in Cummings, *Spenser: The Critical Heritage*, 271.

11. Thomas Birch, "The Life of Mr. Edmund Spenser," in *The Faerie Queene* (London: J. Brindley and S. Wright, 1751), xxiv.

12. William Duff, *Critical Observations on the Writings of the Most Celebrated Geniuses in Poetry* (London: T. Becket and P. A. de Hondt, 1770), 214.

13. Douglas Bush, *The Works of Edmund Spenser: A Variorum Edition* (Baltimore: Johns Hopkins University Press, 2001), 6:448.

14. Lethbridge, "Spenser's Last Days," 314.

15. Edmund Spenser, *The Faerie Queene*, ed. A. C. Hamilton, 1st ed. (London: Longman, 1977), 711.

16. Andrew Zurcher, "The Printing of the *Cantos of Mutabilitie* in 1609," in *Celebrating Mutabilitie: Essays on Edmund Spenser's Mutabilitie Cantos*, ed. Jane Grogan (Manchester: Manchester University Press, 2010), 48–58.

17. Andrew Hadfield, *Edmund Spenser: A Life* (Oxford: Oxford University Press, 2012), 369.

18. Sebastian Evans, "A Lost Poem by Edmund Spenser," *Macmillan's Magazine* 42.248 (June 1880): 151.

19. Grosart, *Complete Works in Verse and Prose of Edmund Spenser*, 1:508.

20. Herbert Ellsworth Cory, *Edmund Spenser: A Critical Study* (Berkeley: University of California Press, 1917), 360n11.

21. Edwin Greenlaw, Charles Grosvenor Osgood, Frederick Morgan Padelford, and Ray Heffner, eds., *The Works of Edmund Spenser: A Variorum Edition; "The Faerie Queene" Books Six and Seven* (Baltimore: Johns Hopkins University Press, 1938), 433–34.

22. Thomas J. Wise, ed., *Spenser's "Faerie Queene"* (London: G. Allen, 1895–97), 1:lxxix.

23. Northrup Frye, "The Structure of Imagery in *The Faerie Queene*," *University of Toronto Quarterly* 30 (1961): 111.

24. Jane Grogan, "Introduction," in *Celebrating Mutabilitie*, ed. Grogan, 1.

25. Grosart, *Complete Works*, vol. 1, title page.

26. Zurcher, "Printing," 40.

27. Lethbridge, "Spenser's Last Days," 302 and 302n.

28. Cory, "Preface," in *Edmund Spenser: A Critical Study*, unpaginated.

29. Both Lucretius and Bruno now have entries in the *Spenser Encyclopedia*, neither of which mentions Evans (A. C. Hamilton, gen. ed., *The Spenser Encyclopedia* [Toronto: University of Toronto Press, 1990], 118–19, 442–43). Credit for launching the inquiry into Spenser's knowledge of Lucretius and Bruno almost always goes to Edwin Greenlaw, "Spenser and Lucretius," *Studies in Philology* 17 (1920): 455–64; and Ronald B. Levinson, "Spenser and Bruno," *PMLA* 43 (1928): 665, although Josephine Waters mentions Evans as the originator in a footnote to her "Spenser's Venus and the Goddess Nature in the *Cantos of Mutabilitie*," *Studies in Philology* 30.2 (1933): 160n2. For a recent reexamination of the *Mutabilitie Cantos* in the context of sixteenth-century science and the revival of Lucretianism, see Ayesha Ramachandran, "Mutabilitie's Lucretian Metaphysics: Skepticism and Cosmic Process in Spenser's *Cantos*," in *Celebrating Mutabilitie: Essays on Edmund Spenser's Mutabilitie Cantos*, ed. Jane Grogan (Manchester: Manchester University Press, 2010), 220–45.

30. Edward George Harman, *Edmund Spenser and the Impersonations of Francis Bacon* (London: Constable, 1914), 79–80.

31. Grogan, "Introduction," in *Celebrating Mutabilitie*, ed. Grogan, 1.

32. Teskey, *Two Cantos of Mutabilitie*, 335; Greenlaw et al., *Variorum*, 6:445.

33. Grogan, "Introduction," in *Celebrating Mutabilitie*, 1; the lexical and stylistic analyses carried out by earlier scholars are summarized in Lethbridge, "Spenser's Last Days," 313–16.

34. James Shapiro, *Contested Will: Who Wrote Shakespeare?* (New York: Simon and Schuster, 2011), 32–35. On the long history of the Shakespeare authorship controversy, see also Paul Edmondson and Stanley Wells, eds., *Shakespeare beyond Doubt: Evidence, Argument, Controversy* (Cambridge: Cambridge University Press, 2013).

35. William Blissett, "Spenser's Mutabilitie," in *Essays in English Literature from the Renaissance to the Victorian Age Presented to A.S.P. Woodhouse*, ed. Millar Maclure and F. W. Watt (Toronto: University of Toronto Press, 1964), 26.

36. Frank Kermode, *The Sense of an Ending: Studies in the Theory of Fiction with a New Epilogue* (Oxford: Oxford University Press, 2000), 75.

37. Blissett, "Spenser's Mutabilitie," 26.

38. James Nohrnberg, "Supplementing Spenser's Supplement, a Masque in Several Scenes: Eight Literary-Critical Meditations on a Renaissance Numen Called Mutabilitie," in *Celebrating Mutabilitie*, ed. Grogan, 85.

39. Walter Scott, 1805 letter to Anna Seward, quoted in John Gibson Lockhart, *Memoirs of the Life of Sir Walter Scott* (Cambridge: Riverside Press, 1902), 1:436–37.

40. Robert Southey, letters to Chauncey Hare Townsend, February 10, 1816, and July 22, 1816, in Charles Cuthbert Southey, ed., *The Life and Correspondence of Robert Southey* (London: Longman, 1849–50), 4:152, 191–92.

41. Henry Melmoth, *Letters on Several Subjects. By the late Sir Thomas Fitzosborne, Bart. To which is added, (translated by the same Hand) A Dialogue upon Oratory* (London, 1749), 2:104–10.

42. William Shenstone, letter to Lady Luxborough (1748), in *The Letters of William Shenstone*, ed. Marjorie Williams (Oxford: Basil Blackwell, 1939), 131.

43. James Boswell, *The Life of Johnson*, ed. G. B. Hill, 6 vols. (Oxford, 1934–50), 3:422–24, 4:272n; Thomas De Quincey, "Notes from the Pocket-Book of a Late Opium-Eater"; both quoted in the entry on William Melmoth (1710–99) in the *Dictionary of National Biography*.

44. John Callander, handwritten annotations to *The Works of Edmund Spenser* (1611/1612), in the Osborn Collection at Yale University's Beinecke Library (Osborn fpb57 1–2). Discussed in Eve Houghton, "'A piece said to be Spenser's': Spenserian Forgery in the 1740s?," *On the Margins* blog post, April 24, 2015, https://beineckemargins.wordpress.com/. I am grateful to Houghton for sharing this—and so many other wonderful archival finds—with me.

45. Ibid.

46. Wallace Stevens, *The Necessary Angel: Essays on Reality and the Imagination* (New York: Alfred A. Knopf, 1951), 50.

INDEX

NOTE: *TFQ* stands for *The Faerie Queene* in this index.
Page numbers followed by *f* indicate a figure.

Act of Union of 1801, 203
Adagia (Erasmus), 118
Adams, Hazard, 266n56
Addison, Joseph, 79
Aeneid (Virgil), 294n6
"Against Whoredome and Vncleannesse" (Cranmer), 158
A Gaping Gulph (Stubbs), 285n24
Alcott, Bronson, 21, 58–63, 93, 275n21
The Allegorical Temper (Berger), 20, 115–17
allegory in *TFQ*, 50–107; adaptations for children of, 85, 88, 90–101, 278n59; Arthur's role in, 31–32, 113, 161; assumptions of childish reading of, 58–63, 77–85, 90, 277n43; gendered dichotomy in, 58; historical forms of, 182–87, 193–97, 200–201, 207, 289n15; interruption by ordinariness of, 62–64; on marriage, 148, 161–64, 167, 283n10; reception history of, 50–56, 145, 274n5; Spenser's ambivalence about, 93; Spenser's explanation of, 57–58; Spenser's self-reflexive practice of, 53, 74; stories of the Redcrosse Knight and Una as, 61, 64–77, 101–3, 156, 161, 276n24, 276nn31–32; tension with realist narrative of, 56, 147–48. *See also* Una and the Legend of Holiness
The Allegory of Love (Lewis), 50, 52, 152, 154–55
Allott, Miriam, 109–10
Allott, Robert, 121–25, 139, 142, 280n31, 281n33

Alpers, Paul, 156, 286n30; on how to read *TFQ*, 20, 31–32; review of Cheney by, 234–39; on Una's allegorical function, 66, 70
Amis, Martin, 24
Amoretti and Epithalamium (Spenser), 149–51, 158, 171–75, 286n30
Analogy of "The Faerie Queene" (Nohrnberg), 20
The Anatomy of Criticism (Frye), 19–20
Anderson, Judith, 270n17; on historical contexts of book 5, 183; on learning to read with *TFQ*, 2, 4–5; on Spenser's allegorical intent, 50–51, 145
Anglo-American imperialism, 200–202, 205
Anne, Queen of Great Britain, 198
annotations. *See* hand-annotations
Another Original Canto of Spencer (Roberts), 292n51
anthologies, 119–26, 139, 201, 280–81nn31–32
Antiquitee of Faerie Lond, 1–3, 22–25, 135
Apollonius of Rhodes, 189
Apteker, Jane, 192
Apter, Emily, 194
Arcadian Rhetorike (Fraunce), 111, 120–21, 126
Areopagitica (Milton), 10, 200, 264n24
Argonautica (Apollonius of Rhodes), 189
Ariosto, 132, 220, 226, 294n6
Artegall, 187–91; betrothal to Britomart of, 154, 160, 187–88, 215; dependency on Talus of, 208–10, 214; as surrogate for Lord Grey, 182–84, 200

Arte of English Poesie (Puttenham), 111, 172
artificial intelligence. *See* digital humanities
attentiveness, 22–24, 268–69nn90–91
Augustine, 134, 158–59, 164–65, 186–87
Austin, William, 141
avid readers, 108–12, 117–19, 142–44. *See also* Legend of Temperance

Bacon, Francis, 253–55
Baldick, Chris, 14
Baldwin, Edward, 230–33, 240
Baldwin, William, 121
The Bankette of Sapience (Elyot), 121
Barret, J. K., 188
Barthes, Roland, 178
Basu, Anupam, 29–30, 33–35, 48
Bates, Catherine, 32
Beers, Henry A., 9
Bell, John, 44, 143
Bellamy, Elizabeth Jane, 184–85, 192
Bel-vedére, or, the Garden of the Muses, 121, 280n31
Bercovitch, Sacvan, 105–6
Berger, Harry, Jr., 20, 115–17, 167, 267n70, 280n22
Best, Stephen, 185, 269n91
Bethurst, Theodore, 39
Birch, Thomas, 41–42
Bismarck, Otto von, 205
Blair, Ann, 23
Blank, Paula, 180–81, 270n13
Blissett, William, 255–56
Boaden, James, 27
Bodenham, John, 280n31
The Book of the Duchess (Chaucer), 43
book reviews, 234–39
Books of the Governors, 132
Bowes, Robert, 195–96
Bowker, Geoffrey C., 293n71
Boyle, Elizabeth, 149–50, 171
Bradburn, Eliza Weaver, 90–93, 100, 101
Brady, Ciaran, 180, 183, 288n7
Brawne, Fanny, 143, 209
Bridges, Eleanor, 284–85n23

British imperialism, 200–202, 205
Britomart, Knight of Chastity, 58, 160–71, 176, 210, 284n19, 288n53; betrothal to Artegall of, 154, 160, 187–88; half-envy of Amoret and Scudamore of, 152–56, 160–61, 223; in revised ending of book 3, 148, 167, 226, 242–43; Talus and, 187, 210, 214–15. *See also* Legends of Chastity and Friendship
Brooks, Cleanth, 18–19, 267n70
Brown, Charles, 143, 209, 293n68
Brown, John Russell, 46
Browne, William, 296n6
Bruno, Giordano, 253, 296n29
Bryskett, Lodowick, 149–50, 174–75
Bunyan, John, 50, 275n14
Burby, Cuthbert, 121
Burkhardt, Sigurd, 293n72
Burlinson, Christopher, 208
Burrow, Colin, 152

Callander, John, 259–60
Calvin, John, 67
Cambridge University Library SSS.22.27, 228–230
Campana, Joseph, 274n5
Canny, Nicholas, 288n7
The Canterbury Tales (Chaucer), 44–45
Carruth, Hayden, 19
Catholic Emancipation Act of 1829, 203
Cave of Mammon. *See* Mammon's Cave
Cecil, William, Lord Burghley, 128
The Cenci (Shelley), 108–9
Certeau, Michel de, 111–12
characterological reading, 4, 50, 145–46
Charles I, King of England, 39, 136, 142, 197–98
chastity. *See* Legends of Chastity and Friendship
Chatterton, Thomas, 46
Chaucer, Geoffrey, 114; editing of spelling of, 43–45, 272n55; Lounsbury's study of, 47; Spenser's rewriting of, 213–14
Cheney, Donald, 152–53, 234–38

Cheng, Anne Anlin, 269n91
child readers, 51–64, 77–83; adaptations of
 TFQ for, 53–54, 56, 85, 88, 90–101, 278n59;
 Alcott's teaching of *TFQ* to, 58–63;
 nineteenth-century attitudes towards,
 92–93; passive impressionability of,
 57–58, 61–62; quasi-allegorical notions of,
 54–55; response to beauty by, 54. *See also*
 allegory in *TFQ*
children's literature, 54–56, 92
Christian allegory. *See* allegory in *TFQ*
The Chronicles of Narnia (Lewis), 52–53
Church, Ralph, 42–44, 47
City of God (Augustine), 159
Clarke, Charles Cowden, 109–10
close reading, 31–32, 185, 194, 270n17
Coleridge, Samuel Taylor, 50, 77–78
Colin Clouts Come Home Againe (Spenser),
 148–51
Collected Works of Edmund Spenser (The
 Oxford Edition), 29–30
commonplace books, 119–21, 139
*Complete Works in Verse and Prose of
 Edmund Spenser* (ed. Grosart), 14, 200,
 204–5, 248, 251
compositorial analysis, 37, 47–48,
 272nn36–37
conspicuous consumption, 115, 280n22
conversation, 220–22, 294n7
Copernicus, 246
Cory, Herbert Ellsworth, 209, 248, 252
Cory, Kenneth, 213
courtesy, 169–71, 219–20, 226, 236. *See also*
 Legend of Courtesy
Cowley, Abraham, 56–58, 64, 78, 80, 90
Craig, Martha, 31–32, 270n16
Crane, D.E.L., 280n31
Crane, Walter, 95f
Cranmer, Thomas, 158
Crawforth, Hannah, 288–89n9
crisis and criticism, 179–82; as hermeneutic
 strategy for book 5, 207; Irish colonialist
 context of, 183–87, 208; Talus as symbol
 of, 197–99, 205–7, 292n51

"Criticism, Inc." (Ransom), 18
Cromwell, Oliver, 197–98
Croxall, Samuel, 198–99
Cummings, R. M., 244

Daniel, Samuel, 13, 121
deconstructive analysis, 20
De Copia (Erasmus), 110–11, 119
De Doctrina Christiana (Augustine), 134, 186
de Grazia, Margreta, 47–48, 272n59
Delia (Daniel), 13
Deneef, Leigh, 32
De Quincy, Thomas, 258
Digby, Kenelm, 136–44, 282nn50–51
digital humanities, 178–82, 207–15,
 293nn71–72; *Early English Books Online*
 database, 33–34, 181, 270n14; EEBO-TCP
 N-gram browser, 29–30, 34–35, 181
discipline, 1, 3–6, 25, 194
Discourse Concerning Edmund Spenser
 (Digby), 136–37
Discourse of Civill Life (Bryskett), 174
distant reading, 23, 34–35
Dixon, James, 196–97, 291n44
Dobson, James E., 211, 214, 293n72
Dolan, Frances, 158
Dolven, Jeff, 6, 62–63, 112–18, 151, 167–68,
 274n5
Dowden, Edward, 200–201, 204–5
Drayton, Michael, 13, 121
Drucker, Johanna, 208
Dryden, John, 80
Duncombe, William, 40

Early English Books Online (EEBO), 33–34,
 181, 270n14
Early Modern Print website, 181
Edmund Spenser's Poetry (Norton Critical
 Edition), 28–29, 145, 236, 243
EEBO-TCP N-gram browser, 29–30, 34–35,
 181
Eikonoklastes (Milton), 197–98, 200
Einstein, Albert, 247, 250
Elias, Norbert, 294n7

Eliot, T. S., 17
Elizabethan spelling, 29–31, 39–40, 42–43, 45–46
Elizabeth I, Queen of England, 37, 145–51, 172, 194–97; conflict with James VI of Scotland of, 195–97; Irish policies of, 182–87; as Raleigh's Cynthia, 149–50, 172–73; Spenser's accommodations for, 147–51, 155, 174–75; as Spenser's ideal reader, 147, 151, 162, 174, 283n9; views on marriage of, 155, 284–85nn23–24
Elyot, Thomas, 121
Empson, William, 17, 20
Endlesse Worke (Goldberg), 20, 295n18
Englands Helicon, 121, 280n31
Englands Parnassus, 121–26, 139, 280–81nn31–32
English scholarship, 194, 263n2; on conspicuous irrelevance, 112–18; critical culture of, 238–40; digital technology and, 177–82, 207–15, 293nn71–72; discipline of, 3–4, 25; entering the conversation in, 220–22, 294n7; establishment within the university of, 248–49, 252–53; etymological moment in, 180–81, 288n9; expedience and the ideal of slow reading in, 194–95; foundational role of *TFQ* in, 4–6, 9–10, 14–22, 31, 79, 120–21, 248–49, 266n49, 266nn51–52; hostile book reviews in, 234–40; on lyric poetry, 18–19; New Criticism in, 17–20, 22–23, 114, 116, 234, 270n17; on poetic excess, 110–12; professional exclusivity of, 14–17; resistance to reading *TFQ* in, 17–25, 80–81, 116, 234; role of belle-lettres in, 44; on Spenser's spelling, 28–36, 43–49, 270nn16–17, 274n64; on *TFQ* as children's book, 77–83; turn to close reading in, 31–32, 270n17. *See also* readers of *TFQ*; reading well
Enquiry into the Authenticity (Warton), 46
envy, 160–61
epic form, 113–14
Epigrams (Harington), 13
epithalamia, 172
Epithalamion (Spenser). See *Amoretti and Epithalamium*
Erasmus, 110–11, 118–19
Essential Articles for the Study of Edmund Spenser (ed. Hamilton), 236
etymology, 180–81, 288n9
euhemerism, 186–87, 290n29
Evans, Sebastian, 245–56, 296n29

The Faerie Leveller (Anonymous), 39, 197, 272n42
The Faerie Queene (Spenser), 1–25, 263n1; 1590 and 1596 editions of, 3, 8, 30–43, 47, 147–48, 152–56, 160–63, 167, 216, 225, 242–44; 1609 edition of, 42, 129, 133, 196, 209–10, 230, 242–45; 1617 edition of, 36, 126, 136, 138; 1715 annotated edition of, 13, 39–44, 78, 113, 218–19, 245, 247; 1758 annotated edition of, 41–44, 200, 216–19, 244; adaptations for children of, 53–54, 56, 85, 88, 90–101, 278n59; advice on reading well in, 1–6; allegorical intent in, 50–107, 145; anthologized extracts of, 120–26, 280–81nn31–32; contemporary editions of, 21–22, 29–30, 145, 202, 243; dedication to Elizabeth I of, 37, 145–51, 155; explanatory supplements to, 3, 5, 7–11, 21, 37, 57–58, 123, 161, 243, 274n64; foundational role in literary scholarship of, 4–6, 9–10, 14–22, 31, 79, 120–21, 248–49, 266n49, 266nn51–52; imitation and exploitation of, 26–28, 45–46, 108–44, 257–59; Knevett's *Supplement* to, 39; length of, 8, 21, 241–42; on manners and mores, 216–40; missing original manuscript of, 36; numbering of stanzas in, 129, 209–10, 293n71; poetic disunity of, 113–18, 241–45; reception history of, 6–14, 50–56, 110–12, 145, 264n16, 264n24, 274n5; rumored additional six books of, 243–45, 247–49, 296n6; spelling in, 26–49; Spenser's intention of fashioning

a gentleman in, 1, 3, 16, 58, 121–23; *Two Cantos of Mutabilitie* and, 242–60; uncertain ending of, 241–60. *See also* English scholarship; readers of *TFQ*; Spenser, Edmund
The Faerie Queene book 1. *See* Una and the Legend of Holiness
The Faerie Queene book 2. *See* Legend of Temperance
The Faerie Queene books 3 and 4. *See* Legends of Chastity and Friendship
The Faerie Queene book 5. *See* Legend of Justice
The Faerie Queene book 6. *See* Legend of Courtesy
The Faerie Queene books 1 & 2 (Spenser) (Odyssey Press), 29
The Faerie Queene (Spenser) (Penguin Classics), 28
The Faerie Queene (Spenser, ed. Hamilton) (Longman), 28–29, 37, 47
Fairy Queen Express, 211–12
fairy tales, 55
"Faults escaped in the Print" (Spenser), 37
feminist theory, 20
Ferguson, Margaret, 32, 271n23
Field, Richard, 37, 47
Fish, Stanley, 23
Fisher, James C., 230, 295n16
Fitzosbornes Letters (Melmoth), 257–60
Fletcher, Angus, 20, 32, 187, 283n10
Florimell, 152, 162–64, 177
forgeries and hoaxes: Chatterton's "Thomas Rowley" poems as, 46; Ireland's Shakespeare Papers as, 26–28, 45–46, 255, 272n59; Melmoth's *Fitzosbornes Letters* as, 257–59
Fowler, Alastair, 62–63
Fraunce, Abraham, 111, 120–21, 142
Freedgood, Elaine, 193–94, 213
friendship. *See* Legends of Chastity and Friendship
Frost, William Edward, 83, 87f
Frye, Northrop, 19–20, 207, 249, 294n5

Fumerton, Patricia, 166

Garber, Marjorie, 109
Gascoigne, George, 19
La Gerusalemme liberata (Tasso), 125
Giamatti, A. Bartlett, 284n22
Gill, Alexander, 10, 21, 38, 264n24
Gillis, John R., 168
Gilmont, Jean-François, 263n2
Gless, Darryl J., 61, 276n24
Gloriana, 20
Goldberg, Jonathan, 20, 32, 178, 196, 295n18
Gough, Alfred B., 201–2, 205
Graff, Gerald, 5, 15, 266n49
Grafton, Anthony, 2, 45–46, 263n2
The Great Tradition (Greenlaw and Hanford), 16, 201, 266n57
Greenblatt, Stephen, 20, 183
Greene, Thomas, 171–72
Greenlaw, Edwin F., 15–17, 19, 201, 205, 266nn56–57, 296n29
"Greenlaw trust," 15–16, 266nn56–57
Gregory, Tobias, 184
Greville, Fulke, 19
Grey, Arthur, 47, 174, 180–86, 200, 203–4, 206
Grogan, Jane, 222, 249–50, 254–55
Grosart, Alexander, 14, 200, 204–5, 248–49, 251
Guillory, John, 44
Guyon, Knight of Temperance, 8; appearance in book 5 of, 131–32; in the Castle of Alma, 135–44; destruction of the Bower of Bliss by, 20, 24, 116, 127–28, 183; Hoby's tracking of adventures of, 129–32, 281n38; in Mammon's Cave, 108–12, 115–18, 125, 129–30; Phaedria's shallow temptation of, 124–26; reading of *Antiquitee of Faerie Lond* by, 1–3, 22–25, 135. *See also* Legend of Temperance

Habermas, Jürgen, 156
Hadfield, Andrew, 145, 184–85, 245, 283n1, 285–86n29

Haec Homo, Wherein the Excellencie of the Creation of Woman is Described, By way of an Essay (Austin), 141
Hamilton, A. C., 37, 184, 192, 236, 245, 294nn5–6
hand-annotations, 126–35, 216–19, 281n38, 281n42; Hoby's tracking of plot in, 126, 128–32, 135, 281n38; Jonson's tracking of figurative language in, 126–28; readers' rivalry and debates in, 228–233, 240, 295n16, 295n18; in Upton's 1758 edition, 216–19, 244; Warton's tracking of alliteration in, 126, 133–35, 281n43
Hanford, James Holly, 16, 201, 266n57
Hanoverian succession controversy, 198–99
Harington, John, 13
Harley, Robert, 198–99
Harman, Edward George, 253–55
Hart, John S., 92
Harvey, Gabriel, 12–13, 38, 220, 254, 294n6
Hausmann, Alexander, 247
Hawthorne, Nathaniel, 102–7, 278n66–67, 279n69
Hawthorne, Sophia Peabody, 102–6, 278n66–67
Hawthorne, Una, 102–7
Hayes, Thomas, 121
Hayles, N. Katherine, 34
Hazlitt, William, 10, 14, 81, 90, 200
Heaney, Seamus, 207
Heisenberg, Werner Karl, 250
Helgerson, Richard, 286n30
Herrick, Robert, 19
Herrnstein Smith, Barbara, 242–43, 257
Hillard, George S., 93, 102–7, 279n69
Hilton, William, the Younger, 83, 86f
Hoby, Thomas Posthumous, 126, 128–32, 135, 281n38
Holiness: or The Legend of St. George: A Tale from Spencer's Faerie Queene, by a Mother (Peabody), 93–102, 278n65
Horace, 3, 119
Hough, Graham, 196–97
Houghton, Eve, 230, 259
Howard, Edward, 39, 272n42

"How to Read *The Faerie Queene*" (Alpers), 234–39
Hughes, John, 13, 39–44, 78, 113, 218–19, 245, 247
Hughes, Merritt, 19
Hume, David, 10–11
Hunt, Leigh, 54, 82–83

Imagination and Fancy (Hunt), 82–83
imagined readers, 146, 283n5
imitation and exploitation. *See* Legend of Temperance
imperialism, 200–202, 205
Indian Sepoy Mutiny of 1857, 200–201, 212
indiscipline, 6
Inescapable Romance (Parker), 20
Inquiry into the Authenticity of Certain Miscellaneous Papers and Legal Instruments (Malone), 27–28
Iraq invasion of 2003, 207
Ireland: Great Hunger of, 206–7, 213; incorporation into Great Britain of, 203; nineteenth-century independence movement in, 202–7, 292n61; Spenser's colonialist views on, 182–87, 208, 213, 288n7; Spenser's historical allegory of, 182–87, 193–97, 200, 205, 208, 213, 289n15
Ireland, William Henry, 26–28, 45–46, 255
irrelevance, 112–18, 280n22

James, Heather, 192–93
James, Henry, 275n21
James VI, King of Scotland, 195–97
Johns Hopkins University Press Monographs in Literary History, 16
Johnson, Samuel, 40, 258
Jonson, Ben, 13, 36; Digby's *Observations* and, 138–43, 282n50; hand annotations of TFQ by, 126–28
justice. *See* Legend of Justice

Kearney, James, 64
Keats, John, 9, 108–12, 117, 143; addition to book 5 by, 209, 293n68; imitations of

INDEX 305

Spenser by, 110, 112; on *TFQ*'s linguistic richness, 108–10
Kellogg, Robert, 29–30
Kelly, Matthew, 202–7, 292n59
Kermode, Frank, 255
Knevett, Ralph, 39, 272n42
Kramnick, Jonathan, 44, 113–14
Krier, Theresa, 286n30
Kucich, Greg, 143

Lady Lizzie Eustace (Trollope character), 8–9
Lamb, Charles, 82
Landor, Walter Savage, 12
Lang, Andrew, 98*f*
Lang, Jeanie, 99*f*, 278n62
Larkin, Philip, 9
Latour, Bruno, 238
Lavoisier, Antoine, 246
Leavis, F. R., 17–18, 19
Legend of Constancie. See *Two Cantos of Mutabilitie*
Legend of Courtesy (*TFQ* book 6), 170, 216–40, 294n5; Caliore's detachment in, 222; on entering the conversation, 220–22, 294n7; escape of enemies in, 237; ethics of scholarly critique and, 234–40; Nohrnberg on virtue in, 170; readerly rivalry and, 226–33, 295n16, 295n18; shame and humiliation in, 219–20, 225–27, 294n5; threats of the Blatant Beast in, 222–26
Legend of Holiness (*TFQ* book 1). See Una and the Legend of Holiness
Legend of Justice (*TFQ* book 5), 131–32, 176–215; 1918 Clarendon Press edition of, 201–2; crisis as hermeneutic strategy for, 207; Cymoent's urgency in, 176–82, 187; digital speed and, 207–15, 293nn71–72; as historical allegory of events in Ireland, 182–87, 193–97, 200, 203–5; machine enhanced reading and, 182; presentist readings of, 181–82, 193, 196–207; Talus and temporalities of reading in, 178, 187, 189–95, 291n32, 291n34; temptation for speedy reading of, 181, 187–89, 194

Legend of Temperance (*TFQ* book 2), 108–44; avid readers of, 110–12, 117–19, 142–44; commentaries on the Castle of Alma in, 135–44, 282n50; destruction of the Bower of Bliss in, 20, 24, 116, 127–28, 183; Hoby's annotations on plot in, 126, 128–32, 135, 281n38; Jonson's annotations on figurative language in, 126–28; metaphorical spaces of, 118–19; on the perils of conspicuous irrelevance, 112–18, 280n22; poetic excess and, 108–12; satire of anthological reading in, 124–25; Warton's annotations on alliteration in, 126, 133–35, 281n43. See also Guyon, Knight of Temperance; Mammon's Cave
Legends of Chastity and Friendship (*TFQ* books 3 & 4), 145–75; accommodation of Elizabeth I in, 147–51, 155, 174–75; allegorical function of marriage in, 148, 161–64, 167, 283n10; ambivalence towards marriage in, 152–64, 171–75, 284n22; Britomart's chastity in, 152–56, 160–71, 284n19, 288n53; on courtesy and magnanimity, 169–71, 226; Florimell as image of beauty in, 152, 162–64, 177; Garden of Adonis in, 161; interlaced story lines of, 152, 154, 160, 163; Marinell's crises in, 176–82; partial absorption of readers of, 151–60; on privacy and lust, 164–70, 287n44; revised ending of book 3 in, 148, 167, 226, 242–43; on rivalry between friendship and marriage, 168–69, 287n51
Legends from Spenser's "Faerie Queene," for the Children (Bradburn), 90–93
Lethbridge, J. B., 251–52, 255, 296n6
Letter concerning a new edition of Spenser's "Faerie Queene" (Upton), 41, 43–44, 218–19
"Letter of the Authors expounding his whole intention . . ." (Spenser), 3, 5, 7–9, 37, 243; on allegory, 57–58; on fashioning a gentleman, 3, 58; on poetic excess, 123
"Letter to Raleigh" (Spenser), 161

Levinson, Ronald B., 296n29
Lewis, C. S., 7, 20, 102; on allegory in *TFQ*, 50–53; on humiliation in book 6, 220; on marriage stories in *TFQ*, 152–54, 160, 163, 284n22; on political context of book 5, 183, 185; on reading book 5, 179
The Library of Entertainment (ed. Scammell), 85, 88
Lindley, John, 228–229
Ling, Nicholas, 121
Lionel Asbo: State of England (Amis), 24
literary criticism. *See* English scholarship
"Little Annie's Ramble" (Hawthorne), 106
Loewenstein, Joseph, 29–30, 33–35, 48, 269n10, 286n30
Logonomia Anglica (Gill), 38–39
Longman edition of *The Faerie Queene*, 28–29, 37, 47
Loose Fantasies (Digby), 136
"A Lost Poem by Edmund Spenser" (Evans), 245–56
Lounsbury, Thomas Raynesford, 47
Love, Heather, 185, 239
Lowe, Lisa, 213
Lowell, James Russell, 14, 54, 83–84, 200
Lowell, Robert, 18
Lownes, Matthew, 242–55, 288n8
Lucretius, 253, 296n29
Lupton, Christina, 23
Luther, Martin, 158–59

MacCaffrey, Isabel, 3, 50–51
MacCauley, Thomas B., 7, 264n16
MacLehose, Sophia L., 92, 278n62
MacPherson, Tara, 208
Maley, Willy, 32, 184–85
Mallette, Richard, 158
Malone, Edmund, 27–28, 30–31, 45–46, 255, 281n43
Mammon's Cave, 108–12, 125, 129–30; as invitation to imitation and exploitation, 109–12; perils of conspicuous irrelevance and, 115–18, 280n22

manners and mores, 216–20
Mao, Douglas, 54
Marcus, Sharon, 185, 269n91
marginal annotations. *See* hand-annotations
marriage: concepts of privacy in, 156–59, 164–71, 286n30, 287n44; Elizabeth I's views of, 155, 172–75, 284–85nn23–24; Protestant ideals of, 155–56, 158–60, 164–65, 286n32; Spenser's ambivalent depictions of, 152–64, 284n22; in Spenser's *Amoretti and Epithalamium*, 149–51, 158, 171–75. *See also* Legends of Chastity and Friendship
Marxist theory, 20
Mary, Queen of Scots, 195–97
Masten, Jeffrey, 272n37
Matthiessen, F. O., 105, 279n71
May, Thomas, 142–43
Mayer, Julius Robert, 246
McCabe, Richard, 196
McCulloch, Lynsey, 189, 291n32, 291n34
McElderry, Bruce, 29, 270n13
McEleney, Corey, 221
McKeon, Michael, 55, 275n14
McLeod, Randall, 35, 272n57
media theory, 208, 293n71. *See also* digital humanities
Melmoth, William, 257–60
Miller, David, 32, 148, 283n9, 284n22
Miller, J. Hillis, 176
Milton, John, 10, 43, 51, 91, 197–98, 200, 264n24
Minos (Pseudo-Plato), 189
miscellanies, 119–25, 139, 280–81nn31–32
Montrose, Louis, 20, 147, 286n30
More, Henry, 78
Moretti, Franco, 34
Moshenska, Joe, 68, 136
M.R. (*Spectator* letterwriter), 6–7
Mulcaster, Richard, 4–5, 166–67
Mutabilitie. See *Two Cantos of Mutabilitie*

Nashe, Thomas, 13
Neuse, Richard, 171, 294n5

Newbery, John, 56
New Criticism: on lyric unity, 114, 116; resistance to reading *TFQ* in, 18–20, 22–23, 234, 270n17
New Historicism, 20
The Noble Voices (van Doren), 19
Nohrnberg, James, 8, 20; on Calidore's detachment, 222; on Malbecco, 167; on the *Mutabilitie Cantos*, 244, 256; on the restoration of Guyon's horse, 132; on Talus's classical namesakes, 189; on virtue, 170
Norton Critical Edition of *Edmund Spenser's Poetry*, 28–29, 145, 236, 243
the novel, 55–56, 63

Observations on the 22. stanza in the 9th. canto of the 2d. book of Spencers "Faery Queen" (Digby), 136–44
Observations on the Faerie Queene of Spenser (Warton), 15, 40–41, 113–14, 116–17, 133–34
O'Connell, Daniel, 202–3
O'Connell, Michael, 184
O'Driscoll, Dennis, 292n63
Odyssey Press edition of *The Faerie Queene*, 29
"Of Myself" (Cowley), 56–58
Of the Orthographie and Congruitie of the Britan Tongue (Hume), 33–34
Ong, Walter, 146–48, 283n5
Oram, William, 73
An Original Canto of Spencer (Croxall), 198–99
Orlando Furioso (Ariosto), 132, 294n6
Orlando Furioso (Harington), 13
Orlin, Lena, 166, 168
orthography. *See* spelling
Osborn Z76 O75, 230–33, 295n16
Ovid, 189
The Oxford Edition of the Collected Works of Edmund Spenser (ed. Cheney, Fowler, Loewenstein, Miller, and Zurcher), 29–30

Padelford, F. M., 255
The Pain of Reformation (Campana), 274n5
"Panic's Castle" (Dolven), 274n5
Parabolae sive similia (Erasmus), 119
Paradise Lost (Milton), 10, 91
Parker, Patricia, 20, 61
parody, 170–71
partial reading, 151–60
Pask, Kevin, 53
Peabody, Elizabeth Palmer, 59–60, 93, 275n21
Peabody, Eliza Palmer, 93–102, 278n65
Peabody, Nathaniel, 278n65
Pelican Guide to English Literature, 114, 280n19
Penguin Classics edition of *The Faerie Queene*, 28
Pentecost, Stephen, 29–30, 34
Perrot, John, 180
Pfeiffer, Julie, 91
The Phoenix Nest, 121
Pickering, Samuel, 54–55
Pilgrim's Progress (Bunyon), 50, 59, 275n14
Pitts, Joseph, 83–84, 89f
Plato, 132
plural reading, 35
Plutarch, 119
The Poetry of "The Faerie Queene" (Alpers), 20, 31–32, 234
"Poets of Great Britain from Chaucer to Churchill" (ed. Bell), 44
Poly-Olbion (Drayton), 13
Ponsonby, William, 37, 148, 242, 245, 254
Pope, Alexander, 77, 79, 277n43
Pope, Emma Field, 29, 270n13
postcritical reading, 238
"Preface to the Fourth Edition" in *Edward Spenser's Poetry* (Hadfield and Prescott), 145, 283n1
Prescott, Anne Lake, 145, 283n1
privacy, 156–59, 164–71, 286n30, 287n44. *See also* Legends of Chastity and Friendship
The Prophetic Moment (Fletcher), 187

Proposal for printing by subscription a new edition of Spenser's "Fairy Queen," with notes by John Upton, 218
Prothalamion (Spenser), 157–58, 285n29
The Province of Literary History (Greenlaw), 15–17
puns, 32–34, 270n16, 271n23
Puttenham, George, 111, 172

Quilligan, Maureen, 20, 147, 151
Quin, Michael Joseph, 202–3
Quint, David, 155

race, 208
Radcliffe, David Hill, 15, 266n51
Raleigh, Walter, 3, 148–49, 155, 172
Rambuss, Richard, 184
Ramsay, Stephen, 210, 213–14
Ransom, John Crowe, 18, 19
Read, William A., 109
readers of *TFQ*, 216–40; avid reading by, 108–12, 117–19, 142–44; characterological reading by, 4, 50, 145–46; children as, 51–64, 77–85, 90–101, 277n43; close reading of spelling by, 31–36; commentaries on the Castle of Alma by, 135–44, 282n50; conjectural status and remoteness of, 146; continual conversation among, 220–22, 294n7; Elizabeth I as first among, 145–51, 155, 162, 174, 283n9; extraction of quotable jewels by, 118–25; hand-annotations by, 126–35, 216–19, 281n38, 281n42; hostile book reviews by, 234–40; imitation by, 108–18; insatiability of, 241–60, 296n6; on knowing what not to read, 193–94; partial absorption of, 151–60; rivalries and debates among, 226–33, 240, 295n16, 295n18; slow pace required of, 176–82, 194; social networks and bonds among, 142–43; Spenser's friends as, 175; Spenser's instructions to, 1, 3–5, 25; Una's appeal to, 51; uncritical reading by, 21–25, 117, 268–69nn90–91. *See also* English scholarship; resistance to reading *TFQ*

reading: close reading, 31–32, 185, 194, 270n17; cultivated inattention to beauty in, 54; in the digital age, 178–79, 181–82, 207–15, 293nn71–72; distant reading, 23, 34–35; idyllic childhood imaginaries of, 51–52; plural reading, 35; postcritical reading, 238; recuperative power of, 186–87; reparative reading, 238–40; slow reading, 194–95; surface reading, 185, 238; time and attention requirements of, 22–24, 176–82, 268–69nn90–91
reading well, 1–6; as improvisatory practice, 6; Spenser on development of discipline in, 1, 3–5, 25; surviving the narrative in, 2, 263n2; vs. uncritical reading, 21–22. *See also* English scholarship
the realist novel, 55–56, 63
real reading, 174
Record of a School (Peabody), 59–60
Redcrosse Knight, 47, 49, 190, 274n5; allegorical function of, 59, 62–77, 101, 156, 161, 276n24, 276nn31–32; Archimago's plot against, 32–35, 53, 56, 68–75; defeat of the dragon by, 63, 64–65; encounter with Orgoglio of, 31, 34; true identity of, 64; vision of New Jerusalem of, 76
Red Romance Book (A. Lang), 98f
Renaissance Realism (Fowler), 62–63
Renaissance Self-Fashioning (Greenblatt), 20
Renwick, W. L., 17
reparative reading, 238–40
resistance to reading *TFQ*, 17–25; among New Critics, 17–20, 22–23, 234, 270n17; archaic spelling and, 31
Reynolds, Joshua, 83
Richards, I. A., 17
Richardson, Samuel, 12
Ricoeur, Paul, 238
Riddell, James A., 138–42, 282n50
Riemer, A. P., 140–41
right reading, 2
Roberts, James, 292n51

Robinson, T. H., 96f, 97f
Roche, Thomas P., 168, 284n22
Rockwell, Geoffrey, 210
Romantic Spenserians, 77
Rowe, George, 222
Royde-Smith, N. G., 96f, 97f, 278n62
Rymer, Thomas, 79

Sanchez, Melissa, 158
Sánchez-Eppler, Karen, 54–55, 61, 92
Sanders, David, 79
Sawday, Jonathan, 291n32
Scammell, John Chilton, 85, 88
scanning, 177–82, 207–15. *See also* digital humanities
The Scarlet Letter (Hawthorne), 105–6
Schmitt, Cannon, 193–94
Schoenfeldt, Michael, 170, 220–21
Scott, Walter, 12, 79–80, 256, 277n48
Scribner, Dora Ana, 121
Scudamore, James, 155
"The Secret Wit of Spenser's Language" (Craig), 31–32
Sedgwick, Eve, 238–40
Seneca, 119
Sermon on the Mount, 112, 125–26
Seven Types of Ambiguity (Empson), 17
Shakespeare, William, 43, 253, 255, 272n57; amateur study of, 46; modern-spelling versions of, 45, 47–48, 271n30; spelling patterns of, 27
Shakespeare Papers, 26–28, 45–46
Shelley, Percy, 108–10, 143
Shelton, Mary, 155
Shenstone, William, 258
The Shepheardes Calendar (Spenser), 38, 39, 44, 155, 156–57, 272n40, 286n30
Shore, Daniel, 35
Sidney, Philip, 148, 285n24
Silberman, Lauren, 168
Singleton, Hugh, 155, 285n24
Sircy, Jonathan, 91
Smith, Roland M., 47
Smyth, Adam, 117–18

Songes and Sonnets, written by the right honorable Lorde Henry Howard . . . (Tottel), 119–20
South African apartheid, 207
Southey Robert, 12, 80–81, 241, 257, 296n2
Special Exposition of "The Fairy Queen" (Hart), 92
spelling in *TFQ*, 26–49; archaic impression of, 28–30; close reading of, 31–36; comparisons to Chaucer of, 44–47; compositorial analysis of, 37, 47–48, 272nn36–37; eighteenth-century debates on, 39–46; Ireland's imitation of, 26–28, 45–46, 255; modernized versions of, 29, 48; purist approaches to, 29–31, 270n13; role in English scholarship of, 28–36, 43–49, 270nn16–17, 274n64; statistical analysis of, 29–30, 33–35, 48, 269n10; threshold standard of orthographic rarity in, 35; variability in early editions of, 36–39, 47, 272n36, 274n64
Spencer Redivivus (Howard), 39
Spense, Joseph, 277n43
Spenser, Edmund: career of, 47, 174, 180, 182–83, 203–4, 221, 226; colonialist perspective of, 182–87, 208, 213, 288n7; death in 1599 of, 242–44; on discipline through reading, 1, 3–4, 25; education of, 221; first mention of *TFQ* by, 12–13, 265n39; intellectual context of, 6, 155–56, 158–60, 186–87, 246, 263n2, 286n32; Irish estate of, 183, 244, 248, 289n11; as literary scholar, 14–15; marriage to Elizabeth Boyle of, 149–50, 171; as "poet's poet," 82–83, 108–12, 143; published occasional verse of, 148–51, 157–58, 171–75, 285n29, 286n30; publishing of *TFQ* by, 36–39, 148; on recuperative power of reading, 186–87; reputation for archaism of, 28–30, 247–48; scientific interests of, 253; secretarial spelling of, 47; *The Shepheardes Calendar* of, 38, 39, 44, 155, 156–57, 272n40, 286n30; treatise on Ireland by, 180, 183, 186, 193, 203–6, 288n8. *See also The Faerie Queene*

Spenser, Edmund, collected editions: *Complete Works in Verse and Prose of Edmund Spenser* (ed. Grosart), 14, 200, 204–5, 248, 251; *Edmund Spenser's Poetry* (Norton Critical Edition), 28–29, 145, 236, 243; *The Oxford Edition of the Collected Works of Edmund Spenser*, 29–30; *Variorum (The Works of Edmund Spenser)* (ed. Greenlaw et al.), 16, 17, 37, 47, 136, 248–49, 272n64; *Works* (1611), 38; *Works* (1679), 38, 39–40; *The Works of Edmund Spenser* (Routledge), 202; *The Works of Mr. Edmund Spenser* (ed. Hughes), 39–44, 218–19

"Spenser, The Poet and Teacher" (Dowden), 200–201

"Spenser and British Imperialism" (Greenlaw), 201

Spenser for Children (Towry), 93, 94f

Spenser's Faerie Queene (illus. Crane), 95f

Spenser's Image of Nature (Cheney), 234–38

Sprat, Thomas, 57, 78

Stallybrass, Peter, 47–48

Steedman, Carolyn, 54

Steele, Oliver, 29–30

Stevens, Wallace, 260

Stewart, Stanley, 138–42, 221, 282n50

Stirling, Brents, 266n56

Stoll, Abraham, 214–15

Stories from "The Fairie Queen" Told to the Children (J. Lane), 99f

The Story of "Paradise Lost," for Children (Bradburn), 91

St. Paul, 158

Stradling, Edward, 136, 139

Stradling, John, 296n6

"The Structure of Imagery in *The Faerie Queene*" (Frye), 207

Stubbs, George, 83, 86f

Stubbs, John, 285n24

A Supplement of "The Faerie Queene" (Knevett), 39, 272n42

surface reading, 185, 238

Tales from Spenser (MacLehose), 92, 278n62

Talus, 178, 189–99; Britomart and, 187, 210, 214–15; digital speed and, 207–15; instrumental function of, 189–95, 291n32, 291n34; as symbol of crisis, 197–99, 205–7, 292n51

Tate, Allen, 18

The Tears of Fancie, or Loue Disdained (Watson), 125

technology theory, 208. *See also* digital humanities

temperance. *See* Legend of Temperance

Teskey, Gordon, 58, 143–44, 163, 243, 245, 253, 255, 283n10

thin description, 185–86

Throckmorton, Elizabeth, 155

Tillyard, E.M.W., 17

time to read, 22–24, 268–69nn90–91

"To Clytander" (Melmoth), 259

Todd, Henry John, 44, 277n48

Tome of Homilies, 158–59

Tottel, Richard, 119–20

Towry, M. H., 93, 94f

"The Transformation of Lycon and Euphormius" (Melmoth), 257–60

Traversi, Derek, 18, 114

The Treatise of Moral Philosophy containing the Sayings of the Wise (Baldwin), 121

Trollope, Anthony, 8–9

Trumpener, Katie, 56

Tuve, Rosamund, 20, 63

Two Cantos of Mutabilitie, 242–60; critical reception of, 245; differences from TFQ of, 254–55; Evans's account of, 245–56; Lownes's account of, 242, 250–51, 253–54; Mutabilitie's quest for power in, 244; sense of an ending in, 255, 260; speculation on authorship of, 253–56; as Spenser's poetic fulfillment, 248–50

Tyrwhitt, Thomas, 44–45

Una Alarmed (Frost), 87f

Una Among the Fauns (Frost), 87f

Una and the Legend of Holiness (*TFQ* book 1), 32–33, 35, 51–107; Alcott's explication of, 59–60; allegorical function of, 51, 64–77, 101–3, 145, 156, 161, 276n24, 276nn31–32; beastly companions of, 53, 56, 62, 67–69, 72–75, 100; children's adaptations of, 90–101, 278n59; critical affection for, 77–78, 81; Hawthorne's realist versions of, 102–7, 278n67, 279n71; opening description of, 65–67; ordinary virtues of, 62; proem to, 146–47, 149, 220, 225–26, 228; queries of Arthur's identity in, 216–20; realist adventures of, 62–65, 106–7; reception history of, 53–56; satyrs' worship of, 61–62, 74, 83, 100; visual portrayals of, 83–89, 94–99*f*
Una and the Lion (Mary Hall in the Character of Una) (West), 84*f*
Una and the Lion (Portrait of Isabella Saltonstall) (Stubbs), 86*f*
"Una and the Lion," 88*f*, 98*f*
Una and the Red Cross Knight (Royde-Smith), 96*f*, 97*f*
Una Entering the Cottage (Hilton the Younger), 86*f*
uncritical reading, 21–25, 268–69nn90–91
University of California series in Modern Philology, 248
Upton, John, 41, 43–44, 46, 200, 216–19, 237, 244, 260
Urry, John, 43, 44

van Doren, Mark, 19
Van Es, Bart, 290n29
Variorum (The Works of Edmund Spenser) (ed. Greenlaw et al.), 16, 17, 37, 47, 136, 248–49, 272n64
Veblen, Thorstein, 280n22
Veblen, Thorsten, 115
Victoria, Queen of England, 83, 204
"View of Mr. Alcott and the children conversing" (Alcott), 60*f*
A View of the Present State of Ireland (Spenser), 180, 183, 186, 193, 203–6; surviving manuscript of, 288n8; Ware's 1633 preface to, 40, 243–44
Virgil, 220, 226, 294n6
The Vision of the Red Cross Knight (Pitts), 83–84, 89*f*

Walpole, Horace, 12, 83
Walsingham, Francis, 285n24
Ware, James, 40, 243
Warner, Michael, 21–22
Warner, William, 121
Warren, Kate M., 182, 183, 191–92, 201, 294n5
Warton, Joseph, 133, 281n43
Warton, Thomas, 13–14, 30, 46; annotations to *TFQ* by, 126, 133–35, 281n43; *Observations on the Faerie Queene of Spenser* of, 15, 40–41, 113–14, 116–17, 133
Waters, Josephine, 296n29
Watson, Thomas, 85–86, 125
The Well-Wrought Urn (Brooks), 18–19
West, Benjamin, 83, 84*f*
Wilcox, Phineas Bacon, 230–33, 240
Wilde, Oscar, 54
Wilkinson, Hazel, 112
Williams, Kathleen, 155, 284n22, 287n51
Winters, Yvor, 19
Wise, Thomas J., 249
Wiseman, Nicholas, 202–3
Wofford, Susanne, 65
Wolfe, John, 37, 47
Woolf, Virginia, 1, 11–12, 14, 241–42, 257
Works (1611) (Spenser), 38
Works (1679) (Spenser), 38, 39–40
The Works of Edmund Spenser (Routledge), 202
The Works of Mr. Edmund Spenser (ed. Hughes), 39–44, 218–19
World War I, 201–2
Worthington, John, 244
Wurstbaugh, Jewel, 16–17

Yamashita, Hiroshi, 47, 272n36
Yeats, William Butler, 183

Zurcher, Andrew, 37, 208, 245, 251–52, 254

A NOTE ON THE TYPE

This book has been composed in Arno, an old-style serif typeface in the classic Venetian tradition, designed by Robert Slimbach at Adobe.

GPSR Authorized Representative: Easy Access System Europe - Mustamäe tee 50, 10621 Tallinn, Estonia, gpsr.requests@easproject.com

www.ingramcontent.com/pod-product-compliance
Lightning Source LLC
Chambersburg PA
CBHW021649230426
43668CB00008B/560